Elementary Social Studies

Organized around four commonplaces of education—learners and learning, subject matter, teachers and teaching, and classroom environment—*Elementary Social Studies* provides a rich and ambitious framework to help social studies teachers achieve powerful teaching and learning results. By blending the theoretical and the practical, the authors deeply probe the basic elements of quality instruction—planning, implementation, and assessment—always with the goal of creating and supporting students who are motivated, engaged, and thoughtful.

Book features and updates to the fourth edition include:

- Two new chapters on using the Inquiry Design Model (IDM) to understand inquiry-based teaching and learning and to develop IDM inquiries.
- Revised chapter on ideas and questions.
- Revised chapter on literacy to more fully incorporate media literacy and digital citizenship.
- Real-classroom narratives introduce chapters and provide in-depth access to teaching and learning contexts.
- Practical curriculum and resource suggestions for the social studies classroom.
- End-of-chapter summaries and annotated teaching resources.

S.G. Grant is Professor of Social Studies Education in the Department of Teaching, Learning, and Educational Leadership at Binghamton University, State University of New York.

Bruce A. VanSledright is Professor Emeritus of History/Social Studies Education in the Department of Reading and Elementary Education at the University of North Carolina, Charlotte.

Elementary Social Studies

Constructing a Powerful Approach to Teaching and Learning

Fourth Edition

S.G. Grant and
Bruce A. VanSledright

Routledge
Taylor & Francis Group

NEW YORK AND LONDON

Fourth edition published 2021
by Routledge
52 Vanderbilt Avenue, New York, NY 10017

and by Routledge
2 Park Square, Milton Park, Abingdon, Oxon OX14 4RN

Routledge is an imprint of the Taylor & Francis Group, an informa business

© 2021 Taylor & Francis

Third edition published by Routledge 2014
First edition published by Wadsworth Publishing 2000

Library of Congress Cataloging-in-Publication Data
Names: Grant, S. G., author. | VanSledright, Bruce, author.
Title: Elementary social studies: constructing a powerful approach to
teaching and learning / S.G. Grant, Bruce A. VanSledright.
Description: Fourth edition. | New York, NY: Routledge, 2020. |
Includes bibliographical references and index.
Identifiers: LCCN 2020015198 (print) | LCCN 2020015199 (ebook) |
ISBN 9780367855963 (hardback) | ISBN 9780367855857 (paperback) |
ISBN 9781003013808 (ebook)
Subjects: LCSH: Social sciences–Study and teaching (Elementary) |
Learning. | Classroom environment.
Classification: LCC LB1584 .G75 2020 (print) |
LCC LB1584 (ebook) | DDC 372.83–dc23
LC record available at https://lccn.loc.gov/2020015198
LC ebook record available at https://lccn.loc.gov/2020015199

ISBN: 978-0-367-85596-3 (hbk)
ISBN: 978-0-367-85585-7 (pbk)
ISBN: 978-1-003-01380-8 (ebk)

Typeset in Sabon and Helvetica Neue
by Newgen Publishing UK

Brief Contents

Contents

Preface

Why this Book is Different

Students of all ages have long described social studies as lifeless. We think that part of this problem is an unmanageable, neutralized curriculum, one that lists every person, place, and event of note, but treats them with equal importance. Another part of the problem is the overwhelming pressure to give more and more time to the teaching of reading and mathematics to the exclusion of subjects such as science and social studies. One other part of the problem is that state standards and standardized testing often promote a "just the facts" approach to social studies, an approach that students have long and loudly decried.

These are all serious issues, yet we know that the potential for powerful teaching and learning exists. This book—through the in-text features and the accompanying instructor's and student's websites—strives to help all teachers achieve that potential.

We initially wrote *Elementary Social Studies: Constructing a Powerful Approach to Teaching and Learning* largely because we were dissatisfied with the elementary social studies methods books we reviewed for our courses. In our eyes, these books failed to capture the vibrancy and power we see in school classrooms where social studies is well taught. So, we built our respective methods courses around articles, book chapters, and conference papers that spoke to the issues we thought important. In this book, we offer a text that explicitly frames and develops a coherent, practical, and engaging approach to teaching and learning elementary social studies. We encourage our colleagues to supplement and extend their use of the text with additional materials designed to further enrich their students' course experiences.

Although other textbooks bombard students with a huge array of possible approaches, techniques, and teaching tools, our book tells a single coherent story, one that offers prospective and practicing teachers a way to realize the power of ambitious social studies teaching and learning. Where most texts begin with abstract discussions of goals and objectives, we build the case for powerful social studies teaching and learning chapter by chapter through the key elements of any teacher's classroom, the commonplaces of education.

A Commonplaces Approach

Central to ambitious social studies teaching and learning are thoughtful and reflective teachers who understand the learners with whom they work, who know their subject matter well, who possess a wide instructional repertoire, and who work to create powerful learning environments. This view of teaching reflects the *commonplaces of education*, a framework for classroom decision-making that we adapted from the work of Joseph Schwab. The individual commonplace elements—*learners and learning, subject matter, teachers and teaching*, and *classroom environment*—are useful ways for teachers to think about dimensions of their classroom practice. Taken together, however, the commonplaces are even more powerful. In interaction, the commonplaces offer a means of understanding and responding to classroom problems and situations and of planning effective units of study. They also ensure that all areas of pedagogical practice are examined in the process of learning to teach. The commonplaces, then, form part of the conceptual backbone of this book.

Organization of the Text

We use the commonplaces to orient our own instructional practices and to shape our course syllabi. The value of that approach led us to use the commonplaces as the organizational framework for this book. Part One consists of an introductory chapter explaining the commonplaces, followed by chapters devoted to each of the commonplaces in turn. These commonplace chapters are followed by a chapter on literacy within social studies. Part Two examines the commonplaces in action, with chapters on purposes and goals, the Inquiry Design Model and constructing curriculum inquiries, and teacher reflection.

The Commonplaces of Education

In Chapter 1, "Creating a Framework for the Social Studies Classroom," we present an overview of the commonplaces, both individually and in interaction. To do so, we dissect a case study of a first-grade social studies lesson, pointing out how each common place element comes into play. We also use this chapter as an opportunity to introduce other ideas that figure prominently throughout the book. Those ideas include a constructivist view of learning, the integrative "threads" that connect subject matters, big ideas as a way of framing teaching units, and the development of genuine classroom communities.

Learners and Learning

Chapter 2, "Learners and Learning: Understanding What Students Know and How They Come to Know It," is devoted to the first commonplace—*learners and learning*. Research on general teacher education shows that prospective teachers tend to focus first of all on trying to understand their students: Who are these children, and how do they learn? In this text, we explore what it means to learn before delving into what it means to teach.

There has been considerable recent research on what children know about social studies ideas, particularly in terms of historical understanding. We draw heavily on this research and on cases of classroom learning to explore what elementary-age students know about social studies concepts, where their knowledge comes from, and how they learn new ideas. In each instance, we contrast constructivist and behaviorist theories of learning. We conclude that, although constructivist approaches are not problem free, they provide a more powerful lens on how learners learn than behaviorist theories do.

Subject Matter

The second commonplace, *subject matter*, is the focus of Chapter 3, "Subject Matter: A Threads Approach." Although the traditional "expanding communities" curriculum model has been much tinkered with, it shows little fundamental change. In fact, it is the basis for many of the new state social studies standards. This model has its uses, but we encourage teachers to closely examine the underlying assumptions, especially in light of the preceding chapter on learners and learning. One way to do this is through the *threads*, a subject matter framework that features geographic, political, economic, sociocultural, and global dimensions. Using a threads framework, especially during the construction of classroom lessons and units, should help students more fully understand the subject matter under consideration. Moreover, the ability to bring the different threads perspectives to bear on a historical or contemporary issue or event should help students envision multiple perspectives. Finally, most state curriculum standards incorporate explicit references to the content areas represented by the threads categories.

Teachers and Teaching

Although all of the commonplaces are important, this is a social studies teaching methods book. Consequently, we dedicate three chapters to the third commonplace, *teachers and teaching*. As in each of the preceding chapters, we draw from rich classroom examples to illustrate the point that teaching social studies is more than just having a grab bag filled with interesting strategies and fun activities.

In Chapter 4, "Teachers and Teaching: Working with Ideas and Questions," we explore the relationship between ideas and questions. Ideas can take any number of forms—facts, topics, and concepts. Ideas are the stuff of social studies: the people, places, and events that define the social world. But, knowing a bunch of ideas is not enough. Students also need to understand the role that questions play in thinking about and acting in social situations. Questions also give students and their teachers the opportunity to move from a traditional, "just the facts" kind of social studies to an inquiry-based approach. To conclude this first teaching chapter, we discuss the use of big ideas within Lee Shulman's "Phases of Pedagogical Reasoning," a framework that we find particularly valuable as a way of thinking about teaching.

The focus of Chapter 5, "Teachers and Teaching: Choosing Strategies, Curriculum Materials, and Influences on Teaching," is on two major elements of instruction: *teaching strategies* and *curriculum materials*. The teaching strategies section features descriptions of a wide range of methods associated with individual, small group, and whole class instruction. The curriculum materials section is similarly wide ranging as we describe the various textual, representational, and computer resources on which teachers and students can draw. We conclude this chapter with a discussion of the influences on teachers' content and pedagogical decisions. Using a case study, we explore and categorize those influences as personal, organizational, and policy factors, and we demonstrate how they interact.

In Chapter 6, "Teachers and Teaching: Assessment," we explore one final element of teachers' work and the practice of teaching—assessment. Although we discuss standardized testing, we are most interested here with the thorny question of "how do we know what kids know?" This question refers to the practice of regularly assessing students' growing understandings to see how they relate to our teaching goals in social studies. We refer to this form of ongoing assessment as diagnostic. Diagnostic assessment bridges goals, curriculum, and teaching practice with learning. The sharper and more useful our assessments are, the better they help us monitor and diagnose learning difficulties. The more skilled teachers are in that diagnosis, the more likely they will be to adjust their teaching practices to help alleviate those learning difficulties. In this sense, assessment of student learning becomes an extension of teaching and links directly back to it.

Classroom Environment

The fourth commonplace—*classroom environment*—is the focus of Chapter 7, "The Classroom Environment: Creating a Genuine Community." Teaching, learning, and subject matter are all important, but so too is the environment in which these activities occur. The notion of classroom environment or climate can be fuzzy, though, so we talk about it in terms of *discourse, classroom organization*, and *dispositions*. By discourse we mean the kind of classroom talk that occurs between teachers and students. Classroom organization refers to the ways in which teachers organize students for classroom activities. And dispositions are those values and attitudes that teachers hope to foster in class. To ground these ideas, we draw a contrast between a traditional classroom environment and what we call a *genuine classroom community*. In our view, traditional classrooms reflect a factory model of schooling where the norms of quiet, efficient, individual work are valued. Genuine classrooms, we argue, focus on ideas, inquiry, and active participation. As the students who sit in classrooms become increasingly diverse, the need for a more powerful view of the classroom environment becomes even more important. We conclude the chapter with a discussion of how teachers can negotiate the construction of a genuine community in their classrooms.

Literacy

We conclude the first part of the book with Chapter 8, "Social Studies and Literacy." Here, we recognize the influence that the Common Core State Standards, particularly the standards for English Language Arts, are having on teaching and learning in elementary classrooms. The chapter is broken into two major sections. The first highlights the key elements of the Common Core–English Language Arts standards; the second focuses in on the notion of *literacy through social studies*. Here, we talk through the general and specific implications for weaving literacy into one's social studies practice. We end the chapter with discussions of media literacy and digital citizenship.

Purposes and Goals

In Chapter 9, "Purposes, Goals, and Objectives for Teaching and Learning," we take up the bigger aims of social studies. While most methods books begin with this chapter, we believe that it makes more sense to examine the purposes of social studies *after* readers have thought through some of the more practical issues of teaching and learning. The central issue of this chapter is the idea that, even if there is something of a consensus that social studies aims at citizenship education, there is neither a consensus on how to define "good" citizenship nor on how to reach that goal. We illustrate this situation through case studies of four teachers and the goal frameworks they employ. To help readers construct their own goal frameworks, we discuss resources to which they might turn, such as curriculum standards and definitions of social studies, and we suggest issues to be mindful of as they make their decisions.

An Inquiry-Based Approach to Teaching and Learning

Chapter 10, "The Inquiry Design Model," offers an insight into one approach to inquiry-based teaching and learning. Reflecting the tenets of the *C3 Framework*, the Inquiry Design Model (IDM) focuses on the key components of any classroom inquiry—questions, tasks, and sources. The chapter unfolds around an early elementary curriculum inquiry on needs and wants. Using an inquiry with the compelling question, "Why can't we ever get everything we need and want?" we demonstrate how questions (compelling and supporting), tasks (formative and summative), and sources (primary and secondary) support and extend the idea that even young children can engage in powerful learning opportunities.

Constructing Inquiries

In Chapter 11, "Constructing Curriculum Inquiries," we put you in the position of crafting your own curriculum inquiry. We describe a ten-step process that illustrates the development of an IDM blueprint, a one-page representation of the questions, tasks, and sources students need to engage with in order to complete an inquiry. Along the way, we invite you to construct a blueprint based on a topic germane to your students.

Reflection

Chapter 12, "Becoming a Reflective Social Studies Teacher," serves as a capstone to the book. Reflectivity, we believe, is the core of good teaching, for, without it, teachers are little more than instructional robots. Thus, the ideas developed to this point—the commonplaces, threads, big ideas, and the like—will only be meaningful if teachers adopt a reflective stance. We discuss reflection in three ways. First, we describe the importance of personal and professional growth. We argue that teachers who grow personally are also growing professionally, and the reverse. Second, we discuss the nature of reflection. To do so, we use an email exchange between us to demonstrate what reflection can look like and to serve as a background for a discussion of teacher educator Linda Valli's useful categories of reflective practice. Finally, we talk about "breaking the silences." The sociologist Dan Lortie decried the "egg-crate" design of school buildings for its tendency to undermine teachers' interactions with other adults. This silence tends to be destructive because, while self-reflection is essential, so too is reflective conversation with others. To that end, we strongly encourage teachers to break out of their classrooms and to find colleagues who will listen to, challenge, and respect them.

Key Coverage in the Text

Throughout the book we keep in the foreground four aspects of teaching that are crucial for teachers entering today's classroom.

Research

Throughout this book are connections to recent relevant research about teaching and learning social studies. We believe that a teacher who knows something about what the research says is in a much better position to reason soundly and effectively about the many teaching choices to be made. Listening to social studies teachers talk about their teaching—along with our own experiences as social studies teachers—convinces us that a healthy working knowledge of the social studies research fosters higher levels of reflectiveness about teaching. In other words, the more ideas about classrooms, teaching, and learning teachers acquire, the better off they are.

Among the ways in which we incorporate research findings into the book is the use of actual teaching episodes. We want readers to dig deeply into classroom life and see real-life illustrations of the points we make. In such classroom examples, we show what ambitious social studies teaching looks like. We want teachers to come away from these vignettes knowing that real social studies teachers are out there inviting and challenging their students to seize on the power and excitement of learning about big ideas. We hope that these sorts of research-based examples provide encouragement for our readers to become similarly ambitious social studies teachers.

Theory-to-Practice

A second distinctive aspect of the book is the consistent linkages between theory and practice. Part of ambitious teaching is constructing powerful teaching lessons and units that push both teacher and students to greater understandings. To this end, we offer a range of practical suggestions on how to incorporate constructivist principles into everyday teaching.

Diversity

One of the most powerful and positive developments in recent years is the understanding of student diversity. Classroom teachers in all school settings are realizing that the students sitting in front of them may represent a wide range of socioeconomic, ethnic, racial, and religious perspectives. This fact presents a challenge largely because the curricular materials available either ignore diversity or treat it in a superficial manner. Understanding the different kinds of diversities in one's class is a real benefit, especially in a subject such as social studies. History and the social sciences form the backbone of the social studies curriculum. Central to each of the fields is the notion of interpretation—that is, the need to "make sense" of the world around us.

For example, historians examine artifacts and written records to interpret our past; political scientists examine survey data and voting records to interpret our political behavior. With interpretation comes the idea of multiple perspectives, or the realization that different people may interpret the same data in different ways. Two historians or two political scientists may each look at the same set of records and yet construct equally defensible, but quite different, interpretations. For example, one historian might interpret Columbus's diary as evidence for his navigational skills, while another might interpret it as evidence of his cruelty to the native populations. (And these are just two of the many interpretations of Columbus's life!)

The notions of interpretation and multiple perspectives are important to develop in all social studies classrooms. They become especially easy to develop in diverse classrooms where the range of children's beliefs and experiences should help them see both the similarities and the differences in their understandings. While ensuring that social studies content accurately reflects diverse populations is a worthy challenge in itself, equally important is cultivating strategies and techniques for making sure every voice is heard. New teachers must develop the awareness that gives them a disposition for diversity.

Standards

Discussion of national and state standards is also widely covered in this book. Much of the buzz today in classrooms, PTA meetings, school board sessions, and the like is around standards. A good deal of the attention is on literacy and mathematics, for these are the areas given most attention in recent legislation such as the No Child Left Behind act and in the Common Core State Standards. That said, most states have also revamped their social studies curriculum and many have added the assessment of social studies to their state-level testing programs.

Although the emphasis on standards, and particularly the notion of raising standards, is sound, the effects of that emphasis may leave some teachers more confused than enlightened. As new standards documents, curriculum resource guides, sample tests, and the like pile up in teachers' mailboxes, some are tempted to let them stay there. We encourage readers to avoid that temptation! As we show in several places throughout this book, standards and curriculum documents can be transformed into meaningful social studies ideas and plans. Doing so may take more effort, but students will be the beneficiaries.

Let us make one additional point about standards. While we were writing the third edition of this book, we were involved as writers on a state-led social studies standards project that ultimately became *The College, Career, and Civic Life (C3) Framework for Social Studies State Standards* (National Council for the Social Studies, 2013). The *C3 Framework* represents a powerful step forward in terms of the potential for developing state standards that reflect the kind of ambitious teaching we describe in this book. We invite you to take a look at the *C3 Framework* and think about the many intersections between that work and this one.

Useful Pedagogical Aids

Elementary Social Studies offers an array of practical features designed to illustrate, support, and extend teachers' pedagogical thinking.

Resources

Good social studies teachers have good resources. This simple truth spurred us to include in each chapter an updated list of the best resources for teaching elementary social studies (Internet sites, trade books, articles, and multimedia resources) we have come across. Long lists of resources can be off-putting, so we offer these resources only in the context of how they might be integrated into social studies learning opportunities.

Reflection Questions

Part of ambitious social studies teaching is constructing powerful teaching lessons and units that push both teachers and learners to greater understandings. Good teachers are able to step back and reflect on ideas, issues, and situations that arise both in their classrooms and in the nature of schooling writ large. To this end, we include a number of stopping places in the text where we use the issue at hand to pose questions for further thought.

In Your Classroom Boxes

Having a wide instructional repertoire is invaluable, so we include a range of practical teaching suggestions through our "In Your Classroom" feature. In these boxes, we describe teaching strategies such as jigsaws, book talks, mini-lessons, learning centers, and other proven activities that both teachers and students will find valuable.

Appendix: Children's Literature

The growth of trade books provides a powerful tool for teaching and learning social studies. Using trade books can be a valuable opportunity to combine reading and language arts development with greater understanding of social studies content. Rather than provide an encyclopedic, arbitrary listing, we present a carefully selected and updated list of approximately 100 children's trade titles that correspond to the various unit ideas we present throughout the book.

Glossary

Although we worked to write a jargon-free book and to define those terms that we employ in the text, we also provide a glossary of key concepts.

Changes to the Fourth Edition

In the third edition of *Elementary Social Studies*, we expanded on the original nine chapters by including new reference citations and extended attention to a number of ideas and practices. We added new children's literature titles and many new web resources. We also added new chapters on assessment and literacy.

In this fourth edition, we again updated the references, resources, and children's literature titles. We also added one new chapter and substantially revised three others.

One of the revised chapters—Chapter 10, "The Inquiry Design Model"—describes an approach to the kind of inquiry-based teaching and learning that is rooted in the *C3 Framework*. The criticism of classroom inquiry has been that teachers have trouble understanding what it looks like. In this first of two related chapters, we take you deeply inside a curriculum inquiry based on the Inquiry Design Model. That model features components that have long been associated with inquiry-based teaching and learning: questions, tasks, and sources.

The new chapter—"Constructing Curriculum Inquiries" (Chapter 11)—serves as a companion to Chapter 10. Here, the idea is to walk you through the ten-step process of building an Inquiry Design Model blueprint and guide you through the construction of an inquiry based on a topic of your choice.

In addition to these changes, we have also revised Chapter 4, "Teachers and Teaching: Working with Ideas and Questions," to make the connection between ideas and questions more explicit and to introduce the idea of a "compelling question" as a way to frame a curriculum inquiry.

Finally, we revised the chapter on literacy in social studies (Chapter 8) to reflect the topics of media literacy and digital citizenship.

Acknowledgments

Teaching and learning are among the most human of activities. We are who we are in large part because we have been taught by and learned from others. Acknowledging all those who have taught us would be as exhaustive as it would be humbling, for it would include both those whose ostensible role was teacher, as well as those whom outsiders would define as our students. The simple truth is that the soil from which we have grown as teachers has been as enriched by our interactions with our students as it has by our interactions with our teachers. A hearty "thank you" goes out to those who put up with our "studently" fumblings in their classes and to those who put up with nascent "teacherly" fumblings in ours.

Although we cannot possibly thank all those who helped us to this point, we can express our appreciation to those who were directly responsible for making this book as good as we hope it is. We offer our thanks to the many teachers who have invited us into their classrooms to observe and to interview them about their classroom practices. Several of these teachers figure prominently in the classroom examples that appear in this book and without them the text would suffer greatly. Their actual names have been changed to pseudonyms as a requirement of confidentiality. However, if they read this book, they undoubtedly know who they are. We thank them for teaching us much about social studies teaching.

Next, we thank the folks at Routledge whose patience and expertise we surely (and sorely) tried over this edition of the book: Matthew Friberg and Jessica Cooke, as well as our copy-editor, Maartje Scheltens, and the folks who, behind the scenes, set up the pages, and worked to market this edition.

Finally, we thank our families who put up with our doubts, whining, and long hours at the computer. Bruce wishes to thank his family for their support and encouragement while writing this book, and for listening to him grumble about the work involved. He also thanks S.G. for his patience and calm demeanor around manuscript deadlines and for his stellar editorial and assembly efforts. Without him, this book would never have been possible. Lastly, he wishes to thank the many elementary teachers he has had the privilege to work with over the years. He has learned much from them. S.G. would like to begin by thanking Bruce for his insights, thoughtfulness, and continued efforts to improve the teaching of elementary social studies. He would also like to thank Anne, Alexander, and Claire. He's indebted to Anne for her patience, good humor, and encouraging words, and he's indebted to Alexander and Claire and their significant others (Cassidy and Jose) for their willingness to let their dad hang with them when he needs a break from writing.

S.G.G.
B.A.V.

The Commonplaces of Education
A Framework for Powerful Social Studies Teaching

Creating a Framework for the Social Studies Classroom

It is 10:00 a.m. on a blustery March morning as the first graders begin their social studies lesson. "Right now we're doing some traveling," the teacher says, and the class calls out, "to China?" "to Ethiopia?" "to Africa!" A child whispers to a visitor, "We cooked chicken from Nigeria!" Two months later, the first grade has "traveled" all the way from China and Nigeria to Australia. They gather in a semicircle on the floor as their teacher reads a story that introduces some of the history of the Australian rain forest. As she reads, the bell rings, and several students sigh. A boy says, "I'd just like to stay and stay."

(Levstik, 1993, p. 1)

Linda Levstik's snapshot of this first-grade classroom illustrates the power of an engaging social studies lesson: Teachers dream of students saying, "I'd just like to stay and stay."

Why does this first grader feel this way? Several factors are in play:

- **Teachers** who excite children's imagination and curiosity through a range of instructional experiences that include reading stories, asking questions, and even cooking.

- **Learners** who are consistently encouraged to participate actively in their own learning.

- **Subject matter** that goes well beyond the traditional elementary-school emphasis on self and family and beyond the limits of the children's neighborhood, state, and country.

- **A classroom environment** where teacher and learners talk with one another, where children learn in a variety of contexts, and where all hold values that support active engagement in powerful ideas.

FIGURE 1.1 This photograph depicts a first-grade teacher reading a book to her students. What clues about teaching, learning, subject matter, and classroom environment can you infer?

Classes that exhibit these factors make strong impressions on children's hearts and minds and become the stuff that future generations of citizens will recall as meaningful. And that is why social studies matters: It can and should be the site of powerful teaching and learning experiences, a place where children want to "stay and stay."

In this chapter, we present an adaptation of the **commonplaces of education** described by Joseph Schwab (1978).[1] Understanding and using the commonplaces—*teachers and teaching, learners and learning, subject matter,* and *classroom environment*—will help you begin building a powerful framework for teaching and learning. When you have completed this chapter, you should be able to answer these questions:

1   What are the key elements of each commonplace?
2   How do the commonplaces work in interaction?
3   How does an understanding of the commonplaces help me think about teaching and learning?

Introducing the Commonplaces

Schools and classrooms are busy, diverse, and complex places. Children bring a range of physical, emotional, social, and academic strengths and needs;

parents ask many questions and express many concerns; administrators hold various expectations of teachers and learners; the several subject matters elementary-school teachers are responsible for threaten to overwhelm them. In addition, district- and state-level standardized tests, local, state, and national curriculum standards, as well as reforms such as longer school days, the rise of charter schools, and the role of the Common Core compete for teachers' attention. In and around this swirl, it is easy for teachers, even veteran teachers, to lose focus.

Our experience tells us that good teachers are those who are thoughtful and reflective, who can adjust to changing circumstances, and who can see both the big picture and the details. That is a lot to ask, especially of novice teachers. How might you focus your time, attention, and energy? How can you become the best kind of teacher you can imagine?

Part of answering these questions lies in constructing a dynamic approach to teaching and learning. Central to that approach is a guiding framework. The one we advocate features the commonplaces of education: learners and learning, teachers and teaching, subject matter, and classroom environment. Taken separately, these constructs allow teachers to focus on key elements of classroom life. For example, teachers can dig deeply into questions of what it means to learn social studies, what content is appropriate to teach, what teaching approaches they might use, and what kinds of classroom environments foster engaged and thoughtful teaching and learning. These are useful questions, and we have more to say about each of them as this book unfolds.

The commonplaces are even more useful when teachers consider them in interaction—that is, when teachers plan, teach, and assess in ways that reflect attention to all four elements. In classrooms such as the one profiled at the beginning of this chapter, we see a seamless merging of the four commonplaces: The *classroom environment* reflects the *teacher's* sense that *learning* is a social and active process that is abetted by dynamic instruction and powerful *subject matter* ideas. Firing on all four commonplace cylinders is no small feat, and even good teachers flop sometimes. But those same teachers will tell you that much of what keeps them fresh is the sense that they are always encountering new situations and learning new aspects of how they think about and do their work.

The commonplaces are neither a substitute for experience nor a substitute for the passion and thoughtfulness good teachers bring to their craft. Understanding the commonplaces can, however, help you to make sense of the complexity that surrounds teaching and learning and to think your way into the role of social studies teacher. Figure 1.2 is a diagram of the commonplaces. The arrows indicate the interaction among the commonplaces as they operate in educational settings.

Before we talk about the commonplaces in interaction, let's look at each of them in turn and see how they play out in the actions of the first-grade teacher, Ruby, whose classroom is described in the opening vignette.

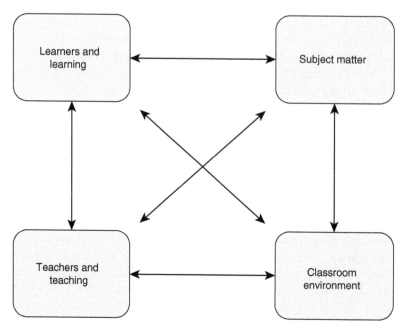

FIGURE 1.2 The commonplaces, both individually and in interaction.

Learners and Learning

When you see yourself teaching, who are the learners sitting in front of you? How are they similar and how are they different? What do they know and care about? How do they learn, and where do their ideas come from? How do they feel about learning social studies, especially as it compares to learning other school subjects?

Although we address these questions in Chapter 2, our purpose here is to prime your thinking about one of the key elements or commonplaces in education—learners and learning. As odd as it may seem, teachers sometimes become so focused on what they are teaching and how they are teaching it that they almost forget that teaching is not the same thing as learning. Think about it: How many times have you sat in a class where the teacher is teaching something, and yet you were not learning anything? Now, it may have been your fault—perhaps you were not prepared for the class or maybe you were not paying attention. But it's also possible that the teacher forgot about or misunderstood those whom she or he was teaching.

Part of remembering and understanding the students in front of you is thinking about the kinds of questions we listed above. There is no such thing as a generic kid. Each shares some commonalities with others, such as race, ethnicity, and gender. But these factors do not always matter, because every child is also an individual. Girls may generally act in a certain way compared to boys, but that does not mean Kara, Shaneeka, and Lucy always think and act in the same ways. Similarly, African-American, Chinese-American, and Native-American children exhibit traits indigenous to their cultural roots (e.g., Epstein, 2009). Yet, to see those children only in terms of their ethnicity is to misunderstand the many influences on their behavior and the power that children have to define themselves.

Teachers face a tough task: They need to understand the cultural backgrounds of their students while also honoring the individuality of each student. In doing so, however, they come to know how their learners are similar and different and what they know and care about. Teachers who prepare social studies inquiries and lessons that help students think and learn find this kind of information invaluable.

But there is more to it. Understanding who the learners are in front of you is key. So too is understanding the learning process. How students learn, where their ideas come from, and how they learn different school subjects is a prime area of educational research (Donovan & Bransford, 2005). Some important findings are emerging, which we will discuss in more detail in Chapter 2. Here, we preview two of the most salient.

One finding relates to the distinction between *behaviorism* and *constructivism*. If you remember Psych 101, you will recall that **behaviorism** is a theory about what causes people to do the things they do. In brief, behaviorists argue that all behavior can be explained as a series of stimulus–response actions: Sunlight (stimulus) hits your eye and you blink (response). Rewards and punishments figure into the mix, in that responses that are rewarded tend to persist; those that are punished tend to fade. Applied to schooling, behaviorist theory surfaces in myriad ways: the division of knowledge into discrete, easily digestible bits; direct instruction of those bits; lots of student practice on the bits; lots of testing to ensure that the bits are memorized; and lots of praise when students recall the bits quickly and accurately.

Current thinking about learning challenges much of behavioral theory. The theory of **constructivism** assumes that people play a much more active role in the development of their lives: What people know and do is an active construction rather than a passive response to an external stimulus. This theory does not discount the importance of environmental stimuli: Constructivists blink when the sun is in their eyes, too! Constructivists differ from their behaviorist colleagues in defining a stimulus and in understanding how people make sense of that stimulus. Put simply, constructivists believe that a wide range of stimuli, both external and internal, influence our behavior and that different people may make very different sense of and respond in very different ways to similar stimuli.

These ideas have profound implications for schooling. Constructivists believe, in part, that knowledge is complex and multifaceted, and that something is lost when it is always broken down into its most basic elements; that teaching is about creating opportunities for students to think about and work through big ideas; and that learning is about understanding rather than simply memorizing ideas. Although these are but thumbnail sketches of two complex theories, you can see that they represent significantly different views of what learning is all about and what learners can and should be able to do.

A second finding that concerns learners and learning revolves around how learners respond to social studies as a school subject. Surveys of students' attitudes toward social studies consistently report the same dismal finding: Most students hate social studies (Haladyna & Shaughnessy, 1985; McGowan, Sutton, & Smith, 1990). Several factors figure into this conclusion. Students dislike the dull nature of many of the social studies ideas presented, most of which they already know. They resist the boring textbooks and worksheets they are handed. They object to teachers who give them no opportunities to talk about their nascent ideas and who promote a singular view of the world. In short, few students find much of value in the traditional approach to social studies, an approach that attempts to pour discrete bits of content into their heads and then simply asks them to recall those bits at a later date. Can we blame them?

Teachers such as Ruby represent the possibilities for social studies. Think about what Ruby knows about learning and the learners in her classroom. First, although her first graders have had little experience outside their own community, she knows that they are deeply interested in how other people live. Ruby understands that by helping her students look into the lives of others, they will be better able to understand their own. Second, although these children need opportunities to learn some specific ideas, Ruby knows that they also need opportunities to play with ideas, to have direct experiences, to ask lots of questions, and to try out their emerging understandings. Finally, Ruby knows that first graders make few distinctions between "social studies," "language arts," and the like, so her lessons invariably take an integrated tack. Students study key social studies ideas such as geography, exploration, and culture using the tools of literacy (reading, writing, speaking, listening) and science (for example, understanding that differences in climate and terrain influence where and how people live their lives). In these several ways, Ruby demonstrates her sensitivity to and her deep interest in her students' learning.

IN YOUR CLASSROOM

PROBING STUDENT ATTITUDES

To develop a sense of your students' feelings about social studies, construct a survey that asks them

- What they remember about their social studies class last year.
- What activities they learned the most from.

If you listen carefully and probe gently, students' responses to these simple questions not only will tell you a lot, but they will also demonstrate to your students that you care about what they think.

Subject Matter

The learners and learning commonplace is an important one, but just as important is the notion of subject matter or the ideas you want learners to learn. Several questions help frame the subject-matter commonplace:

- What is the content of the social studies?
- What content is appropriate to teach children?
- How is social studies content typically organized, and what modifications can teachers make?

We discuss these questions in some detail in Chapter 3. Here, we want to preview some issues that underlie these questions.

One of the first issues teachers confront when teaching social studies is the impossibility of the task. Think about it: Social studies includes the geographic, political, economic, and cultural history of all humankind. That's a lot of territory to cover! Of course, no one teacher can teach it all. (However, S.G. once taught a high school course entitled "World History." His approach: "Buckle your seat belts, kids. We've got five hundred years to cover today!" Needless to say, this wasn't the most successful social studies teaching.) Even so, teachers can feel overwhelmed by the content assigned to their grade level.

Although state standards, textbooks, and other teachers offer suggestions, in the end, you, the teacher, must decide what to teach, how long to teach it, and in what detail. Along with this real responsibility is a real opportunity to choose content that builds on what your students know and that pushes them to greater understandings.

How to do that? Two ideas will help. One is considering the **threads of social studies**. With so much content to teach, it is easy either to give up or to simply start marching through a textbook page by page. Good teachers, however, use a framework to think about and organize the content at hand. The framework we propose divides the social studies into geographic, political, economic, sociocultural, and global threads.[2]

Taken separately, these threads can help learners to look deeply at the important elements of social life. Taken together, the threads help learners to look broadly at how individuals and social groups operate and to compare and contrast one social or cultural group with another.

To see the threads in action, let's return to Ruby's first-grade classroom, where attention to several threads is immediately obvious. First, Ruby encourages attention to the geographic, cultural, and global threads as she and her learners explore a range of world cultures. Second, she promotes the economic and geographic threads when she turns students' attention to the resources present in the Australian rain forest. Finally, although it is not apparent in the vignette above, Ruby and her learners attend to the political thread later on when they discuss government decisions made about the rain forest.

■ ■ ■ ■ THE THREADS OF SOCIAL STUDIES

- **Geographic**: ideas related to where and how people live.
- **Political**: ideas about how people make decisions that affect themselves and others.
- **Economic**: ideas about how people use the land and resources to meet their needs.
- **Sociocultural**: ideas about how people communicate, learn, relax, and find meaning in their lives.
- **Global**: ideas about how people interact across cultures.

Using these threads to frame and organize the subject matter of social studies makes a lot of sense. Another approach that makes sense is the construction and use of a compelling question. A **compelling question** is a question that helps you, the teacher, decide what to focus on in a curriculum inquiry. Compelling questions engage learners' interests by being meaty, complex, and open to diverse perspectives and interpretations. The questions "What is freedom?" (for an inquiry on American slavery), "How do we know what we know?" (for an inquiry on the nature of history), and "How can I impact my community?" (for an inquiry on children's local communities) function as powerful ideas because they enable learners to wrestle with real and important issues.

Compelling questions are also powerful because they help frame the inquiry at hand. Slavery and the nature of history are huge topics, ones that could take most of a year to explore. Using questions such as "What is freedom?" and "How do we know what we know?" provides a focus for the respective inquiries. Teachers and learners can explore a range of issues in these areas, but if they keep returning to the compelling question, they are more likely to find deeper meaning in their explorations. Often the social studies teaching that kids complain about is aimless; they do activities every day, but they cannot see what those activities add up to. Compelling questions help eliminate such complaints.

Turning back to Ruby's first-grade classroom, we see how a compelling question can play out even in first grade. For example, in the unit on cultures outside the United States, Ruby uses the question "Where do we come from?" to frame class discussions. Ruby knows that students make sense of ideas through personal connections. She also knows that, at first, foreign cultures can seem remote and unintelligible to her first graders. So, she uses the construct of a neighborhood to help her students connect their lives to those distant others. She and the children explore dimensions of the diverse cultures found in their local neighborhood—family life, language, traditions, celebrations, and the like. In so doing, Ruby provides both opportunities for her learners to explore their interests and a framework to help them make sense of what they learn.

▶️◀ REFLECTION: WHAT *DON'T* YOU KNOW?

Think of an interesting event in history that you know something about (for example, the Salem witch trials, the Renaissance, the 1960s). On a sheet of paper, list all the things that you know about that topic and divide them into the thread categories. That is, what do you know about the religious situation in seventeenth-century Salem (sociocultural), the forms of government found during the Renaissance (political), or the growth of the consumer culture during the 1960s (economic).

As you work through the five threads, you may be surprised to realize that you remembered more than you might have thought. You may also discover what you don't know or don't remember well. This realization is important, because you will want to help your students understand that (a) no one knows everything and (b) a framework like the threads can help you figure out what you don't know. Understanding what we *don't know* is key to understanding what we *can learn*.

Teachers and Teaching

The third commonplace is teachers and teaching. Because this book is primarily for prospective and practicing teachers, we spend a lot of time talking about what teaching social studies is all about. In fact, we devote three chapters—4, 5, and 6—to that task. In this section, however, we foreshadow some of the relevant questions and issues.

Among the key questions are these:

- What elements make up the act of teaching?
- What is the array of teaching methods available and how do teachers decide among them?
- How do teachers know what their students are learning?
- What materials might teachers use?
- How do influences such as state social studies standards and the Common Core influence teachers' instructional decisions?
- What does powerful teaching look like?

As this list suggests, teaching is a richly complex activity that goes far beyond the act of delivering instruction. Planning units and lessons, organizing students for learning, choosing curriculum materials, and creating forms of assessment are big chunks of the teaching process. The instructional phase alone is complicated by choice. Recitation and seatwork, individual reading and note taking, small-group and whole-class discussion, role-playing and simulation, individual and small-group projects, report and essay writing, journal keeping, learning centers, lectures … the list of possible instructional approaches is endless.

As we have suggested above, good teachers take into account their learners and the subject matter at hand. But other influences are at work as well. Parents' and administrators' expectations, state and local curriculum standards, school and district policies, and state and local tests may affect teachers' practices.

Teachers can feel buffeted by the various winds that blow through their classrooms, and they can feel frustrated when those winds blow in contradictory directions. Consider a quick example: Many of the new standards in social studies call for meatier content, higher-level thinking, and greater expectations of students (e.g., National Council for the Social Studies, 2013). And yet, many state standardized tests still reflect basic content, low-level thinking, and require little effort by students (VanSledright, 2014).

Such mixed messages can confuse teachers. Looked at differently, however, they may liberate teachers because they mean that teachers can be held to no single criterion. In other words, with multiple (and often conflicting) influences in the air, teachers have considerable **autonomy** to carve out their own instructional paths. Admittedly, the downside here is that some teachers can find the uncertainty paralyzing, and others may use their autonomy to do little more than the required minimum. Thoughtful, committed, and energetic teachers, however, will find few real drags on their instructional creativity. The choices teachers must make are not easy, but those choices are theirs.

FIGURE 1.3 On the left, a first-grade teacher works individually with one of her students. Although many believe that teaching consists largely of whole-class instruction, good teachers know that much of their work involves one-on-one interactions with their students.

Consider how Ruby uses her classroom autonomy to make good instructional choices for her first graders. For example, she faces the same state and local curriculum standards that most teachers face, yet these guides are expressed in such general terms that she can tailor her teaching around goals that seem much more important—the development of empathy for others, students' interests, and future learnings. Now, it's true that Ruby might feel she had fewer choices if her students had to take a standardized test in social studies. As we will see in the case of Don Kite (Chapter 5), however, standardized tests have no particular influence on teachers' work.

REFLECTION: TALKING WITH TEACHERS

Talk with a practicing teacher about how she or he decides what to teach and how to teach it. Expect to hear references to tests, textbooks, curriculum standards, past experience, and the like. Encourage the teacher to talk about how she or he weighs each of these factors and what trade-offs result. Reflect on what these influences might mean for your teaching.

Classroom Environment

Teachers and teaching, subject matter, learners and learning—it's hard to believe a teacher's job can encompass much more than that. And yet, good teachers also pay attention to the fourth commonplace, one that goes by many names—milieu, climate, atmosphere, environment. All refer, however, to the sense or feeling one has while in a classroom. In some ways, this is the hardest commonplace to talk about because it seems so diffuse. And yet, certain features of classrooms provide ways to examine the nature of a classroom setting.

First, a few questions to think about:

- What does a good classroom environment look like?
- What goes into creating a good classroom climate?
- How does a teacher know whether it's achieved?

You have undoubtedly had many experiences in **traditional classroom settings**. You probably worked under a set of classroom rules that emphasized laboring silently and individually on simplistic tasks with lots of rewards and punishments. Conversely, you have probably had far fewer experiences in classrooms that emphasize working with others on complex assignments that carry both internal and external rewards. When asked, most teachers say that they want to promote this second kind of classroom environment. But, with little personal experience in such settings, it makes some sense that many teachers replicate the kinds of traditional classrooms in which they were schooled.

It doesn't have to be that way, however. Creating the kind of **genuine class-room community** that we envision as the second classroom described just above is no mean feat—especially since both you and your students are so used to the traditional setup. We suspect, though, that making clear distinctions between traditional and genuine classroom environments should make it easier for teachers to work toward the latter.

We have a lot more to say on this point in Chapter 7. For now, however, let us highlight some key components of the classroom environment. Three elements of classroom life seem most appropriate: discourse, classroom organization, and dispositions.

Comparing these elements across traditional and genuine classrooms reveals some startling differences. In traditional classrooms, much of the discourse follows two predictable patterns: The teacher talks and the students listen or the teacher asks a question, a student answers, and the teacher evaluates the answer as right or wrong. Classroom organization in traditional settings is also fairly predictable in that students do most of their work quietly and individually at their seats. Finally, the values or dispositions evident in a traditional class-room emphasize hard work, efficiency, deference to authority, and external rewards. Each of these elements contributes to a **factory model of schooling,** in which teachers are plant managers and students are laborers whose job it is to produce—that is, learn—quickly, quietly, individually, and in response to rewards.

Although they are not as easily characterized, genuine classrooms tend to feature a greater balance between teacher talk and student talk, more diversity in the substance of that talk, and a greater balance in terms of who controls the conversation. The latter two points are important because we want to increase the opportunities children have to air their views and to increase the focus on their ideas and interests. Genuine classrooms also emphasize more balance among activities. Rather than rely on whole-class instruction and individual seatwork, teachers in genuine classrooms use a wide variety of instructional settings, depending on the task at hand.

■ ■ ■ ■ ELEMENTS OF CLASSROOM LIFE

- **Discourse** refers to the nature of the talk that goes on in a classroom, that is, who talks in the classroom and what do they talk about?

- **Classroom organization** concerns the ways in which learning activities are structured. For example, how are learners organized for teaching and learning, and who decides? What classroom rules are evident, and who chooses them?

- **Dispositions** are those values and attitudes a teacher and his or her learners create and practice during classroom activity. For example, is there an honest respect for and commitment to inquiry, open respect for and commitment to ideas and people, and patient respect for and commitment to argument and evidence?

TABLE 1.1 A Comparison of Traditional and Genuine Classrooms

	Traditional classrooms	Genuine classrooms
Discourse	Teachers do most of the talking; students listen or teacher talks and students answer direct questions	Greater balance between teacher talk and student talk
Classroom organization	Whole-group recitation and individual seatwork	Wide variety of whole-group, small-group, partner, and individual activities
Dispositions	Emphasis on hard work, efficiency, deference to authority, and external rewards	Emphasis on ideas, people, inquiry, argument, and evidence

Finally, genuine classrooms reflect values that promote respect for and commitment to ideas and people, inquiry and argument, and evidence. Because genuine classrooms emphasize student learning and understanding rather than the amount of work students produce, it makes sense that the discourse, classroom organization, and dispositions differ greatly from those found in traditional classrooms. Table 1.1 summarizes the differences between traditional and genuine classrooms.

One reason students dislike social studies is that they tend to study it in traditional settings. In fact, we have too often seen a teacher do exciting work in reading or mathematics only to become "Traditional Teacher" when it is time for social studies. Whatever the reason for this transformation, if we want to avoid replicating the kind of social studies classrooms that we all disliked, we need to rework the discourse, organization, and dispositions evident in them.

And that is yet one more reason why we are so impressed with Ruby, for here is a teacher who clearly is pushing beyond the traditional. First, she encourages student talk rather than monopolizing the classroom conversation. For example, first graders in Ruby's class who have discovered new information or have a special expertise can become class "experts" who share their knowledge and skills with others. Second, Ruby organizes students' work in a variety of ways rather than emphasizing individual seatwork. Depending on the activity, students may work in pairs, small groups, or as part of the whole class. Finally, Ruby discourages competition in favor of sharing, cooperation, consideration, and participation.

Ruby takes seriously what she calls her students' "hunger to learn" (Levstik, 1993, p. 19). To that end, three dispositions are key: The first is inquiry—building on the children's expressed *need to know*; the second is providing multiple ways to *find out*; and the third is *providing opportunities* to share discoveries, understandings, or misunderstandings. In these several ways, we see a teacher working toward the kind of genuine classroom community that serves all her students well.

Although thinking about your own experience in this way might have seemed new and awkward at first, we bet that the ideas fairly tumbled out once you got started. With practice, analyzing classroom situations using the commonplaces framework should become easier. We also expect that this framework will prove useful as you begin to prepare classroom inquiries.

▶I◀ REFLECTION: CLASSROOMS YOU HAVE KNOWN

Reflect on some of the classrooms you have been in. What were they like? Were some more conducive to genuine learning than others? What factors might have contributed to that sense? Conversely, what factors do you think were at play in classrooms where it was more difficult to learn? What kind of classroom environment will you try to foster?

Now think back to a memorable learning experience you have had. It could be something you learned last week or when you were five, it could be something you learned at school or at home or on a playground. The key is that you learned something that has stayed with you as an experience. Once you have an experience in mind, analyse it through four commonplaces: learners and learning, subject matter, teachers and teaching, and environment.

- What did the teacher know about you as a learner (and if it was a class situation, what did she or he know about the other learners)? What assumptions did she or he make about learning the task at hand?

- What did the teacher know about the subject matter? What ideas and questions did the teacher want you to think about?

- How did the teacher "teach" you? How did she or he represent ideas? How did the teacher know when you had learned what she or he could teach you?

- What did it feel like to learn in this situation? How did you and the teacher interact?

With so much to think about, how can anyone manage to teach? We were not kidding when we warned you that classrooms are complex places. The simple fact is that there is way too much going on in the typical classroom for any teacher to attend to it all, all of the time. If we had to give individual attention to each commonplace at every moment during the school day, the job would be too big indeed. But as we will see in the next section, using the commonplaces actually gets easier when you look at them together.

■ SECTION SUMMARY:
THE FOUR COMMONPLACES

- The individual commonplaces provide a useful framework for analyzing and understanding classroom situations.

- The *learners and learning* commonplace focuses on how students are similar and different, what they know and care about, and how they learn (behaviorism and constructivism).

- The *subject matter* commonplace focuses on the content of social studies (the threads) and how to make it appropriate for students.

- The *teachers and teaching* commonplace focuses on how teachers plan their instruction (compelling questions) and the factors that play into their decisions.

- The *classroom environment* commonplace focuses on classroom "feel" in terms of discourse, organization, and dispositions (traditional and genuine classrooms).

Looking at the Commonplaces in Interaction

If the commonplaces help us focus on individual elements of teaching and learning, they are even more useful in helping us understand the complex dynamics of classroom life. Teachers, no less than children, can get lost in the swirl of the school day. We see the commonplaces in interaction as an anchor, a way of making sense, of holding strong, and of seeing new possibilities.

For example, consider the question of what learners know and care about. The most obvious connection here is to the *subject matter* commonplace. As a school subject, social studies emphasizes people, places, and events the world over from the beginning of time until today. Wise teachers know well their diverse students' particular interests and the subject matter content they are responsible for, and they are able to highlight instances where those interests and that content intersect.

Asking what learners know and care about also raises questions about the *classroom environment*. Kids know and care about many things, only some of which are academic. They also care about concepts such as fairness and justice, and about having opportunities to think and talk about their developing ideas. If learners are to thrive, the environment in which they learn matters as much as the subject matter taught. Good teachers know that they cannot simply tell students about ideas. Instead, they create classroom environments where learners can become immersed in those ideas and where they feel comfortable expressing their emerging understandings. Those understandings may rarely sound "right" to adult ears, so good teachers are careful not to quash young thinkers' spirits and their participation by judging their contributions too quickly and too harshly.

Finally, if thinking about what learners know and care about raises issues of subject matter and environment, it also raises issues related to *teaching*. "Knowing" and "caring" are related, but they are not the same thing. Many teachers zero in on what students need to know, and consequently their teaching tends to emphasize direct instruction—telling students what they need to know, assigning worksheets to reinforce that knowledge, and using objective-style tests to evaluate what students know. Although there is nothing inherently wrong with such an approach, in our view, it seems a little thin. Knowing is important, but so too is caring about what one learns. For example, it is important to know the particulars about Columbus's encounters with New World natives. At the same time, it is important to encourage students to empathize with the historical characters and to understand what motivated them, how those motivations played out, and the implications of those events for children for whom 1492 seems a million years ago. Teachers who want their students to know *and* care about history think and act differently from their colleagues who are interested in knowledge alone. They are more likely to offer multiple and varied opportunities for tackling new ideas, to encourage learners' multiple interpretations of events, and to use a range of assessments for understanding what learners know.

To demonstrate the power of the commonplaces in interaction, let's return one more time to Ruby's first-grade classroom. In the following vignette, the researcher, Linda Levstik, describes the classroom activities that develop around the artifacts she brought back from a trip through Scotland and England. As you read, think about instances in which each of the commonplaces surfaces and how each of them interacts with others:

> The class is putting the finishing touches on a story about things to see in Scotland and England. They are anxious to see if I have brought anything back with me, so Ruby suggests we share pictures, books, and some artifacts (hats, brass rubbing kits, coins).
>
> DARREN: What is this book about?
> LINDA: Vikings. It comes from an excavation of a Viking village.
>
> The teacher allows several students to work with English money. Jake and Angel try counting out money:
>
> ANGEL: Did you buy these things with this money?
> LINDA: Yes. You can't use American money in English stores.
> MITCHELL: Could you use this here? (He joins Jake and Angel as they continue to try to count the money, reminding themselves of what each coin represents: "That's like a dime.")
>
> Six other children have gone to the back of the room to work on brass rubbings, and Erin wants to know if he can show Ms. Jones's class the bobby's hat he is wearing. Another group gathers around a pile of books, pictures, and magazines the teacher had been sharing. She adds the new brochures, and the group begins to discuss the age of some of the buildings:
>
> DARREN: Some of those are real new, they just make them look like real castles.
> LINDA: Well, we do that in this country, don't we. The one you're looking at is pretty new. It's only one hundred fifty years old.
> CATRINA: One hundred fifty years! That's old!
> MITCHELL: The Vikings are older than that.
> RUBY: How long ago were the Vikings? Does anyone remember? (No one can recall. They think it was "long, long ago, back when they had those ships.")

Darren is working on his own, again, reading the Viking activity book and carefully copying something on a large sheet of manila paper.

DARREN: Look what I've done. (He shows how he has written his name using the Viking alphabet.)
ROGER: Let me see that. (He tries his name, too.)

Others gather around to see the writing. Within minutes, about half the class is trying to write in the Viking script. Darren has moved on to discover a plan for building a Viking village.

DARREN: Mrs. Y., you should run this off.
RUBY: All right, we'll see if we can get copies. (The Viking writing group decides it would also like copies.)
RUBY: Would everyone like to do this? We'll run enough copies.

(Levstik, 1993, p. 11–12)

Reflect on the following questions about this vignette.

- What does Ruby seem to understand about the children in her class?
- How does she approach the subject matter of Viking life?
- What teaching approaches and materials does she use to teach the class?
- What do the classroom discourse, organization, and dispositions look like?
- How do these instances of learners and learning, subject matter, teachers and teaching, and environment interact?

■ SECTION SUMMARY:
THE COMMONPLACES IN INTERACTION

- Classrooms are bustling places, with much for teachers to think about and do.
- Considering the commonplaces in interaction provides a more comprehensive means of analyzing and understanding classroom activity.

Elementary-school children contribute so much in their enthusiasm to think, learn, and grow that teaching them is truly rewarding. What other profession offers so many opportunities to touch the lives of others on a regular basis? At the same time, the hustle and bustle of an elementary-school classroom offers teachers plenty of opportunities for confusion, frustration, and anxiety. With so much to think about and react to, it is easy to feel overwhelmed. Time and experience help, but approaching the classroom with a framework such as the commonplaces in mind should help as you fashion and refashion yourself as a teacher.

Chapter Summary

1   **What are the key elements of each commonplace?**
    ■   *Learners and learning* highlights similarities and differences among students, what they know and care about, and theories about how they learn, such as behaviorism and constructivism.
    ■   *Subject matter* highlights the concepts and ideas of social studies and ways, such as the threads, to transform them for instruction.
    ■   *Teachers and teaching* highlights the big ideas teachers use to develop their instruction and the influences on their teaching decisions.
    ■   *Classroom environment* highlights the differences between traditional and genuine classrooms in terms of discourse, organization, and dispositions.
2   **How do the commonplaces work in interaction?** Classrooms are complex places. Evidence of the individual commonplaces can be detected, but most situations can be understood by looking for the intersections of one commonplace with others. Thus, a teacher's view of learners and learning has implications for the subject matter she or he teaches, the instructional strategies she or he chooses, and the classroom environment that develops.
3   **How does an understanding of the commonplaces help me think about teaching and learning?** Good teachers see connections. A framework such as the commonplaces helps teachers to plan their instruction and to analyze and work to remedy problems.

Notes

1   This list represents an adaptation of Schwab's conception of the commonplaces, which were learners, teachers, subject matter, and milieu. Schwab's conception focuses on the "translat[ion] of scholarly material into curriculum" (Schwab, 1978, p. 365). We are interested in the curriculum development process, but we believe Schwab's ideas can be expanded to encompass a way of thinking about all that goes on in a classroom.
2   The idea of using social science constructs to provide a conceptual framework is an old one. Our presentation of the threads is adapted from that developed by Dr. Patricia Ames. Her version consisted of five elements: physical, political, economic, sociocultural, and international. We develop the rationale for our version in Chapter 3.

Teaching Resources

Print Resources

Barr, R., Barth, J., & Shermis, S. (1977). *Defining the social studies*. Arlington, VA: National Council for the Social Studies.
This classic work is a good place to begin understanding the teaching and learning of social studies.

Jenness, D. (1990). *Making sense of social studies*. New York: Macmillan.
A short history of the field, this book offers a grounding in the founding ideas and ideals of social studies education.

Levstik, L.S., & Barton, K.C. (2015). *Doing history: Investigating with children in elementary and middle schools* (5th ed.). New York: Routledge.
This book offers pre-service and practicing teachers a range of ways to think about teaching history to young children.

Good sources for current articles on teaching and learning social studies are the National Council for the Social Studies journals, *Theory and Research in Social Education* and *Social Studies for the Young Learner*. Another good source, particularly for practical classroom articles, is the Heldref (now Taylor and Francis) publication, *The Social Studies*. All of these journals are available for subscription, and most libraries carry them.

Technology Resources

- www.ncss.org
  The National Council for the Social Studies is the leading professional organization for teachers of social studies. Their website offers a range of useful information and resources to both beginning and practicing teachers.

Learners and Learning
Understanding What Students Know and How They Come to Know It

Ten-year-old Helen has spent the social studies portion of fourth grade studying the history of the state of Michigan. From this purview, she has constructed a window from which to view the broader landscape of American history. Here, at the end of fourth grade, standing on the precipice of fifth-grade American history, she excitedly offers her version of how the United States came to be:

HELEN'S STORY

The British and the Americans, they fought. The United States was really poor and it didn't have that much, but the British had fabulous stuff and they weren't poor. They had clothes and stuff like that. Then, America was just a poor country. There were people there but they weren't the richest part of the world. The British agreed never to fight the Americans again, and America agreed to that. They never fought again, but the British—I'm not sure about this part—but I think the British went against their promise, and the British left and they had to do something like sign a paper or something to get it together, a promise, and the British left and they never got a chance to sign or do whatever they had to do to make the promise. But this time, America was rich and had a lot of soldiers and the Americans won over the British and that's how we got our country. The British won three or four times, and America won only once. The Americans won so the British—there was only one or two people left.

What does Helen know? What does she do with what she knows? Here, Helen weaves her version of the birth of the United States. She has read about the French and Indian War and the battles fought in Michigan by the British against the French and their Native-American allies. She has some knowledge of the Revolutionary War, waged only a decade or so later between the American colonists and the British. In her tapestry, she weaves these elements together in a rather fanciful, elaborated account (Brophy & VanSledright, 1997). In short, she creates new cloth from old thread.

However, Helen's version of these affairs bears only slim resemblance to the accounts historians have researched and written. Her historical tapestry, compellingly arranged and highly imaginative, places ideas from different histories, different wars, and different combatants into one fabric. Helen's storytelling fails to separate these wars and define the chronological space dividing them. Why? What's going on here? Why has she failed to learn her history lessons?

Helen's account demonstrates the active knowledge construction characteristic of young learners. But fourth grade is Helen's first encounter with chronologically arranged history taught systematically across a school year, a common social studies curriculum pattern in the United States: state history in fourth grade and a survey of US history in fifth grade (see Brophy, VanSledright, & Bredin, 1993; Naylor & Diem, 1987). She is only beginning to think historically and to develop a larger sense of historical understanding. Her account indicates how her thinking about the history she learned, coupled with whatever **prior knowledge** she has picked up from casual reading, television, film, mass culture, and earlier grades in school, coalesces around the idea of war in America.

She is starting to form an active set of ideas about this larger concept of war. However, as young learners often are apt to do, she overgeneralizes the idea of wars fought for American independence to include more than simply the American Revolutionary War. She weaves the Revolutionary War together with threads of the French and Indian War, not surprisingly, since this war played a much larger role in the history of Michigan than did the Revolutionary War.

What has Helen learned? Is she constructing the sort of knowledge that a teacher might want her to construct? Helen's interesting though conflated and naive retelling of the birth of a nation might be reason for concern, particularly if one of your goals is to get Helen to develop a more valid accounting of the American past.

At this point, however, our concern is less with the factual accuracy of Helen's knowledge than with the active, imaginative intellectual process she is demonstrating. When elementary-grade learners read about and study dynamic social studies topics such as the French and Indian and Revolutionary Wars, they are constantly busy creating new ideas in their heads and rearranging old ones as you present new topics and social studies concepts. This is the active and inquisitive, though sometimes bumpy, cognitive terrain on which you will teach social studies to your students. The process of creating new ideas, knowledge, and meaning from the residue of prior conceptions and experiences in a learning context is what educational theorists call constructivism.

We will come back to the idea of constructivism and its rich implications for teaching social studies later in this chapter. For the moment, consider a second story by Rita, another student who also has studied Michigan history in fourth grade. With relish and animation, she talks about why Europeans called the Western Hemisphere the New World, even though it was an old world to the natives who already lived there:

RITA'S STORY

They used to live in England, the British, and ... they wanted to get to China 'cause China had some stuff they wanted. They had some cups, or whatever— no, they had furs. They had fur and stuff like that and they wanted to have a shorter way to get to China, so they took it, and they landed in Michigan, but it wasn't called Michigan. I think it was the British that landed in Michigan, and they were there first so they tried to claim that land, but it didn't work out for some reason so they took some furs and brought them back to Britain and they sold them. But they mostly wanted it for the furs. So then the English landed there and they claimed the land and wanted to make it a state, and so they got it signed by the government or whoever, the big boss [laughs], then they were just starting to make it a state, so the British just went up to the Upper Peninsula [in Michigan] and they thought they could stay there a little while. Then they had to fight a war, then the farmers, they were just volunteers, so the farmers went right back to try to put their families back together again.

What does Rita know, and what does she do with it? Rita, like Helen, conflates pieces of territorial Michigan history with European efforts at finding a shorter, more economical trading route to the Far East. That exploration resulted in the fur trade—well, at least in Michigan—but Rita overgeneralizes this trade a bit. The British play a central role. The French are not mentioned, yet the war to which she alludes (unless she is speaking of the Revolutionary War—we don't know for sure) pitted the British against the French in a seven-year war over control, not only of the Michigan territory, but over these two European powers' dominance of trade around the world. Does Rita understand all this? It's difficult to tell; what she says reads a bit like "fact stew." However, if we realize that she is a novice, we begin to see the active, inquiring, and constructive capability of her mind to combine new learning opportunities with prior knowledge and conceptions of the past.

Also notice how her allusions to the French and Indian War differ from Helen's. Could you tell that both had the same social studies teacher in fourth grade, were taught the same curriculum, and read many of the same books? Their overall experiences were much alike, yet their ideas and the way they build new conceptions differ. Why?

Constructivist theorists believe that learning can be highly idiosyncratic, as different minds with various degrees of prior knowledge about a topic or concept engage new ideas in various ways. The result is often mysterious, making teaching problematic and uncertain, but endlessly interesting and engaging nonetheless. One thing is clear: The old notion that children's minds are like **blank slates** on which the teacher simply writes the appropriate knowledge, and later tests to check for its presence, is seriously misleading, if not just plain wrong. Using prior ideas and understandings, Helen and Rita are busy constructing their own views of things, however idiosyncratic. The idea of the mind being a blank slate simply will no longer do, and Rita and Helen present us with crystallized illustrations that show us why not.

So how do we make sense of Helen's and Rita's stories? Helen and Rita may not have all their facts right, but their responses are animated, interesting, and deeply engaging. Are these two girls the exception? In one sense, they are. Most children report being bored by the dull parade of facts and worksheet instruction they experience in their social studies classrooms. Helen and Rita, however, seem alive with ideas and naive assumptions about what they are learning. We believe Helen and Rita really are like most other grade-school students: They like to think and talk about provocative, meaty ideas. It's not that students cannot or refuse to like social studies, but that much of what passes for social studies in their classrooms seems rather lifeless. Creative teachers can change all that.

In this chapter, we want to focus attention on the commonplace called Learners and Learning. When you have completed this chapter, you should be able to answer the following questions:

1   What do elementary-age children know about social studies?
2   How do children learn about social studies?
3   Where do they learn about social studies?
4   What is constructivism as a learning theory, and what are its assumptions?
5   What are the problems and promises of constructivism for social studies teachers?

Knowing and Learning About Social Studies

What Do Children Know about Social Studies?

What do students know about social studies, where do they learn it, and how? These questions seem simple enough to answer, but as it turns out, we have a number of things yet to learn about what students know concerning subjects such as history, geography, economics, and the like. We have made progress in history but less so in other social studies subject areas (see Levstik & Tyson, 2008). We know even less about how they acquire knowledge, and less yet about where they learn all their social studies ideas.[1] These questions have been more thoroughly researched in reading/language arts and mathematics, and to some degree in science.

Social studies educators, by contrast, have traditionally focused more on theoretical issues of curriculum selection, history of the social studies profession, and social education goals than on issues of what and how students learn. Those researchers who have examined children's knowledge about social studies subjects and topics through surveys have yielded some limited information about what children know. Recently, more detailed studies using interviewing techniques indicate that young children hold little deep knowledge about major social studies topics and subjects, that what they learn develops rapidly and incrementally and is influenced by prior experience and understanding but remains wide open to change.

The latter is particularly true when it comes to how they deal with economic concerns such as banks, money, exchange, and consumer goods (see Berti & Bombi, 1988; Jahoda, 1984); political ideas such as governing processes, political leadership, and the role and influence of the president of the United States (see Coles, 1986; Moore, Lare, & Wagner, 1985); and about how society works in general (see Furth, 1980; Turiel, 1983). Over the last two decades in the United States, we have learned much also about what children know about history (see Barton, 2008; Monte-Sano & Reisman, 2016; VanSledright & Limon, 2006; Wineburg, 1996).

To explore what your elementary students might know, we'll begin by examining several exemplary research studies on children's ideas about economics, politics and government, geography, and common cultural phenomena. Then, in the next section, we'll sample a few studies from a fairly large and growing body of work on children's historical understandings.

IN YOUR CLASSROOM

UNDERSTANDING HOW CHILDREN CONSTRUCT MEANING

The following will help you gain a sense of the active, meaning–construction process young learners engage in.

- Choose a social studies topic that children in elementary school might know something about (for example, Native Americans, school or classroom rules, the Civil War, how people use shelters, where natural resources come from).
- Choose two or three students and find a quiet spot where you can talk to them.
- Begin with two questions: What do you know about [the topic you chose]? and Where do your ideas come from?
- Probe the ideas they suggest by asking them to say more, as appropriate.
- Tape-record their answers.
- Listen carefully to the tape-recordings and compare and contrast the children's responses.

Children's Ideas about Economics

In a detailed and wide-ranging study conducted in the late 1980s, two Italian researchers (Berti & Bombi, 1988) interviewed small groups of working- and middle-class Italian children ages four to fourteen to see what they knew about work, work roles, payment for work, ideas about a "boss," where money comes from, views of rich and poor people, understandings of banks and production and distribution, the value of money in buying and selling, and other general economic topics. Here are three examples of what the researchers found:

■ *How do people get paid for working?* Italian children about age five believe that workers are paid directly by consumers for their work. They also know little about the range of occupations. As they get older, their knowledge of the range of occupations grows rapidly. They begin to differentiate occupations clearly, and a notion of a "boss" emerges around age eight. At this age, the children still struggle with how a boss gets money to pay workers, but by age twelve or so, the children begin to understand that goods and services are exchanged for money used to pay workers and that money "circulates" through an economy.

■ *Who's the "boss"?* The youngest children are fully aware of bosses or owners, but they do not differentiate them. A boss is anyone these children think to be in charge. By age seven, children can verbally differentiate a boss from an owner, and by age ten, they can explain how a boss directs workers based on orders given by an owner. These older children also are quite adept at constructing "pyramids of authority," that is, they can explain who reports to whom in the organization.

■ *Who are the rich and the poor?* The youngest children have little understanding of *rich* and *poor*, thinking that being poor is odd since anyone can get money by simply going to the bank. These ideas change rapidly as children come to realize that people obtain money as a result of working. By ages six and seven, the children think that people who work are rich and that being poor is a result of being unable or unwilling to work. These children also tend to think of their own families as rich. By age eight, the children construct a fairly complex three-tiered hierarchy, placing what they call "normal people" in the middle (middle class). They also develop "degrees of richness" related to how hard one works. By ages eleven and twelve, the children begin explaining that intensity of work does not necessarily translate into greater or lesser "richness." Their views begin to show more sophisticated analyses of richness and poorness with greater levels and degrees of differentiation between them.

Much of this work on children's understanding of economics and how economies work has been reviewed more recently. This review includes more current studies and discusses what we now know that we didn't before. Although our knowledge is still limited, these types of reviews can be very useful in understanding more about who your students are and what ideas they bring to your classroom. See the review about economic understandings by Steven Miller and Phillip VanFossen (2008).

RESOURCES: TEACHING ECONOMICS

A good source of teaching lessons, activities, and curriculum standards related to economics is the National Council on Economic Education. Their home page is at www.councilforeconed.org

"Virtual Economics" is a site where you can explore a demo loaded with interesting in structional activities about economics. For more information go to http://ve.councilforeconed.org

FIGURE 2.1 Economics lessons can occur in many venues, both inside and outside the classroom. What might this child be learning as her parents take the keys to their new car?

Children's Ideas about Politics and Government

Children know about more than the economic world. They are also forming ideas about their political worlds. In the United States, two researchers were curious about young children's political knowledge (see Adelson & O'Neil, 1966). Based on interviews, they report that six- and seven-year-olds could name favorite politicians they knew but could not describe much about how the political process works. These youngsters also have difficulty imagining the consequences of political choices. They think of government in terms of the services it offers (for example, trash pickup), see it as a justified authority, and tend to be insensitive to individual liberties.

In Australia, a similar study on political ideas draws from a much wider range of elementary-age students (Connell, 1971). The study's results suggest that, although younger students do not see politics as a matter of making choices, they later learn that it involves selecting from alternatives. Once this shift occurs, the children quickly begin to take political positions and to develop consistent political preferences. However, notable variation appears in how quickly students make the shift to the new ideas. By the pre-adolescent years, many of the Australian children begin to see themselves as political actors in their own right, capable of making choices with real consequences for themselves (for example, making personal choices about ecological matters such as recycling and understanding how those decisions influence their environment). But again, not all children move to these understandings at the same speed. Some are thinking with more cognitive complexity when others are still having some difficulty with personalizing choices and preferences.

Robert Coles (1986), a noted child psychiatrist, spent years traveling around the United States in the 1960s and 1970s, talking to young children about their views of politics and government. He interviewed Black children and White children, Hispanic and Native-American children, and middle-class, working-class, and poor children. He found that kids' views of politics and government vary considerably. For example, relatively wealthy middle- and upper-middle-class kids give government leaders far more favorable reviews than do poor children. Poor children, even as young as six and seven, can be quite cynical about politicians, noting that they believe that politicians support whatever rich people want. Black children, too, tend to be more cynical about politics than White children. Some Black children Coles spoke with in the deep South think that it is a White world, ruled by and for White people. African Americans, they believe, have little hope of changing that. By contrast, White children, especially those from suburban and upper-middle-class backgrounds, have mostly positive and supportive things to say about the country, politicians, and government, thinking of themselves as inheritors of that positive heritage.

RESOURCES: TEACHING POLITICS AND GOVERNMENT

The Center for Civic Education offers a variety of classroom-based materials for teachers as well as links to standards in civic education. Their home page is at www.civiced.org

Coles (1986) also finds that, contrary to general public perception, children, even young ones, are astute in their observations about political life and the workings of authority in interrelationships. Often, children resort to platitudes when describing interrelationships, power, and politics in school or in casual conversations with adults, but in private, when pressed "children [are] constantly noticing who gets along with whom, and why" (p. 40). In summarizing some of his findings on children's views of political authority, Coles notes, "Children ingeniously use every scrap of emotional life available to them in their ... development, and they do likewise as they try to figure out how (and for whom) the world works" (p. 41).

Much of what Coles reports in his work appeared also in a recent study of young elementary children spanning several middle elementary years in two locations, Ohio and Georgia (Hauver, 2019). Like Coles, the upshot of Hauver's study points to the different ways in which even quite young children pay very close attention to the political and civic messages they receive in school and how those messages help them construct ideas about how the world around them works and for whom.

For more on these lines of research, see also a review of children's understanding of politics and government that builds and expands on some of this earlier work (Hahn & Alviar-Martin, 2008).

Children's Ideas about Maps

Much of the research that deals with children's ideas in geography centers on maps and how children develop the necessary reasoning to understand them. The studies focus on three areas: perspective taking, maps as models of the world, and navigation (Gregg & Leinhardt, 1994).

Much of the early research conducted in the 1950s to mid-1970s with regard to perspective taking—how one uses maps to understand what they show—describes children as going through **developmental stages**. For example, children first pass through a stage where they hold a simplistic perspective, then at a certain age move to a slightly more complex perspective, and so on, with clear age boundaries marking each stage. However, by the 1980s, other studies successfully challenged rigid developmental-stage approaches. This later work on what children know about perspective suggests that, initially, they have difficulty with the idea that a map represents a perspective of an actual space (the world, a country, a state). Researchers claim that this is because children construct understandings of space and perspectives of space gradually. Greater levels of exposure to maps as perspectives on actual space speed up the process of attaining the idea, often regardless of age. Children also initially have difficulty with conventions such as north, south, east, and west. Again, repeated exposure speeds up how quickly even younger children learn the conventions. This is especially true with north and south, because educators can assist by using north-as-up and south-as-down conventions, something even young children know. East and west are more difficult because their orientations on a map are always relative to where the child is positioned.

To understand maps as models of the world, children need to know what the different symbol markers on the maps represent. Children who have not been exposed to maps struggle with the symbol system. For example, Liben and Downs (1989) found that children variously describe urban centers on maps—frequently shown as yellow dots—as eggs or firecrackers going off. But again, with repeated exposure to the map symbols, children at young ages can master their meaning. It does take them longer, though, to obtain the idea that the symbols stand for some actual real-life objects. The speed at which they attain the latter understanding depends largely on the amount of detail found on the map; simpler maps help them grasp the idea more quickly (Bluestein & Acredolo, 1979). Symbols such as latitude and longitude lines can pose problems for young

FIGURE 2.2 Although researchers tell us that young children have some difficulty learning some geographic concepts, good teachers know the power of providing a variety of physical world representations for children to explore.

children if they are presented on a rounded surface, such as a globe. However, children as young as six and seven do quickly learn the idea of latitude and longitude if they are presented on a flat surface. Scale is another symbol that can confuse children. However, one study demonstrates that children with exposure to three-dimensional models that represent larger objects (such as a toy truck model of the real thing) quickly understand scale.

The work on children's knowledge of navigation using maps is relatively sparse. Navigation refers to using a map to plan a route or trace where one is going. As you can imagine, young children who have had experiences with parents and relatives using maps to navigate, say, on a vacation trip, learn rather quickly to interpret navigation aids on maps. These children can have some fairly good map-reading and navigation skills by the time you see them in second or third grade, when maps and map skills are often taught. Research documents that children as young as three years old know how to navigate a room using a map to find a hidden object, provided the map is simple, is accurately oriented to the room from the child's viewpoint, and includes clear landmarks, such as doors, furniture, and windows (Bluestein & Acredolo, 1979). Other studies confirm similar results, noting that the presence of clear landmarks is a key to navigation for younger students. The studies also indicate that as children grow older, their sophistication in map use grows quickly with extended exposure.

For more on such studies, read the review done by Avner Segall and Robert Helfenbein (2008).

RESOURCES: TEACHING MAPS

You can find many classroom lessons and activities that use maps at TeachersNet: http://teachers.net/curriculum/socialstudies.html

Children's Ideas about Common Cultural Phenomena

During much of the 1990s and into the early 2000s, researchers Jere Brophy and Jan Alleman studied what they call "cultural universals" among young children in kindergarten through third grade in the United States. Brophy and Alleman sought to understand what children at these grade levels already knew about common cultural phenomena such as the nature of human shelters, where clothing comes from, and how government and economic systems work. They studied the children's ideas as they entered school and how ideas changed as a result of typical units of social studies taught them on these topics in the early elementary grades.

In one study, Brophy, Alleman, and O'Mahoney (2003) explored 96 children's knowledge and thinking about food. The children were predominantly White from a middle- and working-class town in the upper Midwest. In summarizing their data, the researchers concluded that the students had a fairly keen grasp of the physical appearance of food items but lacked a broader understanding of how, for example, processed foods had become finished products. In other words, students from kindergarten to third grade demonstrated a "black box" understanding of the land-to-hand relationships involved in putting food on the table at home.

The children could identify the foodstuffs with some precision and could say that much of the food derived from growth on the land, but they had difficulty explaining what process was involved in getting it from the land into consumers' hands. Some students, however, displayed reasonably sophisticated causal thinking, noting that technology and geography both play a role in which foods are available to us and help account for differences in the food eaten in different cultures.

Brophy et al. (2003) noted that older students generally had more sophisticated ideas. However, the transcript data the researchers provide demonstrates that some younger children can hold more sophisticated ideas than older children. Experience and sociocultural location (e.g., city versus farm, upper-middle class versus lower class) contribute heavily to differences among children's knowledge and thinking about food. These same patterns emerged in Brophy and Alleman's (1997) earlier study on children's ideas about shelter.

RESOURCES: TEACHING ABOUT COMMON CULTURAL PHENOMENA

In the early grades, US social studies curricula typically focus on teaching about common cultural phenomena such as food, clothing, and shelter. Using their research studies as a base, Alleman and Brophy have produced a three-volume set of lesson plans for teaching these topics:

Alleman, J., & Brophy, J. (2001). *Social studies excursions, K–3, Book One: Powerful units on food, clothing, and shelter*. Portsmouth, NH: Heinemann.

Alleman, J., & Brophy, J. (2001). *Social studies excursions, K–3, Book Two: Powerful units on communication, transportation, and family living*. Portsmouth, NH: Heinemann.

Alleman, J., & Brophy, J. (2002). *Social studies excursions, K–3, Book Three: Powerful units on government, economics/money, and childhood throughout history*. Portsmouth, NH: Heinemann.

Drawing Conclusions about What Children Know

In just these few research-based illustrations, we've seen that children know a surprising amount about varied aspects of their social worlds. They also display sometimes startling growth in their ideas about sociocultural, economic, and political topics. We can conclude that elementary-age children's ideas change and expand, almost overnight it seems, highlighting their capacity and desire to actively build and modify their knowledge. After reading studies such as the above, we wonder what elementary teachers mean when we hear them say, "Kids can't do or can't learn" when it comes to social studies. Even young children can learn many things in fairly quick order if teachers take time to assess the ideas they hold and help them construct ideas built upon what they already know, even though, as we have seen, these ideas can be naive and distorted.

From these preceding studies we can draw a second conclusion. It appears that children's ideas quickly become more sophisticated and differentiated as they actively construct new meaning from concepts and experiences they encounter in school. As the studies of the Italian, US, and Australian children suggest, children also pick up a host of ideas about their social, economic, and political worlds independent of school, from their parents, friends, popular culture, television, and their own personal experiences.

We also can draw a third conclusion. Even young children show almost unlimited capabilities to learn ideas, concepts, and principles about their present world and that of the past. Sometimes educators are tempted to think that children are moving through some sequential, fairly rigid developmental-stage process. You may have heard about **Piagetian theory**, used to describe children as "being in a certain stage." We want to argue that making this claim is short-sighted. We know of no neat, agreed-upon method of labeling students by developmental learning "stage," or of any method on the immediate horizon. Yes, children do appear to move in some type of progression from understanding simple ideas to having much greater command of complex concepts and questions.

However, children appear to move along at different speeds, and most seem to be willing to grapple with almost anything that's interesting, even if it's a difficult idea. The variation in children's development defies any simple method of categorizing them by age-specific stages. And we have no real clear sense yet, based on social studies research, of how challenging them with complex ideas in classroom contexts can speed along what they learn.

And one last conclusion: Children do have difficulty understanding and retaining the new ideas they encounter if those ideas are not connected to their prior knowledge, lack coherence, and are not embedded within a meaningful context. Take, for example, the National Assessment of Educational Progress (NAEP) done by the US government. These assessments are administered every five years or so in the social studies areas of history and geography, as well as in reading, science, and mathematics. To get a look at some of the more current test results, consult this website: https://www.nationsreportcard.gov/hgc_2014/

In the late 1980s, Diane Ravitch and Chester Finn (1987) published a book that analyzed results of the US history portion of the NAEP. They noted that students do poorly, are unable to remember many key historical events and important figures, and even have difficulty placing an event as memorable as the Civil War in the correct part of the nineteenth century. Since then, there have been several additional administrations of the NAEP history test that have turned up largely the same kinds of results.

If we take a closer look at the analysis and results, however, and couple them with what we know about how history is typically taught in US classrooms, the poor results make our point. In the typical approach to teaching history, students read a standard, often difficult-to-understand textbook, answer questions at the end of the chapters, listen to a teacher lecture about the facts in the textbook, and take a multiple-choice test on Friday (see Goodlad, 1984; Shaver, Davis, & Helburn, 1980; VanSledright & Limon, 2006). Students receive little help in connecting new historical ideas to their prior knowledge and usually receive little historical context in which to situate what they're supposed to learn. Rather, they are asked simply to memorize "the facts" and spit them back out on the tests. Nothing much sticks, and this comes as no surprise. Learning about social studies turns out to be much more than simple memorization. We discuss how to teach social studies as more than memorization in Chapters 4 and 5.

Generally speaking, the results of these studies suggest that, though young children can possess underdeveloped and naive ideas about societies and their economies, the situation changes dramatically in a few short years, from the time the children are about five and six to the time they leave elementary school. As we have said about Helen and Rita, children are active inquirers and meaning makers, busily constructing an understanding of their worlds. The richer those ideas are and the more tightly connected to what children already know, the more robust are children's understandings and the quicker their development. This is especially true in the area of history, where a spate of studies has emerged recently. But before we explore where children acquire their historical knowledge and how they learn it, let's review the research-based ideas we've touched on so far. We then devote a separate section to the topic of ideas about history because so much recent research has emerged on it.

■ SECTION SUMMARY:
WHAT CHILDREN KNOW ABOUT ECONOMICS, POLITICS AND GOVERNMENT, GEOGRAPHY, AND COMMON CULTURAL PHENOMENA

■ By the time children enter elementary school, they know a surprising amount about their social worlds. Not all their ideas are entirely accurate, and often they can be characterized by their "black box" nature (i.e., they see the box and still don't know what goes on inside). But children have formed some fairly sophisticated models of social life already.

■ Children's ideas about economics, politics, and government change and expand almost overnight, indicating their capacity and desire to actively build and modify their knowledge.

■ Children's thoughts on these subjects quickly become more sophisticated and differentiated as they actively construct new meaning through the process of being challenged with interesting ideas.

■ Children's capacity to learn ideas, concepts, and principles about their present world and that of the past appears almost unlimited, even though some "age-specific developmental stage theories" claim that young children cannot manage complex ideas that have abstract elements.

Children's Ideas about History

Perhaps one of the most systematic studies done in the US of what elementary students know and learn about American history was a year-long project that followed ten middle-class White students across their fifth-grade year (Brophy & VanSledright, 1997). The researchers interviewed the students in depth before and after seven different commonly taught history curriculum topics. A similar and detailed long-term study was conducted in Great Britain (see Lee & Ashby, 2000), but here we focus only on a quick summary of the results from the US study.

Students' knowledge of the history content of each unit before studying it was relatively sparse. Students often reported that they knew nothing. When they claimed to know something, their ideas were often loosely structured and under-developed. This is not surprising, because they had not studied American history in any systematic way before. However, after studying the material in class using textbooks and **trade books**, and listening to the history stories their teacher told, they reported significant gains in what they knew. In short, across the span of one school year, their knowledge of history increased significantly. Several of the ten children interviewed persisted in retaining certain naive conceptions (for example, that Native Americans had completely disappeared, that Johnny Tremain signed the Declaration of Independence), but overall, their knowledge growth was rather remarkable, thanks in part to a skillful, dynamic history teacher. Helen and Rita were both involved in this study.

A study done with six US eighth graders about to embark on a lengthy exploration of British colonization in North America further underscores what is likely happening for kids who take the history NAEP referred to earlier, namely, that historical facts, shorn of a compelling explanatory context such as a story or narrative, make little sense to learners. The researcher found that, even though the students had covered this same material in fifth grade, they had difficulty remembering much of what they studied (VanSledright, 1995). In interviews, five of six students recalled the name Jamestown from fifth grade, but they could say little more about it. This was the case with most of the questions regarding what they remembered from their fifth-grade study of colonization.

The one exception concerned Plymouth Rock and the early Plymouth colony. Students were able to tell the common, celebratory (and often distorted) story about the colonists' arrival there and the first Thanksgiving. They claimed they remembered this so well because they had heard the story in several elementary grades as part of the Thanksgiving holiday celebration. The other historical material got "all jumbled in my head," said one of the students, because it seemed like all he did in class was memorize facts that made little sense because they lacked a meaningful historical context.

For years, researchers and teachers thought that history was too abstract and complex a subject for young children to understand. They often cited children's trouble with dates and historical chronology as evidence for this conclusion and cited the Piagetian developmental stage theory (we say more about this in a moment) to claim that youngsters could not understand the abstract concepts inherent in historical study. To further examine the basis for this idea, two researchers explored how 58 US elementary students (approximately eight students in each of grades K–6) constructed understandings of historical time (in contrast to clock time or contemporary calendar time) (see Barton & Levstik, 1996). They were interested in testing further the claims that children below ages seven or eight often cannot make reliable distinctions about events in the past. What they found is intriguing.

The 58 students were asked to place nine pictures taken from a variety of historical time periods (for example, colonial era, the late nineteenth century, the 1950s) in the order they occurred chronologically. Not surprisingly, the responses varied by age. The youngest children, five- and six-year-olds, were able to make quite clear distinctions in historical time, but placing the pictures by actual dates had little meaning for them. They relied on picture context clues such as clothing and hairstyle and their background knowledge of such cultural artifacts to make

FIGURE 2.3 Children learn in many ways. As this third grader dresses up in traditional Russian costume and samples tea, she is experiencing history first-hand. Think about how you might extend the power of this learning opportunity when she returns to her classroom.

their choices. For example, "Kindergartner Mickey ... explained that the colonial picture was the oldest because 'they don't got nothing to wear 'cept those clothes,'" and first grader Mindy "noted that the colonial picture was the oldest 'cause there isn't anything to move and they walked all the time'" (Barton & Levstik, 1996, p. 431).

Not until about third grade did dates begin to make sense, and not until fifth and sixth grades did children begin to link dates with their background knowledge about event periods, such as colonization of the Atlantic seaboard by the British. For instance, fifth-grade Rodney "compared the 1920s and 1950s pictures by observing that 'in the thirties and twenties, that's when the cars like these start coming out, and these cars come out in the '60s'" (Barton & Levstik, 1996, p. 433).

The authors conclude that such sizable agreement across grade levels in placement of the pictures indicates that children have a large body of chronological history knowledge at their disposal. They use this outcome to dispute earlier claims that young children are not ready for historical study. Elementary-school teachers, they contend, can help to enhance young learners' ideas of the past and historical chronology by building on their existing knowledge of changes in popular culture such as clothing, technology, and hairstyles and by not relying exclusively on dates as organizers.

IN YOUR CLASSROOM

ESTABLISHING HISTORICAL CONTEXT

If you teach a unit on the English Pilgrim settlers who arrived in North America on the *Mayflower*, you might begin to establish historical context by using pictures of

- current forms of water transportation, to compare with ships such as the *Mayflower*;
- supplies that present-day explorers might take with them, to compare with pictures of tools and such materials the Pilgrims had taken along;
- Pilgrim clothing, to compare with present-day attire.

Engage students in a discussion of the differences, helping them to explain why such differences have developed.

Many of these studies suggest that young children have a tendency to oversimplify aspects of both the past and present, especially if the ideas they develop are heavily influenced by popular culture and not offset by other more balanced learning experiences. Although their ideas become more differentiated and less simplistic over time, children may continue to hold overgeneralized conceptions that can be difficult to dispel. Nonetheless, children appear game for almost any big, rich idea—known or unknown—that can engage their minds, regardless of age. Yes, some students will struggle more than others with powerful ideas, but how teachers present these ideas, not student age, seems to be the most important factor. For recent and helpful summary reviews of students' ideas about history, see also Barton (2008), Monte-Sano and Reisman (2016), and VanSledright and Limon (2006).

All of the conclusions we have drawn so far underscore our point about curious, active children's minds busily constructing meaning from almost everything they see, hear, and read as they build understandings. They also suggest that children can persist in retaining naive or misconceived ideas that make sense to them if those ideas are not countered with different conceptions. We will return momentarily to these points and what they might mean for you as a social studies teacher.

■ SECTION SUMMARY:
WHAT CHILDREN KNOW ABOUT HISTORY

- Children tend to oversimplify aspects of the past (and also the present) if the ideas they develop about history are heavily influenced by present-day popular culture.
- Children can hold and retain overgeneralized conceptions about history that may be difficult to change.

- Children, regardless of age, appear game for almost any big, rich idea—known or unknown—that can engage their minds.

- Some children will struggle more with historically complex ideas, but how teachers present these ideas seems to be the most important factor, not age.

How Do Children Learn about Social Studies Ideas?

Despite a fairly sizable pool of research studies on what children know about social studies, how children learn it exactly remains somewhat of a mystery. Current learning theories, such as constructivism, show promise in helping us understand how learning occurs, but much more research must be done. For now, constructivism suggests that children, as we have noted, are active, meaning-making, and thinking creatures who build understandings from their experiences and then continually use those understandings to refine and construct new ones. Thinking begets understanding, so students need to know how to think before they can fully understand, although both parts must fit together. In the area of social studies, research has focused on how children learn from text material, especially in history, because children's access to the past is so heavily mediated by books. As it turns out, social studies (and especially history) is all about reading, which provides elementary teachers with a crucial opportunity to teach reading strategies. Let's examine a sample of this research.

Two researchers explored what fifth graders learn from commonly used US history textbooks (McKeown & Beck, 1990). They interviewed the fifth graders before and after a unit on the American Revolution in which a textbook was the major source. They also interviewed sixth graders who had taken the same fifth-grade history course the year before to see how well they retained what they had learned. The interviews indicate that many of the fifth graders had serious trouble making sense of the textbooks they read, and that the sixth graders had trouble recalling what they learned in fifth grade. Again, this should come as no surprise—try remembering what you learned from your history textbooks. Are you having trouble?

The researchers point out that textbook authors often assume too much background knowledge on the part of students. Textbook authors also use an impersonal "language of objectivity" that dehumanizes the content and distances the students from the ideas. In addition, textbook authors frequently write passages that lack coherence (that is, they leave out key connecting words such as "meanwhile," "and then," "in order to," and so on). As a result, these problems encourage youngsters who lack the prior knowledge to overcome them to back away from the history textbooks, and possibly from the study of history altogether, setting the stage for the dislike of history and social studies we mentioned earlier.

The same two researchers later used what they call **repair strategies** to fix the textbook passages to see whether those helped students learn the information any better (McKeown & Beck, 1994). The repair strategies included (a) providing more background historical context information in the passages to help overcome students' limited prior knowledge and (b) actually rewriting sections of the textbooks to make them more coherent. Both repair strategies were helpful. The researchers conclude that students would benefit by studying a curriculum with fewer historical topics, covering those topics in greater depth, and encountering more of the added contextual information that enhances coherence.[2]

▶️◀️ REFLECTION: CHOOSING CLASSROOM RESOURCES

Social studies teachers will need to exercise caution in selecting and using textbooks because of their adverse influences on learning. You probably will need to augment your use of textbooks with narrative accounts and perhaps fictional trade books, of which the classroom book market offers many (see the list of children's literature titles in the Appendix). However, switching away from textbooks and embracing these alternative books, although it carries distinct advantages, requires you to remain vigilantly reflective and thoughtful about your choice of texts and teaching practices.
▶️◀️

In one study, researchers investigated the relationship of children's responses to textual narratives about the past—the sort of storytelling style found frequently in *historical fiction* and trade books—and their understanding of the history they read about (Levstik & Pappas, 1987). The study looked at small groups of US students in grades 2, 4, and 6. The authors concluded that (a) young learners are quite capable of constructing their own historical narratives, (b) even the youngest children are open to and interested in historical information and find aspects of social history appealing, (c) ample historical context and style of presentation in the texts are both key elements with respect to what students learn, and (d) researchers and teachers consistently underestimate young children's capacity to make sense of the past and think intelligently about it.

As a case in point, consider the story of Jennifer, a fifth grader from Kentucky. Linda Levstik (1989), a researcher at the University of Kentucky, examined the relationship between Jennifer's learning of history and the **narratives** or stories (for example, historical fiction) she read in class. Jennifer found narratives more appealing than textbooks because they provided a sense of wholeness and moral resolution and emphasized the humanness of history. Jennifer's embrace of historical narratives caused her to use them as a reference point from which to judge the quality of the history textbook:

> The social studies [text]book is old and doesn't have as much information in it like [fictional] books do ... and they give you a lot of information that no social studies book ever tells you ... The social studies book doesn't give you a lot of detail. You don't imagine yourself there because they're not doing it as if it were a person. That would be a very interesting social studies book if they told a few things about the people as if it were from their own eyes ... But the textbooks don't like to be interesting, especially.
>
> (Levstik, 1989, p. 114)

Levstik concludes that it is important to provide students with more than just textbooks as sources of historical information. She recommends integrating language arts with historical study as a means of joining the learning of history with the art of interpretation and the creation of narratives, two processes taught more commonly in language arts, yet closely linked to history. However, Levstik does say that reliance on the fictional narratives to teach history can lead to distorted understandings if students are not clear about the distinctions between historical accounts and fictional recreations, or if they are exposed to fictional selections depicting events that are not historically valid.

Another study yields some evidence to support Levstik's concerns (VanSledright & Brophy, 1992). Interviews with ten fourth graders who had read historical fiction accounts during their exploration of state history that year indicated that some of them, particularly the lower achievers, produced stories and fancifully elaborated accounts as responses to questions about what they had learned. The students appeared to equate storytelling with history, so that if an account was based in the past, was dramatic, contained action, was personalized, and was constructed around a **story grammar** framework (conventional beginning, middle, and end), then, to them, it constituted history. These students seemed unaware that historians and novelists often have different goals in mind when they write.

For these fourth graders, the use of narrative or storytelling, especially in fictionalized accounts of history, operated in two opposing directions. It motivated the students to read and engage with the past because the students found the fiction interesting. But it also fostered beliefs about history and historical evidence that are at odds with how historians do their work.

Investigators have further explored how kids make sense of history when they read from textbooks and alternative trade book accounts (e.g., VanSledright & Afflerbach, 2005). Researchers conducted several detailed interviews with six fifth graders about what they were learning from the texts and also used a **think-aloud protocol**, in which students talked out aloud as they read. The six students read two accounts of the Boston Massacre, one taken from a history text that contained eyewitness testimony, and a more general account taken from a text that had no eyewitness reports.

The researchers drew several conclusions from their results: First, students view history as an objective, fact-based account of the past and see their task as being to get those facts; on the other hand, they demonstrate virtually no sense about ways to judge the credibility of the various historical accounts they read. Second, students are unsure about what to do when ideas in one text conflict with ideas in another. And third, students are unaware of the various ways that evidence from the past, such as diaries, artifacts, and letters, has been used in constructing the different types of history texts. This causes most of them to believe that any type of text—textbook, fictional account, diary, letter—is equally credible in representing the past. But when the students are pressed to choose the most accurate type of text, they select the textbook because its apparent objective nature fits more readily with their similar objective view of history, and because their classroom activities involve the search for historical facts and information. These fifth graders constructed a view of history as an objective retelling of past events. Despite evidence that different retellings sometimes contradict each other, making the objective, retelling view suspect, the kids resisted giving up the idea.

Some evidence does indicate that several of the students made judgments about the history texts they read based on an author's point of view. These students assessed the texts' descriptions of an event by building a mental model of the various ways an event might have occurred, depending on one's perspective. For example, one student explained how events of the Boston Massacre look different depending on whether you are a British soldier being charged by a mob of Bostonians, or a Boston citizen being threatened by British soldiers with bayonets and loaded guns. These results are encouraging, for they suggest that students, if given the opportunity to make judgments about historical accounts and coached how to do so, can make some fairly sophisticated analyses of the history they read. Again, the moral of the story seems to be that it's unwise to sell kids short; many of them are much sharper than we think.

■ SECTION SUMMARY:
DRAWING CONCLUSIONS ABOUT HOW CHILDREN LEARN SOCIAL STUDIES IDEAS

- Children (like adults) are meaning-making creatures who take what they have learned from past experiences and use it to make sense of new ideas and experiences they encounter. Exactly how this works in a child's mind remains something of a mystery.

- Although how children learn is in part mysterious, we can speculate that how they learn social studies occurs in relationship to activities such as watching TV, playing games, listening to parent talk, going to the store, going to school, and the like. From research studies, we know that how kids learn comes from interactions with social studies texts of various types.

- Textbooks have been repeatedly criticized for their inconsideration of young readers, their inability to sustain coherent ideas, their emphasis on details at the expense of overall main ideas, and their often dull expository style.

- Textbooks must be supplemented with other texts (historical fiction, trade books, letters, biographies) if learning is to occur in meaningful ways for students.

- Using a variety of texts provides an important set of learning opportunities for students, requiring that they develop an understanding of how to read different types of texts.

■ Multiple accounts of historical events are crucial in enabling students to understand how historians (and others) construct these accounts and what rules they follow about how to use evidence.

■ Books used thoughtlessly, whether fact-based views presented in textbooks or those views from, for example, historical fiction, can distort students' perspectives and prevent them from developing critical, interpretive, and constructive thinking capacities.

Where Do Children Get Their Ideas about Social Studies?

Where children get their social studies ideas has been less actively researched than what children know and how they learn. Before looking at a few research studies, we should note that it is easy to speculate about where children get their ideas about the sociocultural world. For example, because children are busily trying to make sense of their experiences in the world (as are adults), they are curious about most everything around them. As a result, play is a rich source of learning about social organization, social norms, and hierarchies of authority and power. Popular culture, with all its messages about the values and norms of daily life, makes its way into a child's world via television, radio, film, videotapes, games, newsprint and magazines, and the Internet.

Parents and community life also are robust sources for childhood learning. We know, too, that the local context in which a child learns (such as the country, the social class, the community—urban or rural) makes a significant difference. For instance, what children come to understand about banks and work roles in Italy can be different from what same-aged children learn about banks and work roles in, say, a developing country such as Cameroon. Or similarly, a child who grows up in an impoverished inner-city neighborhood likely will have different ideas about work than a child who lives ten miles away in a comfortable, wealthy suburb. Social class and cultural differences among children greatly influence the kinds of resources and experiences to which they are exposed (e.g., access to the Internet as a research source in the home, exposure to print material). They bring these differences to your classroom door. Of course, the systematic experiences children encounter in school and with text material—as we noted—can teach much about the current world, the past, and what a culture values.

One study of where children's social studies ideas come from examined how fifth graders made sense of the arrival of English settlers at Jamestown (Afflerbach & VanSledright, 1998). In the study, seven fifth graders were asked to read from two different texts, one a traditional textbook account of the early colonial settlement, and a second one that described the early colonial events from the perspective of how the colonists, despite having what appeared to be ample food supplies, almost died of starvation in the winter of 1609–1610. Students were asked to think out loud as they read and to explain how they were making sense of the texts.

The textbook passage included a brief description of John Smith's encounter with the Powhatan Indians and the role Pocahontas had in convincing her father, the chief of the Powhatans, to spare Smith's life. All seven students had seen the

Disney film *Pocahontas* and used it to filter their understanding of the account in the traditional textbook. For the students, the film, despite being an animated fictionalized account, held greater authority than the textbook account. Several students took issue with the textbook description, noting that they thought the book was getting some of the ideas wrong because it left out details they had seen in the film.

The authors dubbed the way the students used the film to judge the textbook (in contrast to the other way around, as is often the case) the **Disney effect** (Afflerbach & VanSledright, 1998). This Disney effect indicates, as we have been arguing, that children create meaning from an array of sources. Children use those ideas to filter new ideas and construct new ways of thinking about concepts they encounter in the classroom. This example demonstrates the power of film in popular culture to influence this meaning construction process.

ASSESSING CHILDREN'S IDEAS

IN YOUR CLASSROOM

If you have an opportunity to teach a topic that has been the subject of a recent children's film, you might begin by assessing your students' ideas about the topic, based on what they have seen. You could start by holding a question-and-answer session—an informal type of assessment—in which you ask who has seen the film, what they have learned from it, and how accurate they think the film was. Listen carefully, because the understandings that your students describe will be what you have to build on as far as teaching them new ways of thinking about the topic. This exercise also should help motivate them to study the topic, because many of your students likely will already know something about it and will have ideas to offer. In short, the topic hooks into their existing experience. But, again, listen carefully to what they tell you so you understand how their ideas may differ from or resemble what you intend to teach. After you teach the topic, you might revisit the film and compare what the film conveys and what you studied in your classroom.

Robert Coles's (1986) work supports some of the speculations made about where children's ideas come from. Specifically, he notes the power of the local culture to influence children's ideas about their social worlds. In one rather touching illustration, he notes:

> In the South, for years, I heard Black children speak of sheriffs and policeman as "devils," without picking up the hint that they were giving attitudes long held. In 1965, in McComb, Mississippi, I asked a six-year-old child who was President. She said she didn't know, "but they killed President Kennedy and they killed Medgar Evers."[3] I asked who "they" were. She said, "the people who don't like us."

(p. 28)

Coles points out the power local customs and cultural norms, such as segregation and discrimination by Whites against Blacks in the days before and during the Civil Rights movement, have in shaping young children's perceptions and ideas of social life. At six years of age, this African-American girl from the deep South, Coles observes, already knows a "great deal about what social scientists call the subject of 'race relations,'" and "is fully capable of a firm political judgment: The relatively well-off people don't themselves want to be reminded too pointedly how things work in their favor [because] it is a discomforting accusation" (p. 28). On similar results, see also the study of young children by Hauver (2019).

Terrie Epstein (2009) worked with a group of African-American and White fifth graders from the Detroit area in the late 1990s. She interviewed the students at the beginning of the school year and again at the end, observing how their teacher taught them about the history of US national development in between. In one telling example concerning the study of slavery, the African-American children understood it to be about slaves being treated harshly by their White, European masters and having to work long hours without pay. Although the White fifth graders recognized at the beginning of the year that slavery was a harsh institution, they neglected to note that it was instituted and maintained by White Europeans. By the end of the year, the teacher had successfully helped the White fifth graders realize that European settlers were responsible for American slavery.

In another example, the White and African-American fifth graders had different entering conceptions of the Civil Rights movement. White children understood Civil Rights leaders such as Dr. King as fighting for "rights and justice for all," whereas African-American children thought King's purpose was to end racial violence and strife. Epstein argues that these variations arise from the different types of national development narratives kids are taught at home, in their communities, and at church, which in turn reflect how the past is experienced differently by various groups and, as a result, how they come to define what's most significant.

If recent research is beginning to help us understand what students know, it is also helping us understand how they have come to know what they do in particular contexts and settings. We hope questions about what children know about social studies, where they learn it, and how they learn it will continue to drive research efforts. From what we do know, though, we can begin to shape some theories about how children learn social studies, and about how the sources of their ideas influence the way they construct meaning.

■ SECTION SUMMARY:
WHERE CHILDREN LEARN ABOUT SOCIAL STUDIES

■ Clearly, children learn from text material and ideas they encounter in school, but they also learn from a variety of other sources outside of school. These include parents, film, TV, neighborhood play and community activities, church, popular mass culture, local culture, and so on.

- The power of non-school activities and sources to influence children's thinking about social studies sometimes can be stronger than in-school sources. However, classrooms are highly influential sources of learning.

A Constructivist View of Learning Social Studies

Consider for a moment how you learn and when that learning is most powerful. Are you a "blank slate" on which someone or something "writes" so that you can later reproduce that knowledge? Or do you learn best when you actively integrate new ideas with your prior knowledge, assumptions, and experiences? We suspect that your most powerful learning experiences are more akin to this latter characterization. So too for your students.

This talk of learning and knowing leads us back to exploring constructivism—a theory of how people learn, supported by plenty of evidence. To reiterate, constructivism suggests that your sociocultural context and prior knowledge and experience interact with new ideas to influence how you create new understandings. As evidence accumulates, researchers and educators increasingly believe that learning primarily consists of ongoing sense making. Rather than simply absorbing ready-made classroom information, students need to make sense of what they learn and construct meaning for themselves if there is any hope that they will be able to remember it. The recent *College, Career, and Civic Life (C3) Framework for Social Studies State Standards* document (National Council for the Social Studies, 2013), and the inquiry and teaching arcs embedded in it, works directly from this view of learning.

Behaviorism: Assumptions about Learning

Research about what students know and how they learn has led many educators to rethink their views of learning. Until recently, most believed in behaviorist theories. These theories trace their origins to the latter part of the nineteenth and early part of the twentieth centuries, and especially in the United States to the psychologist **B.F. Skinner**. Behaviorists such as Skinner are interested in how people learn but focus on the measurable aspects of that learning. They shun such unmeasurable cognitive processes as the unconscious, popularized by **Sigmund Freud**. Their concern with measurable learning activity and behavioral outcomes gives rise to the term *behaviorism*.

Skinner thought that humans learned best when they were on a **positive reinforcement** schedule. In other words, people encounter and respond in various ways to learning stimuli. The learning **stimulus** might be anything—a new book, a lecture, a film—that a teacher introduces in class. If a learner encounters the learning stimulus coupled with some sort of reinforcement—praise from the teacher, a reward of some sort, a good grade—he or she learns. Even if learners receive reinforcements only part of the time a stimulus is presented, they will

Stimulus ⟶ Learner's response + Teacher's reinforcement = Learning

FIGURE 2.4 The learning process in behaviorism.

still learn. Learners neither learn nor retain stimuli that are not followed by some reinforcement. A simplistic overview of this learning cycle is depicted in Figure 2.4.

To "undo" **responses** that are deemed inappropriate, the teacher can do one of two things: create a situation in which the learner encounters an unpleasant result when he or she responds incorrectly to a stimulus, or simply ignore the incorrect behavior and thus not reinforce the response. For example, if a student encounters the unpleasant result of poor marks on a test, it would be designed to make the student stop doing poorly, change his or her behavior so he or she did better on the tests, and thereby learn what was expected. Using a reinforcement schedule comprising rewards and unpleasant experiences, Skinner, in a heralded experiment, taught pigeons to play ping-pong. Unfortunately for school-age children, who have much more complex mental processes than pigeons, behavioristic ideas and operations soon found their way into the classroom.

Behavioristic theories rest on certain assumptions. We center our description on several that relate specifically to how educators employ the behaviorism model for thinking about learning in schools. Behavioristic models applied in school settings assume, first, that learners need information broken into small, easily digestible bits of information and procedures to be learned. These manageable stimuli can be built one atop the next in a simple progression that allows the teacher to design a reinforcement schedule.

Second, those information bits and procedures are arranged in hierarchical and sequential order: simple facts first, then more complex facts, followed by these facts arrayed around concepts, and so on toward complex modes of thought such as critical thinking. Any disruption in this order causes inappropriate learning that must be undone. "Undoing" is considered an inefficient use of classroom time, so the stress is placed on establishing the proper order of learning stimuli.

Third, given similar learning stimuli or inputs, one can expect learners to produce similar outputs, or learning outcomes. Learners and outcomes can vary somewhat, but this is considered an aberrant result and one to be avoided. The teacher wants all the students on the same page at the same time, so to speak.

Fourth, because of their assumption that learning something precedes being able to think intelligently about it, behaviorists argue that a student needs to learn or memorize facts before thinking about and ordering them into more complex wholes.

Fifth, learning is considered a largely passive, or at best a reactive, activity in which students have their mental slates written on in such a way that they are unaware that learning is actually occurring. Finally, reinforcement schedules using rewards or unpleasant experiences are to be arranged carefully to maximize learning outputs.

As you can see, teachers in this scheme are like learning engineers in charge of arranging learning stimuli and managing learning outputs by the rules of behaviorism. Students are relatively passive recipients of these stimuli–response arrangements and reinforcement schemes. If you think about your own school experience, especially in elementary-school social studies, you will probably recognize how much of your classroom conduct was shaped by teachers who bought into these assumptions and built learning opportunities around them. When you think back, was social studies about learning an endless array of facts about which you were tested in some sort of paper and pencil manner? If you scored well, you were rewarded with praise and good marks. If you did poorly, you experienced the discomfort of thinking you were not learning effectively or at all.

Constructivism: Assumptions about Learning

As many good social studies teachers know (and educational researchers are now figuring out), these behaviorist assumptions just do not hold up very well. Go back and examine Helen and Rita's comments about the birth of the United States and the search for a trade route to the Far East. They demonstrate quite clearly that young minds are hardly passive, blank slates but rather active and cognitively busy learning systems. Because students' prior knowledge varies, sometimes significantly, teachers can hardly assume that variation is aberrant behavior. Variation is the rule, not the exception. Helen and Rita, in theory at least, experienced the same set of fourth-grade social studies learning opportunities (stimuli), taught by the same teacher, using the same set of social studies texts. Yet they developed different ideas about similar events (outputs), leading us to seriously question the viability of behaviorist learning assumptions.

As we have been saying, young learners actively use what they already know to make sense out of new ideas they encounter. Reinforcement schedules and rewards fail to work if these learners make no sense of the ideas and knowledge the classroom offers them. Teacher-as-learning-engineer, who erects knowledge on the flat, blank slate of the child's mind, hardly seems an apt metaphor either. Instead, the learning-coach-facilitator approach appears more appropriate by constructivist lights.

Before proceeding, we should take a moment and clarify the difference between Piagetian and Vygotskian constructivism. In many ways, Piaget was the forerunner of constructivism. His studies demonstrated, particularly in the area of learning about physical science ideas, that children construct new ideas on the conceptions they already hold. Children simply are not the blank slates the behaviorists assumed they were. Piaget and his followers developed a stage theory in which they argued that school-age children move more or less in tight sequence from the pre-operational stage to the concrete-operational

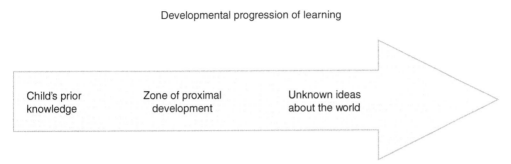

FIGURE 2.5 The zone of proximal development.

stage and finally to the abstract-conceptual stage. Age was considered a key marker on this developmental path. After additional studies demonstrated that age was less a crucial determinant and that children often appeared to be in two stages simultaneously (something Piaget's theory would not allow), **Vygotsky**'s sociocultural developmental view and his idea of the *zone of proximal development* were accepted as a better explanation of the learning process (see Figure 2.5).

The **zone of proximal development** (ZPD) refers to the idea that children can be more experienced and expert in some areas than others, that prior knowledge and experience in a particular area or on an idea count as much or more than age, and that, at any given point, a child possesses a developmental range of capabilities (the zone of proximal development) marked off by prior knowledge at one end and the incomprehensible at the other. Knowledgeable others, such as parents and teachers, once they understand the developmental zone or range a child currently (proximally) inhabits, can push a child forward and expand her or his capacities and prior knowledge, therefore shifting the ZPD forward toward greater expertise, regardless of the child's so-called age-specific developmental stage.

Constructivist learning theorists—such as Vygotsky and his followers—also make certain assumptions about how young children learn. The following are several we consider central to teaching social studies.

Learners Are Inquiring Sense Makers

First, young learners are sense-making creatures. From our adult perspective, they are naive in their knowledge and assumptions. This should be no big surprise, for children's experiences, although rich in many ways, lack the depth and breadth of adults' experiences. Children's accounts of ideas and events often seem fragmentary and disparate. Helen and Rita's historical reconstructions are good illustrations, as are many that emerge from the research. They take what makes historical sense to them initially and wed it with new ideas about the past that they encounter in their Michigan history course. The result is a curious mixture of accurate historical conceptions, fanciful elaborations, and odd **conflations**.

However, their accounts are disparate, elaborated, and conflated not because they do not "know" enough; rather, they are struggling both with making sense of ideas that they have not quite grasped and with the newly found activity of sense-making itself.

Learners Construct Meaning Using Language

Second, children (and adults, for that matter) make sense by constructing meaning. Language is their most important tool here. Students use talk of facts, concepts, principles, and, yes, theories of their own to construct around them a world that has meaning and appears to hold a degree of coherence. Although Helen and Rita's remarks may seem to us somewhat incoherent, they do in their own ways make perfectly good and coherent sense to the girls.

Learners Are Cognitively Active

Third, learners actively make powerful associations among and between facts, concepts, and principles. One way to think about this is in terms of *webs of meaning*. For example, Helen may approach her study of the birth of the United States with established ideas regarding the concepts of war, poor and rich, country affiliation, Michigan, Americans, and perhaps the British. She probably possesses some facts that help anchor these concepts (for example, war involves conflict and fighting, Americans live in Michigan, the British come from England), and she most likely holds some partially formed theories and principles, uniquely her own, that allow her to interconnect the facts and concepts (for example, wars are fought between rich and poor countries).

In the classroom she heard stories about the birth of the United States that interacted with and modified her preliminary associations in ways represented by her response (for example, the Americans and British were once friends, but later they fought because the British broke a promise not to fight). To assess how her understanding of Michigan and US history changed, we would need to have a picture of what her understanding looked like before her classroom study of Michigan history. Because we don't have that, we can only speculate here about how Helen constructs meaning.

Learners' Ideas Vary

Learners' understandings are hardly static or fixed. Each day, in a variety of ways, these webs of meaning and understanding are modified and reconstructed by experiences both in school and certainly out of school, all in ways difficult to predict and anticipate. Because of this, you will need to listen closely to students' ideas and theories about their worlds. The ideas learners bring to the learning context are the raw materials—not the blank slate—you have to work with. This is a fundamental difference in assumptions about learning that demarcate the older behaviorist approach from the newer constructivist one.

We are encouraged by the implications of constructivism for teaching. Yes, it makes teaching more complex and difficult in some ways, but it also makes it more engaging and rich in many others. We're further encouraged that many constructivist learning/learner assumptions have been borne out by emerging research results, especially in the area of history education. However, some features of constructivist assumptions complicate teaching and make it problematic in actual practice. As we continue our examination, we will suggest strategies for addressing those problems.

The Problems of Constructivist Views

The constructivist view of learning social studies has far-reaching implications. Some of those implications show great promise, whereas others are problematic. Many of your students will be able to make sense of the learning opportunities they create on their own, but experienced teachers know that others will need help. This is an important point; the constructivist story, as we have said, is not entirely rosy all the time.

First, we explore four interrelated problematic features of constructivism:

1   How do you, as their teacher, know what your children know?
2   How can you learn to hear what your students are saying about what they know and are learning?
3   What do you do if students have naive, misconceived, or conflated ideas about social studies?
4   How do you validate what your students know and the meanings they construct while still attempting to influence their naive, inaccurate, or conflated concepts?

How to Know What Your Students Know

By now it should be clear that in order to help your students build new ideas and construct new meaning, you must first figure out what your students already know. If Helen and Rita are any indication, we can draw several conclusions. Your students' prior conceptions will be varied, most likely naive, and overgeneralized, and they may show conflations of one cluster of ideas with other, generally unrelated ones. Some of your students will have a fairly rich array of concepts that make good sense by adult and academic disciplinary standards, and others will have little knowledge. All of this complicates planning your social studies classes and predicting what your students can and will learn.

One of the most effective methods for finding out what your students know is to ask them. But taking the time to talk individually with twenty-five or so students is a luxury few teachers can afford. Classroom discussions of what your children know about a topic as you begin its study can help create an impressionistic portrait of their prior knowledge. Yet, some students will say little in such discussions, which leaves you guessing. Other approaches are necessary.

Your work here is to help your students tell you what they already know. This will complicate your next task of structuring learning opportunities, because you will quickly discover that what students know is quite varied and can change in unpredictable ways, as we have seen with Helen and Rita. But this is much better than assuming that their minds are blank, that all you need to do is provide a carefully engineered set of learning stimuli, and that they are learning, and then suddenly the test lets you know otherwise. You are better off building on and working from what your students already know, even though it might be unstable knowledge.

IN YOUR CLASSROOM

USING K-W-L EXERCISES

One strategy we have seen successfully employed in social studies classes is the **K-W-L** exercise (Ogle, 1986). This exercise can be done in two parts, often as a paper-and-pencil activity. The letters represent each of three questions: "What do I Know about this topic or subject?" "What do I Want to learn about it?" and "What have I Learned?" You ask the K and W questions of students at the beginning of a topic study and the L question after you've finished the study. If the students can write well enough, they can write their responses in a **journal**, or you could prepare an activity sheet on which they could write. The many variations on this approach are limited only by your imagination.

How to Hear What Students Are Saying

We cannot overestimate the importance of learning to hear your students, to understand the sense they are making of the social studies they encounter with you. Learning to hear your students will take time. You must come to know them individually as well as in a group context. You must hear what they say when they tell you about the prior conceptions they hold. Reread Helen and Rita's accounts of the past. What is going on in these two fourth graders' heads? What are they actually saying about what they know? What about Levstik's Jennifer? What is she saying? Learning to hear will require asking questions and pondering what your students reply. You can enhance your understanding of children by using several means of recording what students do with what you ask them to learn.

IN YOUR CLASSROOM

PROBING STUDENTS' IDEAS

Asking your students to keep journals could be very helpful, as well as getting them to draw pictures of their social studies ideas. Some teachers audiotape their social studies classes; others assign group projects that allow them to sit in on discussions of ideas students exchange as they accomplish a social studies activity. Some children's language can be awkward and inarticulate. Their ideas may be ill-formed or inchoate. They will need your help to draw the ideas out, which can be difficult and time-consuming, but is crucial to good social studies teaching.

We should caution, though, that learning to hear your students is an ongoing task, never perfected or complete. Why? Because you filter what others tell you through your own understanding of the world, through the assumptions you make, and through the knowledge you hold. **Empathy**, the ability to put yourself in your students' shoes, so to speak, is at best only an approximation. We can never walk away from our own two feet entirely. But that should not stop you from trying to hear what your students are saying. Hearing them, even if only partially, will make your planning and teaching more effective. What you hear will be the floor on which you can build the **scaffold** of social studies learning.

What If Students Don't Have the "Right" Ideas?

Much traditional elementary-school learning in social studies can be characterized as the pursuit of clusters of unrelated facts: the correct names, dates, and events in history; the "right" ideas about how cultures function; how people buy and sell goods in the marketplace; how governments govern; and so on. In elementary school, you probably took social studies tests and filled in worksheets, and most likely, your teachers graded your efforts right or wrong. In many elementary schools, teaching students to produce correct answers is a real concern for teachers, especially in an educational climate that holds students, teachers, and schools accountable for such test results. You will face this same issue.

As we have seen, the wide variation in students' prior knowledge about a given topic, the naive conceptions they bring, and the different approaches they take to constructing meaning all make it difficult for you to move them to a place where they can begin to construct more accurate and less naive understandings. Doing so, after all, is a worthwhile goal. Students need to know about and draw upon the centuries of knowledge we have constructed about sociocultural, historical, political, geographic, and economic events. Much of this knowledge helps us solve social problems and make sense of our world. Jerome Bruner (1996), the educational psychologist, calls this knowledge the **cultural toolkit**. He argues that this toolkit provides the means by which people navigate the sociocultural world. Without it, people cannot function successfully in society.

However, as much as we might wish it were so, knowledge of a culture cannot be reproduced simplistically in children's minds, for at least two reasons. First, as we have seen, learning does not work that way. And second, cultural knowledge is both itself constructed and therefore constantly changing. We continuously modify our culture as we invent new ways of solving our problems (such as the changes in the way we communicate wrought by the digital and technological revolution).

John Dewey was thinking about these ideas when he referred to human minds, their individual and collective learning processes, and the culture they produce as "evolutionary" in nature. All of this makes teaching doubly difficult. You want kids to learn about all those important ideas the culture holds dear. But students as well as ideas evolve; if learning is to occur for them, you must also ensure that your students have ample opportunities to make sense of it in their own way, and above all, to learn how to learn.

Much of our response to this problem is to suggest that it will be virtually impossible to influence all your students in the same way, to get them all on the same page at the same time, and to ensure that they are constructing the "correct" ideas. Tension will be ever present in your classroom between how your students construct knowledge and the knowledge from history and the social sciences that many of us take as given. We refer to this as a **dilemma**, one that all teachers face and do their best to manage (VanSledright & Grant, 1994; see also Cohen, 1989b). But to manage it effectively depends upon taking time to understand the ideas your students have constructed and are in the process of rebuilding. It will also depend on how you "listen" and thus "hear" what your students are saying about the way they construct an understanding of the social world they encounter in social studies and also away from it.

▶️◀ REFLECTION: CONSIDERING NAIVE CONCEPTIONS

The following exercise is one method of examining the dilemma of what happens when "kids don't have the 'right' ideas." Although it won't necessarily tell you "what to do," it will help you better understand the different avenues available to you for managing the dilemma. This also is a great exercise in being reflective about your teaching.

Go back and reread both Helen's and Rita's comments at the beginning of this chapter. Look for naive conceptions and jot them down on the left half of a separate piece of paper, leaving ample space between them (four or five lines). Select six to eight that you think are especially problematic. Divide the right half of the paper in two columns. In the left of these two columns, describe how you might address these naive conceptions through your teaching. In the right of the two columns, speculate on what might happen for both girls if you did not attend to their naive conceptions at all.

▶️◀

Which Children's Ideas Do Teachers Validate?

This, too, is a difficult question because it relates closely to the dilemma we just considered. In its more extreme form, constructivism maintains that no ideas are wrong, that, by school and test standards, wrong ideas are only alternative conceptions. These alternative conceptions are grounded in students' different levels and types of background knowledge and constructed around the way old knowledge interacts with new knowledge. As we have seen, how this works is uncertain at best. So therein lies a powerful tension.

Alternative conceptions are real and legitimate, and they form the backbone of potentially new and creative ways of thinking. To invalidate them, by constructivist lights, is to invalidate the person who holds them, retard imagination and creativity, and chase away some potentially valuable and valid insights. Yet, many of your students' alternative conceptions remain inaccurate and can create learning conflicts that lead to untenable ideas. Thus, you face the same dilemma we just described. And once again, part of managing the dilemma involves you getting students' ideas—as fuzzy and potentially inaccurate as they are—out on the educational table and working with them.

Start by thinking of Helen. She appears to conflate the American Revolutionary War with the French and Indian War. These were historically distinct events, separated by more than ten years. Should Helen's alternative view of these wars be allowed to continue? If so, might it give her trouble later as she encounters historical texts that dispute her view? If she continues to retain it, how entrenched will her idea become? Will it grow increasingly resistant to change? We have no good answers to these questions, but some research suggests that alternative conceptions can be quite impervious to change, even to direct instruction, if held for long periods. Therefore, your task as a social studies teacher will be a delicate one.

▶|◀ REFLECTION: LISTENING TO STUDENTS

You will need to balance the competing demands of students' ideas against the knowledge adults accept as accurate (that is, Bruner's "cultural toolkit"). You will need to listen to your students. You will need to pepper them with questions in order to learn about their alternative ideas. And, if they hold untenable cultural and historical understandings, you will have to challenge them without simultaneously invalidating who they are as curious, cognitively active learners. Occasionally, you will need to fight the temptation—provoked by frustration over your students' stubbornly inaccurate conceptions—to give in and simply provide your students with the "right" answers, the ones that appear on tests or worksheets. At the beginning of Chapter 3, we will provide a vignette drawn from an actual classroom in which the teacher, Ramona Palmer, holds a discussion with her fifth graders about the Bill of Rights. We encourage you to flip forward to that chapter for a first-hand look at how a good social studies teacher asks her students questions to lure their ideas out onto the educational table and challenge some of them without also invalidating those students.

Problems	Promises
Knowing what your students know	Shifting control for learning to children
Hearing what students are saying	Enhancing motivation
When students lack the "right" ideas	Increasing expectations
Validating children's ideas	Increasing the joy of teaching
	Building interdisciplinary connections

FIGURE 2.6 The problems and promises of constructivist social studies teaching approach.

Managing classroom dilemmas is perhaps one of the most demanding tasks that face social studies teachers who embrace a constructivist perspective. But this embrace is not all tension and dilemma management; it includes promises of great rewards for social studies teachers. Figure 2.6 lists both the problems and the promises of constructivist teaching. We've discussed the problems; now let's explore the promises.

The Promises of Constructivist Views

The problems of a constructivist view are real and important, but so are the promises. We already have alluded to the promises, but here we briefly sketch out five that we believe make a compelling case for its embrace.

Shifting Control for Learning

First, constructivist approaches can help your students feel more in control and responsible for their education. By validating your students' ideas and allowing them expression, you send the message that their thinking is respected and important, that they too can contribute something valuable to the learning process. This allows you to create a learning climate in which students can account for why they think as they do. This, in turn, sends the message that they are accountable to you and fellow students for the nature of and the reasons behind their thinking. This shifts the onus for building understandings onto students; your responsibility is to act as a facilitator and coach of a learning process.

Enhancing Motivation

Second, shifting a good share of control and responsibility for learning to students can enhance their motivation to learn. Your students will see that they are in charge of and must direct their own learning. They will learn to make reasoned choices about the way they construct their understandings. They will become more engaged and persistent in the learning tasks they set for themselves.

Increasing Expectations

Third, you can increase your expectations of what students can accomplish and so introduce more complex social studies ideas and concepts earlier in a child's learning experience. In turn, this supports a generally more powerful and robust overall curriculum that can lead to better-informed students who are more cognitively adept at earlier ages. This is crucial to a culture that continues to become more information-driven and -dependent.

Increasing the Joy of Teaching

Fourth, a constructivist approach to learning can increase the joy of teaching. If students are in greater control of their learning and demonstrate stronger motivations to learn, you have before you an eager audience, waiting for you to provide resources and learning opportunities. You end up spending less time on disciplining students and generating an array of rewards to cajole them into the drudgery of learning facts about which they have little interest or control.

Building Interdisciplinary Connections

And finally, a rich, robust curriculum made possible by this approach provides more opportunities to build **interdisciplinary** connections. You can connect ideas across disciplines and school subjects, such as between reading and social studies or between social studies and science, which might otherwise be impossible because of the time required to lay down basic facts in each area. Students get excited about these connections. Light bulbs go off in their heads in ways that stimulate the production of new ideas and enhance their desire to learn more.

You are probably entertaining all sorts of questions about another of the commonplaces—teachers and teaching. But before exploring those questions connected to teaching, let us look at a commonplace that bridges learning and teaching—subject matter—the stuff students have opportunities to learn and teachers are charged to teach.

Chapter Summary

1   **What do elementary-age children know about social studies?** Elementary-age children come to school knowing a surprising amount about their social worlds. Although their ideas are not always accurate, children have formed some fairly complex notions of social life. These ideas can change, expand, and grow even more sophisticated as children construct new meanings.

   - Children's capability to learn ideas, concepts, and principles appears to be almost unlimited, especially if those ideas, concepts, and principles are coherent, embedded within a meaningful context, and connected to the students' prior knowledge and experiences.
   - Children's prior knowledge can interfere with new learning, however: Old ideas can be hard to shake! At the same time, children are interested in and can comprehend complex ideas.

2   **How do children learn about social studies?** Children (like adults) are meaning-making creatures who take what they have learned from past experiences and use it to make sense of new ideas and experiences they encounter. We don't understand this phenomenon well, but we can speculate that how they learn social studies occurs in relationship to activities, such as watching TV, playing games, listening to parents talk, going to the store, going to school, and the like.

   - Considerable research on the use of textbooks, particularly history texts, indicates that textbooks should be supplemented with other texts (historical fiction, trade books, letters, biographies) if learning is to occur in meaningful ways for students. Using multiple texts is an especially important means of presenting varied perspectives on historical ideas and events.

3   **Where do they learn about social studies?** Children learn from text material and ideas they encounter in school, but they also learn from a variety of sources outside school. These include parents, film, TV, neighborhood play and community activities, church, popular mass culture, local culture, and so on. The power of non-school activities and sources to influence children's thinking about social studies sometimes can be stronger than that of in-school sources. However, classrooms continue as influential places of learning.

4   **What is constructivism as a learning theory, and what are its assumptions?** The principal tenets of constructivism include the notions that learners are primarily sense-making creatures who construct meaning primarily by using language and are cognitively active, busy making sense of their world. Learners' ideas vary as each child uses his or her distinct prior experience, knowledge, and understanding of the world to construct new meaning.

5   **What are the problems and promises of constructivism for social studies teachers?** The problems include knowing what your students know, hearing what students are saying, understanding when students lack the "right" ideas, and validating students' ideas. The promises of constructivism include

shifting control for learning to children, enhancing motivation, increasing expectations and the joy of teaching, and building interdisciplinary connections.

Notes

1 Clearly, we can speculate that children's ideas come from their everyday experiences of going to the store or the post office or the bank or listening to parents tell stories of their experiences. And of course, children learn much in school. Our point is that researchers have not examined as closely the "where" question. For the most part we are left to our speculations.

2 To read several critiques of social studies textbooks, see Beck, McKeown, and Gromoll, 1989; Larkins, Hawkins, and Gilmore, 1987; and McCabe, 1993.

3 Evers, an African-American civil rights leader, was assassinated.

Teaching Resources

Print Resources

We highly recommend that you read the research studies we cite both in the chapter text and in the reference section. Our summaries of these studies are limited because of space. A wealth of additional information can be gleaned by consulting the primary sources themselves.

Web-Based Resources

- www.historicalthinkingmatters.org
  This is the website address for Historical Thinking Matters. It contains links to a variety of materials gleaned from the research on teaching and learning history. Many of the suggestions and ideas represented at this site come directly from the research on learning in history. Much of the content of the site is worth consulting, because it can help you better understand the nature of your students' ideas about history and where they come from.
- https://sheg.stanford.edu
  The website for the Stanford History Education Group, a repository for detailed lesson plans, curriculum suggestions, assessments, and other teaching resources focused on history teaching.

3

Subject Matter
A Threads Approach

Ramona Palmer, a fifth-grade teacher, is deeply engrossed, along with her eager and active students, in considering the Bill of Rights. Palmer's 28 students include 18 girls and 10 boys. Most of the children are European American, as is Palmer, but the class also includes three African-American and two Asian students. Palmer has been teaching for almost 15 years in this suburban school in a moderately large northern midwestern city.

To better understand what her students already know, Palmer asks them to explain in their own words the meaning of each amendment in the Bill of Rights. Next, her fifth graders take several minutes to write down one amendment they would be willing to give up if someone passed a law requiring it, and the reasons for their choice.

After several minutes, she says, "If you're willing to give up the First Amendment, stand up." Cameron, a small, wiry boy, rises. He stands alone. Palmer smiles and says, "That's all right, Cameron. There are no right or wrong answers with this; it's what you believe." Palmer repeats the process for each of the next seven amendments, with small groups of students standing for each.

A discussion of Cameron's willingness to give up the First Amendment ensues. Palmer asks him to read the amendment from the book. As soon as he finishes, he shrugs his shoulders, smiles, and claims he has changed his mind; he no longer wants to give this one up.

> PALMER: But why were you willing to give it up in the first place? I'm really curious. This amendment protects the rights of free speech, the press, and personal opinion.
> CAMERON (bashfully): Well, I just liked the other ones better.
> PALMER: If you gave it up, how would this affect you?
> DAVEY (interjecting): You wouldn't be able to give your opinion!
> PALMER: How many of you think that if we gave up this right it would infringe on some very basic American principles? (almost everyone's hand goes up immediately)

What would it be like if we didn't know about this, couldn't read about it in the newspapers? I'm going to take Cameron's position for a minute. What about those papers like the Star or the Enquirer?

SEVERAL STUDENTS: Yeah, they exaggerate!

PALMER: Yes. Should there be rules for supplying evidence in these papers?

CAMERON: No!

ADRIENNE: I think there should be guidelines for what they can print.

PALMER: What about 2 Live Crew (a rap group)?

MARVYN: They're okay! If it bothers some people, they don't have to buy it. They put those labels on there that say there's obscene words and stuff on the record. I guess that's okay.

SAM: I think that the swearing and the words that they use are okay. Everyone does it.

The class erupts into a polyphony of voices. Students compete to be heard above the rapidly rising volume. Palmer tells them to stop. She asks them to raise their hands and speak one at a time.

DAVEY: I agree with Sam.

JARRON: You could bleep out the bad stuff.

PALMER: But then some records would be all bleep.

DAVEY: Well, it's okay because people are doing it. It's not really hurting anybody.

PALMER: But it's not really okay to say so just because everyone is doing it. What if everyone was murdering? Is that okay?

STUDENTS: No!! That's not okay.

ABIGAIL: I think it's unfair to people who like their music.

PALMER: Davey, you said it doesn't hurt anybody. I disagree with you. The lyrics in some songs—I'm just arguing with you—make me out to be a bimbo. I'm offended.

DAVEY: But you don't need to listen to it.

PALMER: But what if people start to believe this stuff? I'm just giving you an example.

ADAM: But in PG movies, they all swear. What's the difference?

FREDERIC: I've never heard a song about women's right to vote.

PALMER: I'm just saying, what do you do if it insults women? What about Blacks? Marvyn?

MARVYN (a Black student): Well … well, if you want to listen to it, it's okay.

PALMER: Marvyn, are you hedging? Should we allow it if it insults Blacks? Yes or no, Marvyn?

MARVYN: Well, if … yes.

ADAM (a White student): There's a movie out right now called "White Men Can't Jump." And some Black people call each other n—s.

PALMER: Should that be allowed?

ADDIE: You should be allowed to do it in the privacy of your own home.

PALMER: Should we allow a parade … if someone was a member of the KKK and wanted to have a parade down the streets of our city, is that allowable? (five hands go up).

BARRY: That's freedom of speech!

PALMER: I want you to talk this over with your parents tonight. We have to go on to number two, the right to bear arms. Lots of you are ready to give this one up. Why?

The class shifts to a discussion of the Second Amendment: the right to keep and bear arms. This one creates as much disagreement as the first. Throughout the ebb and flow of the discussion, many students sit up in their desks on their knees. Their hands often slice the air in a frenzied effort to attract Palmer's notice. Aware of their eagerness, Palmer moves around the room calling on students. As soon as one student finishes his or her statement, she calls on another. At one point she asks students to address each other.

The students debate the pros and cons of owning and carrying guns. Several boys defend the practice on the grounds that people need to protect themselves from would-be terrorists, warmongers, and burglars. Two girls attempt to counter that position by suggesting that guns are more apt to cause accidental shootings than to protect those holding them. One boy, advocating open gun ownership, has a father in the state House of Representatives fighting for more stringent gun control. Palmer asks if the class thinks it acceptable if their classmate disagrees with his father. They all agree, citing First Amendment protections.

With class time quickly running out, Palmer reminds the students that she wants to cover the additional amendments the following day. She wants them to re-examine their positions and come to class prepared to make statements. With two minutes remaining, Palmer pushes on to a brief consideration of the Fourth and Fifth Amendments (search and seizure limitations, due process), for the moment skipping over the Third. In the process of considering these amendments, several students become confused about the due process rule, "innocent until proven guilty." Palmer tries to set the record straight by asking students to reread the actual amendment.

The next day Palmer resumes the discussion. She asks Adam to read the Third Amendment (quartering of soldiers) from his book. Four students had elected to drop this amendment in the earlier lesson segment. Palmer notes this and asks why. Several students who oppose dropping this amendment object to the possibility of soldiers entering and living in your home. Drew argues that the soldiers could be controlled. Sam raises the possibility of harm to civilians if our enemies knew soldiers were quartered in our homes. Palmer acknowledges Sam's point, then pushes on to the Fourth Amendment (search-and-seizure limitations), considering it a second time. Students discuss the nature of arrest warrants for several minutes. After that, Merry reads the Fifth Amendment from the textbook (due process provisions).

A discussion ensues concerning the double jeopardy clause. Palmer asks several students to explain their understanding of this clause. Students appear confused about how the amendment requires the prosecution to prove guilt and how the double jeopardy clause protects the accused from being tried repeatedly for the same offense. After several analogies and direct explanations extolling the protective features of the amendment, Palmer seems convinced that students understand its rudimentary qualities. Students, many again up on their knees in their desks, protest as Palmer asks Cameron to read the Sixth (additional due process provisions), Seventh (right to jury trial), and Eighth (prohibitions against cruel and unusual punishments) Amendments from the textbook. Eyeballing the clock, Palmer insists that they push on if they are to consider all the amendments. As Cameron finishes the Eighth Amendment, several students sing out, "cruel and unusual punishment!"

> PALMER: We could discuss this one for a long time. Some people would object that capital punishment is cruel and unusual.
> SEVERAL STUDENTS: So, what's your opinion? Tell us!
> PALMER: The [school] district says if I tell you then I run the risk of letting my values influence you. I can't …
> STUDENTS (objecting): Oh, we won't tell … tell us anyway … Just get on with it!
> ANOTHER STUDENT: My mom will understand!
> PALMER: Okay. (Students fall completely silent; watching Palmer.) But this is just *my* opinion. I have a lot of trouble with this. It's not black-and-white for me. I really struggle … It seems very cruel on the one hand, but if it was my child … I think then I'd want to have capital punishment.

As Palmer pauses, Adam interjects his opinion, arguing an eye-for-an-eye approach. Palmer turns to an analogy. One of her female friends was murdered in an altercation with someone being pursued by the police. Her friend's brother now frequently objects about paying taxes to keep this murderer alive in prison.

> SAM: Is he in prison for life?
> PALMER: Yes. And he had a record for killing others. The reason I'm telling you this is to explain how opinions about capital punishment vary a lot.
> FREDERIC: What if it was your job to pull the lever?
> PALMER: It wouldn't be! I could never do that! I'm too afraid of the possibility of executing the wrong person. That's a strong argument against capital punishment.
> ADAM: What if someone killed your students? Could you do it then?
> PALMER: I don't know! My emotions might have the better of me. That's so hard for me to say.

As she finishes her sentence, Palmer begins passing out several review sheets for an upcoming test. Several students near the front receive the papers, groan, and say, "Oooh, worksheets! This is capital punishment!" Palmer smiles wryly.[1]

COMMONPLACE CONNECTION

- What does Palmer seem to think is important about the *subject matter* of the Bill of Rights?
- What view of *learners* does she seem to hold?
- How would you characterize her *teaching*?
- How would you describe the classroom *environment*?

What is going on here? A lot. This is a wonderfully rich and powerful set of lesson segments conducted by an astute social studies teacher. Look at how excited the students seem, how well behaved they appear even though the discussion is animated and threatens to explode into chaos any minute, and how skillful Palmer is in conducting this extended treatment of the Bill of Rights. In this chapter, we will use Ramona Palmer's Bill of Rights lessons as a means of exploring a second commonplace, subject matter.

We thought about talking of the commonplace teachers and teaching next. In fact, we argued ourselves into and out of that tack several times. But then we realized that, in some ways, it didn't really matter: If the commonplaces are as integrated and recursive as we believe, then we could take up subject matter, environment, or teaching and still make the points we think are important.

That made us feel better, but it didn't solve our problem. We gave the matter some more thought and concluded that it makes better sense to think about subject matter as an important bridge between learning and teaching. That is, on the way to constructing your teaching practice, you will bring together your ideas about what your students know and how they learn with your ideas about what you might teach them. We'll be exploring the subject matter of social studies and the question of "What will I teach?" When you have completed this chapter, you should be able to answer these questions:

- What does the traditional social studies curriculum look like, and what problems are inherent in it?

- What are the threads of social studies, and how do they relate to the notion of teaching with rich ideas?

- How much latitude do teachers have in making curriculum choices?

But There's Just Too Much Here!

How did Ramona Palmer know she should teach the Bill of Rights? How did she know in what depth to teach it? Such questions are central to understanding the subject matter of social studies. But they are not easy questions. Perhaps you have heard teachers talk about how much they are required to "cover." They sometimes complain vociferously that they have too much subject matter to deal with and not enough time. The question arises about what and how to choose.

Defining the Social Studies

All teachers, and especially new teachers, find that the first step to answering questions about the subject matter of social studies is to get a clear definition. Recall this definition of social studies offered by the National Council for the

Social Studies (NCSS), a large national organization of teachers, curriculum specialists, and researchers:

> Social studies is the integrated study of the social sciences and humanities to promote civic competence. Within the school program, social studies provides coordinated, systematic study drawing upon such disciplines as anthropology, archeology, economics, geography, history, law, philosophy, political science, psychology, religion, and sociology. The primary purpose of social studies is to help young people develop the ability to make informed and reasoned decisions for the public good as citizens of a culturally diverse, democratic society in an interdependent world.
>
> (National Council for the Social Studies, 1993, p. 7)

As you can see, the conceptual range of what social studies is to include is daunting. According to NCSS, social studies embraces history and the social sciences (for example, economics, geography, political science), while including connections to religion, philosophy, literature, and so on. Broad enough to encompass about everything one might teach? It certainly appears so. How are teachers to choose what to emphasize, what's important for students to know and learn? Definitions such as this give teachers considerable latitude, but they are not particularly useful for making classroom decisions.

The Traditional Social Studies Curriculum Pattern

Ramona Palmer's Bill of Rights unit clearly fits under the umbrella of the NCSS definition, but so do many topics. A second, more definitive source of ideas about the subject matter of social studies is a curriculum guide. **Curriculum guide** is a generic term for a document that expresses a set of subject-matter goals and objectives. Also referred to as a **scope and sequence**, a curriculum guide tells teachers what broad content areas they are responsible for (the scope) and in what order they should be presented (the sequence). Curriculum guides may be produced by state departments of education and local school districts.

If you were to read elementary-school social studies guides from around the United States, a pattern would emerge. Figure 3.1 illustrates the traditional pattern of a social studies curriculum.

During the 1940s and 1950s, a curriculum theorist named Paul Hanna (1963) advanced a curriculum sequence. He dubbed it the **expanding communities** model because the child begins learning first about herself and immediate community and gradually expands outward, considering larger and more experientially remote communities as she gets older. As Figure 3.2 suggests, you can think of this as a series of concentric circles, with the child at the center.

Grade	Focus	Examples
Kindergarten	Self	Him/herself and the most immediate environment
1	The family	Similarities and differences across families
2	The immediate neighborhood	School, post office, fire station
3	The local community	Government, services, city and rural life, geography of the community
4	The state	Its history and geography
5	The United States	Its history and geography, sometimes in connection with Canada and Mexico
6	The world	Its history and geography

FIGURE 3.1 The traditional K–6 social studies curriculum pattern.

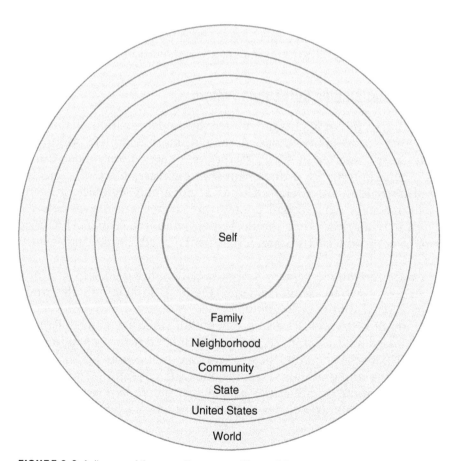

FIGURE 3.2 A diagram of the expanding communities model.

▶|◀ REFLECTION: RECALLING SCHOOLING EXPERIENCES

Recall your experiences in elementary social studies classrooms. How closely did the subject matter parallel the expanding communities model illustrated above? What do you remember about the lessons and units your teacher taught? How might your experiences as a learner inform your practice as a teacher?
▶|◀

Since Hanna first advanced the expanding communities approach, it has become the standard elementary-school curriculum sequence across the country. In many school districts, social studies curriculum sequences follow this expanding communities model in some form. Typically, social studies elementary textbook series also follow this sequence.

Hanna bases his curriculum idea on two principles, both tied to the work of psychologist Jean Piaget (see the discussion of Piaget's work in Chapter 2). One involves the assumption that children learn best when they deal with ideas *known* to them and related to their immediate experiences (for example, themselves, their family, their neighborhood) and then gradually move to ideas that are *unknown* to them (for example, history of the country or world). Ramona Palmer's Bill of Rights unit seems to fit within the expanding communities model. The Bill of Rights is a big part of US history and, as indicated above, this is a common fifth-grade curriculum area.

Hanna's second assumption involves the belief that children reason from the concrete to the *abstract*. This principle implies that students are more comfortable with tangible and familiar ideas and that they have difficulty dealing with conceptual matters until they reach an advanced stage of thinking. This notion has some intuitive appeal, but we have already seen a few classroom examples that challenge this premise. Recall the first-grade classroom Linda Levstik (1993) reports on in Chapter 1. Concepts such as "rain forest," "resources," and the "excavation" of Viking sites are clearly abstract notions, and yet these first graders hardly seem confused. Similarly, Ramona Palmer's fifth graders are handling some pretty powerful ideas: censorship, due process, and the like. Yet, although they undoubtedly have a less than adult understanding of these ideas, we get no sense from the vignette that they are befuddled.

Not only does Hanna's second principle seem problematic, but as we see it, so does the first. Again, we point to the first graders profiled in Chapter 1. According to Hanna's scheme, these youngsters should be unable to understand world cultures, a subject typically reserved for grade 6. The point is that research on how children make sense of social studies ideas simply contradicts Hanna's conception of their development. As we reported in Chapter 2, quite young children appear able to make some sense of both unknown and abstract ideas. Working from the known to the unknown and from the concrete to the abstract may help, but one shouldn't approach a social studies curriculum with rigid ideas about this sequence.

The expanding communities model that forms the basis for many social studies curriculum guides may be common, but it is not especially helpful in understanding how teachers such as Ramona Palmer make curricular decisions.

Other Curriculum Sources

Beyond definitions and curriculum guides, teachers can also draw on state and national curriculum standards, tests, and textbooks for curriculum ideas.

Curriculum Standards

"Standards" for teaching social studies have been developed by individual states (for example, California Board of Education, 1988; New York State Education Department, 1998) and by national-level curriculum groups and organizations (for example, National Governors Association Center for Best Practices and Council of Chief State School Officers, 2010; National Council for the Social Studies, 2010; National Center for History in the Schools, 1996).[2] Everyone appears to be in the game of generating curriculum standards, and the array of standards in social studies borders on bewildering. The ones that appear to matter most are state standards, which we describe below. We offer some examples, but it would be most useful for you to go to your State Department of Education's website and examine your state's standards.

Such **curriculum standards** documents typically offer little detailed information to teachers. Consider, for example, the following references to the Bill of Rights in the Social Studies Resource Guide (New York State Education Department, 1998) and in the *National Standards for History* (National Center for History in the Schools, 1996):

> Legal, political, and historical documents define the values, beliefs, and principles of constitutional democracy. In the United States these documents include the Declaration of Independence, and the United States Constitution and the Bill of Rights.
> (New York State Education Department, 1998, p. 12)

> Analyze the significance of the Bill of Rights and its specific guarantees.
> (National Center for History in the Schools, 1996, p. 89)

Neither of these references would prevent Ramona Palmer from teaching the Bill of Rights as she does, but neither do they offer much in the way of teaching guidance. Think about all the questions a teacher might want to have addressed: For example, what particular "values, beliefs, and principles of constitutional democracy" and "specific guarantees" do these curriculum authors suggest teachers teach? Into what level of detail should teachers and students delve? What constitutes an adequate level of student understanding? How are ideas to be represented to accommodate the diversity of students in the classroom? Like definitions and curriculum guides, standards documents tend to provide general rather than specific guidance.

RESOURCES: CURRICULUM STANDARDS

To get a sense of the wide array of curriculum standards available, take a look at these websites:

- https://ed.sc.gov/instruction/standards-learning/social-studies/standards/
- www.doe.mass.edu/instruction/literacy-humanities.html
- www.ncss.org

Standardized Tests

State-developed **standardized tests** are probably even less useful for daily planning. We will have more to say about the influence of testing on teachers' practices in Chapter 6. Here, we suggest that tests are not necessarily a strong indicator of what your classroom curriculum ought to be. Several related considerations drive our thinking. One is the fact that no test can adequately cover the length and breadth of a school subject. Think about it—how many questions would you imagine necessary to get a real sense of what sixth-grade students know about world cultures? 20? 50? 100? Now add a second consideration: Most standardized social studies tests span multiple grades. For example, the typical fifth-grade social studies test is designed to assess not only students' understanding of the fifth-grade curriculum, but the K–4 course of study as well! Add that such tests rarely ask more than 50 questions, and that the questions generally change from year to year, and you begin to see the problem with expecting standardized tests to set your curriculum.

Another problem is that most standardized tests in social studies tend to be biased toward ways of knowing and cultural ideas and icons that are traditionally Anglocentric and middle class. Therefore, they tend not to represent the diversity of students and cultural differences you are likely to find in your classroom. Finally, consider that the current emphasis in standardized testing and accountability is on reading and mathematics achievement, a point made especially obvious by the fact that the No Child Left Behind (NCLB) legislation explicitly left out social studies.[3] As a result, social studies standardized testing in many states has been dropped.[4] In these states, then, testing practices provide no guidance at all.

Textbooks

Although they are often decried as dull and banal (e.g., Beck, McKeown, & Gromoll, 1989; Loewen, 2010), social studies textbooks are a common source of classroom curricula. And that makes sense, because in this one resource teachers have a large amount of information about their subject.

We take up the issue of textbook use in Chapter 5. Here, we want to emphasize the point that, although textbooks can be useful resources, they can prove limiting if they are a teacher's only resource. Just as a teacher of reading would never dream of using a single text to teach all aspects of reading, neither should a teacher of social studies ever think that a single text can define the full set of issues she or he might want to pursue with learners. A more sensible approach, then, is to use a textbook as part of a palette of resources that can help teachers make informed curriculum choices.

So how does Ramona Palmer make curriculum decisions? With the exception of a state-developed, standardized test, she reports that she draws primarily on three sources. Her school district curriculum guide, which features an expanding communities sequence, is one reference point. As she explains:

> We have to follow those district guidelines, and if we go over and above any of those, we have to follow a policy from the Board of Education in which it [our own policy decision] has to meet certain curriculum standards.

Palmer also uses a textbook as a source of curriculum ideas. Her units generally reflect the chapter sequence in her book, but she also makes liberal use of trade books, both to supplement points the textbook makes and to explore ideas and issues it does not. Finally, Palmer relies on her professional judgment. Rightly, her school district refrains from prescribing all elements of the curriculum; as long as a topic meets "certain curriculum standards," she can follow her pedagogical nose. Although this is easier for veteran teachers than it is for novices, the point is the same: Although curriculum guides and standards, tests, textbooks, and the like may seem to direct teachers' curriculum choices, in fact, teachers have considerable instructional latitude (Priestley, Edwards, Priestley, & Miller, 2012).

■ SECTION SUMMARY:
DEFINING THE SOCIAL STUDIES

- As defined by the leading professional organization, the social studies cover a wide range of ideas, topics, and issues.

- The expanding communities curriculum model has been in place for some time, but the principles that underlie that model are open to question.

- In addition to the expanding communities model, teachers can draw on curriculum guides and national standards documents, standardized tests (to a limited degree), and textbooks for curriculum ideas. None is all-inclusive because they vary widely, so teachers must still use their professional judgment in making decisions. After all, you are the one who knows your students and their learning needs most intimately.

The Threads Approach

Curriculum guides and standards, tests, and textbooks, although they do not hold all the answers, are important factors in choosing what to teach. Teachers sign contracts to teach what school districts deem important, which may be expressed in curriculum guides or textbook series. You most likely will encounter some version of the expanding communities approach, which will give you, as it did Ramona Palmer, some direction in terms of the subject matter that you teach. How to teach the topics, under what classroom circumstances, and with which embellishments fall under your professional discretion. In short, you have considerable instructional room in which to maneuver. We like to think of the act of converting the topics in the curriculum guide into powerful social studies ideas and teachable representations as transforming the curriculum. That will be one of your central professional tasks.

Transforming the Social Studies Curriculum

Like the study of mathematics, literature, and science, the study of social studies gives children powerful ways to make sense of the world. As we have seen, the social studies deal with wide conceptual ground. In order to learn how their world works, children need to explore how and why people behave as they do (from psychology), how people operate in group settings (from sociology), how cultural groups are similar and different (from anthropology), how economic and political systems function (from economics and political science), how people interact with their physical environments (from geography), and how people make sense of the past (from history).

As this list indicates, teachers can look to these **social science disciplines** and to history for rich ideas to help them shape what we want children to understand and accomplish. Remember Ramona Palmer's Bill of Rights discussion: Her students were deeply engrossed in some powerful ideas. Students seem to love rich, weighty ideas and questions. But what ones do teachers look for?

In each discipline, key ideas and questions animate the work. These ideas and questions come from the traditional academic disciplines you probably studied in college. For pedagogical purposes, however, we have translated these disciplines and the ideas and questions they represent into a more convenient form, the *threads*. The threads are a conceptual framework by which teachers can give their students insights into social and cultural phenomena. Figure 3.3 shows the five threads and their respective ideas. The 2013 NCSS C3 *Framework* (www.socialstudies.org) also makes use of a type of threads approach. Considerable guidance can be found in this document by way of many concrete examples.

Now let's consider each of the five threads individually. Remember that the key ideas and questions listed below are meant to be illustrative rather than exhaustive. In other words, we expect you will expand these lists as you work with the thread categories in the context of your curriculum.

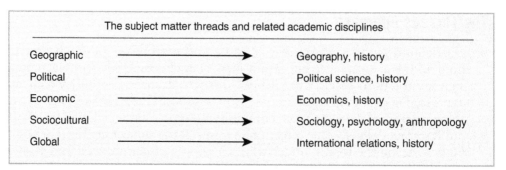

FIGURE 3.3 The threads and their related disciplines.

Thread Name: Geographic

Disciplines: Geography, history
Key ideas/questions:

- *Landforms*—What are the surface features of an area? Which features matter to the inhabitants and in what ways?
- *Location*—Where are people, places, and surface features located? How does the location of one entity influence that of another?
- *Climate/Weather*—What are the prevailing weather and climatic conditions? How do these conditions affect life in a particular area?
- *Resources*—What natural resources are available and in what supply? Which of those resources do the inhabitants use?
- *Population*—How are people distributed across an area, and how densely are they concentrated? How do the people of an area interact with their physical surroundings?
- *Land-use change*—How has people's use of the land changed over time?

Thread Name: Political

Disciplines: Political science, history
Key ideas/questions:

- *Decision making*—How are rules made, interpreted, and enforced in a society?
- *Power*—Who holds power in a society and who doesn't? How has this changed (if it has) over time?
- *Structure of government*—How have people decided to organize themselves to make decisions? What benefits and drawbacks to these forms of government are apparent? How has the structure of government changed?

Thread Name: Economic

Disciplines: Economics, history
Key ideas/questions:

- *Property*—What do people own? How do they come to own it?
- *Means of exchange*—What form of exchange (for example, money) do people use to obtain what they want? How have forms of exchange changed?
- *Labor/Management*—Who works for whom in a society? How does that relationship work? How are these relationships different today than they were 100 years ago?
- *Scarcity/Surplus*—Which goods and services are plentiful in a society and which are scarce? How does the scarcity or surplus of something influence its cost?

Thread Name: Sociocultural

Disciplines: Psychology, sociology, anthropology
Key ideas/questions:

- *Class*—How is the society organized? Which groups have more power and influence than others? Is it possible to move from class to class?
- *Race/Ethnicity/Gender*—How do these factors influence the way people are perceived throughout the society? How have people's ideas and perceptions of these factors changed over time?
- *Education*—How do people transfer the accumulating knowledge and experience from one generation to another?
- *Arts*—How do people represent themselves and their lives in writing, art, music, and dance?
- *Recreation/Leisure*—How do people spend time when they are not working or attending to family matters?

Thread Name: Global

Discipline: Anthropology, international relations, history
Key ideas/questions:

- *Competition/Cooperation*—How do cultural groups interact? In what ways do they cooperate and in what ways do they compete? How has technological and industrial change influenced how people cooperate and compete over time?
- *Conflict*—How do cultural groups handle conflicts between themselves?

- *Change*—How do norms, values, and institutions of cultural groups change over time?

You may have wondered, as you read these lists, why we do not include history as a separate thread. Instead, we add it to the categories because we believe the threads are equally useful for understanding *both* current phenomena and past events, as we noted in the questions we generated. In other words, working through the thread categories can contribute as much to children's understandings of the Industrial Revolution as to their grasp of recent situations such as the US role in Afghanistan and Iraq.

The discipline of history also contributes a key set of ideas and questions about *how* people go about examining what interests them: how historians gather information about the past, how they decide what happened, where they look for evidence that events occurred, and what they do with evidence when they find it. Historians make claims that events happened in certain ways. How do they know? Are their claims trustworthy? If so, on what grounds? It is essential that children learn to ask these questions if they are to become thoughtful consumers and creators of ideas in their own right.

IN YOUR CLASSROOM

LEARNING HISTORY BY DOING IT

To help your students not only to learn history but also to investigate it, you can construct a unit around a local history project. A good example would be to invite your students to explore the history of their school.

Using the threads approach, assign groups to find out when the school was originally built and why on this particular location (geographic thread). Ask another group to investigate the economic and political changes in the surrounding neighborhood that necessitated the building of the school (economic and political threads). Encourage a third group to explore how the school population changed over time, examining such issues as ethnic and racial makeup and the like (sociocultural thread). Finally, assign a fourth group to survey the school and local population to determine the ethnic character of the area (global thread).[5]

Such an approach might require using the local library, city hall, and the Internet to locate documents and records, many of which can be found online. In addition to understanding the documents, you will need to help your students learn how to interpret these documents by teaching them to pay attention to (1) who the authors were, (2) when they were written, and (3) why they might have been created in the first place.[6]

Understanding the Threads: Returning to Ramona Palmer's Classroom

The case of Ramona Palmer's teaching that opened this chapter demonstrates several of the threads. Reread the vignette that opens the chapter, asking yourself what evidence you see of the threads.

As we see it, the discussion and debate in Ramona Palmer's classroom broach serious *political* issues. The primary focus of this analysis is on governing, a central issue for those involved in political science: How do people govern themselves? How is power to make choices distributed across a society? What regulates the system? What is the proper relationship between the governors and the governed? Much of the talk in the discussion hinges on students debating and making sense of these deep questions.

The issue of capital punishment is tied to *sociocultural* and *economic* issues. Why do people murder? Is it related to socioeconomic class? Who will act as executioner? What does it cost the government to exercise the act of capital punishment allowed by the Bill of Rights? Is the cost worth the effort? If not, what are more cost-efficient alternatives? If so, why don't more states use capital punishment? These questions raise serious economic and sociological issues.

Reviewing the thread connections in Palmer's lessons raises two important points. One point concerns the interrelatedness of the threads. As we see in the paragraph just above, discussing the practice of capital punishment leads us to consider political, sociocultural, and economic threads at the same time: The laws that govern the administration of capital punishment reflect the norms and values of our society, but they also reflect the economic costs and benefits of punishment. One might study capital punishment as a purely political, sociocultural, or economic issue. As Palmer's presentation suggests, however, the issue is enlivened when considered from multiple thread directions.

Yet, the second point is that a teacher need not always address every thread category in every lesson. Did you notice, for example, that Palmer leaves aside the geographic and global threads? She does so largely because they are not directly relevant to this discussion of the Bill of Rights. However, if the class extended the capital punishment discussion to other nations, they would be asking questions that deal with the global thread. If the class went on to consider how the practice of capital punishment is distributed across the United States, they would be dealing with geographic questions.

Palmer doesn't take the time to deal with all the possible threads, but the discussion is laced with many of them nonetheless. She could stop at any point and broach them, as she does when her students push her on her position regarding capital punishment. Ramona Palmer is making crucial decisions about how to allocate classroom time while working with the richest ideas, questions, and threads that time allows.

Other Examples of the Threads Approach in Practice

Consider this common curriculum guide dictum for fourth-grade state history:

> Students are to know the Native-American tribes that inhabited the state and where they lived.

We would argue that if taught as expressed, this would be impoverished instruction. What are the rich ideas and understandings your students can dig into? What evidence of the thread categories is apparent?

We don't see much power in asking students to memorize a bunch of names and locations. Simply teaching topics, lists, names, and places and events that can be counted off on worksheets and multiple-choice tests provides little incentive for your students to learn. Most importantly, research strongly suggests that your students quickly forget these lists and names and topics. Instead, what would happen if you began with the question: What was life like for Native-Americans in this region before colonization, and how has it changed since then?

If you asked your students to consider this question, they would have much digging to do. They would need to learn something about Native-American social life (sociocultural thread), where they lived and why (geographic thread), how they made rules to live by (political thread), how they satisfied their basic needs (economic thread), and how they interacted with other native groups and with the Europeans (global thread). Digging into how Native-American cultures changed over time would include additional elements of the historical. Cast this way, the question becomes a vehicle to explore both historical and contemporary circumstances and events, in effect tying the past to the present.

The threads here are unmistakable and help weave together what students need to understand. By taking the initial topic, Native-American tribal names and locales, and reframing it around a penetrating question, you gain considerable power in what you invite students to do. By choosing topics and developing rich questions around them that focus on the threads, you are helping yourself select from the welter of teaching choices. The NCSS *C3 Framework* (www.socialstudies.org) begins with this very idea of asking rich questions and can provide considerable guidance in thinking about how to frame them in the way we are suggesting here.

▶️◀ REFLECTION: MAKING CONNECTIONS

A rich social studies curriculum lies in the connections you help students make between ideas and questions. The threads' conceptual framework is designed to help you think about those ideas and questions. As you look at the various curriculum resources available, push yourself to reflect on the potential thread connections you might make with learners.
▶️◀

APPLYING THE THREADS APPROACH

Now it's your turn to try out this selecting and transforming process using the threads approach. A common social studies topic in early elementary school is "the nature of local communities." Think hard for a few minutes about this topic and make some notes. Draw on your subject-matter knowledge from history and the social sciences and on the thread category descriptions above.

■ What rich ideas concerning communities surface?
■ How might you make these ideas engaging and suitable for, say, second or third graders? Generate a list of ideas and questions that make use of as many threads as possible. Write your questions in the spaces below.

Topic: _____

Ideas/Questions: _____

_____

_____

_____

_____

_____

_____

_____

If you have difficulty with this exercise, you may need to read up on the topic to figure out the subject-matter connections. This shouldn't be any big surprise; good teachers frequently read about the subject matter they teach to gain depth of knowledge and to understand more about the connecting threads. You should expect to have questions about your subject matter. This is both natural and good; no one can know deeply every topic or issue. And your own curiosity in pursuing your questions may turn out to be highly infectious in your classroom.

To help with the process, you also may want to include your students' questions by asking them directly to talk about their curiosities before you begin a unit (for example, using the W of the K-W-L exercise we mentioned earlier). Finally, the more experience you have in this, the more effective you'll become. We encourage you to be patient but persistent. Persistence is really the key.

In several respects, the threads approach resembles a "thematic" or "integrated" curriculum, in which teachers choose a large theme and draw from a variety of subject matters (mathematics, social studies, literacy/language arts) to build a thematic and integrated unit. However, these thematic units involve cross-subject-matter integration; they integrate social studies with an entirely different area, such as mathematics. We are talking about within-subject-matter integration; that is, we stay within the social science/history realm.

There is nothing the matter with thematic units and cross-subject integration. In fact, when you teach you may wish to expand on our thoughts about the threads approach to include other subjects beyond the social studies, especially given the importance of the Common Core State Standards for English Language Arts. However, our emphasis here is on the integrative power of working *within* the social studies through the threads.

■ SECTION SUMMARY: THE THREADS APPROACH

- ■ The social sciences and history provide the disciplinary background for the social studies. For pedagogical purposes, we have translated these disciplines into *threads*.

- ■ The threads are: geographic, political, economic, sociocultural, and global. Each thread category represents a particular set of ideas and questions.

- ■ Social studies topics can be broken down by individual threads, but the real power of the threads approach is when a teacher and students see the interconnections among the threads.

What to Teach? You Must Choose

Let's begin this section by returning, once more, to Ramona Palmer's Bill of Rights unit. Palmer's choices reflect how she wants her students to confront and build understandings of the subject matter. She is constantly choosing and acting on those choices.

Why? The most immediately noticeable reason in this cascade of lessons is the relationship between the time available to teach and what she knows about representing her subject matter. She could dig deeply and explore all the threads and their many rich questions, but she also must pay attention to the clock. For now, let's focus on the way she chooses to represent the subject matter.

Ramona Palmer opts to cover the first eight amendments, skipping the ninth and tenth—an important choice. These last two, she notes, are more complex than she wishes to deal with at the moment. She decides to concentrate her attention on the threads contained in the first eight amendments, threads rich enough to make the points she wants. We see that she avoids a strictly textbook-dominated approach. Like many social studies teachers, Palmer could push on after students read and recite the textbook-inscribed amendments, but she doesn't. She wants her learners to explore the ramifications of these amendments for their personal lives. She does so through a give-and-take discussion in which she asks students about their implications for topics the students know about (rap music, movies, gun laws, capital punishment).

In this way she breathes life into a document that is at once both over two hundred years old and of very present importance. She represents the subject matter of the Bill of Rights as having clear present-day political, social, and economic implications. Her students see the connections and run with them in a highly engaging conversation. The point here is that Palmer is choosing how to represent the subject matter at almost every turn. That's what teachers do.

Yes, the social studies curriculum *is* in your lap, and you *must* choose. Making these choices about social studies subject matter can be daunting, and even downright frightening. But if you learn to use this threads approach, and with it the process of generating questions that your students will find intriguing, you will be well on your way. Remember, you are after the rich, meaty ideas that make social studies subject matter such an interesting area of the curriculum. (See the list of technology resources at the end of this chapter for assistance with choosing rich ideas.) And remember that avoiding the process of choosing is really still choosing. What do we mean? Consider the following.

Choosing by Default

For various reasons, some social studies teachers fall prey to the seductive temptation to slavishly follow the curriculum guide and to teach social studies as though it were a set of simple topics comprising a vast array of facts for students to memorize. We have pointed out how such teaching lacks power and results in quick forgetfulness on the part of students. Let's examine a few reasons why teachers fall into this trap, along with some different ways to think about your teaching that may help prevent you from being so tempted.

Substantive Content Knowledge in Social Studies

History and the social sciences, from which the social studies draws much of its subject matter, are heavy on what some call **substantive** or **propositional knowledge**. We can think of social studies as a collection of facts about how the world works, objective knowledge that makes up a portion of our cultural knowledge base. And we might assume that if students merely memorize this knowledge, they will know what they need to know and teaching has been successful. But, as the last chapter and Ramona Palmer's Bill of Rights discussion suggest, other choices exist for thinking about social studies knowledge and learning.

Think back to Helen and Rita, introduced in Chapter 2. The girls produced widely different interpretations of the American history they studied in fourth grade. You have no guarantee that, if you reduce the social studies curriculum to a set of facts students need to memorize, all students will learn the same ones or interpret them the same way. Learning, as we saw in the last chapter, is much more than memorizing facts; it's about thinking with and about ideas and constructing understandings of them. Children bring different prior ideas to the learning context, ideas that interact in unpredictable ways with the new ideas they encounter in your classroom. Asking children to memorize social studies facts and propositions simply ignores this important aspect of the learning process and limits student achievement. We cannot stress this point enough. Trying to deny that children learn this way will only greet you with endless disappointments at assessment time.

Moreover, many of the so-called social studies facts and propositions that we tend to take for granted and find piled on top of one another in social studies textbooks are really "somebody else's facts" (Holt, 1990, p. 2). Who produced the knowledge in social studies school textbooks? Frequently it has been White men with a decidedly Western outlook on culture, history, economic systems, and so forth. What is Marvyn, an African-American student in Palmer's class, supposed to think about this? What if his ideas about our culture and history—and he gives us some interesting possibilities in the discussion of the Bill of Rights—differ strongly from those he gets from the textbooks and from his teachers who ask him to memorize what it holds? Can he trust the book and his teacher and the facts each convey? Are they his "facts"? In other words, are the circumstances of his life as a Black youngster, with a history that traces its roots to slavery, the same as those of the European American or Asian American children sitting around him? Do they all agree on the so-called "facts"?

Although one could argue that there should be agreement, we disagree because we know that it is simply impossible to shove these ready-made textbook facts into Marvyn's head, especially if they oppose those he already holds and run contrary to his experience (for other clear examples, see Epstein, 2009; Levstik, 2008; VanSledright, 2015). His different ideas and perspectives growing out of a different history must be respected and allowed to interact in an open forum with the ideas he encounters in class. Reducing the curriculum to a set of memorizable facts will sell short students of color such as Marvyn, girls, Asian Americans, Latinos and Latinas, and even White, middle-class students. Chances are, you won't get away with it, either. Expect students to turn off to your teaching, act bored, act up, challenge you, or any combination of these.

The point here is that social studies knowledge is produced by human beings to help them understand their worlds. This knowledge reflects the perspectives of its authors and therefore can reflect multiple cultural experiences or purviews and biases. Historical and social science knowledge is always open to interpretation and reinterpretation, depending on one's perspective and the evidence one can muster to change an accepted view. Children must have opportunities to bring their ideas, perspectives, and evidence to this changing knowledge table as well. As we argued in the last chapter, this doesn't mean that teachers need to accept as valid all the ideas students hold or construct. Clearly, it would be better if children jettisoned untenable ideas and replaced them with ones that are based on careful argument and evidence. This brings us to a last point.

Creating Social Studies Knowledge

Equal in importance to knowledge of social studies itself is the process of creating knowledge. For example, how have historians figured out what went on during the American Revolution? How have economists figured out that capitalism, as an economic system, functions the way it does? What assumptions do we make and take for granted? In other words, how do we know what we know?

Students need to learn as much about methods of creating knowledge as they do about social studies facts and propositions. They need to learn about the tenuous and problematic nature of creating knowledge. They need to learn that a problem-laden process creates problem-laden knowledge, knowledge that cannot be accepted at first blush. Social studies knowledge and its creation process require close scrutiny. They, too, are part of the connecting threads, as you saw in the previous example of researching history with your students.

Some people refer to research methods as the **procedural** or **syntactic knowledge** of subject matter, that is, understandings of the procedures employed to create knowledge. In history and the social sciences in the Western world, we build knowledge through a process of careful research and data gathering, followed

FIGURE 3.4 Social studies knowledge is a human construction. Adults, through their roles as historians, psychologists, political scientists, and the like, help construct knowledge. What role do children have in the construction of knowledge?

by rigorous analysis, interpretation, and argument based on the accumulated evidence. To the extent that an evidence-based argument is accepted by people, it becomes knowledge and perhaps fact. Children need to learn about this process as well and especially about how it works. This is another point we cannot stress enough.

For a detailed example of how young students can be taught to build their own evidence-based understandings using newly learned procedural knowledge, see the accounts in Chapters 3, 4, and 5 of *In Search of America's Past: Learning to Read History in Elementary School* (VanSledright, 2002). Rather than attempt to pound historical facts into the students' heads, Bruce taught a class of 23 fifth graders how to learn history by doing it themselves, that is, by becoming historical investigators who read and interpreted primary source documents as they constructed their own evidence-based ideas about what happened in the past. He describes in detail how he taught the class and how the students responded. He offers research data that support some successes he obtained in getting the students to read history in a more sophisticated way using their newly acquired procedural knowledge. Doing so deepened their understandings of history.

The social studies-as-fact view ignores the important aspects of how knowledge is constructed. As an unfortunate result, students receive both a limited and limiting view of the social studies that deprives them of the opportunity to assess and evaluate accepted knowledge. They lose the opportunity to understand that knowledge is actually multifaceted, plural, and multicultural.

Yes, you will encounter social studies curriculum guides that stipulate what is to be covered. These guides may also intimate a social-studies-as-fact view and suggest that your teaching must conform to this perspective. But, as we continue to emphasize, you really have considerable latitude in choosing and selecting. Most curriculum guides are vague, and schools lack the resources to hire "curriculum police" to make sure you follow the guide to the letter. They do resort sometimes to pacing guides, but even then, it is difficult to police their use. Nor would they really want to fully. School districts more or less do try to recognize that you possess some professional autonomy and attempt to create an atmosphere in which you can exercise your professional judgment. The choices are largely yours!

Embracing the Choosing Process

We invite you to step up and embrace this choosing process. Exercise the threads approach as a method of enhancing the quality of the subject-matter choices you make. Good social studies teachers with whom we've worked show us that using these threads and engaging their professional judgment in the careful choosing process have profound influences on what and how students learn social studies. These good teachers also know that the process can be difficult and can require considerable outside reading and research, but they tell us that the benefits for themselves and their students almost always far exceed the costs incurred. Ms. Palmer is a fine case in point.

But specifically, what are these benefits?

1   Knowing the social studies subject matter makes it easier to see connections and establish threads and so streamline your work.

2   In a similar vein, knowing the subject matter expands the curricular possibilities upon which you can draw, allowing you richer choices.[7]

3   Knowing social studies subject matter deeply also helps you figure out the important questions, those that people are asking in the disciplines and ones your students might be curious about.

4   Having significant knowledge of social studies helps you "hear" your students, which helps you decide how to respond when they express nascent ideas and misconceptions as you ask them questions in class.

Subject-matter knowledge is the bridge between learners and learning and teachers and teaching. And the bigger, stronger, and wider the bridge, the larger, weightier, and more powerful the ideas that can traverse it.

■ SECTION SUMMARY:
CHOOSING SOCIAL STUDIES SUBJECT MATTER

- ■ The "default" curriculum choice some social studies teachers make is to follow the content and structure of curriculum guides and textbooks and to teach as if the content is but a set of facts to be memorized. We argue, however, that this choice offers little understanding of or benefit to children.

- ■ The benefits of avoiding the default choice include seeing connections and streamlining your work, expanding the curricular possibilities, figuring out important questions, and hearing students as they begin constructing powerful ideas.

In the next chapter we span the social studies subject-matter bridge from learning across to teaching. Specifically, we put to work the threads approach as a means of framing the rich questions you choose, and we introduce this fusion under the notion of teaching with *big ideas*.

Chapter Summary

1   **What does the traditional social studies curriculum look like, and what problems are inherent in it?** The traditional social studies curriculum follows the *expanding communities* model proposed by Paul Hanna in the early 1960s. The model organizes the K–6 course of study by moving progressively away from the child (for example, K–Focus on Self ... Grade 6–Focus on the World).

Two principles underlie Hanna's approach: moving from *known* to *unknown*, and moving from the concrete to the *abstract*. Researchers have raised serious questions about both of these principles.

2   **What are the threads of social studies, and how do they relate to the notion of teaching with rich ideas?** The *threads* are a pedagogical translation of the traditional academic disciplines of the social sciences and history. The threads categories are geographic, political, economic, sociocultural, and global.

The threads, and their attendant academic disciplines, offer teachers a wide range of complex and powerful ideas and questions that can serve as the basis for unit and lesson planning.

3   **How much latitude do teachers have in making curriculum choices?** A lot. Teachers can draw on various resources (see below) as they plan their classroom curriculum. None of the available resources serves all purposes, and they vary widely in focus and goal orientation, so teachers must make a range of curriculum decisions.

Some teachers make a "default" choice to follow, for example, the structure and content of a social studies textbook or the list of topics indicated in a curriculum guide. This default choice, however, seldom succeeds with learners, largely because of how they learn. Choosing is not easy, but the benefits of embracing the choosing process far outweigh the disadvantages.

Notes

1   For more on Ramona Palmer's teaching, see Chapter 5 in Brophy and VanSledright (1997).
2   The Common Core State Standards for English Language Arts are technically not curriculum standards, for they do not prescribe a set of ideas to be taught, but, as we point out in Chapter 8, they are an important document for social studies teachers to consider.
3   The reauthorization of NCLB in 2015, called the Every Child Succeeds Act (ESSA) allowed states considerable flexibility regarding what subjects they test.
4   That said, the state tests developed around the Common Core State Standards for English Language Arts will ask students to read and respond to social studies texts.
5   Although these are social studies-specific questions, they also work well to satisfy the research goals expressed in the Common Core State Standards for English Language Arts.
6   For more on lessons and units like this, see Levstik & Barton (2011).
7   For more on this important benefit, see Wilson (1990).

Teaching Resources

Print Resources

Brophy, J., & Alleman, J. (2008). Early elementary social studies. In Levstik, L.S. & Tyson, C. (Eds.), *Handbook of research in social studies education* (pp. 33–49). New York: Routledge.

Gerhke, N., Knapp, M., & Sirotnik, K. (1992). In search of the school curriculum. In G. Grant (Ed.), *Review of research in education* (Vol. 18, pp. 51–110). Washington, DC: American Educational Research Association.

Hahn, C.L. (1985). The status of social studies in the public schools of the United States: Another look. *Social Education*, 49(3), 220–223.

Thornton, S. (1994). The social studies near century's end: Reconsidering patterns of curriculum and instruction. In L. Darling-Hammond (Ed.), *Review of research in education* (Vol. 20, pp. 223–254). Washington, DC: American Educational Research Association.

Thornton, S. (2008). Continuity and change in social studies curriculum. In Levstik, L.S. & Tyson, C. (Eds.). *Handbook of research in social studies education* (pp. 15–32). New York: Routledge.

Each of these works presents a useful description of how the current social studies curriculum came to be.

Several professional journals regularly provide lesson, unit, and general curriculum ideas for teachers. See particularly *The History Teacher*, published by the Society for History Education, and *Social Education* and *Social Studies for the Young Learner*, published by the National Council for the Social Studies.

Technology Resources

An especially good online resource for understanding the threads approach is *The College, Career, and Civic Life (C3) Framework for Social Studies State Standards*. Examples exist throughout the document, but see especially Appendix A:

■ www.socialstudies.org/c3

In the state of Maryland, the Montgomery County Public Schools district rewrote much of its elementary social studies curriculum using a threads approach. This project could be a very useful model for understanding how the threads can be applied to an existing curriculum that is organized to fit state standards. For more, see the Montgomery County Public Schools website address below and follow links to Academics and the Elementary Curriculum and then on to Social Studies.

■ www.mcps.k12.md.us

Other states and school systems within those states also have developed social studies curriculum standards that follow a threads approach. Search online for possible examples in school systems within your state and/or search for your state's social studies curriculum standards for examples.

For more on building threads approaches that make use of historical connections, see the following website, which also offers guidance on how to conduct a historical investigation that could be modified for use in the classroom:

■ http://dohistory.org/

4

Teachers and Teaching
Working with Ideas and Questions

Sandra Prosy is a fifth-grade teacher in a diverse, urban elementary school in New York State. She is a middle-aged European American; her 21 students are predominantly African American. She begins the first day of a new unit on American government with a recitation:

> Prosy: What kind of government do you think we will talk about?
> Angela: Public schools?
> Rashona: City?
> Prosy: Who runs the city?
> Michael: The mayor?

Prosy writes *city* on the board and asks, "Who is the mayor?" A girl calls out, "Luciano." Prosy nods and writes *Luciano* on the board. "What other kinds of government are there? What other areas need to be run?" she asks.

> Deion: Community.
> Tina: State.
> Prosy: Yes, what state?
> Michelle: New York.
> Prosy: Who runs our state?
> Tom: The governor.

Prosy nods and writes *state, governor, and Cuomo* (the current New York governor) on the board. As she does, a boy calls out, "What about county?" Prosy says, "Well, yes, but I'm looking for something that starts with an F." A girl guesses, "Federal?" Prosy responds, "Right. And who runs the federal government?" A boy offers, "Rush Limbaugh!" while the rest of the class shouts out, "Donald Trump!"

The next day, Prosy begins class by distributing a worksheet entitled "The Government of the United States." She gives the children eight minutes to complete it, instructing them to write "in cursive only." The remainder of class time is spent reviewing the worksheet questions:

PROSY: The _____ is the head of the executive branch?
ANGELA: The president.
PROSY: The courts are in the _____ branch?
WHITNEY: Judicial.
PROSY: The president takes the oath of office on January twentieth. This is called __ _____ day?
DEION: Memorial day?
MICHELLE: Independence day?
PROSY: It's called "Inauguration day." During his years in office, the president lives in the _____?
RACHELLE: The White House.

COMMONPLACE CONNECTIONS

- What does Prosy seem to consider important about the subject matter of US government?
- What view of learners does she seem to hold?
- How would you characterize her teaching?
- How would you describe the *classroom environment*?

Janice Mead is also a White, middle-aged teacher. Unlike Prosy, Mead teaches fourth grade in a largely White, upscale, suburban elementary school. Mead is also different from Prosy in that she uses trade books in addition to a standard textbook, she often groups learners in various ways for work assignments, and she makes learners responsible for the ideas they learn.

On the second day of a unit on American slavery, Mead introduces the Underground Railroad. After a brief recap of the previous day's discussion, she explains, "Now we're going to learn some more facts." She distributes copies of the trade book *If You Traveled on the Underground Railroad* (Levine & Johnson, 1993). Mead announces, "I'm going to give each person a question, and it's going to be that person's job to read the question on the appropriate page and come up with the important points." Continuing, she says, "Now, you should write your important points on a piece of paper or an index card to help you remember. When we're back together as a class, we're going to review the questions, and you're all going to give us the answers. You're going to be the expert on that question."

Although each learner is responsible for one question, Mead organizes the class so that students can work in pairs. She urges them to read the relevant information "a few times" and to "tell your partner the answer to your question, how you would explain it."

Mead allows the class 20 minutes to read the text, make notes in response to their questions, and talk with their partners. She calls the class to order and asks Larry to read his question (How did the Underground Railroad gets its name?) and to give his answer. Larry says, "There once was a runaway slave. He escaped in 1831 and swam in the river to a city in Ohio. His owner searched for him, but he couldn't be found. His owner thought he must have escaped on an underground railroad. And that's how the Underground Railroad got its name." Mead thanks Larry and explains, "Okay. The owner was bewildered because he was so close to him. He knew he (the slave) had to be there somewhere, but he couldn't see him. So, the name 'Underground Railroad' seemed to stick. *Underground* because it was secret and *Railroad* because people on it seemed to move so fast and it was difficult to catch them."

Class continues with learners giving their responses to questions such as: What did it mean to be a slave? Why did slaves want to leave their masters? Where would escaping slaves go first? What dangers did escaping slaves face? What did the Fugitive Slave Law say? How did slaves hear about Canada and freedom?

COMMONPLACE CONNECTIONS

- What does Mead seem to consider important about the *subject matter* of slavery and the Underground Railroad?
- What view of learners does she seem to hold?
- How would you characterize her *teaching*?
- How would you describe the *classroom environment*?

When we compare Mead's and Prosy's instruction, we see some dramatic differences. Unlike Prosy's class, Mead's learners read from rich textual sources rather than from textbooks and worksheets, they work together rather than alone, and they become the "experts" on pieces of the lesson rather than look to their teacher for all the answers. Other differences show up as well. Whereas Prosy focuses on a narrow set of dry, decontextualized facts, Mead encourages learners to think about a series of questions related to slavery and the Underground Railroad. Some are fact-based, such as "What did the Fugitive Slave Law say?" Others, like "Why did slaves want to leave their masters?" call for relatively low levels of analysis. Still others, like "What did it mean to be a slave?" ask learners to think more deeply. Listen to Susan's response:

To be a slave, it meant that you could not read or write. If you did, you would be punished. Being a slave meant that your owner could punish you whenever he wanted. To be a slave meant that you had to do everything he tells you to. To be a slave meant that you had to get your owner's permission to do almost everything. To be a slave meant that you could be sold away from everybody you knew.

With wonderful clarity, Susan defines the desperation of slave life: One must do "everything he [the owner] tells you" and "get your owner's permission to do almost everything." She concludes with perhaps the most wrenching dimension of slavery: "You could be sold away from everybody you knew."

It is not clear that all Mead's learners are making the same substantive connections that Susan is, for diverse learners will focus on diverse ideas. Still, by providing a richer instructional climate, Mead offers her students powerful opportunities to learn deeply.

Before going on to the rest of the chapter, let's consider one more teacher. Pam Derson, a European American in her 40s, is a 20-year veteran whose experience has been in suburban schools with predominantly White children. The learners in this vignette are fourth graders.

Introducing a history unit in which students will research Native Americans in the Tidewater Chesapeake region, Derson asks, "How do we know what we know?" Derson understands that historical knowledge is largely indeterminate because what we know is based largely on traces of the past—residual evidence with gaps and holes. She wants her learners to wrestle with this big idea as they go about researching questions of their own design. Derson knows that the class will encounter numerous facts about native life, and she wants them to know this information, but she also wants her students to become careful, systematic researchers with a skeptical, questioning edge.

As the class considers her question, Derson continues. "Did you ever wonder how we know what we know about these Tidewater Native Americans we are studying? Have you wondered? I think about this a lot. I talk to my relatives about it, too." Students volunteer several sources of information: artifacts, bones, fossils, a wagon. On this last point, Derson asks about what would happen to a wagon over time. It would "rot," one boy replies. Sensing a teachable moment, Derson responds:

> That's right. That's exactly what happens. It makes the work historians and researchers do very difficult, because what's left of the past is so scarce many times, especially if the history you are studying happened a long time ago.

Derson then informs the class that they are going on a scavenger hunt. She tells them to look under their desks, where, taped to the undersides, they find different colored pieces of paper—pink, yellow, green, and white—with drawings of native artifacts on them. Some students have one piece; others find more than one. Derson asks the children to take out a piece of notebook paper and carefully describe the nature of what they found. She draws a map of the classroom on the board and labels the rows and desks in a grid pattern with coordinates.

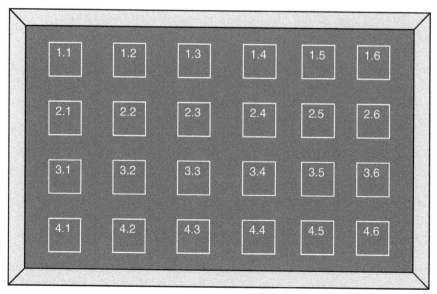

FIGURE 4.1 Derson's blackboard map of the classroom.

Students spend the next 30 minutes charting the location of each piece of colored paper and what is drawn on it. Once finished, Derson explains that the grid is an example of how archeologists map a dig site in order to understand what happened there. Having piqued their interest, Derson asks her students, "What can we say are the advantages and disadvantages of using artifacts to learn more about Native Americans?"

LOUISE: They help us know more about the Indians?

RUDY: They tell us how they lived.

DERSON: Yes, but do they tell us everything? Take a look at this. (She holds up a pottery shard and walks around the room showing it to learners.) What is it?

GINA: We don't know because it's broken.

DERSON: That's right. Sometimes we don't know what these things are. We have to guess, and sometimes we make mistakes. That's the problem when doing research. Often we can't be sure of the answers to our questions because what we find is not very good evidence.

Having demonstrated the difficulty of interpreting bits and pieces of evidence, Derson senses her learners are now receptive to her bigger point about the interpretative nature of history and historical understanding—how we know what we know:

DERSON: What we know about history changes over time. We find new things and figure out different explanations for what went on. You would think history is dead because it happened a long time ago, but it's not. It's very much alive, and it's changing all the time. That's why I like it so much. When you are doing your research, remember to be careful; check your sources. Sometimes the facts aren't what they seem to be.

COMMONPLACE CONNECTIONS

- What does Derson seem to consider important about the *subject matter* of native history and historical evidence?
- What view of *learners* does she seem to hold?
- How would you characterize her *teaching*?
- How would you describe the classroom environment?

This vignette differs from the first two in several respects. First, Derson gives much less attention to traditional, static facts than her peers do. Factual information emerges—for example, wagons rot over time—but the emphasis is on ideas. Second, this vignette represents a more active pedagogy than the first two. Derson makes reading and writing assignments throughout the unit. She begins, however, by grabbing her children's imaginations with an engaging mapmaking activity. The biggest difference between this vignette and the others, however, is that Derson aims at a big, powerful idea—how we know what we know. Her learners will do many activities and encounter a lot of subject matter over the course of the unit. But the planned subject matter and activities support and extend an idea that is substantially more meaty and complex than those attempted by Prosy and Mead.

To this point, we have looked at learners and learning and at subject matter. Here, we turn to the third commonplace: teachers and teaching.

The vignettes above suggest several ideas about teachers and teaching that are worth considering. One is that teachers can choose from a wide variety of teaching methods. In these three vignettes alone, we see evidence of recitation and seatwork, individual reading and note taking, class discussion, and simulation. We can supplement this list with other approaches: lecture, group projects, report and essay writing, journal keeping, learning centers. You may remember your social studies classes largely in terms of worksheets and lectures. Clearly many other approaches are available.

This plethora of available teaching methods brings up a second point: No one "right" approach works for all topics with all students and in all situations. You may hear some people insist that every lesson have a group activity, and others argue that using textbooks is always a bad idea. We disagree on both counts. Group projects can be a good way to teach; using only a textbook can be a pretty awful way. But good teaching doesn't reduce to absolutes. Teachers can take many approaches to build curriculum inquiries, structure lessons, and deliver instruction, and, as the teacher, you must decide which ones to use and when.

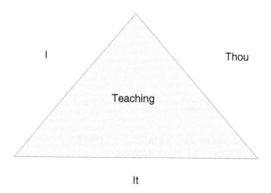

FIGURE 4.2 "I, Thou, and It" triangle: Good teaching lies at the intersection of you, your students, and the subject matter.

The third point is that good teaching demands consideration of a host of factors. In fact, one can get dizzy trying to keep track of the potential influences on one's teaching—educational goals, community needs, parents' expectations, district and state curriculum standards, Common Core standards, statewide tests—well, you get the point. Many factors can and should figure into your instructional decision-making. We argue, however, that two factors rise above the rest: subject matter and learners. Although the other influences are important, the heart of teaching lies in the middle of a triangle consisting of you, your learners, and the subject matter. David Hawkins (1974), who calls this triangle "I, Thou, and It," notes that the "child comes alive for the teacher as well as the teacher for the child ... [when there is] some third thing which is of interest to the child and to the adult in which they can join in outward projection" (pp. 57–58). See Figure 4.2.

Hawkins's observation hints at one more important point: Teaching is more than loving students, managing a quiet classroom, and designing fun activities. Instead, powerful teaching and learning develop when teachers and their learners regularly engage with ideas and questions. Instructional methods are important, but only as they provide a vehicle for bringing students and subject matter together.

In this chapter, the first of three in which we discuss the teachers and teaching commonplace, we consider how your knowledge of subject matter and learners figures into the construction of ideas and questions and how ideas and questions fit within the larger realm of pedagogical action. When you have completed this chapter, you should be able to answer the following questions:

1 What is the relationship between ideas and questions?
2 How does a compelling question differ from most of the questions that teachers ask?
3 What are the phases of pedagogical action, and how does the notion of a compelling question fit into that schema?

Teachers and Teaching

Every teacher wants to think that she or he is teaching students to be smart, thoughtful, powerful knowers and thinkers. And yet observers and students alike report that little of the teaching they see and experience hits this target. Much of the social studies teaching in American schools looks like that in the first vignette above: teacher-centered and textbook-driven, a teacher talking and students listening (or not), discrete bits of information rather than complex, meaty ideas. As one classroom observer notes, social studies topics really do interest children, yet "something strange seems to have happened to them on the way to the classroom." Instead of being vivid and vibrant ideas, he continues, "the topics of study become removed from their intrinsically human character, reduced to the dates and places readers will recall memorizing for tests" (Goodlad, 1984, p. 212). The approach represented in Prosy's classroom may still be the norm, but many teachers are moving toward more ambitious forms of teaching.

David Cohen (1989a) and others (Cuban, 1984; Grant, 1998; Grant & Gradwell, 2010; VanSledright, 2002) argue that most teachers have considerable classroom autonomy, that is, the ability to make subject matter and instructional decisions. That autonomy makes two points clear: Some teachers may be choosing to teach in traditional ways; you can choose differently. To be sure, some days you may want to give the students a stack of worksheets and be done with it. But we cannot imagine how a teacher could do so on a regular basis and assert that she or he is challenging all learners to achieve all that they can.

Although good teachers use various means to develop and maintain a productive learning environment, they manage more than students' behavior: They also *manage ideas* (Shulman, 1987). In this chapter, we define good teaching in terms of managing—planning, developing, and enacting—big ideas in the classroom.

Teaching Is More Than Classroom Management and Teaching Methods

Prospective teachers routinely worry about **classroom management.** Although they fret about knowing enough subject matter and the like, the number one concern new teachers have is managing children's behavior. It's a valid worry. We have all been in classes where the students ran wild, and the thought of them running wild on us is pretty intimidating. Most adults can manage a group of students through some combination of authority, persuasion, diversion, and threats. Indeed, there are some "tricks" to managing student behavior—plan more than one activity per class, provide learners with opportunities to work with their peers, give challenging assignments. Students cannot learn amidst chaos. But an enormous difference exists between keeping students quiet and in their seats and teaching them to be thoughtful, smart, and engaged.

FIGURE 4.3 Classroom management is a concern for every teacher. There are some standard practices that teachers employ, but as the fifth graders in this photograph demonstrate, an engaging assignment often "solves" discipline problems before they start.

If prospective teachers' first concern is discipline, typically their second worry is how to teach—what methods to use and how to use them. In fact, most people associate teaching only with methodology. That is, teachers teach when they lecture, lead recitations, set up role-playing situations, and organize cooperative groups.

▶◀ REFLECTION: "MANAGING" STUDENT BEHAVIOR

Although the idea of managing 20 or more active children can seem daunting, in practice it rarely is. Reflect on the ways you have observed teachers manage students' behavior. Which of those approaches seem more effective? less effective? Which of those approaches do you think you will feel comfortable using?
▶◀

If teaching is more than managing students' behavior, it is also more than a collection of **instructional strategies.** Having a clutch of strategies or methods in your repertoire is important and useful. Teachers need to know, for example, *how* to lecture and *how* to assign group work. Such knowledge will benefit you, however, only if you also know *why* you might use one approach instead of another, and when this approach makes sense and when it doesn't.

Continuum of teaching practices

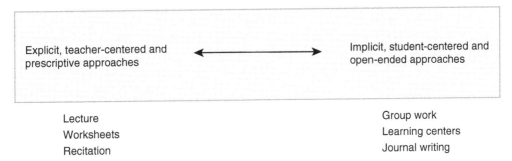

FIGURE 4.4 A continuum of teaching practices.

As Figure 4.4 illustrates, some teaching methods are more explicit (recitation); others are more implicit (group work). Some are more teacher-centered (lecture); others are more student-centered (learning centers). Some are more prescriptive (worksheets); others are more open-ended (journal writing).

Although it may seem obvious that no single method is best, with so many possibilities, how do you decide? You may be tempted to choose the pet method of a favorite teacher or one that you have seen other teachers use successfully. Remember, however, that a method used to teach one idea or with one group of learners may not necessarily work, or work as well, with the students in your classroom.

▶️◀️ REFLECTION: CHOOSING TEACHING APPROACHES

Reflect on the following teaching approaches in light of the continuum in Figure 4.4. Where would you place each one? Is the designation always clear-cut?

group projects	report writing	class discussion
simulations	textbook reading	diary entries
pair reading	role playing	skits/dramatizations
oral presentations	demonstrations	researching

▷◀

Let's now think about the teachers profiled earlier. Sandra Prosy may want her learners to know something about the power and dynamism of American government. She may want them to feel connected to and a part of the governments that represent them. Yet what message does her instruction send? We suspect Prosy's learners only understand government as a set of names and definitions, all of which seem a great distance from their everyday lives.

We think Janice Mead and Pam Derson's instructional approaches mesh more closely with the ideas and learners at hand. Mead wants her class to know some of the "facts" of the Underground Railroad, and, to that end, she poses questions and provides resources for learners to locate that information. But Mead also wants her learners to push below the surface—to know more about the experiences of African-American slaves. She accomplishes both of these aims within the context of the same lesson simply by asking different kinds of questions. It's a subtle difference and one that the casual observer might not catch. But the questions "How did the Underground Railroad get its name?" and "What did it mean to be a slave?" call for profoundly different levels of analysis and insight. The first calls for a factual response and, in that sense, is little different from the questions Prosy asks. The second, however, pushes much further. Here, students must put together an array of ideas to construct a sense of what the term *slave* means. We want our learners to know the "facts," but we also want them to use facts to make sense of bigger and more substantive ideas.

IN YOUR CLASSROOM

BRAINSTORMING

Brainstorming is a teaching strategy designed to elicit the widest array of ideas students can generate around a topic, question, or issue. For example, Janice Mead might have begun her unit by writing "Underground Railroad" on the board and asking students to call out whatever associations they had.

Use brainstorming as a way to uncover and assess the diverse ideas students bring to a topic.

It is on this last point that we see a useful difference between Janice Mead and Pam Derson. Whereas Mead pushes children to consider more of the slave experience than is typical, Derson goes one step further by linking the meaning learners construct to a bigger idea. Derson wants children to understand how archeologists map and interpret evidence. She takes her lessons even further, however, by using this experience to illustrate the interpretative nature of history and historical evidence. In asking, "How do we know what we know?" Derson pushes her learners toward questions and ideas that go well beyond the traditional curriculum. And the implications for doing so, as we will see in succeeding sections, are enormous.

RESOURCES: ARCHEOLOGY WITH CHILDREN

For some neat web sites related to doing archeology with children, see the following:

- ■ www.museum.upenn.edu/new/exhibits/online_exhibits/online_exhibits.html
  This University of Pennsylvania site features a number of virtual exhibits on world cultures both ancient and modern.

- ■ www.archaeology.mrdonn.org/lessonplans.html
  This site provides one-stop-shopping for all things archeological.

The Teaching Act: Two Considerations

Before discussing how to develop ideas and questions and to organize instruction around them, let's talk about some of the factors teachers should consider when planning instruction. These are a few:

- ■ educational goals and objectives
- ■ state and national standards
- ■ local curriculum guides
- ■ curriculum materials
- ■ teaching time
- ■ standardized tests

Although each of these factors is important, two pivotal elements—teachers' knowledge of the subject matter and their knowledge of the children they are teaching—figure most prominently in good teaching (Cohen, 2011).

We have stressed several interrelated benefits of having deep subject-matter knowledge. Teachers find that it makes the process of making connections—finding the threads—between different social science and history disciplines easier and less time-consuming. Deep knowledge helps expand your choices of curriculum possibilities by pointing you toward interesting questions and powerful ideas that can make those choices exciting and learning-worthy for your students. We also noted that deep subject-matter knowledge helps you "hear" your students and decide what to do with their initial and emerging ideas.

Subject-matter knowledge is important—even necessary—but it is not sufficient. Knowing the subject well does not tell you what ideas and questions children find interesting. Nor does it tell you the most sensible teaching approaches. Knowing the subject matter will make you a better teacher, but that knowledge alone cannot help you know what to do when you stand in front of 25 children.

Suzanne Wilson, a university researcher and third-grade teacher, knows well the geography content she wants her students to learn. Her subject-matter knowledge expands "the curricular territory I can explore with my class." She adds, however, that her content knowledge "fails to supply all the answers I need to decide what paths to take." Wilson senses that her learners need to do more than color and fill in map worksheets in order to understand the purpose and value of mapmaking. After several weeks of classwork, however, Wilson concludes that, "knowing the subject matter well and armed with good intentions, I am nevertheless unprepared to teach my learners well" (Wilson, 1990, pp. 12–13). Wilson realized that knowing one's learners is equally as important as knowing one's subject matter.

Teachers could benefit from more research in this area, but, as discussed in Chapter 2, we do know something about what learners know. You can expect your students to have little deep knowledge about social studies concepts and ideas. Moreover, much of what your learners know comes from sources outside the classroom walls—family, television, movies, peers. An occasional child may seem to have an encyclopedic knowledge about state capitals or Martin Luther King, Jr. Most of your students' ideas, however, may sound fragmented, overgeneralized, and naive to your adult ears. These ideas make sense to students, however, and can be hard to shake. The good news is that children can learn powerful ideas during the elementary years, and their thinking can become more varied and sophisticated. To realize these aims, learners need powerful learning environments and multiple opportunities to engage with new ideas that are coherent and embedded in meaningful contexts and that connect with their prior knowledge and experiences.

▶️◀ REFLECTION: THE POWER OF OLD IDEAS

A good illustration of how hard it is to shake old ideas is to say the first thing that comes into your mind when asked the question "Who discovered America?"

If you answered immediately, we bet your response was "Columbus." If you hesitated—fumbling perhaps for a response like Native Americans, Vikings, Irish, or Africans[1]—we bet that you still saw the word *Columbus* in your mind's eye. The point is simple: Although we *know* that Columbus was hardly the first to "discover" the Americas, it is his name that we recall first.

▶️◀

John Dewey (1902/1969) reminds us of the necessary relationship between subject matter and learners when he observes that "the child and the curriculum are simply two limits which define a single process. Just as two points define a straight line, so the present standpoint of the child and the facts and truths of studies define instruction" (p. 11). Other factors, such as state standards and tests, weigh into teachers' instructional decisions. Focusing on subject matter and learners, however, seems like a good place to start.

■ SECTION SUMMARY:
TEACHERS AND TEACHING

■ Teaching is more than managing children's behavior and using a variety of instructional strategies.

■ Although numerous factors influence teachers' practices, subject matter and learners are particularly important.

The Power of Ideas

Several pitfalls await teachers as they wrestle with these issues of subject matter and learners. One is the impulse to dilute social studies content under the assumption that the easier it is, the quicker learners will master it. Another mistake is to focus on classroom discipline under the assumption that children learn more and better only when they are quiet and on task. Still another pitfall is to develop "fun" activities under the assumption that learners will find content more palatable if it is dressed up.

We would never advocate eliminating fun (or discipline or simplicity, for that matter) from the classroom. In fact, we suspect that each of these responses and the assumptions behind them has some salience. We do suggest, however, that teachers construct activities that lead toward a purpose more powerful than entertainment or quiet or ease alone. Students remember and enjoy activities that engage them. But they know and understand even more when you construct learning opportunities that help them connect activities with powerful ideas.

Types of Ideas

Ideas come in lots of forms. Facts, concepts, and generalizations all have their uses. Understanding the differences among them is useful in building classroom curriculum.

Facts

Make no mistake: **Facts**, such as the Alamo is located in Texas, or the US government has three branches, or a community is made up of neighborhoods, are important and useful. By definition, facts express ideas that are provable and are accepted by a majority of people. In that sense, facts conveniently summarize and express ideas that most folks believe.

For example, the statement "We live in an urban neighborhood" could function as a fact, in that it is a verifiable proposition (i.e., the students define

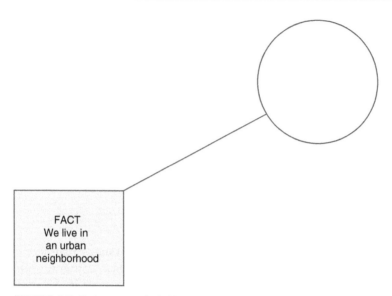

FIGURE 4.5 Facts express single ideas.

where they live and the majority in the class agrees that this idea represents the reality of their lives). See Figure 4.5.

Facts express important ideas, but they are single ideas. The usefulness of facts lies in context, not in isolation. Knowing a bunch of individual facts does not guarantee that students can think about anything in particular. Facts need to be connected in order to make sense.

Concepts

A **concept** allows us to express complex sets of ideas, such as "change" or "justice." Educators often talk about children learning concepts and becoming conceptual thinkers.

Continuing our example in Figure 4.6, "neighborhood" functions as a concept in that it represents a large set of related ideas, such as where neighborhoods are located, how they begin and grow, and why they change over time.

Concepts are useful as placeholders for meaty ideas, but they can be so big and complex that they are instructionally unwieldy. Concepts, like facts, help students think and know, but they are of limited use in constructing teaching inquiries, and they are practically useless for developing daily lessons. Where, for example, would one even begin planning a single lesson on "change"?

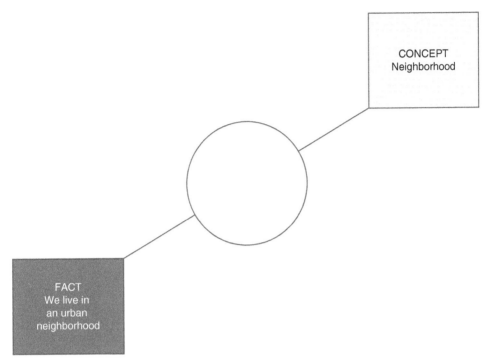

FIGURE 4.6 Concepts express sets of ideas.

Generalizations

Ideas can also be expressed through **generalizations.** A generalization is a broad statement that summarizes a set of conditions. In social studies, those conditions include people's actions and beliefs and the material things around them. Generalizations express ideas that are often widely accepted. But when pushed, such statements may not be true in all circumstances.

Generalizations are useful because they allow us to talk broadly about sets of ideas. In the context of our neighborhood example, a range of generalizations might be:

- Life is simple in rural areas.
- There are more economic opportunities in cities.
- Suburbs combine the best of life in rural and urban areas.

If we were to poll any number of Americans, we might find broad agreement with each of these statements. But if we looked more carefully behind each generalization, we would find examples that challenge its accuracy.

When generalizations over-reach or exaggerate, then they cross over into **stereotypes.** A stereotype expresses an over-simplified idea or trait, typically about a group of people. These over-simplifications often relate to characteristics over

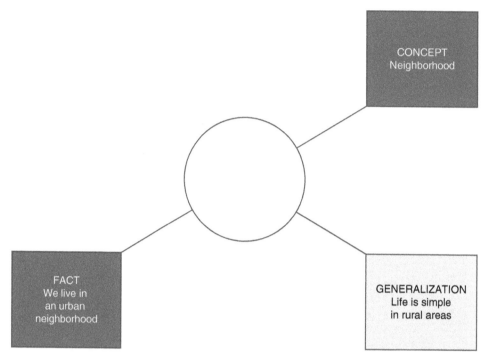

FIGURE 4.7 Generalizations are broad statements.

which people have no control, such as nationality, gender, or race. Stereotypes also typically assert a negative image of the identified group. Some individuals within that group may fit the image, but such statements fail to offer useful information about the group as a whole.

With the caveat about avoiding stereotypes, students will find generalizations a valuable way to express their emerging interpretations of the ideas they encounter. Teachers will find generalizations important, too, in combination with facts and concepts.

■ SECTION SUMMARY:
THE POWER OF IDEAS

- Ideas typically come in three types: facts, concepts, and generalizations.
- Facts have two components: They are ideas that are provable and are accepted by a majority of people.
- Concepts are ideas that allow us to organize and express complex sets of ideas.
- Generalizations are broad statements that effectively summarize a set of conditions.
- Stereotypes are a kind of generalization that oversimplify an idea or trait, typically about a group of people.

Turning Ideas into Questions

Now let's think back to the vignettes that opened this chapter. Sandra Prosy's fifth-grade unit centers on a *concept*—government—and she seems interested in differentiating between governments at national, state, and local levels. As concepts go, American government is both huge and complex. What does Prosy want her learners to know and understand about government in general and government at each of these levels? She asks several questions as a way to quiz students over a range of facts, but where the unit is going seems unclear.

RESOURCES: AMERICAN GOVERNMENT

For some interesting web sites related to studying American government with children, see

- https://edsitement.neh.gov/lesson-plans?keywords=government
  This National Endowment for the Humanities site includes lesson plans, materials, and resources for teaching a variety of lessons related to US government and many other social studies topics.

- www.icivics.org/curriculum/state-and-local-government
  This site has a nice array of offerings related to state and local governments across the United States.

Janice Mead's fourth-grade unit also focuses on a *concept*—slavery in the United States. She, too, emphasizes factual knowledge; the difference is that she does not stop there. Mead pushes her learners to dig below the surface. She wants her learners to know something about the Underground Railroad, but this information serves a bigger purpose—beginning to understand and to create useful generalizations about the institution of slavery. In these ways, Mead's unit appears more connected and coherent than Prosy's.

RESOURCES: SLAVERY IN THE UNITED STATES

The following web sites offer much to students studying slavery in the United States:

- http://www.pbs.org/wgbh/aia/home.html
  This PBS site offers a comprehensive set of materials associated with the four-part series *Africans in America: America's Journey through Slavery*.

- https://www.thirteen.org/wnet/slavery/resources/wpa.html
  One value of this site lies in the access to hundreds of firsthand accounts of slavery collected by the Works Progress Administration during the 1940s.

The problem is, if we asked Janice Mead what she wanted learners to know about American slavery, it's hard to guess what she would say. Her unit seems more comprehensive and substantial than Sandra Prosy's, but in many ways it still lacks a unifying idea that gives the unit conceptual *and* pedagogical focus.

Pam Derson's unit differs from those of her peers. She, too, emphasizes facts, concepts, and generalizations. But she uses a question—How do we know what we know?—to frame the unit of study. And, if students are to become active and inquiring learners, then questions matter.

Framing Derson's unit around a question pays off in three ways. First, the question helps her decide *what content to teach*. Derson draws from the state curriculum guide in her students' study of Native-American tribes, but she chooses to situate their study around understanding the nature of historical evidence and using it to make and support claims. She knows that her students come to class with a variety of ideas about native life and culture, some accurate and sophisticated, most not. Her question—How do we know what we know?—encourages learners to think about the limits of what we know and about the evidence available as they begin their research projects. To that end, she chooses content that illustrates native life and challenges the children's preconceived ideas.

Second, Derson's question helps her decide *what instructional approaches she might take*. Because she wants her students to learn new information about native life and to think about how they know what they know, Derson provides a range of instructional activities. Some activities, like the archeology simulation, are opportunities to emphasize particular points. Others, like the research project, pull the entire unit together. For that project, learners draw on their literacy skills by using a range of trade books and information texts to research an aspect of native culture.

Finally, Derson's question *promotes learners' thinking and understanding*. One of Derson's goals is to help learners understand that native cultures can be viewed from different vantage points. She provides materials from the earlier time period and from today that express the perspectives of natives and others. She urges students to see similarities and differences from the diverse views of those who lived within native cultures and those who encountered them as outsiders. Students are free to choose their own topics for the research project. To demonstrate that they understand it, however, they must show that they have considered the several ways native ideas and actions can be interpreted.

IN YOUR CLASSROOM

SHOEBOX ARCHEOLOGY

Consider providing students with an engaging experience as archeologists by creating a shoebox dig.[2]

1. Lay a thin layer of soil in the bottom of three to five shoeboxes.
2. Place on top some artifacts related to your grandparents (such as photos, coins, perfume bottles, and tools). Lay on another thin layer of soil.
3. Next, lay in some artifacts related to your parents and cover with another layer of soil.
4. Finally, place inside some artifacts specific to your time and top these off with a final layer of soil.
5. Distribute the boxes to small groups of students and ask them to complete the following tasks:
    a. Complete a Shoebox Archeology Observation Sheet (Figure 4.8) on which they describe, sketch, measure, and hypothesize about the importance of each artifact.
    b. Connect the activity to language arts by having students write an Archeologist's Report in which they describe the process they undertook, summarize their findings, and offer conjectures about the people who created and used these artifacts.
    c. Share each group's work through short oral presentations.

Soil layer	Objects (description)	Objects (sketch)	Measurements	Importance
Layer 1				
Layer 2				
Layer 3				

Sketch artifacts found within each soil layer. Then measure, identify, and describe the importance of each artifact.

FIGURE 4.8 Shoebox archeology observation sheet.

Pam Derson's unit is one example of how having a question can help a teacher make content and instructional decisions. When we talked with her, however, Derson was a little irritated. She had set aside several fine ideas and activities because they did not fit with her question-based inquiry. Moreover, she had set aside another set of ideas and activities because she simply did not have enough time to do them.

We sympathize with Derson's frustration. Dropping a good activity because of time constraints is a hard thing to do. Derson realized two things, however: (1) Having too many good instructional options is better than having too few, and (2) she could always use some of the omitted activities with future classes. Like all good teachers, Derson understands that one never throws away a good activity.

Derson's framing question for the Native-American unit—How do we know what we know?—illustrates the power of teaching with questions. Let's look at some other examples developed by prospective teachers in our social studies methods classes:

- *Who Are We?* (kindergarten)
- *How Did My Family Get Here?* (grade 1)
- *What Do Flags Represent?* (grade 2)
- *Can We Unmelt the Melting Pot?* (grade 3)
- *Why Is Albany the Capital of New York?* (grade 4)
- *What Were the Unheard Voices of the Civil War?* (grade 5)
- *What Does It Mean to be Civilized?* (grade 6)

Now let's consider how Janice Mead's unit on American slavery might have been different if she had developed it, as prospective teacher Kristen Stricker did, around a question: What is freedom?

Like Mead, Stricker constructed an array of activities—brainstorming, independent and shared reading of fiction and informational trade books, journals, artifact centers, guest speakers, and mini-lessons—that explored the particulars of slavery. Unlike Derson, however, Stricker developed her inquiry around a genuine question. The framing question—What is freedom?—can be explored in two ways. First, one can examine multiple perspectives. This inquiry "teaches the histories of the many Americans, rather than just one story," Stricker explained. To that end, children learn about slavery from the perspective of an African boy kidnapped into slavery, a White indentured servant, a runaway slave, a White slaveowner, and Abraham Lincoln. Second, slavery can be studied as part of a bigger issue or idea, namely, What is freedom? Stricker said, "to teach slavery by simply saying, 'it is bad to own other human beings' does not do justice to this rich and often difficult period." She wants her learners to understand "how our country could have let the ownership of other humans continue for so long."

She also wants children to think about what freedom from slavery has meant to African Americans since the Civil War. In that light, her inquiry includes readings and discussions that explore the ongoing struggle for rights and freedom for all Americans (e.g., people of color and women). Understanding the topic of American slavery is important, but to fully realize its importance, students need to see it in the context of bigger ideas and issues.

IN YOUR CLASSROOM

DEALING WITH MISCONCEPTIONS

A common misconception many children (and adults) have is that Abraham Lincoln's Emancipation Proclamation in 1863 freed all enslaved Africans. In fact, the Proclamation dealt only with those enslaved in the Southern states, which, having seceded in 1861, were no longer under Lincoln's control. After reading the Proclamation aloud to students, ask students to imagine why Lincoln might have taken this tack.

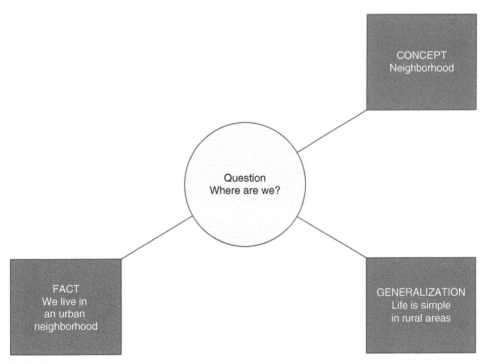

FIGURE 4.9 Questions connect facts, concepts, and generalizations.

Now we can complete the ideas diagram that we began during the discussion of facts. The circle in Figure 4.9 encloses the question Where are we? as a way to frame a first-grade unit on neighborhoods. Asked of a group of first graders, the question likely will produce some giggles; after all, we're right here! And yet, "here" is a relative position. As teacher and children begin to explore the many ways they can define where "here" is, they can build a more sophisticated sense of where their neighborhood boundaries are, what resources are available in their neighborhood, and how their neighborhood fits within the larger community.

It takes time and energy to develop units around questions. The payoffs seem worth it, though: Your learners can benefit from the opportunity to engage with real ideas and the excitement that doing so brings, and you can gain confidence and skill in your ability to create and deliver powerful instruction.

■ SECTION SUMMARY:
TURNING IDEAS INTO QUESTIONS

■ Teaching with questions can help teachers decide what content to teach, what instructional approaches to take, and how to promote learners' thinking and understanding.

Questions and the *C3 Framework*

If you are like our students, you are probably thinking something like this:

> Okay. I can buy the notion that creating units around ideas and questions is probably a good thing, but I wonder if I really know enough about the subject matter and what interests and engages students. Still, I didn't like much of my experience in social studies classes and I don't want to teach my students the way I was taught. So, I'm willing to think some more about this approach.

Fair enough. Let's talk about how you might develop some idea-based questions of your own.

First, you need to understand that you are not alone in the use of questions to frame your lessons. Questions in general and "compelling" questions in particular are prominent in the current national thinking about how to improve social studies teaching and learning. We'll have more to say about the *College, Career, and Civic Life (C3) Framework for Social Studies State Standards* (National Council for the Social Studies, 2013) in later chapters. For now, however, let's focus on the role of questions in developing a more ambitious teaching practice.

As part of the team that wrote the *C3 Framework*, we had a hand in developing the notion of a **compelling question**—a question that is both academically rigorous *and* attends to the things that learners care about.

▶|◀ REFLECTION: QUESTIONS AND THE *C3 FRAMEWORK*

To understand the two components of a compelling question, read Dimension 1 of the *C3 Framework* (available to download free at: www.socialstudies.org/c3). Dimension 1 is on page 17. For a longer discussion of compelling questions, see Grant, Swan, & Lee, 2017; Mueller, 2017.

As we suggested earlier, teachers need to know the subject matter they are responsible for—the major facts, concepts, themes, and patterns—as well as how those ideas were developed. They also need to know their students—what ideas interest them, what kinds of experiences they have had, what kinds of language they are familiar with, the different ways they think about ideas. These two forms of knowledge are critical; good teachers transform social studies subject matter in light of what they know about learners. It is to that process of transforming the subject matter—and constructing a compelling question—that we now turn.

In this chapter, you have already seen several questions that we think fit the criteria for being compelling—Pam Derson's question "How do we know what we know?" and Kirsten Stricker's question "What is freedom?" But how did they get there?

Crafting a Compelling Question

It would be nice if we could offer a list of simple steps to develop a *compelling* compelling question, but we know of no single path. Good teaching is rarely a straightforward process. Ambitious teachers take routes with lots of side trips, dead ends, and reversals as they develop compelling questions of their own. What follows is a general framework for crafting a compelling question. Know, however, that each of you will find your own way.

1. *Begin with an Issue or Idea That Interests You*
One good place to start is with an issue, idea, or curriculum resource that interests, intrigues, or puzzles you. Most teachers, when questioned at this stage, say something like, "well, I've always been interested in Canada," or "I saw this really neat book on immigrants to America that I'd like to use," or "I think I want to do something where the students have to go out into the community." These thoughts might not seem like much, but they represent all you need at this point—an engaging idea and a place to start working. In fact, each of the

inquiries described in this chapter stemmed, in part, from the teacher's personal interest.

For example, Pam Derson transformed her interest in Native Americans and how we have come to know what we know about them into the compelling questions for her inquiry. Similarly, Kristen Stricker said she began with a vague but strong interest in the civil rights movement. Wondering how African Americans could still face discrimination more than 100 years after the end of slavery, she started thinking about the notion of "freedom" and whether Black slaves were really freed after the Civil War.

Other teachers may use a topic from their state's curriculum standards as their starting point. In those instances, teachers generally begin by brainstorming questions about a topic they want to learn more about. One prospective teacher, for example, noticed that recycling was listed in a curriculum guide as a grade 2 topic. Always an active recycler herself, she had long wondered why many people are not. The inquiry she developed around the compelling question *Recycling: Does It Matter?* exposed students to arguments both for and against recycling and reusing products and materials.

No matter what the source, good reasons abound for starting with something that piques your curiosity. If you are interested in the topic, chances are your learners will pick up on that and will ratchet up their own interest.

2. Ask Yourself a Series of Student-Relevance Questions
With a content idea in mind, it's time to start thinking about your students. Some teachers think through a series of questions like these:

- Why do I think students will care about or be interested in this idea?
- What kinds of activities or experiences do I want students to have?
- How will I know if the students understand what I want them to understand?

These can be tough questions, but they can be useful in defining the kid angle of your compelling question.

▶◀ REFLECTION: STATE STANDARDS AND COMPELLING QUESTIONS

To jumpstart your thinking about a compelling question, take a look at the social studies standards for your state. Typically, you can find them by inserting the phrase "state social studies standards (and the name of your state)" into a search engine.

Skim through the standards for one or more grades until you see a topic that interests you and you think will engage your students.

▶◀

3. Draft Your Compelling Question

Given that you have a content topic that you think might appeal to your students, it's time to try your hand at writing a compelling question. Let your imagination and creativity out because the possibilities are endless.

Remember, standard curriculum guide topics like Canada, immigration, and community involvement may not seem very compelling on the surface, but they can be transformed into engaging questions. For example, if you were teaching a fourth-grade unit on Canada, you could explore past, present, and future relationships between Canada and the United States through the compelling question *Canada and the United States: Friends Forever?* An inquiry that highlights the long tranquil border between the United States and Canada might use a question such as *Should the United States and Canada Be One Country?* to push your students into thinking about the advantages and disadvantages of a united North America.

RESOURCES: TEACHING ABOUT CANADA

A number of web sites provide valuable resources for teaching about Canada:

- https://sites.ualberta.ca/~jkirman/
  This site titled "The Canadian Social Studies Super Site," offers a raft of lesson and unit plans on various topics related to life in Canada, including the history of the Canadian flag, aboriginal peoples, and the Canadian Parliament.

- https://k12studycanada.org/resources_teacher_resources
  This site out of Western Washington University offers a huge set of lesson and unit plans for teachers interested in teaching about Canada.

Similarly, a third-grade unit on immigration might support a range of compelling questions. To recognize the many contributions of immigrant groups, you might develop an inquiry around the question *How Would America Look without Immigrants?* Or, if you wanted to explore current tensions over immigration, you might use the question *Has America Closed the Door on Immigration?* to frame your inquiry.

RESOURCES: TEACHING ABOUT IMMIGRATION

- www.loc.gov/teachers/classroommaterials/presentationsandactivities/presentations/immigration/
  Part of the "American Memory" web site developed by the US Library of Congress, "Immigration" is a tour-de-force on this very important issue, offering a range of texts, maps, timelines, and primary sources. Students can explore the experiences of eleven different immigrant groups.

- www.proteacher.com/090154.shtml
  This ProTeacher site offers a range of lessons and activities designed to introduce children to the experiences of immigrants.

Finally, compelling questions can also help you develop inquiries around a standard second-grade topic such as community. An inquiry that focuses on diversity might be based on the question *Who Is in Our Community?* If individual and social responsibility strikes you as a neat idea for an inquiry, you might use the question *Can I Help Make My Community Better?* to frame your inquiry.

RESOURCES: TEACHING ABOUT COMMUNITIES

- www.instructorweb.com/resources/community.asp
  Instructor Web features several sets of lessons and resources for teaching about communities.

- www.geography.mrdonn.org/communities.html
  This site offers a large number and variety of teaching ideas, unit plans, and lesson activities related to local communities.

4. *Start Thinking about How Your Compelling Question Plays Out in Your Inquiry*

We think the compelling question examples above work because they meet the criteria we discussed above. First, they reflect big, meaty ideas. Like the "It" in Hawkins's triangle, they allow teachers and their learners to come alive together as they explore ideas of interest to the child *and* to the adult. Second, each of these compelling questions helps define the important content. As topics, community and immigration are simply too large to teach well. Without a compelling question, teachers may choose content willy-nilly or follow a textbook outline. We would never recommend the former, and, although the latter has some advantages, we believe your learners will find textbook units less engaging than those of your own design. Finally, having a compelling question helps a teacher make instructional decisions. Consider the Canada example—*Should the US and Canada Be One Country?* Learners might participate in many different activities during this inquiry but, if it is framed this way, surely some kind of debate would be useful. Similarly, the question *Who Is in Our Community?* is likely to inspire the use a variety of resources—text, photographs, and audio- and videotape—to illustrate the range of people who live in the local area.

Our point is simple: Teaching is a complex activity, and compelling questions help teachers decide which methods make the most sense. Given the wealth of instructional possibilities, any advantage in choosing one over another is worth taking.

We'll have a lot more to say about compelling questions and the other components of a curriculum inquiry in Chapters 10 and 11. For now, however, remember that teaching is truly a journey, and each inquiry is a new and intriguing path. You are bound to take some wrong turns along the way—every teacher does—but as experienced teachers and travelers know, every trip is an occasion to learn. You will benefit, and so will your learners.

■ SECTION SUMMARY: QUESTIONS AND THE *C3 FRAMEWORK*

- ■ The *C3 Framework* highlights a particular kind of question: a compelling question.

- ■ A compelling question has two components: academic rigor and student relevance.

- ■ A compelling question is academically rigorous if it reflects an important and useful social studies topic.

- ■ A compelling question is relevant to students if it reflects a quality or condition that we know learners typically care about.

- ■ No simple or single pathway can lead a teacher to a viable compelling question, but the process can be described as (a) beginning with an interesting question, idea, or issue; (b) asking a series of student-relevance questions; (c) drafting a compelling question; and (d) thinking about the implications of the compelling question for the rest of the inquiry.

The Compelling Question as Key to Pedagogical Action

Turning compelling questions into actual teaching inquiries is the subject of Chapters 10 and 11. For now, we want to close our discussion of questions by centering it in the larger realm of pedagogical action.

We locate our notion of teaching with compelling questions in the center of what John Dewey (1902/1969) calls "psychologizing" the curriculum and what Lee Shulman (1987) calls **pedagogical reasoning.** Key to these conceptions is the role teachers play in remaking or transforming the facts, concepts, and generalizations of history and the social sciences into instructional representations that reflect both knowledge of the subject matter and of the learners at hand. Shulman's view of pedagogical reasoning is shown in Table 4.1.

Shulman's view of teaching makes a lot of sense. First, we like his emphasis on creating instructional representations that reflect the needs of the learners in the classroom. Many teachers can imagine different ways to teach an idea in the abstract. That's only half the issue, however. Powerful teaching and learning develop when teachers construct instructional representations that fit the particular learners at hand. The second point that stands out is Shulman's emphasis

TABLE 4.1 Phases of Pedagogical Reasoning

Phase One	*Comprehension:* Understanding the subject matter and educational purposes
Phase Two	*Transformation,* consisting of
	■ *Preparation:* Preparing the text of instruction
	■ *Representation:* Conceptualizing the range of ways to represent subject matter to learners
	■ *Selection:* Choosing instructional representations and materials
	■ *Adaptation:* Adjusting representations and materials to accommodate all learners
Phase Three	*Instruction:* Teaching the subject matter
Phase Four	*Evaluation:* Assessing what learners have learned
Phase Five	*Reflection:* Thinking about the successes and limits of the teaching episode
Phase Six	*New Comprehension:* Making plans for next time

on reflection and change. The mental side of teachers' work is well documented (Akinbode, 2013; Bullough, 2008; Clark & Peterson, 1986). Shulman reminds us that reflecting on what went well (and not so well) leads to "new comprehension," a sense of what we might do the same or differently next time. In this way, our instructional practices change and grow stronger.

Our notion of pedagogical action owes much to Dewey's and Shulman's ideas. Where we differ is in our choice of beginning point. Dewey begins with the twin foci of subject matter and learners. Shulman begins with comprehension—understanding one's subject matter and educational purposes. We begin with a compelling question that expresses a conceptual and instructional direction and guides the entire pedagogical process. Educational goals and the like are important, but the heart of teaching or pedagogical action lies in actively constructing a question that is both academically rigorous and relevant to students.

Other factors influence how we flesh out an instructional inquiry: the sequence of activities, the curriculum materials and resources available, state-level standards, the time allotted, the connections to other subject matters, and the forms of assessment planned. These elements are part of pedagogical action, and we discuss them in succeeding chapters. For now, however, focusing on your compelling question should provide the biggest payoff.

Chapter Summary

1   **What is the relationship between ideas and questions?** Ideas come in many forms (e.g., facts, concepts, generalizations) and they are an important source of the kinds of social studies knowledge that we want students to build. But for instructional purposes, teachers can use questions as a way to give their students a purpose for learning.

2   **How does a compelling question differ from most of the questions that teachers ask?** Many of the questions that teachers ask are designed to check students' understandings of ideas. A compelling question has a different

purpose. Because it reflects important content and is relevant to students' lives, a compelling question is useful for framing classroom inquiries.

3 **What are the phases of pedagogical action, and how does the notion of a compelling question fit into that schema?** The phases of pedagogical action include comprehension, transformation, instruction, evaluation, reflection, and new comprehension. We argue that, although comprehension is important, pedagogical action begins with the construction of a compelling question that acts as a guide or framework for the entire process.

Notes

1 All these groups (and more) have been proposed as the "discoverers" of the Americas. By general consensus, Native Americans were the first inhabitants in the Americas (see, for example, Morgan, 1993). After that, the arguments become intense; various authors have pitched the importance of the Vikings (Wahlgren, 1986), Irish (Fell, 1976), Africans (Van Sertima, 1976), and Chinese (Menzies, 2003).
2 Our thanks to Jill Korse of Reading Is Fundamental for this activity.

Teaching Resources

Print Resources

Jorgensen, K. (1993). *History workshop*. Portsmouth, NH: Heinemann.
Levine, D., Lowe, R., Peterson, B., & Tenorio, R. (Eds.). (1995). *Rethinking schools: An agenda for change*. New York: The New Press.
Levstik, L.S., & Barton, K. (2011). *Doing history: Investigating with children in elementary and middle schools* (4th ed.). New York: Routledge.
National Council for the Social Studies. (2013). *College, Career, and Civic Life (C3) Framework for Social Studies State Standards*. Silver Spring, MD: Author.
VanSledright, B. (2002). *In search of America's past: Learning to read history in elementary school*. New York: Teachers College Press.
Each of these books offers useful ideas about teaching social studies with an eye toward subject matter and learners.

Technology Resources

The following are good general sites for social studies lessons and resources:

- ■ www.socialstudieshelp.com/Educational_Links_for_Teachers.htm
  The Social Studies Help Center has various resources on a wide range of topics.

- ■ **www.mysocialstudies.com/**
  "My Social Studies" is a site developed by long time social studies educator Fred Risinger.

- ■ **www.ncss.org**
  The home page for the National Council for the Social Studies, this site contains helpful information about the organization's activities and a link to useful teacher resources.

- **www.socialstudies.com/**
  A commercial site, this is the home page of the Social Studies School Service, a leading supplier of audio, visual, computer, and print resources for teachers and students.

- **www.thegateway.org**
  A massive site developed by the US Department of Education, "The Gateway to Educational Materials" offers a fully searchable database of social studies lesson and unit plans, most accompanied by primary source documents.

- **www.c3teachers.org**
  A website devoted to enacting the goals established in the *C3 Framework*. The site also has numerous resources related to the construction of compelling questions.

Teachers and Teaching
Choosing Strategies, Curriculum Materials, and Influences on Teaching

Don Kite, a European American man in his mid thirties, teaches fifth grade in an urban magnet school with an explicitly traditional schooling mission. His 24 students are predominantly African American and poor. The compelling question for his inquiry on colonial America is "How are we like colonial Americans?" His students will compare similarities and differences between the two eras along six dimensions: housing, schools, occupations, entertainment, family, and travel.

Class begins with Kite passing around an array of artifacts—a pewter candlestick, a wooden hand plane, and a hand-held drillstock—all of which might have been used during colonial times. He says, "We've started talking about colonies … why they were founded. But what I really want to talk about is what life was like." As the objects circulate, Kite encourages students to handle them, ask questions, and raise conjectures. Students fill the air with ideas.

The second part of the lesson is a K-W-L activity.[1] Kite solicits examples of "things you know about colonial life." Students call out an array of ideas—the oldest son inherits property, no electricity, colonists made lots of stuff, freedom of religion—which Kite lists on chart paper under the label "Know." Kite labels a second chart "Want to Know" and asks students to name what they want to know about colonial life.

Students again participate eagerly, offering a range of questions—How did colonists provide food? Were all the kids in the same schoolroom? How did they get heat? How did people live on so little food? Kite records these questions, praises their effort, and encourages more.

■ ■ ■ ■ COMMONPLACE CONNECTION

What does Kite seem to think is important about the subject matter of colonial America?

■ What view of learners does he seem to hold?
■ How would you characterize his teaching?
■ How would you describe the classroom environment?

In Chapter 4 we argue that teaching is more than managing behavior or possessing a collection of teaching strategies. These things are important, but knowing how to manage kids and how to do a group activity is quite different from knowing *if and when* to do these to promote powerful learning. The key to knowing if and when is the construction of compelling questions that help frame and connect teaching and learning across an inquiry of study.

In this chapter, we extend that discussion by looking at how a teacher's **pedagogical plan** develops through the consideration and selection of teaching strategies and curriculum materials and the factors that influence a teacher's content and instructional decisions. When you have completed this chapter, you should be able to answer the following questions:

1   What teaching strategies support individual, small-group, and whole-group instruction?
2   What curriculum materials are available for classroom use?
3   What factors influence teachers' content and instructional decisions?

Pulling Together a Pedagogical Plan

We believe a teacher's pedagogical plan flourishes with a compelling question that represents the content that a teacher intends to teach and the things that her students care about. A compelling question should also help a teacher reflect on two important questions:

1   What teaching strategies will I use to represent the content?
2   What curriculum materials will I use to support my teaching strategies?

Teaching Strategies

Don Kite chose to begin his fifth-grade colonial inquiry with an exploration of artifacts and a K-W-L activity. He picked this **teaching strategy** from myriad possibilities. Before we examine Kite's case more closely, let's imagine some alternatives. For clarity's sake, we organize them in three categories: individual, small-group, and whole-group teaching strategies.

Strategies for Individual Learning

Given his purposes, Don Kite decided to use two **whole-group activities** to introduce the colonial inquiry. Given different purposes, he might have chosen a plan based on **individual assignments,** in which students draw on their own resources as they work alone on a range of tasks.

A typical individual task is for students to read and respond to a piece of text. Language arts and social studies often make good partners, and good teachers use a variety of literary resources to engage their students. Many available resources are textual—books, magazines, diaries, and the like. Making individual reading assignments, in class as well as outside class, helps students understand the different kinds of texts and the different ways of reading them. Kite might have introduced his inquiry by assigning a section from the class textbook, a chapter from a trade book, or a facsimile of a colonial newspaper, and then asking questions that called for definitions, comparisons, analysis, or evaluation.

IN YOUR CLASSROOM

TRADE BOOKS

Trade books are a great way of making language arts connections to social studies and adding textual variety to your lessons. **Trade book** is a generic term for any commercially published book, either fiction or nonfiction, other than a textbook. Trade books come in a range of reading levels. Their chief advantage is their deeper story or conceptual development. Individual and class sets of trade books are available from many book vendors, who typically send catalogs to schools and to teachers. A good source of information about new trade books is the annual review published by the National Council for the Social Studies in *Social Education.*

Another common individual task is a writing assignment. Teaching social studies provides opportunities for students to learn new writing as well as reading skills. Answering questions associated with a piece of text is one form of writing; there are many more. For this inquiry, Don Kite might have asked the students to write two diary entries—one based on their experiences the previous day and one based on their perceptions of an average day during colonial times. Another approach could be to ask students to imagine how life was different for native tribes and for the colonists and to create lists that identify those similarities and differences.

One other individual task might be developed around learning centers. A **learning center** is typically an area of the classroom where the teacher locates an array of materials and activities that children can explore; the area may be either temporary or permanent. For example, instead of letting the colonial artifacts circulate around the room, Kite might have set up a series of centers. One center might have featured carpentry tools such as the drill and plane, while another displayed household items such as the candlestick. Each center could also have specific questions for students to answer, a description of an individual or partner activity involving the artifact, or a longer writing assignment.

Using individual assignments to introduce a new inquiry has advantages and disadvantages. The obvious advantage is the opportunity to get learners on task immediately. The principal disadvantage is that a teacher loses the opportunity to introduce the inquiry through an activity, such as the K-W-L exercise, that draws on all the learners' input. Good teachers vary their approaches depending on the inquiry at hand.

Strategies for Small-Group Learning

Another set of teaching strategies takes advantage of the power of group learning. Despite some misperceptions, the research evidence is clear: **Small-group activities**, those that usually include two to five children per group, help children learn. Moreover, they help *all* children learn.

Research does not bear out the commonly held view that group learning situations enable lower-ability learners and disadvantage higher-ability learners (Johnson, Johnson, & Holubec, 2009; Ningsih & Budi Eko, 2017). **Cooperative learning** groups benefit both those students who learn more slowly *and* those who are faster learners. The explanation for this condition turns out to be quite simple: The more opportunities students have to read, write, think, and talk about ideas, the more they learn. Putting children in groups and giving them challenging activities is good practice because learners of all ability levels benefit from the exposure to the material and the interaction with one another.

How might Don Kite have used small groups to introduce his colonial inquiry? One way might have been to ask each group to develop a list of everyday needs (for example, food, shelter, protection, leisure) and create a T-chart that illustrates how colonial and present-day Americans meet each of those needs. Another small-group task could involve assigning a different reading to each group. The various readings might describe life during the colonial era from different perspectives: a Black male teenage slave, a White male indentured servant, a Native-American boy, and a White woman colonist.[2] After these pieces have been read and discussed, four new groups could be constituted in jigsaw fashion, with each group retaining one or more original members. The new groups' task would be to develop both ideas and questions about how life was similar and different for each individual.

T-CHARTS AND JIGSAWS

Use a **T-chart activity** to capture students' brainstorming on a topic or question. To make a T-chart, simply draw a large T in the middle of a page on which students can record their ideas. A T-chart based on the exercise described above would look like Figure 5.1.

Meeting food needs	
Colonial Americans	Present-day Americans

FIGURE 5.1 A T-chart.

Use a **jigsaw activity** to help small groups of students teach one another. The idea of a jigsaw is that students in each group become "experts" on a particular piece, after which they split up and share their expertise as members of newly formed groups. The piece shared can be a book review, the explanation of a concept, or a draft of a newspaper article— anything that adds to everyone's understanding.

One additional small-group activity is a **WebQuest**. A WebQuest is an inquiry-based research project designed to draw upon Internet resources. WebQuests are useful ways of providing students with a great range of resources and with opportunities to engage in higher-level thinking skills, from comparing and contrasting to analyzing perspectives to creating arguments. Students typically work on WebQuests in pairs or small groups.

Bernie Dodge, the creator of the WebQuest idea, describes its critical features:

1   An *introduction* that sets the stage and provides some background information.
2   A task that is doable and interesting.
3   A set of *information sources* needed to complete the task. Information sources might include Web documents, experts available via email or real-time conferencing, searchable databases on the Internet, and books and other documents physically available in the classroom. Because references to these sources are included, learners are not left to wander through cyber-space completely adrift.
4   A description of the *process* the learners should go through in accomplishing the task. The process should be broken out into clearly described steps.

5 Some *guidance* on how to organize the information acquired. This step can take the form of guiding questions or directions.

6 A *conclusion* that brings closure to the quest, reminds the learners what they have learned, and perhaps encourages them to extend their experience into other domains. (For more on the WebQuest process, see Bernie Dodge's website at www.webquest.org.)

WebQuests can be designed around any social studies idea, but they are particularly useful when set in the context of a compelling question. For upper-elementary-age children, WebQuests have been developed that ask, for example, "Jamestown: Can You Survive?" For this question, see the Webquest at www. questgarden.com/145/85/7/120626075836/. For "What did Lewis and Clark discover?" see "In the Footprints of Lewis and Clark" at www.questgarden. com/104/65/6/100607225552/. Even younger children can get involved. A K–2 WebQuest exploring community helpers asks the question, "Where Do Adults Go When They Go to Work?" See "Our Community" at www.questgarden.com/ 23/04/7/060428171059/.

RESOURCES: WEBQUESTS

The website "QuestGarden" is an online authoring and hosting system for creating and using WebQuests:

■ www.questgarden.com/

Small-group work can be a powerful teaching and learning experience, and many more teachers are now using such groups as a regular part of their teaching repertoire. But there is more to successful group learning than simply assigning a task to a group of students. Four considerations are crucial to successful group work:

■ creating a challenging task;
■ teaching students to work together;
■ selecting groups thoughtfully;
■ honoring the work of learners.

1. Creating a Challenging Task

Many factors go into developing successful group work activities, but probably the most important is the task you assign. A central assumption behind group learning is that students benefit from the ideas involved and interactions that develop. Consequently, assigning low-level tasks—an end-of-chapter worksheet, for example—is a poor use of groups. Such activities quickly turn into a game of

"I'll find the answer to the first question, you find the answer to the second, and then we'll copy from each other." This approach may be an efficient way to complete the assignment, but students learn little more than if they had worked alone ... and maybe less. A better approach is to design activities that both challenge the majority of learners and create situations where they need to work together to complete the task. As we noted earlier, learners will rise to your expectations. This finding is especially true in group situations, where the collective effort will almost always exceed that of any individual. So, aim high.

2. Teaching Students to Work Together

Creating challenging tasks is critical to effective group experiences, but so too is teaching students how to learn together. Children know how to talk to one another in social settings. That's not the same thing, however, as working together in a classroom setting. Moreover, the messages learners typically hear in traditional classrooms discourage the very kind of behavior—talking with other students, sharing ideas and resources, working together to solve problems—we want to encourage in group activities.

IN YOUR CLASSROOM

GUIDELINES FOR COOPERATIVE LEARNING GROUPS

Help your students learn how to talk and work together by constructing a set of guidelines for working in cooperative learning groups. These guidelines might include the following:

- Stay with your group and help others feel welcome.
- Make sure everyone understands the nature of the assignment.
- Construct a plan for how to proceed.
- Divide responsibility for the tasks.
- Encourage others to participate in discussions.
- Discuss, rather than ignore, disagreements that arise.
- Ask for help when necessary.

Remember, though, that two key features underlie any successful rule-making activity. One is involvement. Students follow best those rules that they have some hand in constructing. The second feature is change. No set of rules is likely to cover all situations, so wise teachers sense when rules need to be revised. In the ensuing discussion, teachers can help students articulate the problem, make some possible rule revisions, and describe how the class might decide.

Some learners will come to you having had good group experiences and having learned how to study with others, but not all will bring those experiences and understandings. It's important, then, to talk explicitly about how groups best function together and to give students opportunities to practice together before the first big assignment.

3. Selecting Groups Thoughtfully

The third consideration in successful group work concerns the size and structure of groups. Two points are important here. One is that you should decide on the composition of study groups. Students often will plead to choose their own partners. Be strong! Resist the temptation to relent, especially in the beginning of the school year when you are unsure what your learners know or don't know about group efforts. The benefits of diverse groupings—both academic and social—are well documented; mix the groups as much as you can along academic, gender, and racial lines. A second point to consider is group size. No one size works best; different tasks may require groups of different sizes. For example, the quick sharing of ideas is best accomplished in pairs. Pairing students is also a good first step if you suspect your learners have had little group experience. Three- and four-member groups are better suited to more complex situations where no one student could be expected to accomplish the task alone. Groups of this size also are big enough to yield a range of perspectives but small enough so that all members can participate easily. Finally, for special projects you may want even larger groups. Large groupings of five or more learners can be quite valuable, especially when assignments call for more divergent thinking. Plan to start small, though, because large groups will falter if learners have not had significant experience in smaller groupings.

4. Honoring the Work of Learners

One last bit of advice in making group assignments is to honor learners' accomplishments. Some teachers assign group tasks but then fail to reward learners for work well done. Reflecting traditional views, these teachers assume that jointly produced work is less important than individual work. Consequently, they may weight an individual test grade twice as heavily as the grade on a group project. Think about the message this sends: The effort students put into the group activity is worth only half as much as a test score. You may well want to assign different grade weights to different activities, but if small-group work is important, make sure you show students that you value it.

The advantages of small-group work are several. As we noted above, you should expect *all* of your students to learn more in small-group settings. You should also expect fewer discipline problems as students become engaged in the tasks you assign.

FIGURE 5.2 The key to successful small-group instruction is the careful selection of students for each group. What factors might the teacher who arranged this fourth-grade group have had in mind?

You may find, however, that small-group work takes a lot of time. Your learners will explore issues more deeply, but you may cover fewer topics. Small-group work also can seem chaotic, at least initially. In the beginning of the school year, as students are learning how to learn together, you may see a fair amount of misdirected and off-task behavior. You might think this is a sign of failure; it isn't.

Remember that, for children, learning how to talk and participate with one another around academic topics and to understand and appreciate one another's similarities and differences is a process. Such learning is bound to look clumsy and chaotic early on.

Finally, some teachers find small-group study disconcerting as their role changes from information-giver to facilitator. The better your students become at working and learning together, the less direct assistance they may need. That's good news for them, but you may feel awkward and left out. Remember, however, they aren't really learning without you: They could not do what they are doing if you were not helping them learn how to work in groups, setting challenging assignments, providing a range of useful resources, guiding their investigations, and the like. Small-group work, then, is not only "real" teaching, but it can also be particularly powerful teaching as children come to see themselves as learners and accept responsibility for their efforts.

Strategies for Whole-Group Learning

As noted, Don Kite chose to introduce his colonial America inquiry with two whole-group activities—looking at artifacts and a K-W-L exercise. Depending on his purposes, however, he might have employed other whole-group activities.

If he was primarily interested in assessing learners' prior knowledge, Kite might have given the class a short examination, known as a **pre-test**. A pre-test gives a teacher a sense of what her students already know about a topic. It can also alert learners to the information a teacher thinks is most worth knowing. If the same test is re-administered as a **post-test** at the end of the inquiry, teacher and students can see immediately what knowledge gains have been made.

If Kite had been more interested in giving students some common information, he might have delivered a formal or informal lecture. Lecture gets a bad rap among educators, but if time is short and the information is relatively straightforward, we see no reason to avoid lecturing: It's a quick and efficient way to communicate explicit information.

One form of lecture that is particularly valuable in elementary classrooms is the **mini-lesson**. A mini-lesson focuses on a particular idea or skill that a teacher wants the entire class to learn. Such lessons typically include a piece of direct instruction and a practice session. For example, to teach third graders about geography, a teacher might talk explicitly about the usefulness of lines of latitude and longitude and then have students locate cities on a map of the United States using coordinates. Kindergarten teachers can also "lecture" in this fashion when they pull the class together at the front of the room to talk about ways of settling disputes between students. The chief advantage of a mini-lesson, then, is the ability to focus on a single idea or skill that a teacher wants to introduce to or develop with the entire class.

Thus far we have been considering alternative approaches Kite might use to introduce his colonial America inquiry. He could also use these approaches as the inquiry develops. Two whole-group strategies that work nicely once an inquiry is under way are *role-playing* and *simulation* exercises.

Role-playing refers to teacher-created situations in which students assume roles different from those they normally play. For example, Kite might have had learners role-play the interaction between two colonists—one settled, another newly arrived. Other examples include having children role-play different resolutions to a playground scuffle, the conversation between a police officer and a lost child, or the meeting between a slave and his owner upon the announcement of the Emancipation Proclamation.

Although **simulations** may involve some role-playing, more often they are situations in which learners confront and work through a series of problems and decisions. Simulations usually have no single right answer, but the choices learners make have appropriate consequences. A good example is *Oregon Trail*. This computer simulation software presents students with an array of situations (for example, what supplies to take, how to negotiate with natives), and decision options. Based on their choices, groups of learners travel farther, turn back, or face imminent death.

RESOURCES: SIMULATIONS

Simulations such as the Sim series (*SimCity, SimFarm, SimTower,* and so on) are commercially marketed instructional packages. The Sim series allows children to create an environment such as a city or a farm.

Free, Web-based simulations are also available. For example, one way to help students explore local government is through the "Peaksville Needs a Rec Center" simulation (https://drive.google.com/file/d/0B8GkIS7_tAXFcjFkNWhULTF6NHM/view) through which students play a variety of roles in order to decide if and how to add recreational services to a town budget.

The *Oregon Trail* simulation is also available for free download (https://www.techspot.com/downloads/5839-the-oregon-trail.html). This classic game offers students opportunities to make a range of choices (with various consequences) around travel to the western United States.

Strategies such as role-playing and simulations can take a lot of class and planning time. However, the advantages—the chance to develop multiple concepts in one exercise, more active learner involvement, and the motivation inherent in doing something fully engaging—often outweigh these negatives.

A Caution about "Fun"

Each of the approaches described above can be motivating, and that's good. A cautionary note is in order, though. All too often we hear prospective teachers talk about their teaching largely in terms of doing "fun" things with their classes. A good teacher understands that the search for fun activities can lead to trivial teaching—lots of activity, but little real learning. An inquiry on colonial America, for example, is a great opportunity to develop activities students would enjoy doing—making candles, writing with a quill pen and bottled ink, and the like. Used in the right context and as long as each activity serves the compelling question, such experiences can be terrific learning opportunities. Simply stringing together a bunch of fun projects may help your students enjoy the moment, but they will not be well served in the end. Fun for fun's sake isn't very useful.

Although he might have chosen otherwise, Don Kite's instructional choices seem to work: The artifacts and K-W-L activity capture the learners' attention, provide them with an opportunity to share their ideas, and help Kite understand something of what his students know about colonial life before the formal inquiry begins. Moreover, each activity is fun (in the best sense of that term) and supports Kite's compelling question. Kite's instructional choices should help you begin thinking about the range of teaching approaches from which you can draw.

What Don Kite knows about the subject matter and his students and how this all translates into his practice is pretty complex. In fact, there is even more to it; his teaching decisions illustrate a range of pedagogical issues. In the next section, we look at how Kite uses curriculum materials to support and extend his instruction.

■ SECTION SUMMARY:
Teaching Strategies

- Teaching strategies for individual work include reading and writing assignments and participation in learning centers.

- Strategies for small-group work include T-charts and jigsaw activities. Small-group activities work best when teachers create a challenging task, teach children how to work together, select groups thoughtfully, and honor learners' work.

- Whole-group strategies include pre-testing, post-testing, lecturing, role-playing, and simulations.

- Preference should be given to engaging activities that address the big idea over activities designed only for fun's sake.

Curriculum Materials

Choosing teaching strategies and creating activities around them is one piece of developing a pedagogical plan. Choosing **curriculum materials**—teaching and learning resources—is another. To see how one teacher selects and uses instructional resources, let's continue to watch the development of Don Kite's fifth-grade colonial America inquiry:

> Kite continues the K-W-L activity from the previous day. After reviewing what the students said they knew and what they would like to know, Kite breaks the class into four-member cooperative learning groups and assigns to each group one of several topics—houses, schools, occupations, entertainment, family, travel. As each group meets, the members select relevant questions from the "Want to Know" list. Most groups also develop additional questions.

Students begin researching their questions using a range of texts and videos that Kite makes available. Some students rush to the pile of US history textbooks on a back shelf. Others peruse the trade books Kite keeps on a large revolving stand. Still others ask permission to visit the school library where a large number and range of books, videotapes, and other media representations are reserved.

Before we talk about Kite's use of curriculum materials, notice that he continues to vary his instruction on the second day of the inquiry. Some teachers use only one or two strategies in every inquiry. Kite mixes whole-group instruction (reviewing the list of what students know and want to know) with a small-group assignment (investigating a set of group-selected questions around a topic related to colonial America). Blending instructional approaches is a good way to provide structure to the class day and keep eager minds and bodies busy. Kite knows this, but his intent is more strategic. He knows his students lack experience researching ideas on their own, so he assigns topics to small groups who then capitalize on each member's strengths as they work together. He also knows that his students sometimes have trouble knowing what kinds of questions to ask, so he gathers the whole class to generate as many questions as possible. Kite manages to challenge his students and still provide the assistance they need.

One other point: Notice that the topics Kite assigns—houses, schools, occupations, entertainment, family, and travel—represent geographic, economic, and social threads. As the inquiry develops, the geographic thread is represented in discussions about where homes and schools were located, how the availability of resources influenced which occupations were viable, and how landforms affected the difficulty of travel. The economic thread is represented primarily through the study of occupations. Although they might have explored a range of other economic issues, Kite's students focus on the kinds of jobs held by colonial men, women, and children. The social thread receives the most explicit attention in this inquiry. Students research family arrangements, housing styles, leisure activities, and how children were educated. From his compelling question—How are we like colonial Americans?—Kite astutely uses three key threads to organize his inquiry. This is wide territory; Kite expects his students to cover a lot of ground.[3]

Don Kite uses a variety of teaching approaches to reach his goals. He also uses a variety of curriculum materials. Because his class represents a wide range of reading levels and confidence, he makes available to students a wide range of resources. Some students may seek out textbooks because they are familiar sources and are easy to read. More adventurous students may seek out more challenging materials, such as trade books and Internet resources. Kite believes that his textbook presents ideas too simplistically and is bland. Eventually, he will encourage all his students to seek alternative sources, especially as he encourages connections between language arts and social studies. In the meantime, however, he supports those students who choose the class textbook until they are ready to move beyond it.

Using Textbooks

Like many teachers, Kite uses textbooks as part of his instructional package. Unlike many teachers, however, Kite uses textbooks as but one of several resources available to learners. Just as textbooks do not define the content he teaches, textbook reading, recitation, and end-of-chapter questions do not define his instructional approaches.

Textbooks are much improved since the 1980s, when criticism of school texts in general, and social studies texts in particular, began growing (Fitzgerald, 1980; Loewen, 2010). Textbooks can be used effectively, especially as a quick resource for defining terms and concepts and for gaining background information. These are important social studies and language arts skills, especially in grades K–2. We only caution you to be wary of becoming overly dependent on textbooks.

Using Other Texts

The Common Core–English Language Arts standards encourage educators to become more interested in the interdisciplinary connections between social studies and literacy. For social studies inquiries, teachers can look to both fiction and nonfiction text sources.

Newspapers and Blogs

One often overlooked text source is the *newspaper*. Although studies suggest that adults increasingly get their news from television and the Internet, newspapers (both print and online) continue to be an important source of current events information and thus a vital resource for social studies classrooms.

Newspapers can be used in myriad ways. You might encourage older students to bring in news clippings and to begin each day with a short discussion of these stories. Or you might ask learners to keep a current events journal where they combine their own clippings with comments on all the stories discussed in class. These two strategies help you expand your regular social studies instruction with additional opportunities to read, write, and discuss ideas.

Other strategies allow teachers to integrate newspaper articles more directly into their lessons. For example, a second-grade teacher introducing an inquiry on the local community might ask rotating groups of volunteers to monitor one or more newspapers for relevant articles. (Kindergarten students can ask their adult guardians for help.) The content of the accumulating articles can play an important part in shaping the content of the inquiry. Such a strategy is a powerful student motivator for, as children participate directly in their own learning, they begin to see immediate connections between their studies and the world around them. If one of our goals is to help learners see the relevance of social studies to their own lives, newspapers can be a powerful resource.

Using newspapers can be a little tricky, however. Remember, newspapers are made up of many different kinds of articles—straight news stories, editorials, features, and the like. It is important to teach your class how to identify and read the different pieces.

- *News stories* typically describe current situations and tend to be written in a top-down manner. Reporters put the key information—who, what, when, where, why, and how—in the lead or first paragraph and develop the details of the story as the article unfolds.

- *Editorials* are expressions of opinion. Editorial writers are less concerned with reporting the facts than with interpreting those facts and persuading readers to adopt their points of view.

- *Features* may describe an important issue such as smoking-related illness, highlight an emerging trend such as increases in video game use, or profile an interesting person such as Mark Zuckerberg.

IN YOUR CLASSROOM

SURVEYING NEWSPAPER USE

Social studies and literacy are natural curriculum partners, but other content area connections can also be made. For example, an easy way to incorporate mathematics into social studies is through the use of **surveys**. A survey is an assessment of what a group of people think about a topic at a particular point in time. You can help elementary children explore newspapers with a simple survey composed of questions such as the following:

- Where do you get most of your information about current events?
  - a) Newspapers   _____
  - b) Radio   _____
  - c) Television   _____
  - d) Internet   _____
- Do you read a newspaper on a daily basis?   Yes/No
- Do you receive a hard copy newspaper at home?   Yes/No

- What section do you read first?
  - a) Front page   _____
  - b) Sports   _____
  - c) Comics   _____
  - d) Editorials   _____

Students can administer the survey, tabulate the results, and graph them before discussing in class their interpretations of the findings.

Many online newspaper sites also feature blogs written by staff members. Blogs typically function to amplify newspaper articles or to express the author's point of view on the issue. Young children may need some help discerning the difference between hard news stories and blogs. But the latter provide a useful tool in helping students understand the difference between writing explanations and arguments, a point we discuss in more detail in Chapter 8.

Helping your learners understand these different types of articles should help them become more sophisticated newspaper readers and reinforce an important literacy skill—being able to read informational text.

Reference and Nonfiction Books

Other text sources—reference books such as *encyclopedias* and *almanacs*, and *nonfiction trade books*—require some special literacy skills, too. For example, learners need to understand that different kinds of reference books provide different kinds of information.

Encyclopedias generally offer the most global information, though not always in the most engaging fashion. Almanacs provide more detailed data on a smaller range of subjects. Almanacs provide a special challenge to beginning readers because of the concise presentation and the absence of much descriptive information. Online sites such as Wikipedia offer comprehensive access to topics that encyclopedias and almanacs once provided individually.

RESOURCES: COMPUTER-BASED RESOURCES

The days of searching through library stacks for oversized encyclopedias are not over ... but they are close! For example, Grolier's has produced a CD version of its encyclopedia that allows students to easily navigate the topics of their interest and it has an online version to which your school may subscribe. Visit at: http://teacher.scholastic.com/products/grolier/

The ease of Internet surfing, however, means that students can quickly go beyond encyclopedic information. A few minutes teaching students to use a browser or search engine (for example, Yahoo or Google) combined with an opportunity to practice searching should open students' eyes to the amazing potential of the Internet.

The power of Internet access comes with some important caveats. One is the caution to avoid allowing children unsupervised access to Internet sites and services. Most school computers are equipped with Firewall programs that filter out obviously inappropriate materials. These filters are not perfect, however, so talk with your school or district computer coordinator about how to protect children from objectionable sites.

Two other cautions fall under the heading of Internet literacy. With so much information available, students can easily be overwhelmed by searches that lead to thousands of hits. Helping children learn how to limit the scope of their searches, then, is an important skill. The second issue concerns how to evaluate Internet sites and the information they offer. The Internet is a boon to individuals and groups whose access to traditional means of disseminating ideas has been limited. But that democracy of access means that children need to learn how to evaluate the sources of information they see and read. Good readers always consider the source when trying to understand text; that practice is even more important in this Internet age.

Encyclopedias and almanacs are good sources for quickly finding basic information. Alternatively, learners can turn to nonfiction trade books. Commercial publishers continually add new titles appropriately written for and of interest to elementary-age learners. Most school and public libraries have selections of biographies, histories, and folk legends from which learners can get more detailed accounts of the topics that interest them. (See the Appendix for lists of trade books organized by social studies topic.)

RESOURCES: CHILD-FRIENDLY WEBSITES

Internet literacy is becoming increasingly important as children (and adults) use the Internet. Useful sites for teachers and children are:

- www.yahooligans.com
  Not only is this a child-friendly search engine, but the authors also provide a helpful set of guidelines for teachers and children as they learn to become Internet literate.

- kids.kiddle.co/Ask.com
  Formerly "Ask Jeeves for Kids," this site allows children to ask questions in plain English. Their questions are then confirmed and they are presented with one or two websites (rather than the thousands offered by some search engines!) that provide answers.

- www.factmonster.com
  Fact Monster offers a true smorgasbord of general information and interesting features.

Using Children's Literature

Many teachers believe that only nonfiction sources are appropriate for teaching social studies. Not so! Children's literature and poetry can be as useful for social studies lessons as they can be for language arts.

Historical fiction refers to realistic stories set in the past. Authors combine real events (for example, the American Revolution, the Civil Rights movement) and circumstances such as slavery and immigration with fictional characters, settings, and plots. (See the Appendix to this book for a list of recommended literature titles.) Learners benefit by vicariously reliving the times through each character's feelings, emotions, and experiences. *Roll of Thunder, Hear My Cry* (Taylor, 1976), for example, is a novel about life in the deep South during the Depression. The following passage vividly portrays the frustrations of a family of Black children faced with violent racism when, while walking to school, they were almost killed by a White bus driver:

When the bus was less than fifty feet behind us, it veered dangerously close to the right edge of the road where we were running, forcing us to attempt the jump to the bank; but all of us fell short and landed in the slime of the gully.

Little Man, chest-deep in water, scooped up a handful of mud and in an uncontrollable rage scrambled up to the road and ran after the retreating bus. As moronic rolls of laughter and cries of "N—! N—! Mud eater!" wafted from the open windows, Little Man threw his mudball, missing the wheels by several feet. Then, totally dismayed by what had happened, he buried his face in his hands and cried.

(p. 48)

Many children have difficulty understanding life for African Americans after slavery ended. This passage and many others in Taylor's profoundly moving book dramatically illustrate the daily tensions of African Americans living in a White-dominated world. Although few of your students may have had anything like the experience described above, most will have experienced some of the range of emotion—fear, humiliation, helplessness—Little Man felt.

IN YOUR CLASSROOM

BOOK TALKS

A common language arts approach to exposing children to new books and emphasizing the differences among texts is using book talks. They work well in social studies settings as well. A book talk is a brief presentation that may feature a synopsis of the whole book or a key element or concept. The idea is to give the audience enough of the book's flavor to entice others to read it. After you model a book talk once or twice, your students should quickly pick up on the form and enjoy presenting their books.

Poetry too can be an effective means of bringing life and color to historical events. Francis Miles Finch's (1991) poem, "The Blue and the Gray," offers numerous ways to think about the tragedy of war, in this case the Civil War:

By the flow of the inland river,
Whence the fleets of iron have fled,
Where the blades of the grave grass quiver,
Asleep are the ranks of the dead;—
Under the sod and dew,
Waiting the judgment day;—
Under the one, the Blue;
Under the other, the Gray.

These in the robings of glory,
Those in the gloom of defeat,
All with the battle blood gory,
In the dusk of eternity meet;—
Under the sod and the dew,
Waiting the judgment day;—
Under the laurel, the Blue;
Under the willow, the Gray.
From the silence of sorrowful hours
The desolate mourners go,
Lovingly laden with flowers
Alike for the friend and the foe;—
Under the sod and the dew,
Waiting the judgment day;—
Under the roses, the Blue;
Under the lilies, the Gray.
So with an equal splendor
The morning sun rays fall,
With a touch, impartially tender,
On the blossoms blooming for all;—
Under the sod and the dew,
Waiting the judgment day;—
'Broidered with gold, the Blue;
Mellowed with gold, the Gray.
So, when the summer calleth,
On forest and field of grain
With an equal murmur falleth
The cooling drip of the rain;—
Under the sod and the dew,
Waiting the judgment day;—
Wet with the rain, the Blue;
Wet with the rain, the Gray.
Sadly, but not with upbraiding,
The generous deed was done;
In the storm of the years that are fading,
No braver battle was won;—
Under the sod and the dew,
Waiting the judgment day;—
Under the blossoms, the Blue;
Under the garlands, the Gray.
No more shall the war cry sever,
Or the winding rivers be red;
They banish our anger forever
When they laurel the graves of our dead!

Under the sod and the dew,
Waiting the judgment day;—
Love and tears for the Blue,
Tears and love for the Gray.

(p. 159)

Your learners may come to this poem with a range of ideas about the Civil War. The patterned refrains, accessible language, and vivid images of Finch's poem, however, offer numerous ways to think about and empathize with soldiers who fought more than 150 years ago. A useful literacy activity is to ask students to identify the language Finch uses to compare (e.g., Wet with the rain, the Blue; Wet with the rain, the Gray) and contrast (e.g., Under the roses, the Blue; Under the lilies, the Gray) soldiers' experiences. Then you can discuss why the author chose this language. Another activity is to divide the class into two sets of small groups and ask one set to read the poem as they imagine a Northern veteran might and the other to read it as a Southern veteran might. Ask each group to discuss whether the author supported the Union or Confederate cause and to underline the language that supports their argument.

Using Maps and Globes

Understanding people and events is the key to a good social studies program. Also important, however, is understanding the physical space around us. Just as the different texts described above can be used to help learners understand people and events, so maps and globes can be used to help them understand spatial features and relationships.

The development of Global Positioning Systems (GPS) and websites such as Google Earth might make the idea of maps and globes seem obsolete. Yet maps and globes are amazing representations of the physical world. Consider the Mercator projection map in Figure 5.3.

Mercator projections provide a wealth of information in the shapes and relative sizes of continents, countries, and bodies of water; in location systems that show direction (compass) and that allow us to pinpoint any spot on the earth (longitude and latitude); and in a legend or key to symbols for a wide range of information—physical features, political boundaries, national capitals. In a glance, we can see information that would take hundreds of pages (or many mouse clicks!) to describe in words.

Like any tool, however, maps and globes are useful only if one knows how to use them. Surveys of geographic knowledge are depressingly consistent: Many Americans simply don't know much about the world around them. The good news is that learning how to read and use maps and globes is relatively easy.

For you to effectively teach the use of maps and globes, you will have to feel knowledgeable yourself. If your skills need upgrading, a good resource is the second edition of *Geography for Life: National Geography Standards* (Heffron & Downs, 2012). As you explore geography, you'll discover infinite ways to

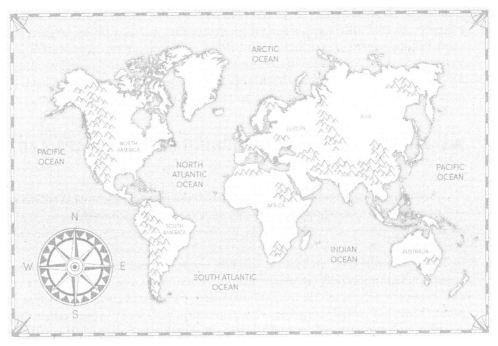

FIGURE 5.3 A Mercator projection. Designed by Freepik.

help your learners become geographically literate. Two activities we find useful are exercises in which children make their own maps.

The first activity introduces young learners to mapmaking. The task involves making a map of the classroom and locating key features such as windows, bookshelves, and teacher and student desks. Especially good for K–2 learners, this activity encourages students to develop their sense of space and relationship as they locate objects on their maps. Learners also can create simple legends to identify objects in the room.

A second activity introduces upper-elementary learners (grades 3–6) to mapping the world. If you have never tried it, take out a piece of paper and draw a free-hand map of the world, labelling as much of it as you can. Go ahead, we'll wait for you …

Okay, so what did you learn by doing this activity? Chances are you had some success—you probably drew some of the land masses fairly accurately and correctly labelled some places. You probably also had some problems; you may have forgotten some lands (did you remember Australia?), misdrawn others (does your South America look like a big drop of water?), or created some locations that don't exist (did you, perhaps, draw in the lost world of Atlantis?). Moreover, you may have discovered that you did not know where to locate many countries, bodies of water, and the like. That's okay; frankly, given the fact that most of you learned geography by coloring in country outlines, we would not expect anything much different. The point is that this activity has terrific potential for all kinds of lessons on locating important places, understanding longitude and latitude, and thinking about where one is in relation to the rest of the world.

Both of these activities fly in the face of the color-in-the-states map and geography work you likely experienced in elementary social studies. Creating a map (and talking about the difficulties in doing so) is a far more powerful learning experience than coloring will ever be. Identifying states or countries on a map is an important skill, but understanding geography and how maps are used to construct that understanding calls for more ambitious instruction.

▶❙◀ REFLECTION: DISTINGUISHING BETWEEN MAPS AND PICTURES

How is a map different from a picture? What features are different? What features do both share? How might your students distinguish between them?
▶❙◀

These mapmaking activities directly expose learners to key geographic concepts. Commercially produced maps (for example, the ones in your textbooks and in sets of reproducible maps) have other uses. For example, learners can get a better sense of which countries share common political borders when they look at a full-color textbook or online map. Reproducible maps, especially outline maps, are useful in assessing whether or not learners can locate the features the class has been talking about. Other good sources of maps and geographic activities are computer programs. Imagine, for example, the excitement learners feel when they use their computers to locate and create maps of the hometowns of their pen pals. Using these resources reinforces the importance of geography and demonstrates another important use for computer technology.

Although many people associate using maps with dull learning, it doesn't have to be this way. Our experience tells us that kids are fascinated by maps and globes. Your students will likely enjoy them, too, if you look for creative ways to introduce them that spark students' imaginations.

RESOURCES: TEACHING GEOGRAPHY

You can introduce your students to a terrific geography tool provided by the Netscape search engine. The "MapQuest" service invites students to enter the name of any destination in the United States and receive a map and directions to that site. An interesting feature is the ability to zoom in and out, decreasing or increasing the size of the map. The site is at www.mapquest.com.

Using Community Resources

The community is a particularly rich resource for building diversity into one's teaching. Much of the elementary social studies curriculum focuses on local and state content, so it makes sense to use the resources that lie just outside the school's door.

Community resources come in at least two forms—speakers who come into class and field trips where students go out and learn on site. Guest speakers are helpful because they can bring to class their perspectives on the issues at hand and can offer children a chance to talk directly with people who are involved. It is also much easier to bring a guest speaker to class than it is to schedule a field trip. The advantage of being able to experience a situation first-hand should not be dismissed, however. Despite their proximity to many community resources, many children may never have visited them. The opportunity to hold or feed an animal at a zoo, to stand on the battlements of a local fort, or to see how newspapers are made is invaluable and well worth the extra effort on teachers' parts.

IN YOUR CLASSROOM

TAKING FIELD TRIPS

Making arrangements for a class field trip can unnerve even experienced teachers. With forethought and careful planning, however, the experience can be as enjoyable for you as it is for the children. The following are some general guidelines:

- Pre-trip administrative plans: Check with your building administrator for school-specific guidelines on taking field trips, including the approval process.
- Pre-trip logistical plans: Visit the site and take note of the physical layout, the coordinator's ideas for the visit, directions to the site, and costs. Compose a permission letter to parents that details the location, objective, and schedule of the trip, including the dress, lunch, and money requirements. Arrange for parent chaperones.
- Pre-trip instructional plans: Identify and discuss with students the objective of the trip, explaining how it relates to the curriculum. Review field trip safety rules and logistics of dress, lunch, and money. Describe the schedule and the components of the site visit, and discuss how to ask good questions of tour guides.
- During the trip: Have students keep a field trip journal in which they enter answers to pre-trip questions, interesting ideas or reactions to site displays, and questions to be followed up in class.
- After the trip: Review students' entries in their field trip journals, and ask for volunteers to pursue questions that surfaced after the trip. Direct students to write individual or group thank-you notes to the on-site coordinator and guides. Make notes to yourself about the trip, including whether it met the objective you established and worked within the time frame allotted. Note also any unanticipated benefits or problems and things that might be done differently in the future.

Of course, not every person makes a good guest speaker, and not every business, museum, or historical site merits visiting. So, it's necessary to do some homework.

Using Computers and Other Technologies Wisely

Although we strongly advocate the use of computers and related technology, we also caution against their misuse. New technologies can open up wonderful new worlds to learners. The Internet, digital resources, computer programs, and the like provide students with far greater access to ideas and information than even ten years ago. So, by all means, use the technology you have available, but use it with an understanding that novelty does not always equal effectiveness.

IN YOUR CLASSROOM

USING VIDEO RECORDINGS

Video is a terrific classroom tool. Too often, however, teachers use more when less can be equally or even more effective. The movie *Dances with Wolves* is a good example. This feature film has great possibilities for illustrating the complex relationships between White and native cultures. The film's length and the content of some scenes undercut the usefulness of showing it in its entirety to elementary-age children, so consider showing small clips of the film. For example, the scene where Kevin Costner's character, John Dunbar, is taught how to say the word *tatonkah* (the Comanche word for "buffalo") can effectively illustrate the problems *and* possibilities of intercultural communication.

IN YOUR CLASSROOM

INTERNET FIELD TRIP RULES

Just as there are rules for taking field trips, so too ought there to be some rules for children as they navigate the Internet.

- Always have permission to go on the Internet.
- Stay at the site(s) your teacher has provided.
- Be respectful of ideas, and be polite.
- Do not give out your name, address, or any other personal information.
- While at school, do not buy anything online.
- If you see anything that is not school-appropriate, hit the Back button and leave the site immediately.

Teachers, who have so many resources available, must use technology wisely. Remember that for thousands of years humans learned real and important knowledge without the use of computers or video. In your excitement to use the latest computer simulation, don't forget that powerful learning still occurs when kids use that oldest of intellectual technology—books. Our goal is not to razzle-dazzle kids, to trick them into learning, but to use the best tool for the job.

■ SECTION SUMMARY:
Curriculum Materials

- ■ Textual resources come in many forms: textbooks, encyclopedias, almanacs, trade books, children's literature, and poetry.

- ■ Maps and globes provide useful representations of the physical world.

- ■ Computers and other technologies have an important place in classrooms, but teachers need to apply to their use the same thoughtfulness used in selecting other teaching resources.

Influences on Teachers' Content and Instructional Decisions

As noted earlier, Colonial Life is a topic traditionally covered in fifth-grade social studies. We have seen, however, that Don Kite's inquiry owes little to traditional approaches. He crafts his inquiry around a compelling question that allows for the exploration of geographic, economic, and social threads. He employs a variety of instructional strategies instead of a single method. He uses the textbook to support the instructional plan he develops, but it does not define either the content or his instruction. He assigns group and individual projects. Kite bases his decisions on a mix of personal, organizational, and policy factors.[4]

Personal Influences

Observers often try to explain the influences on teachers' content and pedagogical decisions in terms of structural factors. Those **structural factors** often include state standards and district curriculum guides, the organization of the school day, the availability of resources, and the norms and expectations of teachers. Although structural factors tend to get more attention (especially from policymakers), the importance of **personal influences** such as teachers' knowledge, beliefs, and experiences is widely acknowledged in the general literature on teaching (Duffin, French, & Patrick, 2012). In this section, we explore the influence of personal factors on teachers' classroom actions.

Personal factors represent the lived character of individual teachers. We can talk about these factors generally as

- personal knowledge and beliefs;
- personal and professional experiences;
- personal history or narratives.

No two people live the same lives, nor are they influenced by their experiences in the same ways. Much like their pupils, what teachers know and do is shaped generally by their unique pasts, and these in turn influence teachers' content and pedagogical decisions.

Don Kite is no different. We see the influence of personal factors on Kite's instruction in two ways. One is that Kite's decisions reflect his *knowledge of history as a school subject*. Kite believes fifth graders are more familiar with social considerations (for example, family, entertainment, schooling) than with any of the other thread categories. Therefore, he puts primary emphasis on social constructs and gives less attention to geographic and economic ideas. Because this is his students' first formal encounter with US history, he focuses on colonial life instead of the structure of colonial government or the nature of colonial economic outputs.

A second personal factor reflects Kite's *belief in interdisciplinary instruction*. One reason he likes social studies is that he can "work it together with some of our other subject matter." Kite often combines his language arts and social studies instruction. This inquiry is no different. For example, during the time allotted for language arts instruction, Kite's students read the nonfiction trade book *A Colonial Town, Williamsburg* (Kalman, 1992) and write sample diary entries that reflect various colonial perspectives—blacksmith, farmer, teacher, child. Kite has a basal reading series that most of his peers use. He uses it too, but sparingly. Instead, he teaches the same skills that the basal covers, but with trade books that support his social studies curriculum.

Kite's personal beliefs in emphasizing social history over political and economic subjects and in linking language arts and social studies influence his teaching. Other personal factors encompass diverse experiences, formal and informal, in and out of school, and current and past. Some of the more influential include a teacher's experiences as a learner, interactions with family members, personal and professional beliefs, and the sense of social studies as a school subject.

You may be surprised to find that teachers make important classroom decisions based on personal beliefs. As a prospective teacher, you can expect some guidance from curriculum guides, textbooks, and the like, but you should expect to balance that guidance with your own important knowledge, beliefs, and experiences.

Organizational Influences

In this section, we begin to build a more dimensional picture of teachers' content and instructional decision making. Teachers do not work in a vacuum.

Instead, they work in a complex system of roles and relationships, norms and expectations, resources and constraints, all mixed in with the personal factors of their lives. A second category of influences on teachers' instructional decisions can be described as organizational, as in the way schools and classrooms are organized for teaching and learning. **Organizational influences** include

- roles and relationships;
- norms and expectations;
- resources.

The colonial America inquiry Don Kite constructed is influenced by several organizational factors. One set of factors involves *roles and relationships*. Although it might seem odd, the role of "student" is an important organizational influence on teachers. As students, the children who sit in Kite's classroom help shape his instructional plans.

Don Kite knows several things about his fifth graders. First, he knows that students find their social studies textbook dull and plodding. Second, Kite knows that, although his students can become engrossed in some activities, their attention span can be short and unpredictable. Finally, Kite knows that different students know different things and that what they know is more or less historically accurate. Diversity in students can surface through characteristics such as gender, race, and ethnicity. But diversity can also emerge in the different ways in which children understand the world and respond to their teachers' practices.

Each of these ideas, in turn, helped shape the inquiry Kite constructed. To take advantage of students' changing attentions, he uses a variety of instructional approaches. To obviate the monotony of the textbook, he offers a range of instructional materials. To address the differences in students' knowledge, he organizes students into groups so that they can benefit from one another's abilities.

These are good strategies in and of themselves. The point here, however, is that Kite takes these actions because of the particular learners he has in front of him. Many factors compete for his attention, but a key factor is the nature of the children he teaches.

A second organizational influence on Don Kite's colonial inquiry involves *norms and expectations* in his school. We might focus on several examples here, but let's focus on Kite's use of the social studies textbook. Many of Kite's colleagues use their textbooks to teach most of their lessons. Kite chooses not to, and an important part of his decision comes from the organizational norm that supports his instructional autonomy. It is not the case everywhere, but in most schools, teachers have considerable say over how they plan and teach lessons and develop inquiries. So, although Kite's peers use their textbooks, he would be shocked if anyone criticized his decision to do otherwise.

Kite's colonial America inquiry is also influenced by a third organizational factor: *resources*. This influence is straightforward; Kite could not put the textbook aside if he lacked other resources to take its place. This is a critical point.

Many teachers would like to move away from their textbooks but, for them, alternative resources are either unknown or unavailable. Kite has no surfeit of available books and videos; as in most urban schools, money is tight. Still, he knows well what is available and, with the help of a resourceful school librarian, he shapes his instruction around the resources he has.

In each of these examples, we see how Don Kite's instructional decisions are shaped by organizational factors. Other teachers work with organizational influences unique to their situations. Their decisions are in part influenced by colleagues, school administrators, central office administrators, and parents. They make choices with reference to school-based norms and expectations, such as the amount of homework to be assigned, how student grades are calculated, and how much classroom "noise" is tolerated. Few, if any, teachers can completely escape the need to consider resource limits such as computer and software availability, equipment for projects, and, in some severely underfunded schools, even a supply of lined paper. Needless to say, lack of resources—especially those basic to instruction—can severely constrain teachers' instructional decisions. Most teachers, like Don Kite, are resourceful: They make good things happen whether or not the latest technology is at hand.

Policy Influences

Policies—national, state, and local—are a third source of influence on teachers' instructional decisions. Schools and school districts are like any large, complex, bureaucratic organization in that certain tacit norms and expectations become formalized and codified as policies. **Policies** include

- curriculum standards;
- tests;
- policy statements.

Policies can take many forms. **Curriculum standards** (sometimes called **curriculum frameworks** or curriculum guides) might come from a national organization such as the National Council for the Social Studies, a state education department such as the California Board of Education, or the central office of a school district. Tests are also a common policy item, since many teachers must administer standardized state and district-level tests. Issues such as the inclusion of special education students into mainstream classrooms may also be covered by state and local *policy statements*.

Just as personal and organizational factors influence Don Kite's decisions, so too do policy factors. Kite teaches the inquiry on colonial life as he does partly because of a district assessment policy: Kite, like his fifth-grade teaching peers, is required to administer a district-developed social studies test. The test includes one question that asks students to compare colonial and present-day life. The question begins, "Life is different today from the way it was in colonial America.

Some things that have changed are houses, schools, occupations, entertainment, family, travel." The question is then divided into two parts. Part A states: "From your list, choose three of the above six, list your choices, and for each of those choices, describe it as it existed in colonial America and describe it as it exists in America today." Part B states: "Using your notes from Part A, write an essay of about one hundred words describing the changes in America from its colonial days until today."[5]

Kite's inquiry shows impressive planning and instruction. The inquiry springs from a decent compelling question with some intellectual meat and kid appeal to it. The instructional activities and materials seem engaging and appropriately diverse. The assessments give learners multiple opportunities to show what they have learned. One criticism might be that Kite focuses exclusively on European settlement. The inquiry ignores native cultures and their views on housing, family, schooling, and the like. Including native perspectives would have enriched the inquiry by providing a third point of comparison.

Upon reflection, basing the inquiry partly on the district assessment question makes sense. Kite really cannot ignore the district assessment; one way or another he is going to have to administer it. Clearly, he brings intelligence and insight to a constrained situation. Policies such as this district assessment test do matter, but as Kite's response suggests, they matter in no particular way. Don Kite "teaches" to this test. He does so, however, in a way that remains faithful to the instructional goals he holds dear. In that sense, Don Kite's colonial America inquiry demonstrates the power of teachers to seize the instructional value from even the most pedantic source. Like good teachers everywhere, Kite turns a sow's ear into a silk purse.

Cross-Current Influences

One way to test the notion that Kite's pedagogical decisions rely not only on the district test requirements but also on personal and organization factors is to imagine how some of Kite's colleagues might have approached the same task. A teacher who believes that children simply need to know the "facts" might have developed lessons and inquiries that focus on imparting basic information through textbook readings, worksheets, and end-of-the-chapter questions. A teacher whose chief concern is getting through the information as quickly as possible might have rejected the notion of constructing an inquiry in favor of delivering a series of short lectures. A third teacher might not have even addressed the test question explicitly. This teacher might have dealt with the issues relevant to the test question—housing, occupations, family, and the like—as part of a larger and perhaps quite different instructional inquiry.

If asked, each of these teachers would likely cite the district exam as influential, but each could also cite other factors, personal and organizational, that influenced her or his decisions, as illustrated in Figure 5.4. As an example of a policy influence, then, testing pushes in no particular instructional direction and ultimately may hold no more authority over teachers' practices than personal

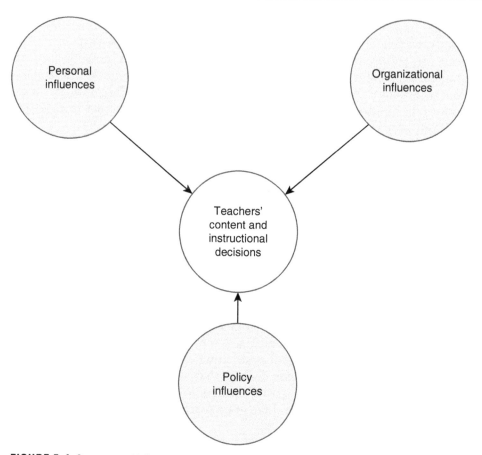

FIGURE 5.4 Cross-current influences.

or organizational considerations. Instead, each teacher's content and instructional decisions likely reflect a mixture of personal, organizational, and policy influences.

Let's look at a few other important points pertaining to the interaction of personal, organizational, and policy influences. One is that influences are potential rather than real. A survey of the influences on teachers' classroom decisions would produce a staggering list. But "influence" is a socially constructed phenomenon; what one teacher counts as influential another might downplay, dismiss, or ignore. Moreover, what counts as an influence may change over time and circumstances. That is, what a teacher counts as influential at one point and in one context may be supplanted by other influences as time and situations change.

If these two points ring true, we begin to see both the promise and problem of teaching: The promise of considerable opportunity to construct engaging and powerful learning situations is balanced by the problem that teachers are likely to feel pushed in multiple directions.

So, what does one do? First, recognize that, although you will discover many potential outside influences on your practice, how real these influences become (that is, how much influence they have over your practice) depends on how you perceive them. Second, understand that the bottom line is that ultimately you must make classroom decisions, and those decisions will reflect as much your own personal preferences as any outside influences. Third, realize that having all this autonomy may feel like a heavy responsibility. The good news, however, is that you really can transform the classroom lives of your learners. It will take a lot of work. Don Kite, like all good teachers we know, puts in long days. Fortunately, the payoff—learners engaged in powerful learning because of your pedagogical decisions—is well worth it.

Chapter Summary

1   **What teaching strategies support individual, small-group, and whole-group instruction?**
    A wide range of teaching strategies can be drawn on to support individual, small-group, or whole-group instruction. Strategies for individual instruction include reading and writing assignments and learning centers. T-charts and jigsaw activities work well in small-group settings. Whole-group strategies include pre-testing, lecturing, role-playing, and simulations.

2   **What curriculum materials are available for classroom use?**
    Curriculum materials are limited only by a teacher's imagination. For simplicity's sake, the most common can be grouped into textual materials (nonfiction and fiction), maps and globes, and computers and other technologies.

3   **What factors influence teachers' content and instructional decisions?**
    Although they can be separated for analytic purposes, personal, organizational, and policy factors interact as they influence teachers' classroom decisions.

Notes

1   Recall that the K-W-L teaching strategy (Ogle, 1986) calls for students to (1) list what they Know about a topic, (2) list What they would like to learn, and (3) after the instructional inquiry is complete, describe what they have Learned.

2   Sources of these readings include *A Colonial Town, Williamsburg* (Kalman, 1992), a story told from the viewpoint of a Black male teenage slave; *From Forge to Fast Food* (Greene, 1995), a history of child labor in New York State from the viewpoint of an indentured servant; *Sign of the Beaver* (Speare, 1983), the story of a native boy; and *Colonial Life in America* (Farquhar, 1962), a story about a White woman's life.

3   We will have more to say on this later, but notice that two threads—political and global—are not mentioned at this point.

4   For a full discussion of this idea, see Grant (1996).

5   This essay is one component of the district assessment. The two other parts are a multiple-choice examination of social studies concepts and a project that each teacher designs individually. Kite's students did individual projects on the states of the United States.

Teaching Resources

Print Resources

Two good resources on the range of issues that surround teaching reading in the content areas in general and in social studies in particular:

Alvermann, D., Phelps, S., & Gillis, V. (2009). *Content reading and literacy: Succeeding in today's diverse classrooms* (6th ed.). Boston: Allyn & Bacon.

Conley, M. (2011). *Content area literacy: Learners in context* (2nd ed.). New York: Pearson.

Two excellent resources outlining the advantages of small-group instruction:

Cohen, E., & Lotan, R. (2014). *Designing groupwork: Strategies for the heterogeneous classroom* (3rd ed.). New York: Teachers College Press.

Johnson, D., Johnson, R., & Holubec, E. (2009). *Circles of learning: Cooperation in the classroom* (6th ed.). Edina, MN: Interaction Books.

This is a useful guide to the issues and approaches around teaching language arts within the social studies:

Finn, P., & Finn, M. (1993). *Helping children learn language arts.* New York: Longman.

Each of these texts offers helpful advice about how to encourage and support students' writing about history:

Jorgensen, K. (1993). *History workshop.* Portsmouth, NH: Heinemann.

Levstik, L.S., & Barton, K. (2015). *Doing history: Investigating with children in elementary and middle schools* (5th ed.). New York: Routledge.

Two useful books on teaching social studies through children's literature:

Irvin, J., Lunstrum, J., Lynch-Brown, C., & Shepard, M. (1995). *Enhancing social studies through literacy strategies.* Washington, DC: National Council for the Social Studies.

Tunnell, M., & Ammon, R. (Eds.). (1993). *The story of ourselves: Teaching history through children's literature.* Portsmouth, NH: Heinemann.

An older but still valuable guide to asking good classroom questions:

Sanders, N. (1966). *Classroom questions: What kinds?* New York: Harper & Row.

Teachers and Teaching
Assessment

In the last chapter, we raised and discussed key two issues central to developing and carrying out a pedagogical plan, teaching strategies and curriculum materials. A third issue is **assessment**—discovering what your students know. It is the focus of this chapter.

As with traditional lecture-and-recitation forms of teaching and traditional materials such as textbooks, traditional approaches to assessing learning such as multiple-choice tests are facing serious challenges. After all, if we are going to use different teaching approaches and materials, we need to think about assessing our learners differently.

The landscape of assessment strategies has begun to change, and quite significantly. Yes, many of the state-level traditional multiple-choice exams kids take as measures of school-level and teacher accountability have not changed much. However, the introduction several years ago of the English Language Arts Common Core Standards (CC–ELA) and Mathematics Common Core Standards have resulted in a re-examination of testing practices.

These new standards, coupled with the introduction of the *College, Career, and Civic Life (C3) Framework for Social Studies State Standards*, strike a different direction than standards frameworks have taken in the past. The emphasis in these new versions is on how children learn and construct knowledge in classrooms that pivot around the kinds of teaching practices we have been describing. It turns out that the traditional and much-relied-upon multiple-choice and fill-in-the-blanks tests are really not structured to assess the sorts of ideas and capabilities these new frameworks and standards promote. As a result, we need to start thinking very differently about assessment.

High stakes traditional testing is usually concerned with overall school-level program evaluation. They are sometimes referred to as **summative assessments**. Although we discuss these high-stakes evaluations here, we concentrate here on what some people call **formative assessments**, the sort teachers use in their classrooms to get a good sense of whether children are actually learning the ideas and thinking strategies teachers want them to.

We will also refer to these formative assessments as **diagnostic assessments,** because we think that, if done well, such assessments can be used effectively to diagnose individual students' learning difficulties. As such, the evidence of learning—or lack thereof—that the assessments generate can be employed to shift teaching practices in ways that help alleviate those difficulties. The diagnostic assessment metaphor is derived from medical practice in which doctors diagnose what's ailing a patient. That allows for the development of a specific solution for treating the ailment. We think, metaphorically speaking, classroom-learning difficulties can be thought of as ailments searching for treatments. Knowing the ailment's source is necessary for providing an effective one. You will be in charge of doing just that. The sharper and more powerful your diagnostic assessment practices, the better you will become at treating learning ailments.

In this chapter, we address the following questions:

1 What forms of assessment will I use to understand what my students have learned?
2 How can I create assessment tasks that let me get close to seeing whether learning is taking place or not?
3 How can I transform the assessment results into evidence that explains what's happening for my students?
4 What kinds of tools (e.g., rubrics) do I need to help me make the best sense I can of my students' learning process?

Assessment Pillars

It might help to begin by talking about the three **assessment pillars** (see Pellegrino, Chudowsky, & Glaser, 2001) on which all good assessment practices depend. Think of this as a triangle with one of the three pillars at each intersecting corner. The beginning point is **cognition**, or thinking processes in which students need to engage in order to come to understand the ideas and elements of the sociocultural world you are teaching them. The second pillar at the second intersecting point is **observation**, a reference to the process of designing assessment tasks and activities that allow you to observe something about these learning processes in action. The third pillar that connects the final intersecting point is **interpretation**. It refers to the ways in which you go about making sense of the tasks that have allowed you to observe learning. It's the space in which you would apply interpretive tools, such as rubrics, to observations and draw evidence-based understandings of learning, or the lack thereof. The interpretations feed back to where you began, with cognition.

The interpretations allow you to assess the strength of your understandings of that cognition and then allow you to modify how you approach it through your teaching practices in order to improve learning. Used well, the assessment triangle is a powerful device for thinking about how assessment works and therefore getting the most from doing it, that is, using assessment data to adjust teaching practice to improve learning.

One thing we want to say about the starting point, cognition, is that it is the hinge. The more robust and clear your understanding of how cognition and learning development works for learners in subjects such as civics, economics, geography, and history, the more robust and effective your assessment practices will be. We spent considerable time discussing learners/learning and subject matter in Chapters 2 and 3, respectively. We won't revisit it all here. But it might do you well to review those chapters before you read on. In what follows, we will focus primarily on the two other pillars, observation (different tasks that allow you to observe learning) and interpretation (the rubrics and other gauging tools you need to consistently make sense of those tasks' outcomes).

To begin addressing the four questions we listed in the foregoing and then taking a closer look at observation and interpretation practices, let's begin by returning to the case of Don Kite and his fifth graders, the one we discussed at length in the preceding chapter. Let's explore in more detail his answer to the question "How do I know what my students understand?"

An Example from Don Kite's Classroom

Don Kite's small groups research their topics for two weeks. Over that period, Kite continually returns to the "Learn" portion of the K-W-L activity, asking students what they are learning as a result of their investigations. As the project draws to a close, Kite reminds the class that they are responsible for two products. One is a group presentation: Each group is assigned twenty minutes to talk about the questions they asked of themselves and the information they gathered. They also should be prepared to answer questions from their classmates. The second product is an individual one. Here, each child must write an essay comparing life during colonial times to that of today. The expectation is that learners will draw information for the essay from the various group presentations.

Just as he uses multiple methods and materials, Kite also uses multiple forms of assessment. Kite knows that conventional measures such as multiple-choice tests tell him little beyond some basic facts about what learners really understand. To provide learners with more opportunities to tell him what they know and are learning, Kite employs the above two less-traditional assignments. His choices feature group and individual components, public and private exhibitions, and opportunities to build writing, speaking, and group-process skills in addition to expressing the content learned.

Group and individual projects such as the ones Don Kite uses represent some of the latest thinking in assessing learners' understandings. These efforts are described variously as "authentic" or "performance-based" assessments. We'll examine more closely the distinctions between these a little later. The point to consider now is that educators are rethinking the traditionally narrow use of tests and grades as they explore the issue of how to know what learners understand, as we just pointed out.

Three ideas are central to current thinking about assessment: viewing assessment as a continuous part of instruction and cognition (for its diagnostic power), using multiple sources of data (from different observations), and looking at a broad range of learner outcomes (through applying scoring rubrics). Percolating throughout these issues is the distinction between assessment and evaluation. Let's look at what these issues involve.

Assessment as an Ongoing Part of Instruction

For far too long, educators have thought about assessment only in terms of **evaluation**, a summative activity that focuses exclusively on what learners know. These attributes of evaluation are a part of assessment, but only a part. We consider assessment an ongoing part of instruction, something we will keep stressing throughout this chapter.

If you wait until the end of a unit to evaluate learners' efforts, you miss important opportunities. One is to understand how learners are responding to the ideas you teach them, and they explore under your guidance, as they encounter it. The results of a short quiz or writing assignment or presentations given midway through a unit offer a snapshot of how each learner is making sense of the unit ideas. Learners who are struggling can receive extra help from you before they fall too far behind and become too frustrated. We cannot overstress the importance of this point in improving learning.

The second opportunity is to modify your instruction based on the outcomes of your assessments. The results of a mid-unit assessment offer an advantage in that they give you a sense of how your unit is progressing. If most of the learners seem to understand the big ideas presented, you can feel fairly confident in proceeding. If most learners seem to be missing the point, however, you can take two actions. One is to do a different sort of diagnostic assessment to check the results of the first. The second is to rethink how the unit has developed thus far and return to those ideas with which learners are having trouble.

In these ways ongoing assessment helps you to understand both how learners are doing and how the unit is progressing. With this information, you can weigh your instructional plan and make adjustments as you see fit. This is the wisdom inherent in using the three assessment pillars; they feed back into your teaching practices in ways that provide you data to make constructive, defensible changes in those practices.

Using Multiple Sources of Data

A second idea that separates assessment from evaluation is using multiple sources of data, or multiple observations of learning in the language of the three pillars. Because evaluation has traditionally meant a summative exercise, educators have generally thought in terms of one measure per unit of study. If we see assessment as understanding what learners know and can do throughout a unit, it makes sense to use as many assessments as is practical.

Probably everyone has experienced the panic of having prepared for one question or type of test and been given another. Maybe you were one of the lucky ones who did well anyway; chances are, you bombed out. The point of recalling such painful memories is not to make you feel badly, but to show that a single measure can produce invalid results. In short, the number and kind of assessments do matter. Some students do well on **objective-type tests**—multiple-choice, fill-in-the-blanks, and matching—but other kids do better on **open-ended tasks** such as writing essays, creating political cartoons, and making journal entries. Relying on any assessment as a single measure can produce invalid results. If, as teachers, we have only one end-of-the-unit evaluation, chances are some learners' knowledge and skills will not be accurately assessed.

▶❘◀ REFLECTION: ASSESSMENT ANXIETY

> Think about your past experiences with assessments, especially those that acted as evaluations, and the anxiety they produced. How did you feel in those situations? How did you respond? How did those situations compare with other assessment experiences you have had?
>
> Just as not all assessments produce anxiety, not all anxiety is bad. The pressure to perform on an assessment can be an important motivation for learning. But good teachers know the importance of being sensitive to student anxiety and of working with those students whose anxiety levels incapacitate them during some tasks.
>
> Because we want all children to have opportunities to succeed, and we want to produce students who can perform well in a variety of situations, we need to build multiple forms of assessment into our teaching. Take a minute to think about the range of possible types of assessments you might actually use.
>
>

Considering a Broad Range of Learner Outcomes

One last assessment issue is the need to consider a broad range of learner outcomes. Evaluation typically implies only one kind of outcome—**cognitive** or academic. End-of-the-unit tests may have objective and open-ended questions, but they typically assess only a learner's knowledge and skill. Other learner outcomes—*affective*, *personal*, and *social*—are often ignored.

We want to make two points here. One is that cognitive or academic outcomes are important. Although we disagree with the conventional view that assessment should focus exclusively on evaluating learners' knowledge, we also disagree with the view that elementary school should focus exclusively on social, personal, and affective goals, and that children will get enough academics in later years. Personal, social, and affective outcomes are vital to children's development, but so too are academic or cognitive outcomes. We are advocating for a balanced approach.

Some observers suggest that the kinds of intellectual experiences children have in elementary schools fundamentally shape their cognitive growth into adulthood (Anyon, 1981; Delpit, 1988). Attending to cognitive outcomes, then—what learners know and can do—is a key component of any assessment plan.

Having said that, affective, personal, and social outcomes are important and should be assessed, if not graded. **Affective outcomes** refer to the attitudes, interests, and dispositions learners bring with them. Of particular concern are those interests, attitudes, and dispositions learners have toward the work they do during social studies. For example:

- Do they enjoy challenges and persist in the face of difficulties?
- Do they have an appetite for learning and a distaste for busywork?
- Do they know how to listen to someone who knows something they do not know?
- Do they understand which questions to ask to clarify an idea's meaning or value?
- Are they open and respectful enough to imagine that a new and strange idea is worth attending to?
- Are they inclined to question past statements that hide assumptions or confusions?

(Wiggins, 1989, p. 48)

Social outcomes are those behaviors that concern how learners work, both individually and in groups. For example, when working on an individual assignment, can learners stay on task and avoid unnecessarily disrupting their neighbors? When working with others, do learners fulfill their responsibilities and take active pleasure in ensuring a quality product? **Personal outcomes** refer to the types of interests learners demonstrate in the ideas you are working with. Are they bored with them? Do they find the ideas compelling enough to go off on their own in search of more on a particular topic, for example?

Few people would argue against the significance of learners' affective, personal, and social development or the importance of understanding them. Instead the concern has been how to assess these behaviors, or observe and interpret them in the vocabulary of the assessment pillars. As noted assessment expert, Grant Wiggins, argues, "*if* you value the outcome that students collaborate effectively on complex tasks, *then* you ought to assess it" (Nickell, 1992, p. 91).

Matching Assessments with Purposes

Bearing in mind these issues of assessment and evaluation, we can now discuss specific assessment measures or tasks (observations of learning). As with teaching methods, you will be able to choose from a range of assessments. And, just as it makes sense to choose teaching strategies wisely, so too does it make sense to consider carefully which form of assessment you use to meet your pedagogical needs.

As we've noted, assessment is a hot topic these days. As teachers rethink traditional methods of teaching, they are also rethinking how they understand learners' work. With the increased attention to assessment, however, has come a somewhat confusing array of ideas and terminology. Depending on the source, you can read about "alternative," "authentic," "constructivist," "performance," "realistic," "formative," and "diagnostic" assessments. We won't try to sort through all this here. Instead, we propose some assessment basics—definitions, examples, and the like—to prompt your ongoing thinking. One basic distinction we want to stress is between *traditional* and *authentic* assessments.

■ SECTION SUMMARY:
FIVE ASSESSMENT CONSIDERATIONS

In the previous section, we traced out five considerations that go into the practice of assessing student learning growth in powerful and useful ways.

First, we started by discussing the importance of relying on a structured approach to assessment. We referred to this structure as the three assessment pillars (Pellegrino et al., 2001). We then offered a brief example to set the stage for thinking about the remaining five issues.

Second, we stressed the idea that assessment needs to be thought of as an ongoing part of instruction.

Third, drawing on multiple sources of assessment data, we pointed out, was good practice because it gives you a variety of windows on student thinking and understanding.

Fourth, multiple sources of data also help you obtain a broader sense of the range of student learning outcomes you might like to consider as part of your overall assessment strategy.

Fifth and finally, we noted that, in order for assessment to work well, its design and practice needs to be carefully and tightly aligned with the purposes you set for student learning in social studies. Without that alignment, the assessment data you gather from students will be difficult, if not impossible to interpret relative to those purposes.

Types of Assessments

Traditional Assessments

Traditional assessments, such as multiple-choice tests, according to Grant Wiggins, "are not authentic representations of subject matter challenges. They are more like checkup tests and quizzes and drills." Wiggins is not saying that students need not know content or that all traditional testing is bad. Instead, he is saying that most traditional measures tell us only "whether kids mastered some facts." This is not the same thing as helping us understand whether learners can perform, for example, "the authentic act of mastering historical analysis and information" (Nickell, 1992, p. 92). In the past, educators seemed content to know whether children had mastered those facts. However, today, the concern has shifted well beyond the question of mastery to one of what children can do with what they know.

The *C3 Framework*, designed to guide shifts in standards development work, reflects this changed priority. No longer are students expected to just know some things about the sociocultural world; they are expected to be able to engage in intelligent and constructive activities with what they know, such as solve real problems and think and reason about societal questions that prompt responses. But before looking more closely at these authentic assessments and their variations, let's talk a bit more about what has typically constituted what are termed traditional assessments.

One form of traditional assessments is often simply termed **test-based assessments**. School tests get knocked pretty hard in the current assessment literature for their over-reliance on these types of tests. Most observers agree with Grant Wiggins that "school-given tests, whether bought from vendors or designed by teachers, are typically inauthentic, designed as they are to shake out a grade, as an evaluation exercise," rather than "allowing students to exhibit mastery of knowledge in a manner that suits their styles and interests and does justice to the complexity of knowledge" (Wiggins, 1989, p. 58). Although we think this makes sense, we recognize that traditional testing can hold a place in every teacher's classroom.

Test-based assessments can retain some importance for two reasons. First, we can construct good tests that measure more than low-level knowledge. Test questions, especially those that call for students to do more than circle the right answer, can be an effective way to get at what students know and can do. The caution is not to rely on such tests as the sole measure of learning.

The second reason tests are important is that standardized testing is a fact of classroom life. Such tests, traditional in their structures, are heavily criticized, and for good reason. Nevertheless, because they are unlikely to go away any day soon, smart teachers must help their learners deal with them. Those teachers study the tests their classes take to understand:

- how the questions are formatted (for example, multiple-choice, essay);
- what kinds of content they cover (for example, content that is part of the school curriculum or general knowledge);

■ what levels of knowledge are tested (for example, knowledge and comprehension versus analysis and synthesis).

Smart teachers also provide learners with opportunities to practice answering the kinds of questions that appear on their state-level exams. The caution here is not to go overboard. Turning your classroom into one continuous practice test not only will bore the class, but it also won't guarantee better test scores (Wiggins, 1993). Learners need practice with different test question formats. More important, however, are opportunities to engage interesting and challenging ideas. Go ahead and give your classes some practice questions, but focus on developing powerful units and more powerful authentic, diagnostic assessments that give you better evidence of what is happening with your students' learning process. That focus leads us to consider such authentic assessments and their variations.

▶️◀ REFLECTION: STATE STANDARDS AND ASSESSMENTS

Most state departments of education now post sample questions from their state tests, and some even offer complete exams. First, go to your state's standards page (for example, www.doe.in.gov/standards/social-studies), which lists links to all of the state standards. Then click on the department of education's home page. From there you should be able to follow the appropriate links to find copies of state test questions.

As you read through the questions, ask yourself:

What thread categories do these questions represent? Are there any patterns in those categories?
What kinds of questions are being asked? Do they represent low-level thinking, high-level thinking, or a mix of thinking levels?
How well do the questions reflect the content emphasis expressed in the state standards?

Authentic Assessments

Authentic assessments are those that push learners to demonstrate their understanding in real and genuine ways. As Wiggins notes, an authentic assessment "would be much more a simulation or representation or replication of the kinds of challenges that face professionals or citizens *when they need to do something with their knowledge*" (Nickell, 1992, p. 92; emphasis added). One of the more important things to realize here is that authentic assessment approaches—that is, asking students to do something with what they know—already presume that they know something. In other words, to do something with what you know requires you to know something and to put it to good use.

FIGURE 6.1 Authentic assessment takes into account performances such as that seen in this photograph. This fourth grader holds his peers' attention as he presents his ideas.

Think of it this way. To obtain a driver's license in most states, you need to pass two different tests: One, a "written test" as it were, asks you to tell what you know about road rules, signs, and accepted driving practices often in a multiple-choice digitized test environment at the Department of Motor Vehicles. The other demands that you *demonstrate what you know*—how to get out there and actually drive a vehicle. The former might be necessary, but it is very likely insufficient. The real authentic assessment is being able to drive a vehicle safely on the road. Knowing details about the road and driving rules is put on display via the authentic performance of proving you can drive, obey signs, and operate the vehicle safely in a real-world context. Both might be necessary, but the authentic performance is critical and it already demands that you know many things. So, the authentic assessment reaches farther and can demonstrate much more than a simple traditional test of knowledge recall.

What do authentic assessments look like? A rainbow of options are available, depending on your pedagogical purpose. For the colonial America unit, Don Kite's fifth graders might write diary entries for various colonial residents, construct maps of important features of colonial towns, or draw pictures of meetings between natives and colonists. Small groups of learners might create a colonial newspaper, assemble a **big book** on colonial life, or write and perform a play dramatizing an interesting colonial experience. Writing tasks can include keeping a daily journal, writing poetry and other creative works (including historical fiction), and writing small pieces of "real" history. Drawing tasks can include making picture books and creating political cartoons. Other tasks might include role-playing, making presentations, and giving speeches. Figure 6.2 illustrates the many ways one might approach assessment. All of these examples can also be called **performance-based assessments**, since they require performance displays of what one knows.

To the extent that they can provide you with evidence of where your students are in their learning progressions, allow you to diagnose learning impasses and difficulties, and help you adjust your teaching practices to provide help for students, we can refer to them also as **diagnostic assessments**. Sometimes this cluster of classroom-level authentic, performance-based, and diagnostic assessments are lumped under the broad category of **formative assessments**. In many ways this is a catch-all term used to describe any assessments given regularly in the course of instruction that provide you with snap shots of where your students are in the *formation* of the ideas and cognitive/affective practices you are trying to teach them.

FIGURE 6.2 Authentic assessment.

You have considerable discretion in choosing classroom assessments. As you do, however, keep two considerations in mind. One is variety. Think about ways to give learners a range of opportunities to demonstrate what they know and can do. You need not include every form of assessment in every unit, but keep track of the assignments you make and rework them over time—a varied diet is always more appetizing than a restricted one. The second consideration is thoughtfulness. Think about what your learners actually might be able *to do* that demonstrates a thoughtful understanding of the material at hand. Not every learner will be able to meet your highest standard, but if you have thought about what constitutes a substantive effort, you will better understand your learners' products.

Informal Assessment

In addition to authentic and test-based assessments, one other way to understand what learners know and can do is through **informal assessment**. The difference between the former and the latter is that authentic and test-based assessments can also be used to evaluate learners' performance. Informal assessment, however, is strictly informative and impressionistic. It is intended to help you understand in real time what sense learners are making of the material to date so that you can adjust your instruction if necessary on the fly so to speak.

Learners cannot always articulate what they do not understand. Sometimes they think they understand something only to discover later that their understanding is thin or flawed. Good teachers help avoid such confusions by using a variety of informal assessments throughout their instruction. The simplest is paying attention to what students say, do, and communicate nonverbally. For example, good teachers "read" the faces and actions of their learners and make educated guesses about whether to slow down, provide another example, or reiterate an idea. But expect to be fooled occasionally: Sometimes learners do understand even when their faces suggest that they don't. Other times they don't understand when it appears they do. Paying close attention isn't fool-proof, but the more you do, the better you will be at gauging learners' understanding.

Another informal assessment method is asking questions. Good teachers ask a lot of questions, and they ask them in a variety of situations—individual, small group, and whole class. Sometimes teachers ask questions to spot-check understanding (and to see who is listening). In those cases, the questions tend to be fact-based, and the emphasis is on right answers. You know the type: "Why did English colonists come to America?" "What hardships did they face?" "Where did they settle?" Though occasionally necessary, these kinds of questions tend to be a bit disingenuous because the teacher asking them already has a preformed answer in his head. We would simply caution against over-relying on these kinds of questions because students get deeply accustomed to hearing them and the game of "guess what I'm thinking" they signify.

FIGURE 6.3 Informal assessment.

Another purpose for asking questions—and a more important and authentic one, we would argue—is to understand children's thinking. Fact-based questions tell a teacher little more than if a learner knows a specific piece of information. To better understand learners' thinking, teachers must ask open-ended questions that push below the surface. Questions such as "How do you know that?" "What makes you think that?" and "Are there other ways to think about that?" push learners' thinking and provide valuable insights into how they come to know what they do. Even a question as simple as "Can you give me another example?" or "Can someone suggest another way to think about this issue?" can yield helpful information about how kids think. Figure 6.3 illustrates the components of informal assessment.

Portfolios

Using portfolios as part of a comprehensive assessment strategy has gained much attention of late. In simplest terms, a **portfolio** is a collection of student work used to demonstrate learning over time.

Any number of student pieces can make up a portfolio (see Figure 6.4). Whether teacher- or learner-selected, these works generally represent the range of assessments assigned throughout the school year. Some items may be individual assignments such as test-based assessments, essays, and drawings. Other items—copies of projects, research papers, videotapes, even computer programs—may reflect work done in group settings.

Portfolios serve a variety of purposes. Learners may see portfolios as a means of charting their own progress and a source of pride and motivation. For teachers, portfolios can clarify a learner's strengths and weaknesses, information that can be passed along to the next teacher. And for parents, portfolios can make clearer the work the class does in general and the work their child does in particular. On first encounter, some parents may seem impatient with portfolios, preferring to look at test scores and grades. Our experience tells us, however, that a teacher's patient explanation pays off. If helped, most parents come to see the value of collecting a range of their child's work and take an active interest in seeing growth over time.

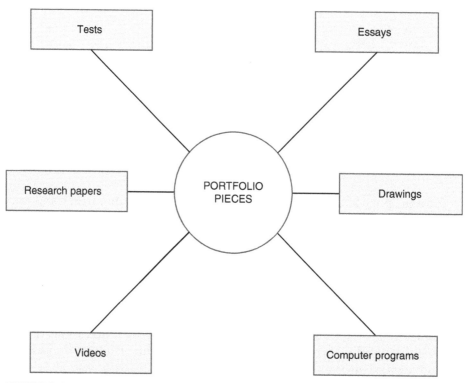

FIGURE 6.4 Portfolio-based assessment.

▶|◀ REFLECTION: DEVELOPING A PROFESSIONAL PORTFOLIO

Think about developing a professional portfolio as a way of capturing your best work and representing yourself to others. Consider including a statement of your teaching and learning philosophy, sample unit plans, examples of classroom assessments, and copies of evaluations of your teaching.
▶|◀

Grading and Rubrics

Before going on, let's look at grading and a recent trend in grading—the use of rubrics. Referring back to the three assessment pillars, we see that rubrics are tied to the third pillar, interpretation. **Rubrics** are uniform ways you apply criteria to gauge the nature of students' efforts, the evidence of learning (or not) that results from the assessment tasks on which you ask students to perform. Rubrics form the method you use to consistently interpret students' learning growth (or the lack thereof). Rubrics should vary depending on the nature of the task and the outcomes the task is designed to produce. But each task's rubric should be applied consistently across students.

It is crucial to realize that assessment is not the same thing as grading. Assessment is about understanding what a learner knows and can do. **Grading,** like any evaluation, is about judging that learner's performance (and often about managing student behavior): His performance on a test might be judged as 88 percent; her performance on a small-group project might be judged an "A."

The more you come to know about assessing learning, the more likely you will squirm at having to render a final judgment. If you are like us, you'll always wonder whether the grades you give truly correspond to the learning that has occurred. Compelling arguments exist for doing away with grades, and some schools have eliminated them. Equally compelling, however, is the tradition of giving grades, and most likely you will teach in a school where virtually everyone expects you to comply to some sort of evaluative grading scheme. We wish we had some good advice on how to deal with this, but we can only try to explain here how we think about the transition from assessing to grading. We do know some social studies teachers who take the time to write short narratives about each child. These narratives go some distance in explaining the letter grade. We think this is a good practice, but it can take a lot of time.

In recent years, many teachers are turning to rubrics as a means of making their grading decisions more coherent and transparent. In general, rubrics help learners by making explicit what is expected of them, and they help teachers by providing a more useful means of diagnosing the quality of learners' work. The rubric-as-scoring-guide allows teachers to examine and assess students' work across a range of criteria. Those criteria can be as general or as specific as a teacher likes. Table 6.1 gives an example of a general rubric that could be used to evaluate a writing assignment. We call it generic because its categories could be applied to just about any writing task.

Compare the generic criteria in Table 6.1 with the specific criteria described in Table 6.2. These scoring criteria apply to a very specific task here—students are asked to draw buildings that are described in a lesson. In this case, the rubric relates to a specific second-grade assignment, the topic of which has been dealt with in class. The teacher has tailored the scoring criteria to the task because he/she wants to know more about what students understand.

TABLE 6.1 General Rubric

4	Student's answer addresses most dimensions of the question; uses appropriate examples; and demonstrates analysis and synthesis.
3	Student's answer deals with most dimensions of the question; generally uses appropriate examples; and demonstrates some analysis and/or synthesis.
2	Student's answer deals with some dimensions of the question; includes examples, though they may not all be appropriate; and demonstrates only literal understanding.
1	Student's answer is missing or unresponsive to the question.
SCORE (e.g., 2)	_____

TABLE 6.2 Specific Rubric

4	The student includes all five of the community buildings described in class.	The student's drawings accurately represent the main features of each type of building.
3	The student includes some (three to four) of the community buildings described in class.	The student's drawings generally represent the main features of each type of building.
2	The student includes only a couple of community buildings described in class.	The student's drawings vaguely represent the main features of each type of building, and/or may contain errors.
1	The student includes only one of the community buildings described in class, or does not turn in the assignment.	The student's drawing does not accurately represent the main features of the building drawn.

SCORE _____
(a 4, 3, 2, or 1)

Specific rubrics tend to be more challenging to create. Their considerable benefit over general rubrics is that, if designed well with clear criteria and applied consistently and accurately, they provide you with significantly more and better information about what your students understand (cognition). As a result, they have strong diagnostic power that general rubrics often lack.

Whether general or specific, rubrics can offer advantages to both learners and teachers. Given to learners when an assignment is made, a rubric allows students to know explicitly what their teacher's expectations are and how they will be evaluated. For teachers, rubrics offer two advantages. One is a more accurate and consistent scoring of assignments; the second is a tangible means of talking with students (and parents) about classroom expectations.

As we said, rubrics can be general or specific; they can use a three- or four-point scale (or any other you create); and they can focus on one or more criteria at the same time. Don't worry about creating the one best rubric. Instead, think about your instructional and assessment goals and how to communicate them to your learners most effectively. Your rubrics should be tied directly to the learning goals you identify. These should come from your understanding of the kinds of thinking (the cognition pillar from which you begin) you want students to put on display.

■ SECTION SUMMARY:
TYPES OF ASSESSMENTS

In this last section, we looked at a variety of different types of assessments. We began by defining and describing traditional assessments that are more often than not referred to as tests. They generally align with a long-running practice of evaluating students, frequently to sort them into different groups by ability.

We then explored the newer forms of assessment, the type we are advocating for use in the classroom. These included a variety of different authentic assessments (e.g., performance-based tasks), informal assessments (e.g., student questioning) used to track student learning growth (or the lack thereof) in real time, and a more recent practice of asking students to build portfolios of their work across a period of time in which to show and describe what they learned. We ended the section by discussing issues and ideas related to the practice of grading and how the use of rubrics can aid in making assessment a more effective and useful endeavor.

Tying it All Together With Another Illustration

By this point, you are probably saying to yourself that all this assessment stuff sounds like hard work. That's true; it is. But it also is absolutely crucial to good social studies teaching. Without sharp assessment practices that link your learning goals (types of cognition in social studies, for example) to generating evidence from tasks that make the learning process and its outcomes visible so that you can apply rubrics to them and see where your students are, you have no real way of determining growth or diagnosing where it breaks down. As such, you cannot do much to repair the problems. In other words, you are handcuffed pedagogically and even general informal assessing will not give you enough feedback to help. Ongoing, more specific assessment is the key.

In an effort to make assessment as clear as we can, we want to provide an example here. The example draws from the three assessment pillars and attempts to show as clearly as we can how the three pillars fit together. It is but one example. But we hope it works well enough so that you can see how the pieces fit and to what end.

Good social studies teaching involves trying to help students understand the subject matter you are charged with teaching them—civics, or economics, or geography, or history, for example. We discussed these subject matters at length in Chapter 3 where you also met teacher Ramona Palmer. We introduced her teaching a lesson on the Bill of Rights. One of her key goals was trying to help her students understand the nature and substance of those constitutional amendments. We focused on the first one especially, her work with students on the idea of freedom of speech, a pivotal and sometimes controversial amendment. Using the three assessment pillars, we can show you how she might go about "seeing" the nature of her students' understanding. We focus here on an assessment approach that targets primarily cognitive understanding, rather than social, personal, or affective. We do this to make our example relatively easy to comprehend in order to get our point across. The other three types of understandings might require a different set of assessment examples, ones we don't discuss here.

It's one thing to simply ask students to restate the First Amendment, either in their own words or by memorizing its key provisions and simply restating them correctly. But, as we have been arguing, that doesn't necessarily mean they understand the amendment. To recall or restate it is a low level cognitive accomplishment, perhaps a necessary one, but also insufficient to demonstrate understanding. If understanding is the goal, a form of authentic assessment is required, even a type of performance assessment that allows you to diagnose learning impasses.

The first pillar, cognition, refers to thinking, the thinking that enables understanding. But what kind of thinking is required to enable understanding? Answering this question carefully lays the groundwork for figuring out what kinds of performance tasks would allow students to put their thinking on display. Answering the question, though, is a complex one. First, a student must be able to *read with comprehension*. Then the student would need to be able to *analyze the meanings* of the words, establish who the *author/s* was/were, what the *intended target audience* was for the amendment's message, and make *evaluations of the nature* of that message (or messages) within its *historical context*. Second, the student should probably be able *to apply* their understanding to some type of realistic example in which the amendment could be related. Doing so would go some distance in showing you how an understanding operated and how deep it ran. Thus, a performance of understanding should follow and provide some evidence of that depth.

The second pillar, observation, needs to follow from the first. In other words, you need to ask, what sort of task could I ask students to perform that would let them display the full nature of their understandings, ones I could carefully observe? Hints for this are embedded in the thinking that must be done. Students would need a task, in this particular case, that required them to read, analyze, think about the amendment's intentions, meanings, and target audiences, and the range of possible applications of the amendment. Then, they would need to describe that thinking so you could observe it.

The third pillar, interpretation, would require that you develop some scoring rubrics to gauge how well students (a) read, (b) analyzed (message, author, audience), (c) evaluated the message (or an example in which the message would apply) within its historical context, and (d) applied those cognitive capabilities to a particular case example in ways that showed understanding. In the best case scenario, the result would be a coherent student performance that addressed a pivotal question or questions in which the First Amendment would come into play. To gauge it would require at least four different rubric categories, one for each of (a) through (d).

Here is our suggestion for how to do all this. It's just one suggestion and you might find equally valuable but different assessment structures that mapped onto the three pillars. First, we would need a copy of the First Amendment and possibly a modern-day translation of it for the less-accomplished readers, who might struggle to make sense of the amendment as originally written. These would need to be situated on a page together and be made available to students while they undertook the task. The task would involve a contemporary scenario, such as the one Palmer discussed with students in class—the censoring of rap music and its "offensive" lyrics, coupled with a series of questions students must address, say on a sheet of paper (or on a handheld or Smartboard), as part of their performance. It all might look like the example in Box 6.1.

With some luck and preparation, students would be able to address each question in enough detail for you to apply some rubrics to their responses and obtain a good sense of what they knew and understood about the First Amendment. What would those rubrics look like?

To check for a degree of reading comprehension, there are a number of good rubrics available on the Internet (see the examples below). The same is

---

BOX 6.1 A FIRST AMENDMENT TASK

A group of concerned citizens in a small town called Atlas has decided that rap music lyrics are obscene and offensive to some people, and therefore the music with those lyrics should be banned in Atlas. They have hired a lawyer and are making their case in court. You have been chosen as a juror and must judge the case.

The citizens' lawyer argues that the music must be banned because it goes against the community's ideas about what is proper and acceptable speech. The lawyer defending rap music argues that the First Amendment guarantees free speech and protects the rights of the rappers to express themselves in whatever words they wish. The lawyer is asking jurors to dismiss the case.

Students: Please answer the following questions:

1 What is this trial all about? Explain in your own words.
2 Why is the citizen group upset about rap music?
3 Do you agree or not with the citizens' case against rap music? Say why or why not.
4 Do you agree or not that the First Amendment protects the rights of rappers to use whatever words they wish? Explain.
5 As a juror, how would you vote in this case? For citizens' rights to get rid of the use of bad language? Or for protecting the rights of rappers to use any words they wanted to use? Explain why you voted the way you did and use examples and details from the case to explain your ideas.

true for different ways of analyzing text. For example, the Smarter Balanced Assessment Consortium (SBAC, see www.smarterbalanced.org) has released both sample items and rubrics linked to reading and analyzing texts and the English Language Arts Common Core State Standards. These might be useful. Responses to questions 1 and 2 could be gauged by using these types of rubrics or modifications of them that you make.

RESOURCES: RUBRICS

The Internet has many resources for teachers who want to learn more about rubrics, examine samples, and create their own. A search for "building scoring rubrics" will yield a variety of options. Here are two:

- www.phy.ilstu.edu/ptefiles/311content/testconstruction/write_rubric.html
  This site provides ideas and information for creating scoring rubrics along with guidance on the characteristics of rubrics.

- http://landmark-project.com/classweb/tools/rubric_builder.php3
  This site allows you to generate your own rubrics for class assignments.

For understanding the First Amendment and its message in its historical context, you would need to develop your own rubric. Box 6.2 contains an example we would suggest. It would be applied especially to question 5. Here, the most established student responses would point out, as one example, that the authors of the First Amendment did not know anything about rap music. Yet, we in the present could evaluate the message of the amendment in such a way that we could apply the free-speech protections to rappers and their lyrical choices in the present, that the amendment could be applied even hundreds of years later.

BOX 6.2 RUBRIC: HISTORICAL CONTEXT

3	Full understanding of historical context; no evidence of presentism in making evaluations of the original message; but simultaneously able to see how it possibly could be applied to situations in the present such as the case example presented.
2	Evaluates message from a past context and a present one but not both at the same time as in a 3 response (see above).
1	Solely evaluated by present perspective, as though authors of the amendment wrote the message yesterday.
0	Does not evaluate message at all.
SCORE _____	

BOX 6.3 RUBRIC: APPLICATION TO A CASE EXAMPLE

4	Response displays understanding of the issues and characteristics of different sides of the case and the arguments made; clearly articulates why s/he takes the position s/he does; provides examples directly from the case and from applications of the amendment to the case.
3	Response displays understanding of the issues and characteristics of different sides of the case and the arguments made; clearly articulates why s/he takes the position s/he does; but does not provide examples directly from the case or from applications of the amendment to the case to justify or explain the position.
2	Response displays understanding of the issues and characteristics of different sides of the case and the arguments made; but does not articulate why s/he takes the position s/he does; nor does s/he provide examples directly from the case and from applications of the amendment to the case.
1	Response displays some understanding of different sides of the case and how the amendment may apply but does not go beyond that to explain, justify or use examples to demonstrate that understanding.
0	No response, confusing response, or very little display of understanding.

SCORE _____

In order to score the overall understanding a student might demonstrate regarding the First Amendment, the application of it to a case would need a rubric. Box 6.3 contains one that we would suggest. As before, however, you could build your own. You would use this rubric especially with questions 3, 4, and 5. In a most accomplished written response, there should some correspondence between scores across the three questions (consistent 3s and 4s).

The application of these kinds of rubrics can provide a good sense of the degree of understanding students have attained. The application to the case itself as represented by responses to question 5, for example, would be the most telling. If students are scoring at the low end of the rubric scale (averaging zeros or ones), then likely they have not understood the different sides of the case and/or how the First Amendment can be applied. Re-teaching would be in order. This is what we mean by a performance assessment holding diagnostic power, the sort that allows you to know something about what your students know and understand. Diagnostic power allows you to use assessment evidence to reshape your teaching practices and obtain better learning results with your students.

Chapter Summary

1   **What forms of assessment will I use to understand what my students have learned?** There are a variety of kinds of assessments that you can use, from formalized, paper-pencil versions you design to more informal strategies such as asking students questions as you proceed through a lesson. Such informal questions will require you to listen carefully to what your students are saying. We recommended that the more formal kinds of assessments be designed to allow your students to perform on what they know, to engage in a task that lets them show you their knowledge while they apply it to an authentic problem or a question.

2   **How can I create assessment tasks that let me get close to seeing whether learning is taking place or not?** We noted that creating such assessments begins with the cognition pillar of the three assessment pillars. We mean by this that you would first need to be very clear about the kinds of thinking and understanding of the social studies subject matter you wish to see them put on display. Knowing what that thinking and understanding looks like allows you to design assessment tasks or performances that permit your students to show you what they know and can do with that knowledge.

3   **How can I transform the assessment results into evidence that explains what's happening for my students?** If the tasks and performances you design are tightly linked to the ways you have taught your students to think and understand, students should readily supply you with examples (i.e., evidence) of their thinking and understanding. This can come in many forms: presentations, writing samples, reports, class discussions, responses to a K-W-L instrument, etc.

4   **What kinds of tools do I need to help me make the best sense I can of my students' learning process?** These tools are often called rubrics. Effectively they are assessment criteria that you can apply consistently to the evidence students give you of what they know and can do. We suggested a number of examples of such rubrics and noted a few good web-based sources to examine other variations.

Teaching Resources

Assessment ideas and strategies are all over the Internet these days, because it is such a hot topic. We recommend going to two websites that deal with current assessment issues in many different forms and exploring the offerings there:

■   www.ets.org
     This is the site of Educational Testing Service. For decades they have worked to develop cutting-edge assessment strategies for use in high-stakes testing contexts, but more recently they have also delved into performance-based assessments and identifying rubrics which can be used with them.

- www.smarterbalanced.org
  As we noted, these are the people (The Smarter Balanced Assessment Consortium) charged with building assessments that map onto the Common Core Standards. Explore their website to see what these latest developments look like.

For a handy print source that deals with the three assessment pillars, designs, strategies, examples, and rubrics applicable to history education and linked to Common Core State Standards in English/Language Arts and the C3, see:

VanSledright, B. (2014). *Assessing historical thinking and understanding: Innovative designs for new standards*. New York: Routledge.

The Classroom Environment
Creating a Genuine Community

We've covered a lot of territory thus far—ideas about learners and learning, subject matter, and now three chapters on teachers and teaching. What else is there to talk about? Well, hang on, for in one sense we are only part of the way there. Although creating question-based inquiries sensitive to all of your learners and your subject matter should make a difference in your learners' lives, encouraging the growth of democratic values and attitudes demands more (Hauver, 2019; Kahne & Sporte, 2008; Rubin, 2011). It goes by many names—classroom climate, atmosphere, milieu—but the point is that the classroom environment itself can have a dramatic effect on how diverse learners experience your class, on what they learn, and on the values and attitudes they develop.

In other words, if you want smart, thoughtful kids who also believe in justice, diversity, opportunity, and the like, you need to think hard about the full range of experiences they have in your classroom and school.

Classroom environment, the fourth commonplace, is a general term that describes the range of activity that occurs in a classroom. Part of that activity is instructional—issues of teaching, learning, and subject matter. Also important is the environment in which instruction takes place. That's a lot of territory, so, for simplicity's sake, we'll talk about three elements of environment: discourse, classroom organization, and dispositions.

Discourse refers to the nature of the talk that goes on in a classroom. For example, what patterns of interaction arise between teacher and learners? What kinds of questions are asked, who asks them, and what do the answers look like? Who decides what the classroom conversations will be?

Classroom organization refers to the ways in which we structure learning activities. For example, how are learners organized for teaching and learning, and who decides? What classroom rules are evident, and who chooses them?

Dispositions refer to those values and attitudes a teacher and her learners create and practice during classroom activity. For example, does the classroom climate reveal an honest respect for and commitment to inquiry? Open respect for and commitment to diverse ideas and people? Patient respect for and commitment to argument and evidence?

Attending to these elements is no easier than attending to the pedagogical plan, and it's every bit as important. Your learners will remember some part of the content you teach; they will remember much more about how your class *felt*—whether or not they all genuinely felt welcome, involved, and respected.

We want students to develop as thinkers and knowers; we also want them to develop as concerned, caring, and socially aware human beings. We can help them on both scores if we work to create genuine spaces where growth can happen.

In this chapter, we unpack the notion of classroom environment and construct an image of these genuine places through extended discussions of discourse, classroom organization, and dispositions. When you have completed this chapter, you should be able to answer the following questions:

1   What discourse, classroom organization, and dispositional patterns are found in traditional classroom environments?
2   What discourse, classroom organization, and dispositional patterns are found in genuine classroom communities?
3   What stakeholders are involved in the negotiation of a genuine classroom community?

The Complex Nature of Social Studies Classrooms

Let's be honest: Few classrooms reflect the kind of genuine classroom environment we envision. Too many are places where teachers try hard and kids try hard (sometimes), but where the classroom environment is a jumble of conflicting messages.

Consider this example from Carol Sheldon's fourth-grade class. Sheldon is teaching a unit on the geography of the United States in which she incorporates a literacy lesson calling for students to construct a story or poem:[1]

The class has been working on a textbook lesson on different uses of land and water resources. Before the students close their books, Sheldon directs their attention to the picture on the last page of the chapter. The picture depicts a harbor scene at dusk. Fishing and tourist boats are tied up to a dock; a large mountain looms in the background. No people appear in the picture.

While students look at the picture with various degrees of interest, Sheldon explains that they are to write a story or poem based on what they see. The assignment clearly excites a few learners; they immediately begin taking out pencil and paper and talking quietly, but enthusiastically, with their neighbors. Most, however, appear uninspired. They roll their eyes, shake their heads, groan. These protests escalate when Sheldon, perhaps feeling the need to raise the stakes, announces, "Maybe we'll have show and tell at the end. Maybe I'll have you go to the front of the room and read your story." She pauses, "That's what I'll do."

A chorus of complaints fill the room. Even some of the children who initially favored the assignment protest. When one student calls for a vote, several classmates come to his side. Calling for order, Sheldon declares, "No, there is no choice this time. There won't be any votes. We already voted once today (on a question involving playground equipment). We'll vote on something later today." As the class quiets, she explains, "You vote on the things you like, not on the things you don't." She pauses and smiles. "Besides, I know I'll get outvoted."

■■■■■ COMMONPLACE CONNECTION

- What does Sheldon seem to think is important about the *subject matter* of geography?

- What view of *learners* does she seem to hold?

- How would you characterize her *teaching*?

- How would you describe the *classroom environment*?

In terms of classroom environment, this is a complex case. Sheldon promotes creativity and freedom of expression when she gives students an open-ended writing assignment. She indicates that she values cooperation as well as individuality when she allows students to work with one another. Other elements are more complex, however.

Consider the mix of messages Sheldon sends around voting. In the playground equipment vote, she sends one message about learners' roles in decision making and majority rule. She sends quite another message in the issue of voting on the classroom assignment.

In the case of the playground equipment, Sheldon implies that because class members have a stake in the outcome, their voices and votes should be heard and counted. Taking a vote is not the only way of resolving such issues, but this is the approach Sheldon uses.

Rather than vote, the class might have devised a compromise that better satisfied all learners' desires. How the issue was resolved, however, seems less important than that the students themselves decided. That's a strong message about the environment of this classroom—the kind of talk, classroom rules, and values that are respected and encouraged.

▶︎|◀︎ REFLECTION: ALLOWING STUDENTS TO MAKE CHOICES

When students have the opportunity to make choices as a class, teachers often allow them to vote on a majority-wins basis. What are the benefits of this practice? What are the drawbacks? How can the diverse interests of the class be respected? How else might children make decisions?

▶︎|◀︎

Sheldon's message becomes muddied later in the day during the story-writing activity. This time the disagreement is over a classroom assignment rather than a playground activity, and the disagreement is between learners and their teacher rather than among classmates. Given the earlier episode, the students' call for a vote is hardly surprising. Sheldon's abrupt response is. In dismissing the call to vote, she not only entertains no alternatives to the assignment, she even seems to suggest that the only votes she is willing to endorse are those that have no real classroom consequence. Individual voice, free discussion, majority rule—all of these considerations fall by the wayside as Sheldon asserts the traditional teacher prerogative of just saying no.

Here's the tricky part: Sheldon had good reasons for her actions in both instances. Although dismissing the call to vote seems harsh, not every instructional decision can be decided by a vote. We do not fault Sheldon for asserting her authority.

We do question, however, the way she handled it, especially given the earlier vote. Two actions she might have taken could have moved the class along (presumably, her main intention) and preserved some of the good from the first incident. She might have explained that the class had to move on. Children understand that class discussion and decisions can take a lot of time and energy, and few would have begrudged their teacher's concern about time if she had explained it. She might also have put the voting idea aside in favor of exploring some alternative assignments. It's not clear why the learners were unenthusiastic about the original assignment, but Sheldon could have defused the situation by taking a few minutes to discuss alternatives and either have the class choose one or allow each student to choose for himself or herself.

Classroom life is often crazy: Teaching is not called the "impossible profession" (Cohen, 1989b) for nothing. Our purpose here is neither to make Carol Sheldon look silly nor to suggest that a teacher can always do the right thing if she thinks about it. Teaching is just not that simple.

Traditional Classroom Environments

The case of Carol Sheldon helps illustrate some of the perplexing issues that arise when one considers the classroom environment. Let's look deeper into those issues by exploring the kinds of discourse, classroom organization, and dispositions that exist in traditional American classrooms.

Discourse

In many classrooms, teachers talk and kids listen (or not). No big surprise there. Studies of who talks and how much yield consistent results: Teachers talk, by some estimates, more than 80 percent of the time (Brown & Campione, 2002; Wilen & White, 1991). When learners talk, they usually speak to a teacher, usually in response to a teacher's question, and usually briefly—a word or phrase at most.

Aside from procedural discourse (e.g., taking roll, giving directions), the prevailing pattern of "school talk" is **recitation**, which looks like this:

teacher Initiation—student Response—teacher Evaluation (**IRE**).

In short, the teacher asks a question, a student answers, and the teacher judges whether the answer is right or wrong. We have already seen several examples of this kind of interaction. Recall this exchange from the first lesson on US government in Sandra Prosy's fifth-grade classroom from Chapter 4:

PROSY: What kind of government do you think we will talk about?
ANGELA: Public schools?
RASHONA: City?
PROSY: Who runs the city?
MICHAEL: The mayor?

Prosy writes *city* on the board and asks, "Who is the mayor?" A girl calls out, "Luciano." Prosy nods and writes *Luciano* on the board. "What other kinds of government are there? What other areas need to be run?" she asks.

DEION: Community.
TINA: State.
PROSY: Yes, what state?
MICHELLE: New York.
PROSY: Who runs our state?
TOM: The governor.

Prosy nods and writes *state*, *governor*, and *Cuomo* (the current New York governor) on the board. As she does, a boy calls out, "What about county?" Prosy says, "Well, yes, but I'm looking for something that starts with an F." A girl guesses, "Federal?" Prosy responds, "Right. And who runs the federal government?" A boy offers, "Rush Limbaugh!" while the rest of the class shouts out, "Donald Trump!"

In Chapter 4, we looked at this vignette in terms of the ideas represented. Here, we return to it as a means of exploring traditional classroom discourse. It is a classic case of the IRE (initiation–response–evaluation) pattern so long a part of US schools (Wilen & White, 1991). Prosy asks the questions: What kind of government do you think we will talk about? Who runs the city? Who is the mayor? Learners answer them: public schools/city; mayor; Luciano. And Prosy evaluates the responses; she nods, says "right," records the answer on the board, or goes on to the next question. So dominant is this form of talk that even primary-grade children can mimic it with ease (Edwards & Westgage, 1987).

But *who talks and how much* is just one component of classroom discourse. A second component emphasizes *classroom questions*: the kinds of questions asked, who asks them, and what the responses look like.

Again, we see no surprises here. Most of the questions asked (upwards of 80 percent in some studies) look like those above—knowledge or fact-level questions to which learners spit back a remembered piece of information (Brophy & Alleman, 2008; Cuban, 1991). Make no mistake: Memory and facts are useful. Humans could not think if they had no memories, and facts bundled together represent the stuff of thinking—ideas. Still, if we only ask low-level questions, we're likely to get only low-level thinking.

Traditional teachers ask the vast majority of questions. In such classrooms, students learn quickly that factual knowledge counts, and so when they do ask questions, their questions tend to look like their teachers'. Questions that probe deeper sometimes become the basis for interesting conversations. More often than not, however, they are perceived by teachers as either "off the subject" or, as in the case above of the boy's question about county government, they are brushed aside. If one sign of a diverse classroom is the range of questions students pose, traditional classroom discourse rarely meets that criterion.

One last element of classroom discourse concerns the nature of *classroom conversations*. Most classrooms are teacher-centered, which means the teacher, like Sandra Prosy above, controls the substance, form, and duration of classroom talk. In other words, the teacher determines what the students talk about, how they talk about it, and how long they talk about it. Learners participate, but their participation is passive—listening, for the most part, and talking only when spoken to.

▶|◀ REFLECTION: CLASSROOM DISCOURSE

> Think about the kinds of discourse you have experienced. How did you feel in classrooms where the discourse was strongly teacher-centered? How did you feel in classrooms where students were encouraged to be actively involved in the discourse?
>
>

Pretty bleak, eh? Such traditional classrooms remind us of old factory scenes where workers do their jobs in drone-like fashion overseen by supervisors whose primary concern is getting the work done efficiently. Few classrooms are quite this bad, but the notion of school as a factory, a place where teachers and learners march through their work, has a long tenure. In fact, Marshall (1990) argues that the "workplace metaphor" is so strongly held that "we hardly notice this root metaphor when teachers talk about 'homework' or 'seatwork' or tell students to 'get back to work' or grade them on 'work habits'" (p. 94). As workers, then, it is the learner's job to accumulate as much knowledge as possible in the shortest period of time. Teachers are the supervisors who push learners to work harder and test them to see if they have succeeded. And the work itself? In reading, it is breaking words into syllables and building oral fluency; in mathematics, it is practicing algorithms; and in social studies, it is gathering facts. (The factory model of schooling also gives us school buildings that look like industrial plants and bells that divide up the workday and keep teachers and students moving efficiently through the halls.)

It may not be fair to lay the prevalence of recitation solely at the feet of the factory model. After all, the notion of education as teachers asking questions and students answering them is at least as old as the ancient Greeks. Nor is there anything particularly wrong with recitation-style discourse per se. But when the factory model of schooling becomes linked with views such as the behaviorist model of learning (Chapter 2), teaching and learning become staid and formulaic. When classroom discourse never pushes beyond mere fact gathering and recitation, problems surface.

Organization

When we think about traditional classrooms, our first image is of teachers talking and students listening. The second is of students sitting in long rows, in individual seats, working quietly on individual assignments. Let us explore another element of classroom environment by looking at:

- how classroom activities are organized;
- how classroom rules support traditional instruction.

The influence of behavioral theory and the factory model of schooling is not limited to classroom discourse. The assembly line—where workers work silently on individual, repetitive tasks—is an American idea. (Quick—who invented this manufacturing approach? Henry Ford? Yes. See, knowing facts can come in handy!) Only recently have American industrialists learned what the Japanese have known for some time—that people working together produce more and often better products than they do as individuals.

Transferring this model to the classroom, traditional teachers *organize their instruction* such that learners spend a good part of the day working quietly at their desks on individual assignments. Doing so provides a means of determining the quantity and quality of each child's output and a way of managing rambunctious children's behavior. Quiet classrooms where learners studiously do their lessons become the model of good teaching and learning. And, as we saw in Chapter 6, standardized tests can reinforce this model.

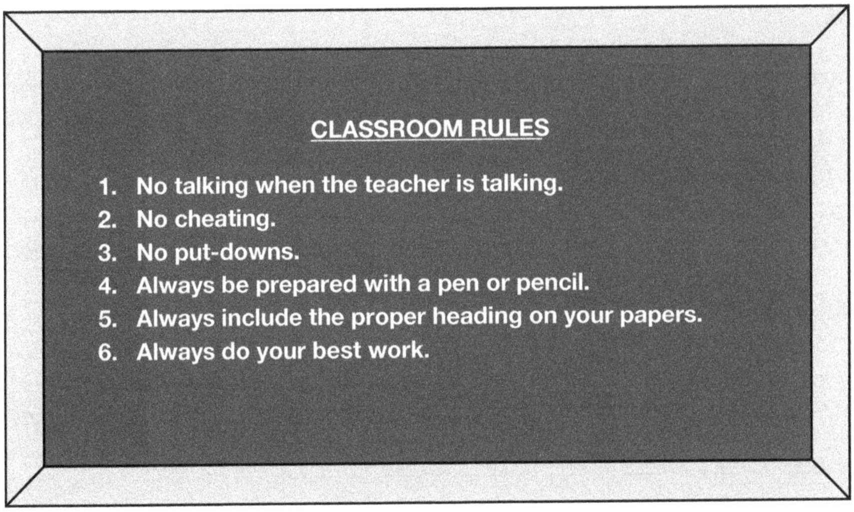

CLASSROOM RULES

1. No talking when the teacher is talking.
2. No cheating.
3. No put-downs.
4. Always be prepared with a pen or pencil.
5. Always include the proper heading on your papers.
6. Always do your best work.

FIGURE 7.1 Rules in the traditional classroom.

Quiet classrooms are still the norm. Many teachers report getting nervous when they schedule group work for fear that their principal or their peers will perceive their class as too loud, off task, or out of control. These teachers typically avoid potential problems by arranging the instructional day around individual assignments that learners do quietly at their desks.

Classroom rules often reinforce the instructional message of quiet, efficient, and individual work. Walking into most traditional classrooms, one inevitably sees a list of rules posted. Many look like the one in Figure 7.1.

Such rules are almost always developed by teachers, and they send strong messages about proper classroom behavior. The sentiments behind admonitions about not putting classmates down and encouragement to do one's best work seem sound, but think about the messages some of the other rules imply. Although classroom rules about being prepared and including proper headings urge students to be responsible and ready to work, such exhortations recall factory rules that tied workers to their tools and closely prescribed and governed their behavior. Rules about no talking and no cheating send even stronger messages. Both rules have long histories in US classrooms that blessed quiet, individual work. The messages are clear: Learners can talk only when their teacher allows them to, and talking to one another is discouraged.

Of course, sometimes teachers need to talk and children need to listen, and sometimes teachers must assess each learner's individual work. These are normal parts of classroom life. But we believe that's all they should be—*parts* of classroom life—actions that arise when necessary. That's much different from *rules* that imply an expectation of every day and every situation. A few classroom rules are probably helpful (especially if they come from the students in the class), but think carefully about the messages that any set of rules send.

Dispositions

The third element of classroom environment looks at dispositions, those *values and attitudes* a teacher and her learners create and practice throughout the school day.

The factory model of schooling promotes a consistent set of dispositions. One is the value of hard work, the notion that learners benefit from diligence and persistence in completing their assignments. A second disposition is efficiency, which emphasizes working quickly, quietly, and without distraction. A third disposition is deference to authority. The traditional classroom has only one power or authority, the teacher. Learners are expected to do as they are told and to ask questions only about those things that interfere with their individual learning. One last disposition is a focus on external rather than internal rewards. Motivating learners, in this view, is a matter of creating the right incentives—praise, grades, promotion. Internal rewards—joy from learning something new, satisfaction from overcoming a problem—are nice, but only explicit rewards produce consistent effort.

Given the world of possibilities, it is hard to argue with any of these values. In fact, none are problematic in and of themselves. Even the goal they support—the efficient acquisition of knowledge—has its purpose. That said, we think this goal expresses a pretty thin view of teaching and learning. We can, and must, do more if all our learners are to be engaged and to succeed.

Few classrooms combine the worst of these features. Moreover, some of these ideas, such as the disposition to work hard, are well worth cultivating. The challenge is for you as a teacher to think carefully about the messages you send through the discourse, classroom organization, and dispositions you create and support.

We have spent time defining the traditional classroom environment because none of us can know where we are going until we understand where we have been. We see elements of these classrooms that are worth keeping, but we also know we can do better. One way to do better is by working toward the notion of a genuine classroom community.

■ SECTION SUMMARY:
Traditional Classroom Environments

- The standard pattern of discourse in traditional classrooms is recitation (initiation, response, evaluation), in which teachers typically control the nature of the classroom conversation.

- Traditional classroom organization favors quiet, individual work.

- The chief dispositions found in traditional classrooms include hard work, efficiency, deference to authority, and external rewards.

The Promise of Genuine Classroom Communities

Those who advocate changes in the classroom lives of teachers and learners often focus on curriculum, teaching methods, assessment, and the like, yet attention to classroom environment is growing.

That attention goes by many names—"learning communities" (Johnson, Johnson, & Holubec, 2009), "democratic classrooms" (Bickmore, 2008; Wood, 1990), and "just communities" (Kubelick, 1982; McDonough, 2005). Our notion of a genuine classroom community shares many characteristics with these models—commitment to inquiry, cooperative learning, democratic values, respectfulness, and trust. Where we differ is that we believe the teaching and learning of social studies is intricately linked to the classroom environment. These other models tend to focus on the environment and either ignore the teaching and learning of subject matter or treat teaching and learning as a generic activity. That's a mistake. Remember, the commonplaces—learning, teaching, subject matter, and environment—must be seen as interactive, each supporting and extending the others. That's the goal in creating a *genuine classroom community*—ambitious teaching that is sensitive to the needs of learners and the subject matter and that occurs in classrooms where discourse, classroom organization, and dispositions encourage the development of thoughtful, caring, and socially aware human beings.

How do you get there? A genuine classroom community is not something one develops by checking off items on a list, and it's not something one achieves once and then never has to worry about again. We can offer some insights into what a genuine community looks like and how to build one. The hard work of constantly working toward that goal, however, is yours.

Teachers who try to understand what their learners know and can do, who develop and teach ideas and questions, and who use an array of teaching approaches, materials, and assessments will inevitably, we believe, establish classroom climates that are significantly different from the traditional norm. In the following sections we use the constructs of discourse, classroom organization, and dispositions to illustrate what we mean by a genuine classroom community.

Discourse

The talk between teachers and learners and among learners sounds different in a genuine classroom. Consider this example from Suzanne Wilson's diverse, urban third-grade class as they explore the purpose, meaning, and construction of maps:[2]

> While working on a class book about the school, Wilson plans three weeks of work with maps. Rather than distribute completed maps, however, she prepares learners to construct maps of the classroom by asking them how

they might use graph paper to aid their work. Several children note that the linoleum floor is made of square tiles and, after counting them, that the classroom is forty squares wide and fifty squares long. Some conclude that they could mark off the requisite number of squares on their graph paper to mark the boundaries of the room. Wilson next asks what features of the classroom might be included in the maps. The list—student and teacher desks, flagpole, bookcases, rugs, and chalkboards—goes on the board. With that, students begin work on their individual maps while Wilson circulates around the classroom asking questions and probing each learner's understanding of what he or she is doing.

After a couple of days and uneven results, Wilson starts a class discussion with a question "What makes drawing a map hard?" The question falls flat as most of the students sit silently. Wilson surmises that those learners who had drawn pictures of the classroom rather than maps simply do not see anything hard about that and therefore see no substance behind the question. She has more luck the next day with the question "What is the difference between a map and picture?" The lively discussion that follows produces a range of hypotheses. Some, such as the idea that maps have keys, are agreed on, while others, such as the idea that pictures are colored and maps are not, are dropped. To test students' developing ideas, Wilson picks up Mary's carefully delineated drawing and asks, "Is this a map or a picture?" When disagreement ensues, Wilson asks, "How can we decide?"

Several students call out, "Let's try to find something!" Sean suggests trying to locate the rug. Agreeing, Wilson asks the class to count the number of squares (fifteen) on Mary's map from the front of the room to the edge of the rug. Eileen then counts the number of floor tiles and announces a match—Mary's drawing, the class agrees, is a map. Melissa's freewheeling drawing is evaluated next. The test—to locate the bookcase—is unsuccessful and the class decides Melissa has drawn a picture instead of a map. The third trial features Ned's drawing. Wilson describes what happened as follows:

> Ned's depiction of the classroom was smaller than Mary's, but my class was sure that it too was a map because they could find things. However, instead of being fifty by forty squares, Ned's map was only twenty-five by twenty squares. "How can this be a map," I asked the class, "when he has twenty-five squares between the front and the back of the room, and there are fifty tiles on the floor?" [After a long discussion] Katharine stood and stated, "If you divide fifty by two, you get twenty-five. I think he made every square two tiles instead of one." Ned nodded smugly. My heart smiled, for I had witnessed the birth of the idea of scale.
>
> (Wilson, 1990, p. 9)

■ ■ ▨ ▨ COMMONPLACE CONNECTION

- ■ What does Wilson seem to think is important about the *subject matter* of mapmaking?
- ■ What view of *learners* does she seem to hold?
- ■ How would you characterize her *teaching*?
- ■ How would you describe the *classroom environment*?

Some observers would object: Surely, Wilson could have saved a great deal of time and frustration by simply describing the concept of scale and having students practice on worksheets. Perhaps, but Wilson's class is directly inquiring about a profound geographic construct. Rather than receiving information, these kids are co-constructing the meaning of scale as they make their diverse views public. Doing so may take more time, but it cannot help but be more powerful than a worksheet approach. And this happens, in large part, because of the way Wilson helps shape the classroom discourse. There is no IRE interaction here where the teacher merely checks to see whether the kids have the same knowledge in their heads that she does. Instead, Wilson uses questions to frame the discussion and her third graders carry the conversation. Moreover, it is a student, Katharine, who observes and describes the key point—Ned's use of scale. Wilson is clearly the teacher in the classroom, but her willingness to share the floor with her learners sends strong messages about the importance of divergent ideas and listening to everyone's voice.

Discourse looks different in a genuine classroom. This is not to say that traditional forms of lecture and recitation are never appropriate. At times, teachers need to transmit basic information to the class and to check students' understanding of basic facts. In those instances, lectures and recitations are in order. The point is that, in a genuine classroom, the discourse frequently moves beyond facts and teacher-centered talk. Wilson is trying to teach her learners about a vital concept—scale. In doing so, however, she keeps two key points in mind. One is that it's better to work with the complexity of the idea than to avoid it. The other is that learners need to make their understandings their own. In using questions and in sharing the talk with her students, Wilson promotes an environment that supports these two points well.

Organization

If discourse is different in genuine classrooms, so too is *classroom organization.* Teaching with ideas and questions demands new kinds of talk and new ways of organizing learning activities and of using classroom rules to support those activities. In traditional classrooms, the demands of keeping learners quiet and on task drive the manner in which activities are structured and classroom rules are developed and enacted. In genuine classrooms, ideas and questions drive activities and rules.

Organizing Classroom Activities around Ideas

In Suzanne Wilson's classroom, we see the power of interweaving individual and whole-class activities. She initiates the unit on mapmaking with a whole-class discussion of how to draw a map of the classroom. Two key aspects of maps surface in the ensuing conversation. One is the notion of size and shape. Students quickly realize that their classroom is rectangular and can be measured by counting the number of floor tiles from front to back and from side to side. Representing the size and shape of objects is a key feature of mapmaking, although it is one that teachers often take for granted.

The second aspect of mapmaking that emerges is the array of objects to include and their relationship to one another. Think about it. No map can include everything, so cartographers must choose what to incorporate and what to omit. Wilson's third graders are no different. For example, some decide to locate their desks but not their chairs; others decide to locate the bookcases but not the individual books. They show a diversity of approaches because the teacher is allowing them to do so.

From the whole-class discussion, Wilson asks students to create individual maps. She often has them work as partners or in small groups but, in this case, we suspect she wants to see how each learner understands the task of mapmaking, especially in light of the preceding discussion. This assignment functions both

FIGURE 7.2 How does this student's drawing of his town fit with the research (described in Chapter 2) on students' understanding of geography?

as a piece of instruction and as an assessment of what each child can do at that point in time.

As so often happens when one assesses, Wilson learns that her students know and can do different things. Some, like Mary and Ned, produce relatively accurate representations of the classroom. Others, like Melissa, do not. Wilson might pull aside Melissa and the others whose drawings look more like pictures than maps for a mini-lesson on mapmaking. Sensing, however, that the whole class would benefit, she asks two questions. The first, "What makes drawing a map hard?" falls flat; the second, "What is the difference between a map and picture?" makes more sense to students and sparks a lively discussion whereby they can test their ideas using classmates' drawings. Out of that discussion comes yet another key geographic concept, the idea of scale.

ENCOURAGING INQUIRY

Early elementary teachers rarely worry about encouraging their children to talk about their ideas; thoughts of all kinds tend to fill the air in most K–2 classrooms. Older students can be more reserved, especially as concerns about getting the "right answer" begin to surface. Although no teacher wants students to come away with inaccurate information, too much stress on right answers alone can stifle children's thinking and undercut efforts to build tolerance for diverse views.

Good teachers distinguish between situations that require factual recitation and those where hunches, conjectures, or guesses are appropriate. In the latter, teachers help students open up their thinking by encouraging divergent ideas and perspectives. Help your students develop and make public their emerging insights by giving them frequent opportunities to brainstorm ideas.

By weaving whole-class and individual activities together, Wilson provides opportunities for learners to try out new ideas individually and with their peers. She might have used other work arrangements such as small groups and partners, but, given her purposes and her sense of her learners, her decisions make considerable sense.

Using Classroom Rules to Support Instruction

Wilson's example helps us understand one more point about the organization of a genuine classroom community, and that involves the kinds of rules or norms that govern this classroom. We don't know what expectations Wilson and her class talked about at the beginning of the school year, but we can infer some of the norms that govern this class, and they seem decidedly different from those common to traditional classrooms.

First, we sense that talk is important—it appears to be a fundamental way of exploring, developing, and negotiating meaning in this classroom. We wouldn't expect Wilson to spend much time scolding her students to be quiet. We expect that she agrees with the traditional norm of no put-downs or meanness between students. It's also clear, however, that she values ideas and she knows that talk may not always be comfortable. Take the case of Melissa and her drawing. Some might worry about showing the girl's sketch, which was clearly not a map. Wilson acknowledges that she chose Melissa's paper deliberately:

> I selected Melissa's on purpose—she had drawn hers freehand, and for a key she had drawn a picture of a house key. Melissa is a smart but lazy student who has been testing my limits. I chose her picture because I thought that she, rather than being devastated by a decision that she had not drawn a map, would pick up the gauntlet and prove that she too could draw one.
>
> (Wilson, 1990, p. 9)

Wilson has two ideas in mind here. On the one hand, she wants the class to see and discuss an example of a picture, as opposed to a map. On the other hand, she wants to challenge Melissa to raise the level of her work. Rather than trying to be mean or expose the girl to ridicule, Wilson believes that the frank examination and discussion of Melissa's work will benefit both Melissa and the class. Talk is an important feature of teaching and learning, and Wilson encourages norms about talk that promote multiple goals.

Second, we suspect Wilson and her third graders think more in terms of sharing than of cheating. We don't know for sure, but we suspect considerable sharing of ideas and approaches occurs while the students work on their individual maps. If so, the possibility exists that one or more children simply copied the work of another without any learning. We think two factors undercut that possibility. One is that Wilson does not sit at her desk while the class works. Instead, she circulates throughout the room, continually stopping to examine and to ask questions about each learner's work. The second mitigating factor is that learning in this classroom is less about getting work done and more about exploring and refining what one knows and can do. To that end, Wilson knows that some of the most important learning that transpires in classrooms is between learners. As a result, she promotes the norm of working together as a means of helping all students learn.

Finally, we sense that Wilson is not much concerned about the nit-picky details that sometimes consume traditional teachers, such as putting proper headings on papers. Maintaining a certain level of structure is important in every class, and we expect Wilson's is no different, but as we see in the vignettes, most important are the multiple, varied, and sustained opportunities children get to work with ideas.

►I◄ REFLECTION: SETTING RULES IN THE CLASSROOM

Wilson has rules for her classroom, but they are not listed anywhere. How might these tacit rules have been made more explicit? Why might Wilson not post a list of rules?

In genuine classrooms, learners and activities take myriad shapes across the school day, and those few rules that do exist encourage rather than discourage a richly diverse and lively atmosphere. These are important qualities, ones that transform a classroom where children simply put their time into one where ideas live and breathe because of the multiple opportunities learners have to engage them.

USING CLASSROOM RULES TO SUPPORT INSTRUCTION

Should you decide to develop a list of classroom rules governing students' classroom behavior, we would encourage you to make this a class discussion and decision. A rule such as "No put-downs" carries much more meaning when it comes from students themselves. Just as important as rules concerning behavior, we think, are rules that support the kind of teaching and learning envisioned in genuine classrooms. You might create this list of rules yourself, but we have another suggestion:

- Soon after the start of the school year, engage your class in a discussion in which you think all or most students will participate. The topic matters less than the opportunity created for everyone to participate.
- Assuming that the discussion goes well, encourage the children to identify features that helped make the conversation work. Examples might include instances where one student tried to understand another's perspective, where all or most students were actively listening, where a student constructively challenged another's point of view.
- Make a list of these actions and decide, with the students, what to call them. Some possibilities include "Our learning rules," "Rules for how we learn," or "How to help everyone be smarter."
- Add to and modify this list each time an activity goes well.

IN YOUR CLASSROOM

Dispositions

Like discourse and organization, *dispositions* are different in genuine classrooms. Dispositions are those values and attitudes teachers and learners work toward that contribute to learners' development as thoughtful adults. A list of those dispositions would be long indeed. Justice, inquiry, freedom, fairness … the list could go on and on. Instead, we collapse that list into three groupings:

- respect for and commitment to inquiry;
- respect for and commitment to ideas and people;
- respect for and commitment to argument and evidence.

These three sets of ideas reflect the values and attitudes we believe are both important and possible in real school classrooms.

As the context for a discussion of these dispositions, let's return to Suzanne Wilson's third-grade classroom. In another set of lessons, Wilson's students try to figure out how the state capital came to be located in Lansing. Students fill the air with possibilities, but when Susie volunteers that it made sense to locate the capital in Lansing, "'cause it's kind of in the middle," Matthew scoffs. "It's not in the middle of the state," he laughs. "Haven't you ever looked at a map?"

Wilson points out that Matthew is correct; if one looks at a map of Michigan that includes the Upper Peninsula, Lansing is nowhere near the middle of the state. (If one considers only the Lower Peninsula, however, Susie's observation makes more sense.) Wilson, however, wants to support Susie's contribution and keep open the classroom conversation. Sensing that Matthew's derisive tone might discourage the offering of other ideas, Wilson subtly reproves him: "We're just making guesses right now, Matthew. Anything goes. Later we'll find out which of our guesses were right." She adds, "Any other reasons why Lansing might be the capital?"

Respect for and Commitment to Inquiry

One disposition found in genuine classrooms is an open *respect for and commitment to inquiry*. If education is about people and ideas, it's also about asking questions and exploring alternative answers. **Inquiry**—the passion for pulling ideas apart and putting them back together—drives learning.

Ideas have power, but that power goes unrealized unless teachers and learners read and think, discuss and argue, compromise and disagree, ask questions, answer them, and then ask and answer them anew. We hear a lot of talk about active learning today. Some people mistakenly believe this means that learners are active only when they are doing something with their hands, feet, and bodies. Active learning, however, is as much about cognition and inquiry as it is about physical activity.

In the vignette above, we see the importance Wilson attaches to inquiry. Although it is convoluted, the "answer" to the question of why Lansing is the

FIGURE 7.3 When trying to figure out why a lesson is not going as you planned, don't neglect an important source of information: your students!

capital of Michigan has something to do with land speculation, bogus maps, and some political wheeling and dealing. Wilson and her learners can develop the complete picture in due time. What is important at this point, Wilson explains, is generating possibilities. She knows that, although her students live in Lansing, few have given much thought to what a capital is and what it represents. She uses the children's developing interest in why Lansing is the capital as a means of generating interest in the larger and more complex issues of government, decision-making, politics, and power. By reminding Matthew that their purpose was to make guesses, Wilson keeps the question open and the ideas flowing.

Respect for and Commitment to Ideas and People

A second important disposition is an honest *respect for and commitment to ideas and people*. We believe, as Hawkins (1974) does, that education is about bringing together people (the "I" and "Thou") and ideas (the "It"). Teachers and learners should hold values and attitudes that promote the power of ideas and the right of individuals to hold diverse perspectives. We are all individuals, and we have a right to hold our own particular views.

But we are also social beings. Classroom groups—whether the whole class, a small work group, or a pair of classmates—have a responsibility to hear and try to understand one another's views, different though they may be. Each member also must understand that holding a perspective confers no special privilege to be mean or inconsiderate to others.

IN YOUR CLASSROOM

DRAWING OUT CHILDREN'S IDEAS

Drawing out children's ideas, especially if they are not fully formed, is not easy. Self-conscious and timid students often remain silent for fear of embarrassment, but even confident children may be quiet if an easy answer is not apparent. Good teachers have a repertoire of questions at hand with which to prompt and encourage students' participation, such as:

- Can you say more about that?
- Can you give me an example?
- Who can add to what has been said?
- Are there any other ways to think about that idea?

In Suzanne Wilson's third-grade classroom, we see a teacher who deftly demonstrates the balance between respect for ideas and for people. Wilson knows that, in some sense, both Susie and Matthew are right in their ideas about Lansing. She accepts both, sensing that each, in turn, should be useful as the class continues to wrestle with this issue. At the same time, however, she clearly disapproves of Matthew's mocking approach in making his point. She knows that students need to feel safe in offering their ideas and that Matthew's behavior may undercut less confident students' willingness to share their thoughts. Think about how she admonishes Matthew, however. Wilson knows that Matthew's words are unhelpful, but she also knows that he's a third grader and that he's still learning how to respect and talk about the ideas of others. Rather than come down hard on the boy, Wilson firmly but gently explains to Matthew that all ideas are acceptable at this point. And though directed at Matthew, Wilson expects her point to resonate throughout the class: We're here to wrestle with hard ideas, but we'll do so thoughtfully and respectfully. As school classrooms become more diverse in terms of race, religion, and ethnicity, respect for ideas and people becomes even more important because it builds trust and trust is crucial to building safe communities.

Respect for and Commitment to Argument and Evidence

Among many other possible dispositions, we believe teachers and learners in genuine classrooms hold one in particular: patient *respect for and commitment to argument and evidence.*

RESOURCES: COMMON CORE–ENGLISH LANGUAGE ARTS

The notion of students making arguments and supporting them with evidence is a big part of the Common Core–English Language Arts standards.

www.corestandards.org/ELA-Literacy

Check out the standards to see how the authors talk about the idea of arguments and evidence.

Sometimes you'll want your learners to begin exploring an idea simply by talking to one another. Other times, you'll want them to brainstorm, a form of inquiry that emphasizes generating as many ideas as possible. Still other times, you'll want learners to be more systematic in their thinking. One key to systematic thinking is the notion of **argument**. Argument, in this sense, is the ability to make a series of claims that build to a reasonable conclusion. **Evidence** is the support one calls on for those claims.

After the brainstorming activity described above, Wilson and her students compare their initial ideas with the resources available as they attempt to construct a satisfactory answer to the question of why Lansing is the capital of Michigan. In the course of their deliberations, students consider whether Detroit would have been a better capital site (rejected ultimately because, at the time, it was too close to French settlements in Canada), whether it should be where other important institutions are located (for example, the state prison and the University of Michigan), and why it might be advantageous to locate a state capital near the geographic center of a state. After considering all the arguments and the evidence behind them, Wilson asks the class to compose letters to then-Governor Greeley making a case for Lansing as the best site for the new capital.

Wilson (1990) notes that Katharine's account is "more sophisticated" than those the class read during their investigation. Her account also demonstrates that Katharine and her peers are "capable of complicated thinking and critical analysis." No one would expect these third graders to handle the full complexity of this issue. Clearly, however, they are on their way to the adult process of making arguments and supporting them. (We have a lot more to say about the

Common Core–English Language Arts in general and arguments and evidence in particular in Chapter 8.)

Actively pursued, the dispositions described above—respect for and commitment to inquiry, ideas and people, and argument and evidence—should help your learners become smarter, more thoughtful, and more reflective people. They should also help your learners become more mindful, responsible, and socially aware members of society.

These dispositions promote a view of the "good citizen" different from the one that emerges from the traditional classroom. There, the emphasis is on passive, respectful obedience. Certainly, there is nothing wrong with obeying laws, respecting authorities, and trying to get along. If we lived in a perfectly just society, that view would probably suffice. But we don't, and while being passive is one way to deal with problems, there are others. In our view, the good citizen is one who embodies the dispositions we describe above. (We discuss the notion of good citizenship more fully in Chapter 9.)

Before this chapter, we focused on the academic side of schooling—the teaching, learning, and subject matter of social studies. Although these elements are important, so too are the less apparent but equally consequential elements of classroom life—discourse, classroom organization, and dispositions. We have talked about those elements by sketching two noticeably different classroom environments, traditional and genuine. As a prospective teacher, you will choose what kind of classroom environment you and your learners will work toward. The traditional classroom may not inspire many learners, but it will be familiar to them and to you. The genuine classroom has the potential to inspire learners, but it demands a lot more work from everyone. Clearly, we believe the extra work is worth it. We hope you do too.

■ SECTION SUMMARY:
GENUINE CLASSROOM COMMUNITIES

- *Discourse* in genuine classrooms is framed by big questions and inquiry, and students play an active role in the conversation.

- In genuine classrooms, ideas drive the *classroom organization* of activities and rules.

- *The dispositions* in a genuine classroom include respect for and commitment to inquiry, ideas and people, and argument and evidence.

How to Know Whether You're Getting There

The image described in the preceding sections is just that—a picture of what a genuine classroom might look like. Images or pictures are important, for they illustrate possibilities, but they can't tell you how to get there. Moreover, once you think you're there, an image can't tell you how to stay there. We'd love to whip out a list of sure-fire dos and don'ts, a prescription for, or a road map to, Genuineville, USA. Instead, we offer some ideas based on our collective experience and that of the several hundred preservice and practicing teachers we have known.

Sometimes it's easy to know whether your classroom is a genuine one:

- A girl approaches you after class one day and says, "You know, I used to hate social studies, but that thing we did in class today wasn't too bad."
- During parent–teacher conferences, a parent "complains" that his child wants him to start buying the newspaper because of the current event issues you and the students have been discussing in class.
- You see kids who seemed to hate each other earlier in the year now hanging out together after working on a group project.
- A boy who hasn't said anything all year offers a comment, asks a question, or does a piece of a group presentation … and he smiles.

These snapshots may reflect little more than moments in time, yet they speak volumes about what is happening in your classroom. In the first instance, the girl is telling you that you've made this subject, social studies, attention-worthy. In kid-talk, if something "isn't too bad," then it's pretty good! In the second case, the parent is saying that his child's interest in the world has so expanded that he wants to read for himself about the events of the day. The child's emerging questions have been validated and given importance, yielding a burst of curiosity. The third situation reveals the big impact you have had on how children view themselves and others and the importance of giving them opportunities to interact with a range of peers. And the last image is one teachers tend to carry around with them for weeks, months, and even years—that time when your patient efforts paid off, and the child you always worried about began stepping out on his own.

You will have many of these moments in your career. They are **psychic rewards,** the gratification teachers experience when they believe that they have positively influenced a learner, which many teachers say mean far more to them than, for example, their principal's yearly evaluation (Lortie, 1975). These moments should confirm your sense that you are doing something right, that learners are benefiting from your teaching and from the classroom environment you are building.

RESOURCES: TALKING WITH OTHER TEACHERS

Check out this site for teacher-developed ideas on classroom management:

- www.weareteachers.com/classroom-management-ideas-resource-guide/

This American Psychological Association site offers a nice array of ideas related to classroom management:

■ www.apa.org/education/k12/classroom-mgmt.aspx

You will have moments of doubt, anxiety, and concern, moments where you *think* that what you are doing makes sense and has value, but the class reactions make you wonder. What do you do? Proceed as if nothing is wrong and hope the kids "get it" later? Switch to a new topic, activity, or instructional approach? Let the kids go to gym early? Give them a quiz? At any particular time, you might do any of these.

We have an additional suggestion: Sometimes, it makes sense just to stop and ask the class what's going on. Doing so sends several important messages.

First, it shows that you care enough about the students' learning to halt the lesson and make sure that they are with you. Good teachers may not worry about their learners being confused and uncertain at particular points in a lesson because they know that greater clarity is around the bend. If that is not the case, however, stopping the lesson tells the class that your purpose is not simply to cover material, but to help them learn and understand. Second, stopping a lesson shows you trust and value what learners think. Although children are not always able to articulate what they are confused or uncertain about, when they do, their insights can prove invaluable. We are reminded of a teacher who, frustrated that her learners did not seem to know or care much about the material at hand, said, "Let's stop here and try to figure what's going on." Five minutes later she understood: The children lacked the necessary background knowledge she assumed they had acquired during the previous year. She learned differently when a student said, "Mrs. Thomas, you're acting like we know what you're talking about, but we don't." She reconsidered what the class needed to learn, made adjustments in her unit and lesson plans, and found the students much more cooperative and engaged.

Not all such incidents have happy endings, but many do. The constant and complex challenges teachers face drive some away after a year or so. Most, however, find those challenges endlessly interesting and the headaches and heartaches well worth the costs.

Negotiating the Genuine Classroom Community

Before we leave the subject of classroom environment, we want to remind you that you're not alone in there. As the discussion above suggests, classroom atmospheres are negotiated (Grant, 1996; VanSledright, 2002). Your stake in that negotiation is important, and much that you do will shape the classroom environment. But other stakeholders' needs and interests, to one degree or another, can also influence the kind of classroom environment that develops. Those stakeholders include:

- students
- parents
- principals and teacher colleagues
- district-level actors
- state departments of education.

Students

One large group of stakeholders is your *students*. Like you, students have a big investment in the kind of classroom that emerges. Nothing good will happen without at least their tacit consent and cooperation. This point is tricky for two reasons. First, although you might expect otherwise, learners may balk in their first encounters with your overtures toward building a genuine classroom. Instead of enthusiastically engaging in real discussions, classroom rule-making, and the like, students may act out, refuse to participate, or remain silent. These behaviors may catch you off-guard because, after all, wouldn't any learner want to be part of a genuine classroom environment? The answer is probably yes, but such an environment may be entirely new to the children in front of you, and when you confront them with a new and uncertain situation, you may see a range of disruptive, unhelpful, and silly behaviors. Take heart. It's not that they don't want to work with you, they just don't know how.

That brings up a second point: Until you help them learn how to act in a genuine classroom, both you and the children may be frustrated. Talk with them about what classroom rules make the most sense, model ways they should talk with one another, and give them opportunities to practice making and supporting arguments. There is no magic formula here, just the idea that if you want learners to think and act differently, you'll have to teach them.

You and your students are the primary actors in shaping the classroom environment. As we described in Chapter 5, however, the factors that influence your teaching may also influence the classroom environment you and the learners attempt to develop.

Parents

Parents are likely to exert some influence on your classroom. Like their children, many parents have only experienced traditional classroom settings. New discourse patterns, classroom organizations, and dispositions may confuse them at first. A call from a skeptical parent is every novice teacher's nightmare. Again, patience and understanding should serve you well. You'll need to listen calmly to the parent's concerns with the knowledge that she or he simply may not grasp your purposes and practices. The vast majority of parents want a good education for their children, and so they typically give you the benefit of the doubt as long as they sense that you are dealing with them honestly. Help them understand what you are trying to do.

WORKING WITH PARENTS

Successful teachers keep the following recommendations in mind:

- Work on building communication with parents early in the school year.
- Seek information from parents about their children's strengths, interests, and home life.
- Provide clear, consistent information to parents about curricular goals and what parents can do to support them.
- Design activities that draw on family resources.
- Help parents understand their child's progress by providing concrete examples.

This list was digested from that offered by the Partnership for Strong Families. The complete list, along with helpful examples and illustrations, is available at: www.pfsf.org/

Principals and Teacher Colleagues

Others who may attempt to influence your class include your *principal* and *teacher colleagues*. Like any social organization, schools have norms and expectations of the people who work there. We would like to think that all principals and teachers support the development of genuine classrooms, but we are not that naive. Some of your co-workers may continue to support traditional aims, and if they set the school norms, you might take some flack. Two realities mitigate that tension. One is that, although genuine classrooms are far from standard, they are increasingly evident, accepted, and promoted through groups such as the Partnership for 21st Century Skills. The other reality is that, despite the presence of school norms, teachers generally hold a wide degree of professional autonomy. A colleague or two may grouse about the "noise" coming from your classroom as your learners actively engage with ideas and each other. You may even find the principal stopping by more often than she or he does in other classrooms. The simple fact, however, is that results—in the form of smart, thoughtful, excited learners—count. You may encounter some grumbling, but you and almost everyone else will see it for what it is: professional jealousy.

FIGURE 7.4 Parents want their children to be well educated, so don't hesitate to enlist their support and cooperation. The key to garnering that support and cooperation is good communication.

District-Level Actors

Less direct influence can come from other quarters. Most teachers work for a school district rather than a school itself, so several actors—*the district superintendent, central office staff,* and the *school board*—may make decisions that influence the classroom environment you strive to create. One of those decisions concerns district-level testing. Like Don Kite in Chapter 5, most elementary-school teachers administer some sort of local test. Group intelligence tests may have little influence; they are presumably un-related to instruction. Subject matter achievement tests are a different story. Some are broad-brush tests of general knowledge and skills (usually in literacy and mathematics) and so, like IQ tests, may have little immediate implication for your practice. Others, however, can be more directly relevant. Recall that Don Kite administered a district-developed test based on the district social studies curriculum standards for fifth grade.

In truth, you will hear many teachers talk about the influence of testing as if it completely and single-mindedly drives their instruction. No evidence supports that claim (Cimbricz, 2002; Grant, 2000, 2001). Recall that Kite still retained considerable autonomy in the way he interpreted the influence of that test.

Testing influences teachers' practices, but like everything else, how it influences teachers depends in large part on how an individual teacher interprets it. We believe its influence should relate to how you construct your classroom community: If testing practices support your goals and approach, they should be quite influential. If not, they should be less so.

State Departments of Education

Testing, along with the state curriculum standards on which it is based, is also a way that another group of actors, the *state departments of education*, can influence your classroom. Like district assessments, state-level tests take various forms, some more basic than others. Testing is one form of state policy. Curriculum standards that describe subject-matter goals and objectives are another form of state policy, but so too are more specific actions that may set maximum class sizes, the length of the school year, and the like.

With the passage of the Every Student Succeeds Act and the adoption by most states of the Common Core–English Language Arts (or a variation of it), the stakes attached to state-level testing have been ratcheted up considerably. The focus of the federal legislation is on literacy and mathematics, but most states have also developed standardized tests for elementary social studies (Buckles, Schug, & Watts, 2001). The stakes for elementary students are not as high as they are for some high school students who may not graduate if they fail even a single state exam. That said, failure on an elementary social studies test can mean that students are labelled "at risk" of academic failure and are shunted off to remedial classes.

We raise these points not to scare you or to send you to the nearest test preparation guide. In fact, there is no research evidence demonstrating a positive relationship between constant drilling of test-like questions and higher test scores. However, research does show a powerful correlation between ambitious teaching and academic performance as measured on standardized tests. In two different studies of student performance on the National Assessment of Educational Progress (Lapp, Grigg, & Tay-Lim, 2002; Smith & Niemi, 2001), the students who scored at the highest levels had *more* opportunities to read multiple texts, participate in class discussions, write, and use technology than did their lower-scoring peers. These research results do not mean that teachers should completely ignore the state-level tests they must administer. They do suggest, however, that beyond reviewing the question formats and taking a practice exam, the surest way to help students test well is to teach them well.

With so many interested parties, it should be clear that a classroom environment is a negotiated affair and that teachers and students are not the only negotiators. Those influences outside the classroom are many and may, at times, seem overpowering. But the nature of teaching remains such that teachers, even untenured ones, retain considerable control over the basics of teaching, learning, subject matter, and environment.

Teaching, learning, and subject matter are all important. In his wisdom, however, Joseph Schwab (1978) saw fit to include milieu or environment as the fourth commonplace of schooling. It's a fuzzy concept, more tacit than explicit. But if we are to believe the research on classroom environments, creating a vibrant atmosphere for learning should energize you and your teaching, your learners and their learning, and the subject matter at hand.

Every classroom has some sort of environment. Most reflect traditional approaches to discourse, classroom organization, and dispositions. Still, we see increasing evidence of teachers promoting what we call a genuine classroom community. In those classrooms, the talk is more open and more balanced between teacher and learners, the learning opportunities are organized in a variety of ways, classroom rules support rather than hinder social learning, and the dispositions that are evident encourage respect for and commitment to inquiry, people and ideas, and argument and evidence.

Creating genuine classroom communities is no mean feat, in large part because doing so challenges much of what we have all experienced as schooling. Teachers who take the leap, who strive to create such classrooms, will find no master plan for getting there. Moreover, they may be discouraged as others struggle to understand their efforts. That said, teachers who do take the initiative to push beyond the norms of traditional schooling will, in the end, sense that they have done something real and important for their learners.

Chapter Summary

1 **What discourse, classroom organization, and dispositional patterns are found in traditional classroom environments?** Traditional classrooms are characterized by recitation, quiet, individual seatwork, and the values of efficiency, hard work, deference to authority, and external rewards.

2 **What discourse, classroom organization, and dispositional patterns are found in genuine classroom communities?** Genuine classroom communities are characterized by active student involvement in classroom conversations, classroom activities and rules driven by ideas, and a respect for and commitment to inquiry, ideas and people, and argument and evidence.

3 **What stakeholders are involved in the negotiation of a genuine classroom community?** Students, parents, principals and teaching colleagues, district-level actors, and state departments of education represent a range of interests in and influences on the classroom environment.

Notes

1   For a fuller account of this vignette, see VanSledright and Grant (1994).
2   See Wilson (1990) for the full version of this and the following episodes.

Teaching Resources

Print Resources

Burke-Hengen, M., & Gillespie, T. (Eds.). (1995). *Building community: Social studies in the middle school years*. Portsmouth, NH: Heinemann.
Although intended for middle school students, this edited book has much to offer elementary-school teachers interested in thinking about how their approach to teaching interacts with the classroom environment.

Cohen, E., & Lotan, R. (2014). *Designing groupwork: Strategies for the heterogeneous classroom* (3rd ed.). New York: Teachers College Press.
In addition to being useful as a guide to constructing small-group instructional opportunities, the authors offer many insights into how to develop and sustain a genuine classroom community.

Fraenkel, J. (1973). *Helping students think and value: Strategies for teaching the social studies*. Englewood Cliffs, NJ: Prentice-Hall.
An older but still useful book that nicely integrates attention to the commonplaces.

Jorgensen, K. (1993). *History workshop*. Portsmouth, NH: Heinemann.
This is an excellent resource for exploring how teacher–student discourse can look in classrooms.

Sapon-Shevin, M. (2010). *Because we can change the world: A practical guide to building cooperative, inclusive classroom communities* (2nd ed.). Thousand Oaks, CA: Corwin Press.
Another excellent resource for a variety of powerful ideas on how to construct a rich classroom community that enables student learning.

Technology Resources

Most of the websites that offer lesson and unit plans for social studies teachers also offer suggestions for various approaches to classroom organization. Some particularly useful sites include the following:

- www.proteacher.net
  This site features over thirty active discussion boards organized exclusively for elementary teachers. There are specialty boards on teaching elementary social studies, classroom management, teaching in inner-city schools, and a wide variety of other topics. There is even one for prospective teachers.
- www.edutopia.org/topic/classroom-management
  A comprehensive site on all things classroom management, teachers should find lots of good ideas and practices here.

Social Studies and Literacy

Social studies is a content-rich school subject. Embracing the fields of history, geography, political science, economics, psychology, and the like, social studies offers rich opportunities to understand why we do the things we do. Yet the beauty of social studies is also its bane. Rich and exciting ideas are one thing, how to demonstrate understanding is quite another. In this chapter, we talk about the ways that students can use literacy to show us what they have learned.

To make sense of the vast subject matter of social studies, students need a conceptual framework to organize their ideas (the threads) and a series of focus questions to make the content real (compelling questions). They also need to develop facility with a range of skills. Some of these skills are content-specific, such as using a key to identify elements of a map, reading tables and graphs to understand economic data, and contextualizing a set of diary entries. But many of the skills students need are literacy-based, as described in the Common Core State Standards for English Language Arts and Literacy (CC–ELA).

In this chapter, we advance the idea of *literacy through social studies*. By this phrase, we mean that key literacy skills can be taught and reinforced through the teaching and learning of social studies. This distinction is important because too often literacy is thought of as a set of generic skills. We argue that the basic skills of identifying the main idea of a passage, writing an explanation, or making a presentation gain a measure of importance and meaning when they are linked with a content area such as social studies.

When you have completed this chapter, you should be able to answer the following questions:

1 What are the key features of the reading, writing, and speaking and listening sections of the Common Core–English Language Arts standards?
2 How is the construct of text complexity expanded in a social studies classroom?

3   In what ways is the line blurred between writing explanations and arguments?
4   What challenges emerge for enhancing children's abilities to speak and listen in social studies classrooms?
5   How are media literacy and digital citizenship related?

The Common Core–English Language Arts

Social studies and literacy have always had a natural affinity. Good teachers have asked students to read **informational** and **narrative** texts and to do so for understanding. They have asked students to write about their ideas through **explanations** and **arguments,** using **claims** and **counter-claims** that are supported with **evidence.** They have asked students to speak and listen in class as a means of understanding each other's ideas and presenting their own. Although some teachers see them as distinct areas of the curriculum, ambitious teachers see social studies and literacy as mutually reinforcing.

The fact that literacy and social studies need each other does not mean that their coexistence has always been easy. In fact, some people saw the emergence of the CC–ELA standards as evidence that social studies was being eclipsed.[1] This sentiment gained traction as one read through the CC–ELA standards and discovered that the authors seemed to push social studies, science, and technical subjects into the background. Social studies (and science) has been losing ground to literacy and mathematics in elementary-school classrooms for the last decade (Rock et al., 2006; von Zastrow & Janc, 2004). Taken together, these two developments suggested that social studies was withering on the vine.

As social studies teachers began to think about the ideas represented in the CC–ELA standards, however, most saw an opportunity: The CC–ELA standards could be used to support the kinds of ambitious teaching and learning that many saw as critical to the field. Literacy (and mathematics) still command the bulk of the elementary-school day. But when teachers and their students *read* narrative and informational texts (e.g., historical fiction and trade books); when they *write* narratives, explanations, and arguments; when they *listen* and respond to speeches, legends, and oral histories; and when they *talk* about their ideas in the form of debates and discussions, they are doing literacy through social studies.

Looking Closely at the Common Core

The Common Core State Standards for English Language Arts and Literacy (CC–ELA) was a project sponsored by the Council of Chief State School Officers and the National Governors Association to help prepare students for college and careers. The standards generated in the CC–ELA focus on four areas: reading, writing, speaking and listening. These standards, though they pertain to all forms of literacy, support the idea of ambitious social studies practice in numerous ways.[2]

RESOURCES: CORE STANDARDS

The Common Core–English Language Arts can be accessed in PDF form at www. corestandards.org/ELA-Literacy

In the next sections, we offer an overview of the key elements of the K–5 reading, writing, and speaking and listening standards, but with a social studies twist.

Reading Standards

The CC–ELA reading standards highlight the importance of key ideas and details, the craft and structure of text genres, the integration of knowledge and ideas, and the range of texts available and their complexity. The authors of the standards focus primarily on literary and informational texts.[3] Although most of the texts teachers use for social studies purposes will be informational, **literary texts** such as historical fiction can also be useful.

We will have more to say about the idea of "text" below. Here, we focus on the kinds of text the CC–ELA authors describe. Those texts include biographies and autobiographies, charts and graphs, maps, and digital sources. As examples, the authors cite *I Read Signs* (Hoban, 1987) for grades K–1, *Ruby Bridges* (Coles, 1986) for grades 2–3, and *A History of US* (Hakim, 2007) for grades 4–5.

Regardless of the kind of text, the CC–ELA standards focus on **text complexity** and comprehension. Text complexity highlights the sophistication of the text along three dimensions: qualitative, quantitative, and reader/text/task. Qualitative evaluation of a text refers to the "levels of meaning, structure, language conventionality and clarity, and knowledge demands" (p. 31). Quantitative assessments of a text involve "readability measures and other scores of text complexity" (ibid.). In matching reader to text and to task measures, the standards focus on "reader variables (such as motivation, knowledge, and experiences) and task variables (such as purpose and the complexity generated by the task assigned and the questions posed)" (ibid.). In each case, the authors of the standards expect students to be reading texts of increasing complexity over their school careers.

IN YOUR CLASSROOM

TEXT COMPLEXITY

Talk with a range of people in your school—other classroom teachers, a literacy specialist, the special education coordinator, the principal—about the issue of text complexity and how they suggest you make adjustments for the array of students in your classroom.

Text comprehension is the idea that a reading becomes real when children are able to understand it. The CC–ELA authors define comprehension as the ability to:

> Discern more from and make fuller use of text, including making an increasing number of connections among ideas and between texts, considering a wider range of textual evidence, and becoming more sensitive to inconsistencies, ambiguities, and poor reasoning in texts.

> (p. 8)

Although it is important to assist young students by offering them texts that fall within their independent reading abilities, it is equally important to increase the textual challenge posed. For example, in a unit on Native Americans, a teacher might ask her students to read Simon Ortiz's *The People Shall Continue* on their own, but pair stronger and weaker readers for John Neihardt's more complex book, *Black Elk Speaks*. Although children need to be offered texts that they can read by themselves, they also need to read, in a supportive fashion, texts that push them.

Writing Standards

The CC–ELA writing standards highlight the production of three main types of text: narratives, explanations, and arguments.[4] The standards also address the development of clear and coherent writing and the ability to conduct research projects in which students demonstrate their capacity to "gather relevant information from multiple print and digital sources, assess the credibility and accuracy of each source, and integrate the information while avoiding plagiarism" (p. 18).

RESOURCES: BACKGROUND

For more background on the differences among narratives, explanations, and arguments, check out the writing section of Appendix A of the CC–ELA standards at www.corestandards.org/assets/Appendix_A.pdf

The two kinds of writing students are most likely to do in social studies classrooms are explanations and arguments. Explanation or informative tasks ask students to describe, illuminate, detail, or clarify an idea, behavior, condition, event or series of events in order to aid a reader's understanding. Students could be asked to describe the route they take from home to school, they could be asked to explain the symbols on their state flag, they could be asked to identify the differences between Native-American tribes in the Eastern and Western sections of the United States during the early 1800s. Young children should be provided with a range of appropriate sources to construct their explanations; older children should be expected to use sources they gather on their own as well as those that the teacher supplies.

Arguments have a different purpose. Where explanations are intended to help readers understand a phenomenon, arguments are intended to persuade readers to accept a point of view. Arguments consist of claims and evidence. In social studies, claims are assertions of ideas that represent judgments about and interpretations of social life. For example, "our town needs a new park," "the US and Mexico should be best friends," and "taxes are a bad thing" are all claims or statements that express the speaker's point of view. The speaker may be convinced that the assertion is true, but until she offers some evidence to back it up, it is only an opinion. Evidence, therefore, is the factual information that supports a claim.

Consider the example of the first claim above: Our town needs a new park. What evidence might be offered to support (or dispute) this claim? We can imagine students looking at the current number of local parks and where they are located around the town, the number of adults and children who use the parks, and what features each park offers. We can also imagine students doing a brief survey of their peers and of the community to determine the interest in and need for a new park facility. After gathering all this information, students could then construct an argument (consisting of claims and evidence) that supports the idea that a new park is essential.

▶|◀ REFLECTION: CLAIMS AND EVIDENCE

People often offer statements that sound like facts but, at heart, are essentially claims that need evidence to be persuasive. The next time you are at a family gathering, listen to the conversations and keep track of the number and kinds of claims that are made … and whether any evidence is offered to support them.

For example, when Uncle Jed starts talking about how politicians are crooks, does he offer specific examples of their wrongdoing or does he just talk louder when questioned?

▶|◄

Explanation and argument are as important to powerful social studies as they are to literacy. Each is a useful means of helping students express their ideas whether it be in the form of an essay, a PowerPoint presentation, a blog entry, or a chart. Reading multiple texts is a key component of learning; writing helps make real what children are reading.

Speaking and Listening Standards

In most standards documents, reading and writing get the headlines. In the CC–ELA standards, speaking and listening receive equal billing and they should: Speaking and listening are critical skills for a well-rounded social studies program.

The CC–ELA speaking and listening standards focus on collaboration and presenting ideas in clear and coherent ways. On the first point, the authors of the standards take a strong stand on the importance of students interacting with others. Far too often, literacy is looked at as a solitary pursuit. The CC–ELA standards, by contrast, require that students prepare and participate in a "range of conversations and collaborations with diverse partners" (p. 22). As we describe in Chapter 5, there are many ways that children can collaborate—as partners, in small groups, and in whole class experiences. The CC–ELA standards also support another key element of powerful teaching: Multiple opportunities for students to express their ideas. The default approach—paper and pencil tasks— is useful, but insufficient. Students ought to be encouraged to use a range of media to present their explanations and arguments.

Let's see how the idea that our town needs a new park plays out in the CC–ELA speaking and listening standards. One obvious connection is the need for students to think and talk through their initial ideas about the value of and need for a new facility. Doing so calls for students to be able to express their individual perspectives, but it also calls for them to be active listeners—that is, to try to understand the ideas their peers bring forward, especially if they disagree with them. Active listening also implies a need to raise questions about ideas offered that seem obscure or off-point. Asking questions, if done in a respectful manner and if done in the pursuit of understanding, is an invaluable way of honing claims and determining what counts as evidence.

As students' ideas begin to crystalize, they need to think about how they present those ideas. Argument-based essays are a traditional venue, one that teachers need to support and encourage. But other venues are also open. Younger children might represent their stances on the question of a new park through drawings of activities such a venue might enable. Older children might engage in an informal debate where the pros and cons of the venture are expressed. Still older students might graph the results of their surveys and put together a presentation that they deliver to invited members of the community. The world that students enter when they leave the classroom values the ability to write a coherent and well-supported essay; it also values the many other ways that we are all called on to articulate our ideas.

▶|◀ REFLECTION: DISCOURSE IN GENUINE CLASSROOM COMMUNITIES

Think back across the classrooms we have portrayed in earlier chapters. Recall that in those instances we described as genuine classroom communities, there was a different quality to the ways in which students interacted with one another and with their teachers. We argued that teachers can foster a sense of shared experience by the ways they organize their classrooms and the kinds of dispositions and discourse that they encourage. How might the teachers in Chapter 4—Sandra Prosy, Janice Mead, and Pam Derson—react to the CC–ELA authors' suggestions about children's abilities to speak and listen?

▶|◀

■ SECTION SUMMARY: COMMON CORE–ENGLISH LANGUAGE ARTS

- ■ The CC–ELA is an ambitious set of literacy standards that focus on reading, writing, speaking, and listening.

- ■ The reading standards highlight two constructs: text complexity and text comprehension.

- ■ Key to the writing standards are the types of text students produce: explanations and arguments.

- ■ Speaking and listening illustrate the need for students to work together as well as independently and for them to present their ideas in a range of formats.

Ratcheting Up Literacy Through Social Studies

Development of the CC–ELA standards has changed the landscape of schools in many ways. The initial worry that this development would completely displace social studies (and science) in favor of literacy and mathematics appears to be unfounded: The English Language Arts portion of the Common Core gives explicit attention to the literacy connections to content areas such as social studies, and informational texts play an increasingly prominent role in the expectations of students as they mature. Rather than see the CC–ELA standards as a distraction or an intrusion, we argue that they offer a means of supporting the idea of literacy *through* social studies. In other words, reading, writing, speaking, and listening can be the vehicles through which social studies ideas come alive in classrooms.

Students do not read and write generically or in a vacuum. Instead, their ability to read a political cartoon, comprehend a speech, draft an argument, or conduct a discussion depends on their knowledge and use of ideas—the physical, political, economic, sociocultural, and global ideas that help students understand the world in which they live. Knowing how to decode words, write complete sentences, and the like are skills that can be applied in any school subject. *Using* those skills to make sense of history, geography, and the other social studies areas exemplifies the notion of literacy *through* social studies.

Reading through Social Studies

Although a wide range of generic reading elements can be supported through good social studies instruction, some of those elements develop a sharper edge when introduced in the context of social studies. In this section, we point out the places where reading takes on a different flavor when students are engaging in a social studies inquiry.

RESOURCES: RECOMMENDED TEXTS

The CC–ELA authors provide a valuable list of recommended texts for K–5 teachers and students at www.corestandards.org/assets/Appendix_B.pdf

Good social studies teachers have always supported students as they develop the vocabulary that is key to understanding social studies ideas; as they gain the skills of gathering, comprehending, evaluating, synthesizing, and reporting information; and as they experience a range of texts in terms of type and readability. Each of these ideas is well described in the CC–ELA standards. The last idea, however, takes on a special significance in social studies classes.

The Complexity of Text

The CC–ELA authors are right to recognize the importance of text complexity in helping students become more sophisticated readers. But the complexity of text takes on a different meaning when discussing the kinds of texts useful in social studies classes.

One issue is with the word "text" itself. Usually associated with the written word, text should more properly be defined as a *source of information*. As the CC–ELA authors note, children should be introduced to a wide range of text types or sources—biography and autobiographies, charts and graphs, historical fiction, and maps—in their social studies lessons. But that list only scratches the surface. Artwork, music, political cartoons, oral histories, documentaries, and blogs are just a few of the sources that push beyond the traditional boundaries of the term "text."[5]

"READING" YOUR CLASSROOM

IN YOUR CLASSROOM

Any human creation can be considered a text to be "read" for meaning. Books, posters, and student artwork can all be interpreted, but so too can the classroom itself. Look around your room—what does the physical space tell you? What does the arrangement of student desks or tables say about the kind of teaching and learning that occurs? What do the forms of technology present in the room say about its use and importance? What do the teacher and student materials on the classroom walls say about what you and they value? Communication can take many forms, so spend some time thinking about the messages broadcast by the physical space of your classroom.

A second consideration related to the complexity of text involves the reader. We talked at length in Chapter 2 about the construct of students' prior knowledge. Rather than being blank slates, children come to school with all sorts of ideas about how the world works. Some of those ideas come from authoritative sources, but many do not. Moreover, because they have had limited life experience, many of the ideas children bring to bear are going to be naive and underdeveloped. That does not mean their ideas are not influential, however. And that is our point: Whether their knowledge is well-formed, accurate, and nuanced—or not—children's prior knowledge influences the ways that they read texts.

The practical implication of this point is that good teachers work hard to understand how their students make sense of texts. Having children read a text and respond to a few comprehension questions is one way of assessing their sense-making, but it is unlikely to be enough. As we note in Chapter 6, teachers need to offer students a range of opportunities to articulate their emergent ideas so that misconceptions and inaccuracies can be detected.

The third way that the complexity of text emerges in a social studies classroom concerns the idea of perspective. The CC–ELA authors advocate that children engage with texts of various degrees of sophistication. We agree, but, if all the texts support the same point of view, then the key social studies concept of perspective is undercut. We cannot think of a single social issue on which there is universal agreement. (Go ahead—try to think of one!) From the definition of family, to the influence of culture on our behavior, to the landing of Columbus in the "new world," people have identified points of both agreement and disagreement. Good teachers introduce texts that vary in their readability, but they also offer texts that vary in the perspectives presented.

Consider these two pieces of text. Each refers to Christopher Columbus's first trip back to Spain after landing in the Americas:

- "In March, 1493 Christopher Columbus sailed back to Spain with gold trinkets, parrots, and a few Indians" (Adler, 1991, p. 22).
- "Soon the *Niña* and the *Pinta* are ready to sail back to Spain. The ships are already loaded with many kinds of food ... Columbus has also forced six Indians to come with him" (Krensky, 1991, p. 41).

Although these two trade book passages are intended for young children, have roughly the same quantitative text complexity, and were written the same year, they present very different perspectives on Columbus's interactions with the natives. In Adler's text, it appears that the Native Americans[6] freely boarded the European ships while, in Krensky's book, it is apparent that they were enslaved. Since most historians support Krensky's interpretation, it is tempting to ignore Adler's. Doing so, however, misses an important point—there are always multiple ways of looking at a social situation.

A fourth way in which social studies teachers need to contextualize reading in their subject matter has to do with the manner in which students read *behind* the text. Every text, no matter the type, reflects something of the human hand and mind that constructed it. A map is created by a cartographer, a movie by a filmmaker, a website by a designer—such that in each case, the text is authored. Even school textbooks, which often seem to be written in an omnipresent voice, have identifiable authors. This point about authorship is important because it means that all texts express a point of view, even if they appear to be neutral.

Maybe the best example of this idea is a photograph. Common sense tells us that pictures are a "true" image of a scene. Yet every photo reflects only what is portrayed in the setting ... and a photographer *chooses* that setting to preserve. She or he might have chosen otherwise—moving the camera ten feet to one side or another might have revealed an entirely different photographic description and therefore communicated an entirely different message.

Our point is both simple *and* challenging. The simple part is that every source of information, regardless of its textual form, is human-made and therefore reflects a perspective on rather than the truth of a situation. If we are to understand any social phenomena, we need multiple perspectives. The complicated part is determining what those perspectives are and how to make sense of them.

In order to understand the perspective behind a text, historians and others offer three tools: *sourcing, contextualization,* and *corroboration* (Reismann,

2012; Wineburg, 1991). **Sourcing** refers to the idea that readers need to know and consider a document's source and purpose. Was a source created by an expert in the field or a casual observer? Was it intended to present a rich and well-supported argument or was it intended to distort facts in order to reach a predetermined conclusion? **Contextualization** is the idea that readers need to understand where and when a text was created. How might the location and/ or the time period in which the source was constructed influence what it says? **Corroboration** represents the idea that readers need to consider any text in relation to others on the same topic. In other words, how might a different text speak to the issue at hand?

▶|◀ REFLECTION: SOURCES

To understand the usefulness of sourcing, contextualization, and corroboration, think back to the two excerpts about Columbus's return trip to Spain. What can you tell about the sources of the two quotes? What hints did we include to help you contextualize the texts? And what benefit is there to looking at the two pieces of text together?

▶|◀

In this section, we have expanded the notion of what counts as a text to be read. The world we live in is a complex place. To make sense of that world, we need to draw on a wide range of sources. Those sources rarely, if ever, support a single point of view. So, we need to help students understand the construct of perspective.

Writing through Social Studies

The authors of the CC–ELA standards talk about the importance of questions as students read and write, especially in the case of doing classroom research. They advocate for students learning how to write explanations of events and arguments intended to persuade. And they discuss the need for students to gather sources for use as evidence to support their ideas. These are valuable prompts for teachers and students across the school day, but they take on a special meaning when applied to social studies.

The CC–ELA authors largely see questions in light of student research projects. For example, Anchor Standard 7 calls on students to base their research on "focused questions, demonstrating understanding of the subject under investigation" (p. 18). Good social studies teachers, however, see a purpose for questions beyond student research projects. As we noted in Chapter 4, framing classroom units based on a compelling question such as "Why do we need rules?" helps students see that questions can serve a larger instructional purpose.

The distinction between writing explanations and arguments is a useful one, at least on the surface. An explanation typically asks students to describe a situation, an event, or an activity in summary fashion. In social studies, students might be asked to explain who an historical actor was, what a map represents, or how money can be exchanged for goods and services. By contrast, an argument calls for students to offer an interpretation of a social phenomenon and to provide evidence to support that interpretation. For example, if asked whether the American Revolution was revolutionary, students have to take a stand on the question (e.g., the Revolution produced a political change but not a social or economic one) and then say why they thought their stand was justified.[7]

The trouble we see with this distinction between explanation and argument is that the line turns out to be fuzzy. Think about it: If students do any more than list the most basic facts about who Martin Luther King, Jr. was, aren't they also offering an interpretation of him? That is, if they explain who Dr. King was in rich detail, then students will have to make decisions about what information to include and what to exclude, what to emphasize and what to skim over. As they make these decisions, their "explanations" of Dr. King begin to take on the form of an argument—an interpretation of his life that reflects a sense of his importance. And to the extent that they back up their interpretations, their arguments may be more or less persuasive.

We make this point about the blurry line between an explanation and an argument for two reasons. First, much of what students do in social studies class should be making arguments rather than writing explanations. The facts that students use to describe the economic goods produced in their state or the impact of a river on their community are important. But those facts only begin to mean something when students use them to make sense of bigger issues. Knowing what agricultural and industrial products a state produces is only the first step in understanding whether those products make the best use of the state's natural resources or whether the state government should develop tax incentives for some businesses but not others. Answering these kinds of questions involves the construction of arguments. And it is the making and supporting of arguments that students find engaging.

The second reason the line between explanations and arguments is blurry has to do with the idea that, although kids can get tangled up in facts, they can still begin constructing persuasive arguments. On the surface, this point does not make much sense: How could kids build an argument if they don't know the facts? We agree. But we have also seen many instances where the relationship between facts and arguments is fluid (Grant, 2007; VanSledright, 1995). Consider the following example.

Bill is an African-American third grader who attends an urban elementary school. Trying to understand how young children think about different perspectives on history, S.G. interviewed him about the relationships between Christopher Columbus and the native peoples he encountered. After asking Bill some initial questions about how he thought Columbus and the natives interacted, S.G. read the two passages (Adler and Krensky) quoted above. What follows is part of their conversation:

[Have you ever heard of Columbus?] We studied him because when he was in his land, he thought, everybody else thought it was, a flat, um, land, so he, he was brave, so he went in his boat and went and bumped into North America and then he thought he, he went to um, India, India, so he called the Iroquoians the Indians.

[Were the Iroquoians in India?] They were in North America.

[Oh?] That was their land and then here comes, um, Europe and they try to go to there and buy the place, they like be trading with [unclear]. They didn't know if, if they were letting them borrow their stuff, but, and they thought, now the land is ours, so they started a war.

[Who started the war?] Um, the, the French, um, the, the, Europe, the Europeans.

[Did Columbus start the war too?] Uh uh, he didn't, he didn't start anything. He was friendly.

Bill's first ideas about Columbus are a jumble of facts, conflations, and wild suppositions. He represents his ideas in a loose narrative that moves into and out of the factual realm. After listening to the Adler and Krensky texts, however, Bill offers a tentative interpretation:

[Some people say that Christopher Columbus is a hero, what do you think about that?] He is a hero, because he found new land and ways they could get food.

In his response, Bill offers the beginnings of an argument: He has proposed an interpretation of Columbus (a hero) and some evidence for that view (Columbus discovered new land and food). Asked to write an argument-based essay, Bill might not be able to write a very long piece and it is likely that he will mix up some of the factual evidence he offers in support of his claims. That said, Bill is on the right track: He shows that he understands the components of an argument and he is giving his teacher something with which to work.

▶|◀ REFLECTION: "HEARING" STUDENTS

One of the trickiest parts of being a teacher is learning how to "hear" what students are saying. Our adult ears need to be trained to hear the often fumbling, inarticulate, and confusing things that kids say. Review Bill's initial comments above: Which of his statements are accurate? Which are inaccurate? Which walk a fine line between the two?

We offer this example of Bill to illustrate the point that children are going to come to the task of writing evidence-based arguments with a range of ideas and experiences. Even the youngest students know something about the need to provide reasons for the claims that they make. It will not be easy for them to transition into articulate and well-written papers but, with your thoughtful and patient guidance, they will make it.

Speaking and Listening Through Social Studies

Although reading and writing get most of the attention in the CC–ELA standards, speaking and listening are important skills for students to learn in general and in their social studies lessons.

Speaking

Children typically come to school with far greater facility to speak than to write. Knowing that, some teachers immediately begin pushing students to communicate their ideas through writing. We understand that impulse—writing is a challenging skill and, for most of us, takes a long time to develop.

Knowing how to speak is not the same thing, however, as knowing how to use one's voice to communicate clearly and convincingly. In Chapter 5, we talked about the need to help children learn how to talk with one another in group settings. We want to echo and expand that idea here.

First, we need to remember that, although they can be quite verbal, elementary-age students are still learning how to use language. They have neither the vocabulary nor the capacity to communicate their ideas that adults have. As noted above, good teachers adjust their ears such that they can "hear" what children are saying as they sometimes fumble in communicating their ideas.

Second, children's voices develop in a range of social settings outside of school, but the kind of talk appropriate to school settings is different enough that teachers need to help them. Outside of school, children may learn that speaking louder, intimidating others through name calling, and even using threats may be the "proof" that supports their points. In school, as in most of adult life, it is the evidence that one offers that provides the support for one's argument. Before they even begin writing, then, students need to learn how to articulate their ideas verbally and how to support those ideas with evidence.

Finally, we want to plug the idea of giving children more rather than fewer opportunities to talk through their ideas. Given the rush of the school day, the heavy curricular expectations of teachers, and the tendency of many children to wander when they are talking, some teachers try to make their instruction more efficient by limiting students' verbal responses. Asking only yes or no questions may help teachers push through the material, but researchers have found that teachers can get fooled into thinking that children understand more than they do unless they are given opportunities to fully explore their ideas (Grant, 2007; Nuthall & Alton-Lee, 1995).

For example, see how S.G.'s questions to Bill, the third grader described above, reveal a whole new set of ideas about the relationship between Columbus and native peoples ... and between Columbus and Bill himself:

> [I was thinking about the piece I read that said that Columbus forced six Indians to come with him. What do you think about that?] That he was real mean to them because they might not have wanted to go with him so he had to force out ... in anger.
>
> [And what does that make you think?] That he was a little mean.
>
> [A little mean? What does that sound like to you?] Like he's, um, half good, half bad.
>
> [Have you ever heard of anybody like that?] Me!
>
> [(S.G. laughs) You!] (Nodding) My brother and sister, everybody I know.
>
> [How is that so?] Because sometimes they get mean and sometimes they be good.
>
> [Can you be a good person and still do some mean things?] I do some good things, but mostly all bad. (S.G. and student laugh).[8]

What is going on here? After being prompted, Bill seizes on the word "forced" from Krensky's text and then describes Columbus's actions as "a little mean." But then he turns the tables on us and makes the intriguing claim that Columbus is "half good, half bad" just like he is and everyone else he knows. Adults often think children see the world only in stark contrasts of good and bad. Bill's words put the lie to that view: Here is a young child who sees Columbus as a real person, a fully figured human being who is neither a mythic hero nor evil incarnate.

It is still unclear what Bill really knows about Columbus and his interactions with the native populations. Some of the inaccurate information he had at the beginning of the interview may have been clarified, but we suspect Bill still clings to much of it. That said, we take heart from the fact that this young boy has made a meaningful connection to an historical actor, one that suggests he may be open to thinking even more positively about social studies in the future.

Listening

We end this chapter on literacy through social studies with what may be the biggest challenge of the four literacy skills—listening. Put simply: How do we know a student is listening? And more importantly, how do we know what sense students are making of what they hear?

▶️◀️ REFLECTION: LISTENING TO STUDENTS

Watch the video clip entitled "Making the Most of Listening and Learning: Ruby Bridges Read-Aloud" at www.engageny.org/resource/making-the-most-of-listening-learning-workshop-ruby-bridges-read-aloud. Think about how the teacher is assessing what her children are hearing as they listen to the story.
▶️◀️

In Chapter 6, we talk about the idea that the most common method teachers use to assess whether or not their students are engaged is observation. It is a solid approach as children's faces often betray their interest and attention. But we can be fooled. In Suzanne Wilson's (1990) study, the boy who was sticking pencils up his nose earlier in the class comes up with a key insight into the idea of geographic scale—he proposes that they use the square floor tiles to measure the area of their classroom. At the same time, children who appear to be listening may be off playing softball or fighting ninjas in their minds. Good teachers, then, supplement their observations with an array of activities through which students can demonstrate their abilities to listen. Such activities may be verbal (e.g., answering direct questions) or physical (e.g., standing beside their desks if they agree with a conclusion) or both (e.g., writing their ideas on a whiteboard and then explaining how they arrived at them).

■ SECTION SUMMARY: RATCHETING UP LITERACY THROUGH SOCIAL STUDIES

- Using reading, writing, speaking, and listening skills to make sense of history, geography, and the other social studies areas exemplifies the notion of literacy *through* social studies.

- The notion of text complexity takes on a special meaning in the context of social studies.

- Writing in social studies classrooms primarily consists of crafting explanations and arguments.

- Students need a range of opportunities to practice their speaking and listening skills in social studies contexts.

Media Literacy and Digital Citizenship

Although "media literacy" and "digital citizenship" might not seem to have much to do with one another on the surface, in fact they are intricately linked. And that linkage highlights a key intersection between literacy and social studies.

As if teaching students how to read generally and within social studies weren't enough, teachers today have the extra challenge of helping students become media literate. **Media literacy** generally refers to the practices that enable people to access, evaluate, and create media. In schools, that means the need to teach students how to gain access to digital media, how to decide the value and credibility of that media, and how to use media to represent their ideas.

In some ways, the challenges of teaching students how to read and use texts that we described above are equally appropriate in the digital world. Students still need to understand that anything they see on the Internet is a human creation and, as such, represents the author's perspective: Just as no article or book is the objective truth, neither is anything on the World Wide Web. Students also need to understand that looking at only one perspective on an issue is unlikely to give them the kind of well-rounded view that they need to form their own views and arguments.

Three factors make digital media especially challenging, however. One of those factors is the unfettered access that people have to post things to the Internet. Magazine and book content typically goes through rigorous fact-checking and editorial review before being published; no such constraints exist on web-based material. The second factor is the deceptive appearance and language associated with digital media. Website images and language can be constructed in ways that give them the shine of credibility and yet be highly suspect. A third and related factor is that some Internet sites can pose real dangers to young students, luring them into situations that put them at risk of involvement in immoral and unlawful activities. Many schools try to shield students from the worst of Internet behavior by creating password and firewall protections. Unfortunately, those efforts do not always work.

RESOURCES: TEACHING MEDIA LITERACY

A number of excellent sites are available to help teachers think about and craft lessons around media literacy:

■ https://www.canva.com/learn/10-creative-methods-to-teach-media-literacy/

The authors of "10 Creative Ways to Teach Media Literacy" present an easy-to-understand and use set of guidelines for addressing concerns about using digital media.

■ www.medialit.org/how-teach-media-literacy

The Center for Media Literacy features a rich array of articles and reports on media literacy as well teaching materials that are free and for purchase.

■ www.edutopia.org/topic/media-literacy

Edutopia has an extensive website archive devoted to helping students develop as wise users and creators of digital products.

■ https://cor.standford.edu

The Civics Online Reasoning project developed by the Stanford History Education Group represents a wide range of interesting and engaging resources for teaching about media literacy.

The notion of **digital citizenship** overlaps media literacy in its attention to the use of technology. But it pushes in a couple of different directions that are worth noting. One of those directions is an expanded notion of media. Where media literacy is largely focused on students' use of the World Wide Web, digital citizenship also covers the use of all forms of social technology, including the various social platforms available on tablets and cellphones. A second useful direction emphasized under the label of digital citizenship is the role and responsibility of students to think and act in ways that promote the common good. The widespread availability and use of cellphones and other social technology have made communication easier, but they have also enabled a host of behaviors that can range from hurtful to destructive. Cyber-bullying, shaming, and inappropriate postings of video material are just some of the ways that technology is used for harmful purposes.

RESOURCES: TEACHING DIGITAL CITIZENSHIP

Digital Citizenship is a website devoted to the appropriate and responsible use of technology.

- www.digitalcitizenship.net/home.html

Among the helpful resources are articles and books, podcasts, and lists of relevant websites. Of particular value is the "Nine Elements of Digital Citizenship" and the synthesis of those elements into the three guiding principles of the "S3 Framework":

Safety—being protected from or unlikely to cause danger, risk, or injury to yourself or others.

Savvy—wisdom and practical knowledge; the understanding to make good judgments.

Social—creating cooperative and interdependent relationships and understandings of others.

New technologies and media outlets have contributed to teachers' ability to enrich their students' learning experiences. Yet, they come with challenges that can complicate students' ability to make sense of text (in the biggest sense of that term) *and* to be good citizens. We think the benefits largely outweigh the problems, but teachers of today must be far more cognizant of those problems than did their peers in earlier decades.

Chapter Summary

1   What are the key features of the reading, writing, and speaking and listening sections of the Common Core–English Language Arts standards? The reading standards focus on text complexity and comprehension; the writing standards highlight crafting narratives, explanations, and arguments; and the speaking and listening standards point to collaboration and presenting ideas in clear and coherent ways.

2   How is the construct of text complexity expanded in a social studies classroom? Text complexity in the context of social studies classrooms highlights the definition of text, the impact of the reader's prior knowledge, the role of perspective, and the significance of helping students to read *behind* the text.

3   In what ways is the line blurred between writing explanations and arguments? The line between explanations and arguments blurs because most of what students do in social studies class will be making arguments rather than writing explanations and because, although students may not possess complete factual knowledge, they may still be able to construct valid arguments.

4   What challenges emerge for enhancing children's abilities to speak and listen in social studies classrooms? The primary challenges to students' abilities to speak and listen hinge on the fact that they are still learning to use language in effective ways and the fact that our observations of students can sometimes be misleading.

5   How are media literacy and digital citizenship related? Media literacy generally refers to the practices that enable people to access, evaluate, and create media. Digital citizenship expands on the notion of what media are useful and speaks to the roles and responsibilities that students have in promoting the common good.

Notes

1   The fact that the National Governors Association and the Council of Chief State School Officers limited the Common Core to literacy and mathematics made both social studies and science teachers nervous. Consequently, efforts were undertaken to provide guidance in those areas as well–the *College, Career, and Civic Life (C3) Framework for State Social Studies Standards* and the *Next Generation Science Standards*.

2   Beyond the four focus areas, the authors of the CC–ELA add in language standards. Those standards focus on generic conventions of grammar and usage and thus, while appropriate for the writing and speaking products that students produce, do not necessarily support the development of social studies content knowledge and understanding.

3   The reading standards also include a section on foundational skills: e.g., phonics, decoding skills, and reading fluency.

4   Social studies teachers may sometimes ask students to write narratives, but, for the most part, they will be interested in having their students write explanations and arguments.

5   The CC–ELA authors use the language of primary and secondary documents presumably to draw a contrast between texts that reflect an original author's perspective (primary) and those that draw on the perspectives of others (secondary). In this view, a diary would be considered a primary source while a textbook would represent a secondary source. This distinction, like some others in the CC–ELA standards, becomes problematic if we assume that every text is authored and therefore represents its creator's perspective. Historians, therefore, drop the qualifiers "primary" and "secondary" and talk only about "historical" sources.

6   The terms "Indian" and "Native American" engender considerable controversy. Although both are accepted in some circles, we recommend use of the phrase "Native American" in school settings.

7   The CC–ELA authors make a distinction between the terms opinion and argument, though the distinction is largely one of grade level and sophistication:

> Although young children are not able to produce fully developed logical arguments, they develop a variety of methods to extend and elaborate their work by providing examples, offering reasons for their assertions, and explaining cause and effect. These kinds of expository structures are steps on the road to argument. In grades K–5, the term "opinion" is used to refer to this developing form of argument.
>
> (CC–ELA standards, Appendix A, p. 23)

We find this distinction to be confusing since the common definition of "opinion" is the making of a claim *without* any evidence to support it. Consequently, we use only the term "argument" in this book when talking about texts whose intent is to persuade.

8   If you would like to read more about Bill and other students' interpretations of the relationship between Columbus and native populations, see Grant (2007).

Teaching Resources

Print Resources

Agarwal-Rangnath, R. (2012). *Social studies, literacy, and social justice in the Common Core classroom: A guide for teachers.* New York: Teachers College Press.

Calkins, L., Ehrenworth, M., & Lehman, C. (2012). *Pathways to the Common Core: Accelerating achievement.* Portsmouth, NH: Heinemann.

Frey, N., & Lapp, D. (2012). *Text complexity: Raising rigor in reading.* Washington, DC. International Reading Association.

Latimer, H. (2010). *Reading for learning: Using discipline-based texts to build content knowledge.* Washington, DC: National Council of Teachers of English.

Technology Resources

The following are good general sites for resources related to the Common Core–English Language Arts and for literacy-related social studies lessons and resources:

■   www.corestandards.org/ELA-Literacy

This site is the home of the Common Core–English Language Arts standards.

■   https://ncte.org/resources/online-learning/the-national-center-for-literacy-education

The National Center for Literacy Education, affiliated with the National Council of Teachers of English, offers a nice array of resources for elementary teachers.

Putting the Commonplaces into Action

Purposes, Goals, and Objectives for Teaching and Learning

In this chapter, we talk about selecting a social studies *goal framework* and how one goes about working from it to construct powerful learning opportunities for students. Our discussions in the previous chapters have explored social studies in a teaching–learning context that we hope will help you reflect on the education process and make the sometimes difficult choices required. We have presented a range of vignettes from classrooms that we trust have given you a distinct feel for this teaching–learning context. Now we offer you some ideas and guidance about choosing and working from goal frameworks so that, in the end, you will feel prepared to make your own choices.

You can build goal frameworks from several options, several of which we describe later in this chapter. These goal frameworks are clusters of goals that help teachers decide how to design and organize learning opportunities and to evaluate their importance. They reflect not only different purposes of education, but also different views of what it means to be a good citizen in society. Each framework tends to make good sense in and of itself. And because each of the arguments may seem persuasive, choosing one framework may be difficult. But if you try to build your own educational goal framework by picking and choosing from the best and most attractive features of all the arguments, you may end up putting incompatible elements together.

We begin with examples from teachers' classrooms. We describe four of the most common frameworks that influence social studies education, illustrate how they play out in those classrooms, compare them, note some of their incompatibilities, and offer some guidance about becoming a reflective and independent decision-maker.

This chapter builds on the commonplaces discussed in Chapters 2 through 7: learners and learning, subject matter, teachers and teaching, and classroom environment. We draw on learners and learning because social studies goal frameworks inevitably center on students and their learning processes. We draw on subject matter because it deals with what students are learning. We fuse these two commonplaces together with teachers and teaching and environment because the classroom is the context in which your goal frameworks take root and grow.

When you have completed this chapter, you should be able to answer these questions:

1 What are several common educational goal frameworks that influence social studies teaching and learning?
2 What arguments support different goal frameworks?
3 Where can teachers go for guidance in choosing a goal framework?
4 What goes into building a goal framework?
5 What is the case for working from the liberal-education goal framework?

Goal Frameworks and Good Citizens

How do seasoned social studies teachers work from goal frameworks in their teaching? This is a tough question. Although teachers rarely talk much about their goal frameworks and sometimes even disparage talk about **goals**, nonetheless teachers do teach toward goals. What do we mean by goal frameworks? A **goal framework** expresses those aims teachers hold for their students that help them decide how to design learning opportunities, what those opportunities should consist of, when to put them in place and in what order, and how to explain to parents, administrators, and other teachers why engaging with these opportunities is important. In many ways, a teacher's goal framework is the very heart of her or his teaching. These crucial learning aims form the basis for making sound decisions about learning opportunities. A teacher simply cannot teach effectively without a goal framework.

In social studies, goal frameworks have been expressed in differing and often competing visions of what it means to develop "good citizens" (see, for example, Engle & Ochoa, 1988; Parker, 2008; Rubin, 2011; Thornton, 2004; VanSledright & Grant, 1994). The debate, as you can probably anticipate, centers on how you define the idea of **good citizenship**. In other words, what does it mean to be a good citizen in this country and in the world? What should good citizens do? What are their characteristics? How you answer these questions makes all the difference in understanding how you will design learning opportunities for your students.

In the next section, we look at four elementary-school social studies teachers who work from different goal frameworks that express competing visions of what it means to develop good citizens. We use these examples to illustrate types of goal frameworks from which you might choose to anchor your own social studies teaching practice.

Let's begin with a series of short stories about four teachers. All four teach units on the American Revolution to predominantly White fifth-grade students. Each teaches in the same school district, so the social studies curriculum guidelines and objectives are identical. We will talk more about curriculum guides and other sources of information about goal frameworks in a moment, but let's first look at the teachers in action.

Tom Simpson: Good Citizens Are Good Workers

The first teacher, Tom Simpson, employs a common approach to teaching and learning social studies. He relies almost exclusively on the fifth-grade history textbook used by the school district, follows its order of contents, has students answer the follow-up questions at the end of each chapter section, and finishes the unit with a slightly modified version of the end-of-chapter test supplied by the publisher. Classroom instruction is a predictable daily dose of reading the chapter and reciting answers to the section questions that have individual students recalling specific facts from the book. This approach is spiced up with an occasional DVD, digital slideshow, or PowerPoint presentation. Students do reasonably well on the unit tests, in part, because the questions are as predictable as the daily order of instruction.

Simpson retains tight control of classroom activities and, should student disruptions arise, he deals with them as quickly as they begin. His management style is designed to create an orderly atmosphere in which the work he assigns gets done efficiently and his students all accomplish the tasks at the same pace. Tom Simpson's classroom is structured in ways quite similar to the factory model we describe in Chapter 7. Students study the history textbook by consuming facts and work to produce good scores on the test in something akin to an assembly line (think here about the behaviorist approach we discussed in Chapter 2). Good citizens, by Simpson's lights, are good workers who follow his rules by diligently consuming and reproducing historical knowledge (that is, the key terms and ideas of American culture as defined by the textbook) as preparation for later adult roles that require similar consumption/production roles.

Ramona Palmer: Good Citizens Are Knowledgeable and Informed

Across town but still within the same school district, Ramona Palmer, whom you met in Chapter 3, is doing something quite different with her unit on the American Revolution. She also uses the textbook, some DVDs, and an occasional digital slideshow or PowerPoint, yet she does so sparingly. Her students read historical fiction accounts for different perspectives on the past and richer, more varied accounts than the textbook provides. They also play the roles of angry colonists writing letters to relatives back home in England on the eve of the passage of the Stamp Act. Palmer engages them in a simulation exercise where she plays King George and collects "taxes" from her students to help them feel what the colonists might have felt. Later, she invites her fifth graders to pursue a deep discussion of the Bill of Rights.

Palmer operates from a much different goal framework than does Simpson. She asks her students to become engrossed with this historical period, to make the period come alive. She pushes them to analyze and assess events as a portion of their historical heritage as American citizens. She encourages them to imbibe the period, wrestle with its events, study it from different angles, judge causal connections, and learn by constructing their understanding of the period and its consequences for Americans.

In short, she urges children to inquire into history with panache and commitment. Why? Because she defines the good citizen as one who is deeply knowledgeable and well informed about many things, including his or her own history and politics. Through history, she believes, children learn deeply about their collective past, a process necessary to helping them become well-educated citizens who know enough about their country and its government to effectively and passionately discharge their roles and responsibilities as thoughtful citizens.

Tina Roberts: Good Citizens Are Well-Rounded Human Beings

Tina Roberts spends much of her non-classroom time at the local teacher store. There, she hunts down activities to use with her students that they find interesting and fun. Roberts wants her students to enjoy school and learn to feel good about themselves. Rather than make schoolwork drudgery, Roberts's goal framework promotes as pleasant and as rewarding a school experience as possible for her students.

The unit Tina Roberts constructs on the American Revolution is less about the history of events that occurred and more about arranging activities that enable children to interact in multiple ways, to learn how to get along with each other, and to develop positive self-esteem. Roberts worries less about the content itself. She is far more concerned with the nature of the activities and whether her students are enjoying themselves and each other.

Roberts begins the Revolution unit with a series of trade book stories about key figures who contributed to the Americans winning independence from Britain. Roberts is careful to avoid the uglier aspects of the war with England, such as the early struggles of Washington's ragged army, the details of the Boston Massacre, attitudes and actions against the Loyalists, and the conflict between slavery and the idea of inalienable natural rights in the Declaration of Independence. Much of the unit features students creating period costumes, art projects, dioramas, and stories designed to ensure that each student succeeds in accomplishing something that he or she can be proud of. Students receive grades, not on the basis of test scores as in Simpson's class, but on the relative quality of their projects. Roberts assists students as much as she can to enable them to get the best grades possible.

The way Tina Roberts organizes learning opportunities for her students differs greatly from both Simpson and Palmer. Tom Simpson focuses on the importance of helping students understand and be prepared for work and their future as citizen consumers and producers in a complex, competitive adult work world. Ramona Palmer trains her eye on getting students to deeply engage in the social studies subject matter because she believes it is important for helping them become articulate, thoughtful, and knowledgeable citizens. Tina Roberts, on the other hand, focuses on her students as human beings with unique talents, personalities, thoughts, and emotions. She is primarily interested in her children as children. Educating good citizens, for her, is about creating well-rounded human beings.

Sara Atkinson: Good Citizens Are Social Activists

In a fourth school in the same district, Sara Atkinson is treating the American Revolution unit differently than any of her three colleagues. Like Simpson and Palmer, Atkinson uses a wide array of resources: the textbook, the Internet, DVDs, political cartoons. The textbook acts as a guide, a method for organizing the order of the content. Students read it and occasionally address the section questions by writing responses in their social studies notebooks. Sometimes, as a form of review, they make a game out of answering the questions, a sort of American Revolution *Jeopardy!* Students also read from alternative texts, such as historical fiction. Atkinson connects these readings to language arts as a method of integrating content.

But what really gets Atkinson excited about teaching history is the opportunity to discuss with students what she often refers to as the "mistakes of the past." She wants her students to see how such events as the Boston Massacre can be understood from different perspectives, that the colonists who were killed in this so-called massacre had been agitating the British sentries who fired their guns. Atkinson wants her students to consider whether this agitation was justified, whether or not it might have been a mistake, and whether the British could have handled the situation differently. Were these all errors in judgment? Could disaster have been averted? What do we learn by these lessons from the American Revolution? In short, Atkinson uses historical knowledge as a tool for getting her students to think about what they might gain from understanding historical mistakes in judgment and how they might avoid repeating similar mistakes. She frequently approaches this task by using analogies to students' lives that reflect bad judgment and unfortunate consequences. She links the past with the present and attempts to extend the lessons learned to the future. She wants her students to recognize and avoid those mistakes, to work to correct those that create injustices.

In short, Atkinson wants to develop students who can detect social problems and do something about them. The content she teaches serves as a vehicle to this end. Students become historical detectives, but detectives with an activist mission to undo the damage that has been done by incorrect or unjust decisions made in the past. What animates Atkinson about history, and social studies generally, is that it serves her purpose of educating young social activists who sense wrong and injustice and who are willing to extend their energies toward change. By her definition, this is what it means to educate the good citizen.

▶|◀ REFLECTION: THINKING ABOUT GOAL FRAMEWORKS

Having read the goal frameworks of the teachers profiled, think about these questions:

> Which of these frameworks have you experienced as a student? How do they seem similar and different?
> Which of these frameworks seems closest to your sense of yourself as a teacher?
> If you are having trouble deciding, think about why that might be so.
> If you could ask any or all of these teachers a question or two about the goals they hold, what would those questions be?

▶|◀

■ SECTION SUMMARY:
GOAL FRAMEWORKS AND GOOD CITIZENS

- A goal framework should help teachers decide how to design learning opportunities, what the opportunities should consist of, when to put them in place and in what order, and how to explain why engaging these opportunities is important.

- In social studies, most goal frameworks center on the education of "good citizens."

- Four common goal frameworks define good citizens alternatively as (a) good workers, (b) knowledgeable and informed thinkers, (c) well-rounded human beings, and (d) social activists.

Educational Goal Frameworks and the Supporting Arguments

In the section above, we have four teachers who all work from the same curriculum guidelines, yet do so through quite different approaches. How do we account for these differences? Why do they have such disparate views of the curriculum, of citizenship? As we discuss in Chapter 5, one part of the answer is the many personal, organizational, and policy influences that affect teachers' decisions about subject matter, teaching approaches, and, most importantly, the goals they pursue. In many ways, these four teachers represent four ways these various influences play out in the social studies classroom.

You may be wondering whether it is good practice for these teachers—all from the same school district and ostensibly following the same curriculum guidelines—to be working from such different goal frameworks, with different definitions of what it means to educate the good citizen. It's a good question, for it illuminates the fact that each of the goal frameworks and definitions of good citizenship is rooted in a long history of arguments about how schools should educate children and create citizens. As a larger culture, we cannot agree on what a good citizen is; it is no surprise that these teachers do not agree either (Parker, 2008).

Arguments are efforts designed to persuade. It is essential to recognize the on-going debate over what makes a good citizen, and that this debate is among groups of people who value certain ideas and try to persuade others to share their values. For our purposes here, we discuss only those arguments that address and support the goal frameworks embedded in the stories of the four teachers you just read. However, these are only four of perhaps twice that many arguments about how schools educate good citizens.

Educating Workers

Because much of adult life relates to being a productive worker in whatever capacity, one could say that the social studies role in educating good citizens ought to focus on training children for life's adult work roles. Those who support this view argue that children should learn to get their work done efficiently and effectively, to follow rules, to listen to authority figures, and to become disciplined, competent members of the work world (see Engle & Ochoa, 1988). Doing so helps to create citizens who participate in the economy via the process of being wise producers and informed consumers.

You have probably encountered much talk recently in newspapers and on television concerning America's place in the burgeoning world economy. This talk spawns increased calls for training students more diligently in school subjects so that they will be better able to help America compete in an increasingly competitive and information-driven world. You may have heard teachers talk about the importance of helping students become good workers in the classroom as a prelude to becoming valued contributors to the life of work after school.

Embedded in Tom Simpson's approach is just such a view: Learners become good citizens when they become good workers. Students learn to consume the culturally authoritative textbook content and reproduce it on worksheets and tests. Simpson's classroom tends to mirror the world of workers going to work and doing their jobs (studying the textbook), producing things (test results), earning their pay checks (grades), and reaping the rewards by exchanging their earnings for what they want (praise from parents, academic degrees, good jobs). Simpson structures his classroom to serve this goal of getting students ready for the world by creating an environment that tries to mirror that world. In short, it is education as work and as preparation for the world of intelligent consumption and competitive production in our democratic, capitalist system.

FIGURE 9.1 Teachers such as Tom Simpson emphasize the importance of individual achievement and good work habits.

Providing a Liberal Democratic Education

A second, rather different way to understand messages about school goals comes from what some call the liberal democratic educational ideal. Liberal democratic education as a goal framework means, generally speaking, that students are taught about society's culture and ways of doing things, such as its political methods and its social and economic interactions. This knowledge, so the argument goes, enables them to become intelligent, creative, adaptive members of their communities and of our democratic society as a whole. It encourages them to be wise consumers, who are actively involved participants in the democratic process. This goal stance can be traced to Thomas Jefferson and to European Enlightenment social philosophers such as John Locke (Engle & Ochoa, 1988; Rothstein, 2004). But it has deeper roots. The early Greeks talked about *phronesis*, the well-educated wise person making informed decisions on the basis of the greatest good for the community. This liberal-education ideal is deeply embedded into American culture, its history, and its cultural institutions. As a goal framework, it drives much of what public schools choose to do, how they organize their curricula, and how they make value choices.

Knowledge in this framework is usually thought of as a product of universities, the end result of scientific research, careful study, and published scholarship. This conception is why schools typically have built their curricula around subject matters that sound like university departments and colleges. Students amass a liberal-education in chemistry, sociology, art, history, literature, and so on, and therefore become capable of accepting their democratic rights and exercising their responsibilities soundly, reflectively, actively, and with respect and concern for their community. Although the stress here is on becoming knowledgeable about ideas already created within the culture, this goal framework also leaves room for students to invent new ways of seeing and understanding the world through a focus on the importance of curiosity about and systematic inquiry into how things work.

You have probably heard some teachers talk about their goal frameworks using these ideas. They might say:

> I want my children to be well educated, so that when they leave school, they can think for themselves and evaluate ideas, political propaganda, sales pitches, and the like. I want them to make wise choices when they vote and become involved in their communities, to do good for others, and participate in making society a better place to live. This requires them to earn a good education and be knowledgeable and also to be curious and inquisitive, to question and assess. And it all starts right here in my classroom.

Ramona Palmer believes that history is one of those academic disciplines that provides a rich store of the knowledge Americans need to be liberally educated, to develop rich habits of mind that allow them to think and reason intelligently about issues they confront in their daily lives and in the world around them. From history they learn about the struggles inherent in building their country, about its political, economic, and social systems, about its successes and its failures. Without this understanding and deep knowledge, Palmer believes that her students simply will not be educated enough to become good citizens in American democratic cultural life.

Although she is working from the same curriculum guidelines and using the same textbook, Ramona Palmer differs from Tom Simpson in that she operates from a goal framework that goes beyond preparation for adult work roles and the consumer–producer environment he creates in his classroom. One could argue that Palmer's approach tacitly encompasses some features of Simpson's work world, but she explicitly goes beyond it by asking students to engage the subject matter more deeply, to think, argue about, and assess what they are learning. Students in Palmer's class are more independent and self-engaged than Simpson's students, because Palmer organizes their learning that way. She interprets the curriculum guidelines differently than Simpson, largely because she is working from different arguments about what good citizenship is, arguments designed to support her quite different goal framework.

Nurturing a Humanist Perspective

Did you ever meet a teacher who talked about the importance of students learning to feel good about themselves, to search for the meaning of their experience and the experiences of others, to develop strong interpersonal skills? This description sounds like Tina Roberts, whose talk is usually coupled with commentary on how these personal growth factors are essential to the development of healthy, competent, well-rounded people who serve society in admirable ways and are therefore exemplary citizens. This view centers on introspection, on learning to appreciate one's self, and on developing a fun-loving sense of self and others that results in a deep commitment to care and concern about human beings. This view of good citizens as well-rounded humans is expressed in schools and classrooms that nurture and support the social growth of children (see Brophy, 1990).

Such is the humanist educational goal framework. It has its roots in much the same period as the liberal democratic educational goal, but with social thinkers such as Jean-Jacques Rousseau. In fact, the two approaches share much common language. The principal difference between them is in the nature of how knowledge is directed and understood. In the humanist stance, knowledge is directed inward, toward knowing one's self, and it is understood, in part, through self-reflection. In the liberal educational approach, by contrast, knowledge is directed outward, toward self-in-the-world, and it is understood largely, but not entirely, through academic scholarship.

Tina Roberts appears committed to the humanist approach in her teaching. She wants her children to develop into citizens who care about others because they have learned to care first about themselves. Because they participate in the pleasant activities Roberts organizes in her classroom to enhance their own self-esteem, they develop into citizens who wish to do well by their fellow citizens, or so Roberts hopes. She develops fun and enjoyable in-class activities that reduce conflict and dispute and that allow budding citizens to work together toward ends that actualize their full potential and, by extension, the potential of the culture as a whole.

Encouraging Social Change

The fourth goal framework sounds something like a call to arms. Here, the argument involves the desire to create citizens who are competent, intelligently informed, and socially engaged precisely because they are activists intent on changing the system locally, nationally, and internationally (see Bickmore, 2008). Educational goals, so this argument suggests, ought to be about showing students the injustices and mistakes we make as a society and as individuals, and what to do to change them. Schools and education are used to leveling the playing field by, for example, providing the poor with opportunities to avoid poverty and obtain the same wealth the rich hold, thus making for a more just and humane society (see Freire, 1998).

Some observers suggest that, in fact, American public schools are the embodiment of equal educational opportunity. Others claim that our schools are stratified into rich and poor just as is society itself, that they perpetuate the status quo, and that fundamental changes need to occur (see Apple, 1993).

You might wish to read Jonathan Kozol's 1991 book, *Savage Inequalities*, as a case in point. Kozol describes educational conditions in a variety of urban centers in the United States. For example, he shows how major corporations settled in East St. Louis, Illinois, in the last century, drawing thousands of blue-collar workers (many of them African Americans from the South), who then began raising families and sending their children to school in the city. The corporation managers and executive officers and their families (most of whom were White) lived in communities on a bluff overlooking East St. Louis. In the late twentieth century, after these corporations had seriously polluted East St. Louis, they abandoned the town, the workers, and their families. Without the tax support supplied by the corporations and the people who worked for them, the town spun into a chronic recession, complete with deteriorating schools and disintegrating infrastructure.

The wealthy, Kozol observes, have the power and privilege to live where they wish, send their children to schools that they control, and abandon a community entirely if it suits their interests. Schools of the less fortunate and less advantaged remain dependent on the choices exercised by the wealthy and can suffer from diminished resources as a result. These educational arrangements help perpetuate the divisions among social classes in society.

Effective citizenship education, in this goal framework, is about creating knowledgeable people who can inquire into, recognize, and challenge the problems and injustices in local (such as those Kozol describes), national, and international

FIGURE 9.2 The students in this photograph are helping to clean a park in their community. Their involvement, facilitated by their teacher, demonstrates that student learning can take place just as easily outside classroom walls as inside.

communities. Such people actively organize themselves to fight for better living, working, and general sociocultural conditions. The Civil Rights workers of the 1960s, by this definition, are a pointed illustration of social change activists.

According to this argument, teachers should help students understand and create knowledge about the world and use it to act upon the injustices inherent in that world. Teachers also have a responsibility to challenge assumptions learners typically have about the world, especially those held by students who come from privileged backgrounds.

This sounds like Sara Atkinson. Compared to Tom Simpson, Atkinson's definition of developing a good citizen is notably different from educating future workers. In fact, she rejects the students-as-future-workers goal framework because she finds injustices in it, such as exploited workers and unsafe working conditions. She differs from Tina Roberts in that she teaches the very content Roberts studiously avoids as a lesson in detecting injustices and moving toward social activism. In some ways, Atkinson is more like Ramona Palmer. However, she worries less about engaging students in the content as deeply as Palmer does. She's more interested in those elements of the American Revolution that allow her to pursue her goal framework and to bypass content that provides no lessons for the future. Atkinson, too, wants knowledgeable citizens, but for a different purpose. Good citizens, to her, are social and political activists; they use their knowledge of history, for example, to seek out and attack social and cultural injustices.

▶️◀ REFLECTION: CHANGING IDEAS, CHANGING GOALS

Reflect on the set of questions we posed at the beginning of this section. After reading the arguments supporting the various goal frameworks, have any of your responses to those questions changed? In what ways? What questions are you now thinking about?

■ SECTION SUMMARY:
ARGUMENTS SUPPORTING GOAL FRAMEWORKS

- The goal frameworks most teachers employ have their roots in enduring arguments about the nature of schooling in general and the education of good citizens in particular.

- The good-worker goal reflects the educating-workers argument; the knowledgeable-informed-citizen goal reflects the liberal-education ideal position; the well-rounded human-being goal reflects the humanist perspective; and the social-change stance reflects the social-activist goal.

Teachers' goal frameworks are also influenced by their own personal histories, their social class background, their gender, and their race or ethnicity. Your choices will likewise reflect your own history and background. This tendency is something to think about as you build a goal framework. You might want to ask yourself how much your choices about goals represent your own background biases and how those biased choices might influence your students, for better or for worse. Asking yourself such questions is an important step to becoming a more reflective teacher, something we discuss in depth in Chapter 12.

Sources for Guidance about Goals

A visit to classrooms in any school is likely to turn up examples of all four goal frameworks; they tend to be fairly common. But which one is right for you? Remember, each goal framework is composed of arguments (and suggested definitions) about what it means to be a good citizen. You must decide which argument (or perhaps none of them) is most persuasive to you, and use it to construct your own goal framework. At the moment, you are probably leaning toward one or more that resonate with your own values, education, history, and community background. Before choosing, however, let's look at several places where you might get further guidance about developing a goal framework. After all, if your framework influences your decisions about the when, what, where, and why of creating learning opportunities for your students, you will want to think hard about formulating it. One way to do this would be to consult a variety of sources about potential social studies teaching and learning goals.

The Standards Movement

From the 1990s on, we have seen a move toward establishing national curriculum standards. Many different organizations have weighed in on this effort, including state boards and departments of education from Maine to California and federally funded organizations such as the National Center for History in the Schools. Let's see what several of these groups say about defining citizenship and establishing a goal framework.

National Council for the Social Studies Standards

The National Council for the Social Studies (NCSS) created a set of standards in 1994 called *Curriculum Standards for Social Studies: Expectations of Excellence*. These thematic standards, listed in the accompanying box, represent ten curriculum target areas in which to situate goals:

■ ■ ■ ■ TEN THEMATIC CURRICULUM STANDARDS FOR SOCIAL STUDIES

1 Culture.
2 Time, Continuity, and Change.
3 People, Places, and Environments.
4 Individual Development and Identity.
5 Individuals, Groups, and Institutions.
6 Power, Authority, and Governance.
7 Production, Distribution, and Consumption.
8 Science, Technology, and Society.
9 Global Connections.
10 Civic Ideals and Practices.

(National Council for the Social Studies, 1994)

Because our purpose here is to provide you with a detailed example of how to look at performance expectations to deduce ideas about goals and definitions of citizenship, let's look closely at just one, Standard 2, Time, Continuity, and Change, to see whether we can ferret out the goals NCSS is recommending. We focus on this standard because the four teachers above teach history and this standard deals with that subject area.

One way to understand the goals behind this standard is to explore student "performance expectations." From these expectations, one can detect specific goals behind each standard. Consider the elementary-level expectations for Standard 2 as listed in the accompanying box.

Here, and throughout NCSS standards, the authors appear to assume that the primary goal of schooling is for students to engage with and learn subject matter. Thus, in line with their definition of social studies, NCSS seems to embed its goal framework primarily in the liberal-educational ideal. But also notice the trace of social activism connected to this target area, as when the authors suggest "taking action on public issues." From a different angle, expectation B could represent what Tom Simpson understands as a primary goal of teaching social studies because it would be an expectation he values.

■ ■ ■ ■ PERFORMANCE EXPECTATIONS FOR NCSS SOCIAL STUDIES CURRICULUM STANDARD #2

A To demonstrate an understanding of how different people describe the same events over time.
B To correctly use language connected with history (change, continuity, timeline, etc.).
C To compare and contrast different historical stories and accounts.

D   To use source material in reconstructing an understanding of the past.

E   To understand how time has shaped our differing views of history.

F   To use knowledge of history and methods of inquiry to help with decision making and taking action on public issues.

(National Council for the Social Studies, 1994, p. 54)

As we have noted, in 2013, following the release of Common State Standards for English Language Arts and Mathematics (www.corestandards.org), NCSS released another type of curricular or standards-based document known as the *C3 Framework* (www.socialstudies.org). This framework also contains an explicit set of goals that follow in some ways the earlier 1994 standards. This time the framework elevates inquiry reminiscent of what Palmer does with her students. It also contains an activist approach tied in some ways to what Atkinson does. By its structure and design, it would not be a workable framework for someone such as Tom Simpson. The *C3 Framework* offers yet another resource for thinking about goals.

▶|◀ REFLECTION: INTERPRETING PERFORMANCE EXPECTATIONS

Think about how each of the teachers presented earlier might interpret these performance expectations. What similarities might emerge? What differences?

▶|◀

RESOURCES: NCSS CURRICULUM STANDARDS AND FRAMEWORK

For more on the ten NCSS Thematic Social Studies Standards and each of the performance targets, plus a look at the 2013 *C3 Framework*, visit the NCSS website at www.socialstudies.org

National History Standards

If, like the four teachers we have discussed, you find yourself teaching a heavy dose of history, you might take a close look at the *National Standards for History, Basic Edition* (National Center for History in the Schools, 1996). In the first chapter of these standards, the authors discuss the importance of understanding history for the "educated citizen." Reading this preface quickly takes one back to Thomas Jefferson; it sounds like a full embrace of the liberal-educational ideal. Again, this should be no big surprise, since this ideal has deep roots in our culture.

At one point, the authors state:

> *Knowledge of history* is the precondition of political intelligence. Without history, society shares no common memory of where it has been, what its core values are, or what decisions of the past account for present circumstances. Without history, we cannot undertake any sensible inquiry into the political, social, or moral issues in society. And without historical knowledge and inquiry, we cannot achieve the informed, discriminating citizenship essential to effective participation in the democratic process ...
>
> (National Center for History in the Schools, 1996, p. 1, emphasis in the original)

This statement clearly attempts to define good citizenship. It expresses the liberal-educational ideal through its view of citizens as knowledgeable, able to inquire about issues, and able to make informed judgments and act on them. In many respects, it relates the importance of history to preparation for life in our democracy, for life as an active participating citizen. It does not spell out a form of social activism per se, but it hints at it nonetheless.

For elementary teachers who teach American history, the *National Standards for History* are well worth reading. These standards go farther than many documents in spelling out important and engaging content and examples of student learning expectations.

RESOURCES: IDEAS FOR TEACHING HISTORY

We recommend that you read *Bring History Alive! A Sourcebook for Teaching United States History* (Ankeney, Del Rio, Nash, & Vigilante, 1996). This book gives insight into how the authors of the *National Standards for History* think history should be taught in schools. It also reveals more about the goal frameworks behind the history standards.

Other Content-Standards Documents

Among the host of other national standards documents, many, like the *National Standards for History*, were commissioned and funded by the federal government. They deal with such subject areas as world history, geography, economics, and civics. We lack the space here to look at all these standards, but they are out there and might be worth reading as you construct your own goal framework. The accompanying Resources list presents some of these other standards organizations, their documents, and the social studies subject areas they address.

National Board for Professional Teaching Standards

The National Board for Professional Teaching Standards (NBPTS) (www.nbpts. org) has also produced a set of social studies–history teaching guidelines. The

NBPTS consists of 11 target areas or standards teachers should attain if they wish to be certified by the NBPTS. These target areas are a rich source of ideas related to creating a goal framework and to developing ideas about what is meant by citizenship education.

RESOURCES: CURRICULUM STANDARDS BY SOCIAL STUDIES SUBJECT AREA

Standards Document (Organization)	Subject	Grade Levels
Geography for Life: National	Geography	2, 3, 4, 5
Geography Standards, Second Edition www.aag. org/cs/education/organizations_and_policy/ geography_for_life_national_geography_ standards_second_edition		Middle School
National Standards for Civics and Government www. civiced.org/standards	Civics/Government	2, 3, 4, 5 Middle School
National Content Standards in Economics www.councilforeconed.org	Economics	3, 4, 5 Middle School
National and State World History Standards whfua.history. ucla.edu/foundations/natl_standards.php	World History	Middle School

Defining Social Studies as Citizenship Education

It should be clear by now that many resources exist to help teachers clarify what they want to accomplish with students in schools. But is this always the case? To take a closer look at this question, return with us for a moment to the definition of social studies offered by the National Council for the Social Studies, which contains some important statements that suggest guidance on goals.

The NCSS Definition of Social Studies

Read the following portion of the NCSS definition of social studies carefully. These two sentences are essentially goal statements that we analyze more carefully as we look for guidance about choosing teaching and learning goals:

Social studies is the integrated study of the social sciences and humanities to promote civic competence ... The primary purpose of social studies is to help young people develop the ability to make informed and reasoned decisions for the public good as citizens of a culturally diverse, democratic society in an interdependent world.

(National Council for the Social Studies, 1993, p. 7)

What do these two sentences mean? What does it mean to "promote civic competence" and to "help young people develop the ability to make informed and reasoned decisions for the public good?" Does the latter phrase define the former? It seems that the root message is about educating good citizens, but what is a "good" citizen? As we have seen, it can be defined according to one of several different arguments about which values are better than others in developing citizens. Also, upon closer scrutiny, we see that the goals implied in this definition are difficult to see clearly, largely because the definition is so broad and all-encompassing. This situation is often the case with such goals and standards documents because, to satisfy many different educational groups, the authors try to include many elements of different goal frameworks at once, and therefore produce goal frameworks that are quite vague. Based on this NCSS definition, it's tough to say for sure what the argument is here, so let's explore it further.

Similarities in language between the liberal and humanistic goals make it easy to read the NCSS definition and its goal sentences as applying to either a liberal education approach or a humanist one. In other words, the NCSS statement is roomy enough to allow a Palmer, or a Roberts, to find herself in it and to claim she is teaching social studies in the name of creating good citizens. At the same time, the NCSS definition language is open enough to suggest other possibilities. A social activist such as Atkinson could appropriate the NCSS statement, claiming that competence is defined as the basis for social action. Yet, Simpson might also feel comfortable with this definition because competence could easily be interpreted to mean learning basic facts. Statements that reflect goal frameworks require careful study. Often what seems good in print means little in practice because terms and statements need further interpreting and defining. Our point is simple: In the pursuit of a thoughtful goal framework, not all resources are equally useful.

Variations on the Definition of Good Citizenship

The debates and discussions around the definition of social studies in general, and around the definition of good citizenship in particular, have fed a small industry of groups who have tried to define with greater clarity what they think good citizenship should be and the social studies' role in helping to shape it. As you develop as a social studies teacher, we invite you to consult the expanse of social studies literature that has grown up around various ways to define and to specify a curriculum for social studies and good citizenship. But for now, let's briefly examine some examples of this literature.

Issues-Centered Social Studies

One example is **issues-centered social studies,** or ICSS (Engle & Ochoa, 1988; Evans & Saxe, 1996; Goodman, 1992; Koeppen, 2010). Advocates of ICSS seek to use the social studies as a vehicle for developing knowledge in students that can enable them to address public issues that need attention in the nation and world. ICSS is rooted in the social-activist goal approach (although this assumption too can be questioned; see Grant & Tzetzo, 1997) that we see most clearly in Atkinson's treatment of the American Revolution. To a large degree, proponents of ICSS believe that the goal of social studies teaching and learning is the education of democratic citizens who are deeply knowledgeable about their world, can use their knowledge to understand social justice issues, and can employ this understanding to address and redress those issues.

Proponents of ICSS seek a social studies curriculum that reflects the goals they believe will create these democratic citizens. Rather than have the curriculum organized around typical subjects such as history and geography, they would welcome courses of study focused on the current problems and social issues confronting Americans. For example, ICSS advocates might ask that a third-grade social studies curriculum that focuses on studying and understanding the students' local community be changed to examine instead the social problems facing that community. These might include troublesome race relations, waste-management difficulties, transportation problems, and air and water pollution issues. Students would use investigative strategies from the standard subject matters as tools to understand the issues and would then work on suggestions for solutions. Students might engage in civic action around their proposed suggestions, writing letters to local leaders about their studies and policy solutions. Teachers might also engage students in community-service exercises; that is, students would contribute time and energy after school and on weekends to local organizations (which might include the students' own school) that were attempting to solve the problems the students had studied.

These efforts, the ICSS advocates argue, would help make students thoughtful, informed "young citizens" who are actively involved in solving community problems. They hope to instill in students a lasting commitment to active, participatory citizenship of the sort that would bring greater degrees of economic and social justice to the world in which they live.

Multicultural Education

Another approach to good citizenship can be seen in **multicultural education,** or MCE (Banks, 1994/2001; Banks & Nguyen, 2008; Ladson-Billings, 1994; Sleeter & Grant, 1994). Proponents of MCE look to social studies as one area of the curriculum that can help students to develop greater awareness of the ethnic and racial diversity of our culture. This awareness promotes a view of good citizenship that turns on a greater appreciation of the strengths of cultural diversity, a tolerance for different world views, and a culture that is free from bigotry, intolerance, and racism.

Over the past decade, MCE advocates have talked about the social studies as a location in which social justice concerns and goals (e.g., eliminating bigotry and racism, increasing social and economic opportunities for those traditionally underserved by cultural institutions, promoting cultural sensitivity and responsiveness) can be addressed. Much of this talk has centered on the idea of culturally relevant or responsive teaching and curricula (for one of the most thorough treatments of this idea that also includes portraits of such teachers in action, see Ladson-Billings, 1994). Advocates call for teachers to become more culturally relevant in their teaching practices so that they can boost the academic achievement of students of color. Increased achievement, proponents argue, is central to effective, thoughtful, and active citizenship. Low achievement relegates students to lower rungs on the social class ladder and potentially marks them for failure. Such results form the antithesis of good citizenship.

This call to change teaching practice and the curriculum is rooted in the understanding that, while much of the teaching force—both practicing and prospective—remains White and middle class, students in the schools served by these teachers are increasingly non-White and non-middle class (Howard, 2003). This arrangement results in sociocultural discontinuities between teachers and students that contribute to the continued underperformance of students of color in public schools. Advocates recommend infusing the social studies curriculum with literature and subjects that are relevant to students of color, including their family life, their cultural history, their social dynamics, and the issues of social justice that touch their lives.

Teaching practice turns on an ethic of care (Gay, 2000), a commitment to the academic success of *all students* through cultural sensitivity and relationship-building (Ladson-Billings, 1994), as well as through continual critical self-reflection about curricula, pedagogy, and sociocultural differences (Howard, 2003). Without these forms of culturally relevant pedagogy and curriculum, advocates argue, students of color will remain underserved by the educational system, and their commitment to good citizenship practices and beliefs will be limited.

Caveat Emptor (Buyer Beware)

All of the above definitions and approaches to thinking about goals are broad. None define good citizenship in specific, behavioral terms; each leaves that to the reader. We can understand why these authors might have avoided this task; there is nothing straightforward about defining the terms. Their potential to provide guidance, however, suffers from such a wide array of possible interpretations. As odd as it may seem, goals and standards documents and definition statements may lack both clear goals and specific definitions, and so they must be studied carefully.

Beginning teachers and many more experienced ones look at all these standards and definitions and wonder, do they cohere? Does one voice unite them all? Unfortunately, the answer is no. As we have said, goal frameworks are about arguments, arguments about what's best for students. Within our culture, we are not in complete agreement about how to educate students for the society at large. We differ politically, racially, ethnically, and socially, and therefore we wrestle with and argue about educational goals. This is the case also among those who recommend goal frameworks for teaching social studies. In some respects, disagreement over goal frameworks gives you some autonomy in choosing them because we have no *final* authoritative source to which we can appeal to settle the debate. This situation may seem like a mixed blessing, particularly when you are first learning to teach. But you will cherish this autonomy after you become more masterful at your chosen profession.

■ SECTION SUMMARY: GUIDANCE TOWARD GOALS

- ■ Teachers have additional sources for finding guidance in developing a goal framework. These sources include, for example, documents emerging from the curriculum standards movement, a definition of social studies developed by NCSS, and several other ways of defining social studies and its relationship to citizenship (e.g., ICSS, MCE).

- ■ None of these sources, however, has a corner on the goal framework market, leaving to you the task of constructing a goal framework for yourself from the resources available.

Building a Goal Framework

By now you can see that making goal choices involves embracing some ideas and letting others go. This is important, for most teachers we know have difficulty attending to a whole mixed bag of goals. You might blend together some of the goals shown by the four teachers profiled, but quite frankly, we suspect that you would end up sending your young students confusing and mixed messages about what is important. A few features of each goal framework may be compatible, but for the most part, the four arguments for good citizenship are different enough that blending *all* of them together would be difficult and futile.

A better approach is to locate your teaching practice primarily within one goal framework and add compatible pieces so that you tailor-make a framework that reflects your values, beliefs, and strengths. The metaphor of a restaurant meal may help you conceptualize this: Think of your primary goal framework as the entrée and the compatible pieces from other goal frameworks as side dishes. *How* you mix your goal framework and compatible pieces—entrée and side dishes—is less important than the product—a complete and satisfying meal, er … goal framework.

Consider how Tom Simpson and Ramona Palmer have seasoned their goal conceptions. Simpson thinks good citizenship is all about competitive, hard work; adept consumption and production; and other such efforts that prepare his charges for their adult roles as workers in a market economy. This stance reflects the goal of educating workers as the means toward producing good citizens. At the same time, however, Simpson adds something of the flavor of the liberal-education agenda in that he expects his students to know the facts of American history. We might disagree that factual knowledge is sufficient, but many observers would argue that Simpson's focus on facts defines a good education (see, for example, Hirsch, 1987, 1999). Ramona Palmer's goal framework also reflects some diversity. Palmer teaches her students the importance of being informed about the past so that they can make better decisions in the present—a standard expression of the liberal-education ideal. Palmer's focus, however, is on elements of the good-worker stance, in that, like Simpson, she values some types of competitive work settings.

Both teachers give attention to the educating-workers and liberal-education positions, yet each focuses on one position. Simpson's goal framework features an entrée of educating workers with a side order of liberal education. Palmer's goal framework is just the reverse; it features educating workers as the side order to her main meal, which is creating knowledgeable and informed citizens in the liberal-education tradition.

Compatible or Incompatible Goals?

Now think about Tina Roberts and Sara Atkinson. What compatible elements—side orders, if you will—can you detect within their goal frameworks? Do any elements seem incompatible?

Thinking about your goal framework as an entrée with complementary side orders should help you begin building your own goal framework. To push yourself to greater clarity on this issue of social studies goals, ask yourself the accompanying reflective questions, and make a list of your responses as you go.

▶|◀ REFLECTION: CLARIFYING SOCIAL STUDIES GOALS

What should be the purposes of social studies teaching?
What should students learn from social studies and be able to do once they learn it?
What is my definition of a "good citizen"?
In what ways do my responses to the first three questions reflect my values?
How are my responses to the first three questions complementary?
In what ways are my responses contradictory?
▶|◀

You also might talk over and perhaps debate these questions with fellow practicing and prospective teachers to get a sense of how others think about these goal issues. Making your ideas public is a good way of deepening your understanding. Doing so also helps you become increasingly reflective and thoughtful about your practice. After all, as a part of your professional responsibility as a teacher, *you are choosing goals for other people's children.* That's a daunting responsibility and one you will need to take very seriously. At some point in your career, you may need to develop a reflective and thoughtful rationale for why you have chosen to pursue the goals you have in your classroom.

■ SECTION SUMMARY:
BUILDING A GOAL FRAMEWORK

■ Building a goal framework is no easy task.

■ When you build your framework, avoid blindly choosing a mix of elements from various other frameworks.

■ A better approach is to build your framework around a primary goal to which you add complementary elements.

Some Parting Thoughts about Goals

So far, our effort here has been to (1) familiarize you with a non-exhaustive range of possible stances you could take, (2) ask how your stance reflects your values, and (3) argue that your goal framework influences the way you make teaching and learning decisions in your social studies classroom. We are hoping this quick trip through the goal menu will help you become more reflective about your goal positions and help you avoid the trap of thinking that teaching is nothing more than teaching technique. Thinking more clearly about your goals will help you think more clearly about what learning opportunities to provide your students, when and how to provide them, and why.

Our Choice: The Liberal-Education Goal

As both school and university teachers, we hold to the liberal-educational ideal argument, for the following reasons:

■ It appears to drive much of what we ideally know schools, teaching, and curriculum to be.

■ It likely will have the most profound influence on you as you move into teaching elementary-school social studies because of its deep roots in American cultural institutions.

■ It holds the greatest promise for allowing aspects of other goals to be embedded within it, such as the goals of issues-centered social studies and multicultural education to the extent that they are aligned.

The liberal-educational ideal is a broad framework, which may account for much of its appeal in a culture that prides itself on the importance of democratic participation in the affairs of community, state, and nation, from political to sociocultural, economic to familial, and so on. We think that appeal is well deserved.

Achieving the liberal-educational ideal requires thoughtful, well-educated, well-rounded citizens who are willing to engage deeply in the lives of their communities, both large and small, close and distant. They value historical and social science inquiries and the knowledge they produce, and, most importantly, use such knowledge to benefit their communities.

They also value constructive debate about courses of action, are concerned that *all voices* are heard in such debates, and are sensitive to the consequences of possible choices. In several ways, Ramona Palmer comes the closest of the four teachers we've profiled in this chapter to working toward this ideal. But Sara Atkinson also embodies many of the goals of the liberal-educational ideal in her commitment to improving the world and teaching her students to do so as well. We consider something like this ideal a worthy place to set up *your* social studies goal framework. It gives you considerable flexibility to adjust and modify it as you go. However, that's *our* argument. We still recognize that it's up to you to decide, and decide you must. We simply hope that you choose wisely, reflecting on your choices as you go.

Chapter Summary

1 **What are several common educational goal frameworks that influence social studies teaching and learning?**
A goal framework is a means by which you decide how to design learning opportunities, what the opportunities should consist of, when to put them in place and in what order, and how to explain why engaging these opportunities is important. In social studies, goal frameworks commonly revolve around definitions of good citizenship. There is no one definition that all teachers work from; instead, numerous definitions are in circulation. These definitions characterize good citizens as good workers, knowledgeable and informed citizens, well-rounded human beings, and social activists. Teachers build goals to match the definition that they most support.

2 **What enduring arguments support different goal frameworks?**
The competing goal frameworks reflect enduring debates about the nature of schooling and of citizenship. The good-workers goal comes out of the educating-workers argument; the knowledgeable-citizens goal comes out of the liberal-educational ideal; the well-rounded human-being goal comes out

of the humanist perspective; and the social-activist goal comes out of the social-change position.

3   **Where can teachers go for guidance in choosing a goal framework?**
Several sources are available for teachers seeking guidance in developing a goal framework. None of these sources—curriculum standards and definitions of citizenship—is perfect, but they serve a useful purpose as ways to provoke teachers' thinking.

4   **What goes into building a goal framework?**
Although teachers may feel comfortable firmly ensconced in a single perspective, many will want to broaden their frameworks. One way to do that is to develop a primary focus (for example, one of the goal positions outlined) and then add complementary elements.

5   **What is the case for working from the liberal-education goal framework?**
Although we can see pros and cons within all goal frameworks, we find ourselves drawn most consistently to the definition of good citizens as knowledgeable, informed, and active, which is reflected in the liberal-educational ideal. The ideal is deeply wedded to our culture, it's had a profound impact on educational practice, and it offers enough room to accommodate other goal framework elements within it. It is also forward-looking in that it represents a never-ending commitment to fulfill its "ideal," one in which citizens become actively engaged in promoting institutions and a culture that reflect the values of justice and liberty for each member.

Teaching Resources

Print Resources

Butts, R.F. (1980). *The revival of civic learning.* Washington, DC: Phi Delta Kappa Educational Foundation.
This classic text on citizenship education offers some valuable insights into the various definitions of the good citizen.

Technology Resources

See the website addresses we listed within this chapter. These sites contain many resources for thinking about goals and goal frameworks, but study them critically and carefully because no single one of them can articulate fully the best goal framework for you or your students. As we have said, we debate such goals all the time because we are different and value different things. The websites reflect the positions of their authors and are unlikely to be completely compatible with one another. Yet, you will still need to choose even though guidance can be limited.

10

The Inquiry Design Model

Purposes, goals, and objectives help center us as teachers: The work we do reflects the positions that we take. To this point, we have argued that those positions can best be understood through the commonplaces of education. In this chapter and the next, we describe the **Inquiry Design Model** (IDM), an approach to teaching, learning, subject matter, and classroom environment that brings students more fully into the world of ideas.

There is a change going on in social studies. Inquiry-based teaching and learning has taken hold at the national level through the *College, Career, and Civic Life (C3) Framework for Social Studies State Standards* (National Council for the Social Studies, 2013). Referred to as the *C3 Framework*, the document was a national effort to help states and school districts generate their own curriculum standards. Coming on the heels of the Common Core State Standards, the *C3 Framework* draws on the English Language Arts portion, but dives deeply into the social studies disciplines of history, geography, economics, and civics.

Rooting the *C3 Framework* are four dimensions: 1) Developing questions and planning inquiries, 2) Applying disciplinary concepts and tools, 3) Evaluating sources and using evidence, and 4) Communicating conclusions and taking informed action. These four dimensions outline a pathway for enacting inquiry-based teaching and learning. A portion of the *C3 Framework* is the **Inquiry Arc**, a brief description of what the four dimensions mean in general and in the context of teaching and learning social studies.

Like our purposes, goals, and objectives, standards are a way of helping us center ourselves as teachers. But the global nature of most standards offers only limited value to teachers in planning their day-to-day curriculum and the instruction and assessments that go with it.

RESOURCES: THE *C3 FRAMEWORK*

Check out this free, downloadable version of the *C3 Framework*:

■   www.socialstudies.org/c3

The Inquiry Arc is located on pages 17–19.

To help teachers bridge the gap between standards and their daily practice, S.G. and his colleagues Kathy Swan and John Lee have created an approach to make inquiry-based teaching and learning a classroom reality. The Inquiry Design Model (IDM) enables teachers to plan curriculum inquiries that invite *all* their students into the inquiry dance.

When you have completed this chapter, you should be able to answer these questions:

1   What are the four dimensions of the *C3 Framework*?
2   What are the primary components of the Inquiry Design Model?
3   What are the two kinds of questions represented in the IDM blueprint?
4   What distinguishes a formative from a summative task?
5   How can teachers adapt sources for their students' use?

Inquiry and the Inquiry Design Model

In Chapter 4, we hint at the three typical elements of inquiry-based teaching and learning: questions, tasks, and sources. The IDM has several components, but central to the entire model are *questions* (compelling and supporting), *tasks* (formative and summative), and *sources* (textual, graphic, and the like). In this chapter, we talk you through an example of an inquiry. Then, in Chapter 11, we walk you through the process of designing your own inquiry. Let's get started.[1]

Before delving into the practice of inquiry-based teaching, let's take a quick look at its history. Inquiry has been advocated as an approach to teaching for over 100 years. Yet, it is taken root unevenly and it has been slow to develop as common classroom practice (Grant, Swan, & Lee, 2017). The reasons are several: Inquiry-based practice demands more planning time, teachers worry that students may not succeed, and standardized testing seems to promote traditional teaching approaches. These challenges notwithstanding, the research literature strongly supports inquiry-based practice as a powerful approach to teaching and learning (Grant, Swan, & Lee, 2017). Moreover, the benefits accrue to *all* students: elementary, secondary, and academically challenged as well as the academically gifted (Grant, 2018).

These research findings will convince few teachers, however, if inquiry-based practice seems more abstract than practical. Even teachers who want to pursue more ambitious instruction have been thwarted, as there have been few effective models for them to employ.

The IDM is intended to meet these several challenges. By offering a concise, practical approach to developing classroom inquiries, IDM offers teachers a way to see their way into inquiry-based practice. And with a bank of over 300 inquiries available (at www.C3Teachers.org), teachers can save considerable planning time.

RESOURCES: C3TEACHERS

C3Teachers is a website (www.c3teachers.org) devoted to all things inquiry. On the site are materials that further explain the Inquiry Design Model, publications that use the *C3 Framework*, and blogs by teachers who are working to bring inquiry into their classrooms.

One of the most used features is the tab that takes you to a searchable database of inquiries for grades K–12. You can also go directly to the inquiries at www.c3teachers.org/inquiries.

Central to the IDM is the **blueprint**, a one-page representation of the common elements of inquiry-based practice: questions, tasks, and sources. Each blueprint offers a visual snapshot of an entire inquiry. Viewers can then see the individual inquiry components *and* the relationship among those components. Those components, listed below, focus on the elements necessary to support students as they address a compelling question:

- Standards (anchor the content of the inquiry)
- Compelling questions (frame the inquiry)
- Staging the compelling question tasks (create interest in the inquiry)
- Supporting questions (develop the key content)
- Formative performance tasks (demonstrate emerging understandings)
- Featured sources (provide opportunities to generate curiosity, build knowledge, and construct arguments)
- Summative performance tasks (demonstrate evidence-based arguments)
- Summative extensions (offer assessment flexibility)
- Taking informed action exercises (promote opportunities for civic engagement)

IN YOUR CLASSROOM

THE IDM BLUEPRINT

If you would like to start playing around with an inquiry, go to the website www.c3teachers.org/inquiry-design-model/ to download a blueprint template. If you would like to see a version of a blueprint with all the components defined, download the IDM-at-a-glance version at www.c3teachers.org/wp-content/uploads/2019/08/Inquiry-Design-Model-at-a-glance.pdf.

In the sections that follow, we unpack the defining elements of inquiry—questions, tasks and sources—relevant to an early elementary inquiry on the economic concepts of needs and wants. As we do so, we highlight the compelling and supporting *questions* that frame and organize this inquiry; the formative and summative assessment *tasks* that provide opportunities for students to demonstrate and apply their understandings; and the featured *sources* that allow students to practice inquiry-based thinking and reasoning (See Figure 10.1).

As you look at this blueprint, what do you notice about the questions, tasks, and sources and about how they are arranged within the blueprint? We will have more to say about each element below, but take a minute to familiarize yourself with the structure of the blueprint and its components.

■ SECTION SUMMARY:
AN IDM BLUEPRINT

- Inquiry has long been promoted as a more ambitious way of teaching and learning, but has not been widely embraced in classrooms.
- The Inquiry Design Model (IDM) is intended to address the challenge of making inquiry-based teaching and learning more practical.
- The IDM is built around a blueprint that features compelling and supporting questions, formative and summative tasks, and featured sources.

Questions in the IDM

Questions are key to any teacher's instructional practice; they are also key to inquiry-based curriculum design. Two types of questions—compelling and supporting—surface in the Inquiry Design Model. These questions differ in form

Kindergarten Economics Inquiry

Why Can't We Ever Get Everything We Need *and* Want?

New York State Social Studies Framework Key Idea and Practices	K.9 People have economic needs and wants. Goods and services can satisfy people's wants. Scarcity is the condition of not being able to have all of the goods and services that a person wants or needs. ✏ Economics and Economic Systems ✏ Civic Participation
Staging the Question	Brainstorm examples of wants and needs and discuss examples of goods and services.

Supporting Question 1	Supporting Question 2	Supporting Question 3
What do we want? What do we need?	How do goods and services meet our needs and wants?	What happens when there isn't enough for everyone?
Formative Performance Task	**Formative Performance Task**	**Formative Performance Task**
Sort and categorize items as needs or wants.	Identify a need or want and determine ways in which it could be satisfied through goods and services.	Participate in a discussion of options people have when faced with scarcity.
Featured Source	**Featured Source**	**Featured Source**
Source A: Image bank: Needs and wants	**Source A:** Image bank: Goods and services	**Source A:** Image bank: Scarcity

Summative Performance Task	ARGUMENT Why can't we ever get everything we need *and* want? In small groups, construct arguments, supported with evidence, that address the question of whether or not we can ever get everything we need and want.
	EXTENSION Create two-sided collages with images of needs (or goods) on one side and wants (or services) on the other.
Taking Informed Action	UNDERSTAND Identify a need or want for the classroom. ASSESS Brainstorm methods of fulfilling the need or want for the classroom. ACT Select and act on a method of fulfilling the need or want for the classroom.

FIGURE 10.1 A Needs and Wants inquiry.

and function. But they work together to build academic rigor and student relevance into an inquiry.

Those two qualities of rigor and relevance define a good compelling question. An academically rigorous question highlights an enduring social issue, concern, or debate worth thinking through. For example, the compelling question for an early elementary inquiry—"Why can't we ever get everything we need and want?"—asks students to wrestle with two of the central components of economics: the things we *need* to survive as human beings and the things that we *want* to have to make life more enjoyable.[2] That distinction seems simple enough. Yet, depending on one's perspective, a bottle of Smartwater might be considered a want or a need.

Kindergartners will have all kinds of ideas about this example of wants and needs. And their debates around those ideas speak to the second quality of a compelling question—relevance to students. Because they have no one right answer, compelling questions invite students into an active and genuine discussion. A compelling question also connects real social studies content to the realities of students' daily lives. Bottled water has certain advantages of being sanitary and convenient. But it can also be expensive and produce excess garbage, ideas that even young students can understand and appreciate.

IN YOUR CLASSROOM

COMPELLING QUESTIONS

A compelling question has to have some academic value, but it also has to spark students' curiosity and interest. Teachers who craft good compelling questions know the content *and* they know their students.

So, give it try: Think about a topic that is commonly taught as part of elementary social studies and draft a compelling question for it.

If compelling questions set out the broad frame for an inquiry, **supporting questions** help teachers build the content that fills that frame. Supporting questions demonstrate a logical flow of ideas. By answering them, students learn the content that enables them to make an evidence-based argument at the end of the inquiry.

The supporting questions for an inquiry on needs and wants might be:

1   What do we want? What do we need?
2   How do goods and services meet our needs and wants?
3   What happens when there isn't enough for everyone?

We think this set of supporting questions works for two reasons. First, the sequence of questions makes sense. That is, in order to understand the idea behind the third question, students need to understand the concepts of needs and wants and goods and services expressed in the first two supporting questions. The second reason we think this sequence works is because, by answering each of the supporting questions, students develop their knowledge and capacity to then answer the compelling question.

Compelling and supporting questions are mutually reinforcing; the compelling question frames the inquiry and the supporting questions give it a coherent structure. That said, there is no one "right" compelling question on needs and wants nor is there a single right set of supporting questions. We can imagine all kinds of alternatives and we invite you to play with them.

To that end, all IDM inquiries available on C3 Teachers (c3teachers.org) are available in both PDF and Word documents so that teachers can adapt the inquiries for their particular classroom contexts.

■ SECTION SUMMARY:
QUESTIONS IN IDM

■ An IDM blueprint features two kinds of questions—compelling and supporting.

■ Compelling questions reflect important ideas, but they also reflect students' interests and concerns.

■ Supporting questions offer students opportunities to build their content knowledge in preparation for answering the compelling question.

Tasks in the IDM

It is hard to imagine doing inquiry with students without a set of questions that are worth pursuing. But questions are not enough. How students respond to questions matters too. And how they demonstrate their new knowledge and understandings emerges through the tasks that they complete.

Because an IDM inquiry begins with a compelling question and ends with students constructing an evidence-based argument, students' summative products are *convergent*—that is, their investigations converge on an answer to the compelling question. The formative performance tasks students complete in response to each supporting question can also be considered convergent in nature as this work helps students develop and support their arguments.

Convergent thinking is important, but it is not sufficient. In IDM blueprint, extension activities and taking informed action exercises offer students opportunities for *divergent* thinking. By divergent, we mean the possibility of expanding on one's original work.

At the heart of each inquiry, however, are two points—the compelling question and the summative argument. The elements in the middle (i.e., supporting questions, formative performance tasks, and sources) help students move constructively between the compelling question and the argument. Note, however, that the summative performance task begins with the compelling question followed by the phrase, "construct an argument." We purposefully chose the verb *construct* to indicate that not all arguments must be expressed in written form.

Students build both their content knowledge and their reasoning skills by working through an inquiry. To that end, formative performance tasks function as content and skill *exercises*. These exercises scaffold students' learning toward the goal of making and supporting their arguments. Although these tasks may not include all of what teachers want their students to know and do, they do provide students with a foundation for their arguments.

In the Needs and Wants inquiry, the **formative performance tasks** ask students to:

1 Sort and categorize items as needs or wants.
2 Identify a need or want and determine ways in which it could be satisfied through goods and services.
3 Participate in a discussion of options people have when faced with scarcity.

Staging the compelling question activity is another type of formative task. In the Needs and Wants inquiry, we recommend having students brainstorm their wants and needs and the goods and services that satisfy them. Doing this exercise at the beginning of the inquiry gives teachers an early insight into their students' familiarity with the concepts and how those concepts are represented in students' worlds.

Formative performance tasks focus on *performances*, opportunities where students demonstrate their emerging understanding of the content. Instead of having students answering end-of-chapter questions or other mundane assignments, formative tasks enable students to directly build the content knowledge and skills they need to make and support their summative arguments.

▶|◀ REFLECTION: PERFORMANCE VERBS

Benjamin Bloom and his colleagues (1956) created a widely used taxonomy of thinking, from the most basic (knowledge) to the most complex (evaluation). In an inquiry, we want students to think on a wide range of levels. But when constructing the tasks students are to complete, we advocate clearly defining what we want them to *do*—actions that demonstrate that students are building the knowledge they need.

Formative tasks help teachers identify their students' strengths and challenges. In that sense, they act to *inform* teachers throughout the inquiry. Teachers can then decide if they need to slow down their instruction, give more examples of an idea, or provide additional sources for students to engage. Summative tasks are opportunities for teachers to assess their students' work at the end of an inquiry. In the Inquiry Design Model, there are three kinds of **summative performance tasks**: arguments, extensions, and taking informed action activities.

An inquiry technically ends when students construct answers or arguments in response to the compelling question. The extension and taking informed action activities are summative in nature. But it is the **argument** that closes the circle around the compelling question.

Arguments matter because it is a rare question or issue on which there is universal agreement. Arguments, then, are our attempts to persuade others how to think about that question or issue. If we simply state a belief about it, then we have offered an opinion. If we back that statement up with evidence, then we have made an argument.

An argument has two parts: a stance and one or more claims. A stance expresses our initial response to the compelling question; a claim explains our stance. Here are some possible arguments that students might come up with for the Needs and Wants inquiry:

- We can get everything we need and want because my mom and dad will get it for me.

- We cannot get everything we want and need because stores can run out of stuff.

- We can get what we need, but not everything we want because there is not always enough money for what I want.

Although they reflect the overall purpose of the inquiry in general and the students' arguments in particular, summative **extensions** offer students a chance to flex their creative muscles. Extension activities can take any number of graphic, textual, oral, and even performance forms. An extension is a new task, but it does not demand new teaching and learning. Instead, students employ their initial arguments into a new form. In the Needs and Wants inquiry, for example, the extension activity asks students to draw on their arguments to create two-sided collages with images of needs (or goods) on one side and wants (or services) on the other.

The last type of IDM task is **taking informed action**. These experiences enable students to apply the content they have learned through an inquiry in a civic form either inside or outside of the classroom. The key word, however, is "informed." In taking informed action activities, students build their knowledge and understanding of an issue *before* engaging in any type of social action.

There are three stages to a taking informed action activity. In the *understand* stage, students demonstrate that they can think about the issues behind the inquiry in a new setting or context. The *assess* stage asks students to consider alternative perspectives, scenarios, or options to address a problem or issue. The *act* stage occurs only after students have learned about a problem or issue and explored possibilities for tackling it. For the Needs and Wants inquiry, the taking informed action sequence is:

UNDERSTAND: Identify a need or want for the classroom.
ASSESS: Brainstorm methods of fulfilling the need or want for the classroom.
ACT: Select and act on a method of fulfilling the need or want for the classroom.

Following these stages of taking informed action enables students to employ their understandings from the inquiry directly to a relevant issue and to make decisions about how they might use their voices to participate in public discourse around the matter.

■ SECTION SUMMARY:
TASKS IN IDM

- Tasks come in two forms: formative and summative.

- Formative performance tasks offer students the opportunity to build their knowledge and skills throughout an inquiry and they inform teachers about their students' emerging strengths and challenges.

- Formative tasks result in performances, products that demonstrate students' knowledge and skills in response to the supporting questions.

- Summative performance tasks offer students the opportunity to pull together their new learnings and for teachers to see the results.

- Summative performance tasks include arguments, extensions, and taking informed action activities.

- Taking informed action activities have three stages: understand, assess, and act.

Sources in the IDM

Sources play a vital role in inquiry. By weaving in and around the questions and tasks, sources provide the glue that holds an inquiry together. Those **sources** can be textual (e.g., books), graphic (e.g., charts), visual (e.g., photographs), or digital (e.g., videos). Where they once had only a textbook and a few trade books, teachers today can draw from a wide range of sources to build their inquiries.

Sources serve three purposes in an inquiry: 1) to spark and sustain student curiosity in an inquiry; 2) to build students' disciplinary (content and conceptual) knowledge and skills; and 3) to enable students to construct arguments with evidence. On the IDM blueprint, sources are listed in the column with supporting questions and formative tasks.[3] But sources can also support other parts of the IDM blueprint such as the staging,[4] extension, and taking informed action activities.

In inquiries aimed at the youngest learners, sources often take the form of images. To build their curiosity during a staging activity on needs and wants, for example, teachers could provide students with the images of a glass of water and a sports drink as a way to prompt students' brainstorming about what counts as a need or a want.

SOURCES

Open up the C3Teachers inquiries site (www.c3teachers.org/inquiries) and survey some of the other elementary-level inquiries to see what other kinds of sources can support inquiry.

Sources play a central role in helping students build their disciplinary knowledge and skills. Content and conceptual knowledge is important, but no more so than disciplinary skills such as historical thinking. The long-standing debate between content and skills is over; students need both. And they can gain both through the use of sources to complete formative and summative tasks.

In the Needs and Wants inquiry, the first supporting question pushes students to think about needs and wants. To help them answer this question, students see images of a container of food, a log cabin, and a coat as examples of needs and a bracelet, a box of toys, a stuffed animal, and a collection of sports equipment as examples of wants. The sources for the second supporting question on goods and services include images of a farmer, a clerk in a store, and a firefighter. And for the third supporting question about scarcity, there are images of empty supermarket shelves.

The third purpose sources serve is to help students construct their arguments. In the Needs and Wants inquiry, students can pull on all the sources of the inquiry to make and support their arguments.

RESOURCES: THE NEEDS AND WANTS INQUIRY

All of the inquiries on the C3Teachers site have a set of narrative descriptions of each component following the blueprint. To see the full Needs and Wants inquiry, go to:

■ www.c3teachers.org/inquiries/needsandwants/

There, you can download either a PDF or a Word version of the inquiry. If you have an idea for how you might modify the questions, tasks, and/or sources, then download the Word version, which allows you to customize the blueprint to your particular students.

Unfortunately, few sources are perfectly suited for use in an inquiry. Most were created for purposes other than inquiry or with elementary-aged students as the intended audience. Some sources—artwork, videos, and photographs, for example—may be used as is in an inquiry. Many others, however, require **adaptation** in order to meet students' disparate academic needs. To that end, we recommend adapting the sources in any of three ways:

- Excerpting—involves using a portion of the source for the inquiry. Excerpts enable teachers to use longer texts by pulling out the relevant section(s).

- Modifying—involves inserting definitions and/or changing the language of a text. Modifying texts increases sources' accessibility for students.

- Annotating—involves adding short descriptions or explanations in order to introduce a text or to explain a challenging concept. Annotations allow teachers to set a background context for sources.

Text-heavy sources, in particular, often need adaptation. High-quality texts can be really useful, though sometimes they need to be excerpted, modified, or annotated in order to be accessible to students of all abilities.

◼ SECTION SUMMARY: SOURCES IN IDM

- Sources useful for an inquiry can come in many forms—textual, graphic, visual, and digital.

- The three purposes of sources are: 1) to spark and sustain student curiosity in an inquiry; 2) to build students' disciplinary (content and conceptual) knowledge and skills; and 3) to enable students to construct arguments with evidence.

- Teachers can adapt sources in three ways: excerpting, modifying, and annotating.

Bringing It All Together

Researchers confirm what most teachers know: There are many ways to engage students, but inquiry-based practice shows that students of all ages and of all ability groups can profit (Grant, 2018). However, inquiry-based teaching and learning requires attention to questions, tasks, and sources, both individually and in interaction. A compelling question serves to initiate an inquiry; a summative performance task, where students address that question, pulls the inquiry together. The beginning and end points are important, but no more so than the elements—supporting questions, formative performance tasks, and featured sources—that comprise the middle ground of the Inquiry Design Model.

Alert readers may notice that the IDM does not result in fully-developed and comprehensive curriculum units or modules. The blueprint suggests instructional approaches, but it does not delve into lesson planning. The guidance within each inquiry around the key components of instructional design—questions, tasks, and sources—is considerable, but it is not exhaustive. Experience tells us that teachers teach best the material that they mold around their particular students' needs and the contexts in which they teach. Good teachers need no scripts and they ignore those who argue that teaching and learning are generic activities. The IDM encourages teachers to draw on the wealth of their teaching experiences as they add to and modify activities, lessons, sources, and tasks that transform the inquiries into their own, individual pedagogical plans.

In this chapter, we have walked you through the components of the IDM blueprint using an example of an early-elementary inquiry on needs and wants. In the next chapter, we guide you through the construction of your own inquiry.

Chapter Summary

1   **What are the four dimensions of the C3 Framework?** The four dimensions of the *C3 Framework* are: 1) developing questions and planning inquiries; 2) applying disciplinary concepts and tools; 3) evaluating sources and using evidence; and 4) communicating conclusions and taking informed action.

2   **What are the primary components of the Inquiry Design Model?** The principal components of the IDM are *questions* (compelling and supporting), *tasks* (formative and summative), and *sources* (textual, graphic, visual, and digital).

3   **What are the two kinds of questions represented in the IDM blueprint?** Compelling questions are one type of question on an IDM blueprint. A compelling question is characterized as academically important *and* relevant to students' lives. Supporting questions help scaffold students' learning by providing opportunities for them to learn new content and skills.

4   **What distinguishes a formative from a summative task?** A formative task illustrates students' emerging understandings; a summative task demonstrates students' understandings at the end of an inquiry. Students' responses to both kinds of tasks help their teachers understand their progress, but formative tasks allow teachers to make mid-inquiry adjustments to meet students' needs.

5   **How can teachers adapt sources for their students' use?** Teachers can adapt challenging sources in three ways: excerpting, modifying, and annotating.

Notes

1   Portions of this chapter draw on Grant, Swan, and Lee (in press).
2   To see the full inquiry on which this Compelling Question is based, go to www.c3teachers.org/inquiries/needsandwants/. The C3Teachers website has some 300

published inquiries that are searchable by grade level and topic: (www.c3teachers.org/inquiries/). All inquiries are available to download and use free of charge.

3   Readers will notice that the phrase "featured sources" is used on the IDM blueprint. The adjective "featured" is meant to imply that the listed sources are useful to the inquiry, but other sources can be used as well.

4   Readers who download the full Needs and Wants inquiry at C3Teachers (www.c3teachers.org/inquiries/needsandwants/) will see that sources (i.e., a glass of water and a sports drink) can be used to help students brainstorm needs and wants during the staging activity.

Teaching Resources

Print Resources

Brophy, J., & VanSledright, B. (1997). *Teaching and learning history in elementary schools.* New York: Teachers College Press. This volume offers deep and thoughtful case studies of three elementary-school teachers and their students as they negotiate issues of teaching, learning, subject matter, and environment.

Grant, S.G., Swan, K., & Lee, J. (2017). *Inquiry-based practice in social studies education.* New York: Routledge. This book presents the background and scholarship behind the development of the Inquiry Design Model.

Swan, K., & Lee, J. (Eds.). (2014). *Teaching the College, Career, and Civic Life (C3) Framework.* Silver Spring, MD: National Council for the Social Studies. This source and the next are companion pieces in which representatives of a wide range of cultural institutions (e.g., The National Museum of American History, the Library of Congress, the National Geographic Society, and the National Museum of the American Indian) have written inquiries using the IDM.

Swan, K., Lee, J., & Grant, S.G. (Eds.). (2018). *Teaching the College, Career, and Civic Life (C3) Framework: Part Two.* Silver Spring, MD: National Council for the Social Studies.

Two other sources of good ideas for lessons and units are *Social Studies and the Young Learner* and *Social Education*, both publications of the National Council for the Social Studies. Both journals feature classroom-ready materials in each issue. A regular column in *Social Education*, "Teaching the C3," offers insights into inquiry-based teaching and learning.

Technology Resources

As noted above, the *C3 Framework* is freely available for download:

■   www.socialstudies.org/c3

Also as noted throughout this chapter, a wealth of resources are available at the C3Teachers website:

■   www.c3teachers.org

The navigation bar at the top of this site offers readers access to a variety of materials that explain the Inquiry Design Model, a series of C3-inspired publications, and dozens of blogs by teachers trying out inquiry in their classrooms, in addition to 300 or so published inquiries from K–12 on a wide range of topics.

Clicking on the "Join" button takes you to a page where you can sign up (for free!) to become a "C3 teacher," which means that you will receive the regular newsletter and learn of opportunities to learn about and discuss inquiry-based teaching and learning with peers around the world.

Constructing Curriculum Inquiries

Classroom observers have long advocated inquiry-based teaching and learning (Dewey, 1938). Some teachers have embraced that call (Fillpot, 2012; Terry & Panter, 2010); most have not. Although various explanations have been offered for that situation (Grant, 2018), one of the most consistent has been the absence of practical applications. Teachers may have wanted to build inquiry into their instructional practices; they just have not known how.

The Inquiry Design Model (IDM) was created to fill that gap. Featuring questions, tasks, and sources—the components of all inquiry-based teaching and learning—IDM offers teachers a vehicle for constructing classroom inquiries.

In Chapter 10, we used the example of an early-elementary inquiry on needs and wants to describe the components of the IDM process. In this chapter, our goal is to take you through the process of constructing your own inquiry.[1]

A note before we start: Although we think there is considerable value in learning how to build your own inquiries, we recognize that you may not always have time to do so. For that reason, we encourage you to use any of the published inquiries on C3Teachers. Those inquiries come in two formats, PDF and Word. If you want to use the inquiry as is, go ahead and download the PDF version. If, however, you would like to tweak the inquiry by changing one or more of the supporting questions, substituting in a different source, or designing a new summative extension, then download the Word version and modify it as you see fit.

RESOURCES: C3TEACHER HUBS

The bulk of the inquiries available to download on C3Teachers (www.c3teachers.org) are available under the "Inquiries" tab at the top of the page. Another group of inquiries can be found under the "Hub" tab (www.c3teachers.org/c3-hubs).

Hubs come in two forms—states and organizations—and are sites where groups of educators can post their inquiry-related work. The inquiries on these sites have not been vetted as thoroughly as those under the "Inquiries" tab. However, if you are looking for ideas for an inquiry, we invite you to peruse those located in the various hubs.

We have a lot to talk about with you in this chapter. Our expectation is that delving deeply into the process will help you construct your own inquiries *and* be a better consumer of published inquiries. So, when you have completed this chapter, you should be able to answer these questions:

1   What are the design steps of the Inquiry Design Model?
2   How can you check the alignment of your blueprint?
3   Where can you go for resources related to constructing inquiries for your classroom?
4   How can you join the conversation around inquiry-based teaching and learning?

Constructing an Inquiry

To get started, go ahead and download the IDM Working Blueprint Template from www.c3teachers.org/inquiry-design-model (see Figure 11.1). You can either work on the electronic version or print and work on a hardcopy. If you do the latter, grab a pencil rather than a pen... and one with a good eraser. Constructing inquiries is hard work and you may find yourself revising along the way.

Recall that the three main components of an inquiry are questions, tasks, and sources. So, as we talk you through the ten steps, recognize that each step features one of these three components. But just as important as getting each of these components right is making sure that they all work together. Let's start.[2]

Step 1: Deciding on a Content Angle

Because all the elements of an inquiry need to work in coordinated fashion, you can actually start anywhere on a blueprint. Got a great source in mind? Make a note in one of the featured sources boxes. Have a taking informed action activity you like to see students do? Note it on the blueprint. Where you start building an inquiry is less important than getting started.

Where many teachers start is with a **content angle**: a social studies topic that is worth your students' time and attention. Many of those topics are big

Grade __ Inquiry			
Compelling Question			
State Social Studies Standard			
Staging the Compelling Question			
Supporting Question 1		Supporting Question 2	Supporting Question 3
Formative Performance Task		Formative Performance Task	Formative Performance Task
Featured Sources		Featured Sources	Featured Sources
Summative Performance Task	Argument	Construct an argument (e.g., detailed outline, poster, essay) that addresses the compelling question using specific claims and relevant evidence from historical sources while acknowledging competing views.	
	Extension		

FIGURE 11.1 The IDM blueprint.

ticket items—rules, the American Revolution, immigration, families—but others may be smaller nuggets that can also help students understand why we do the things we do.

State-level standards and school- and district-level curriculum guides are good places to start. Many seem to be written in the driest possible fashion. Still, as we discussed in Chapter 4, even the seemingly dullest topic can be transformed into a viable question.

▶|◀ REFLECTION: FINDING A CONTENT ANGLE

Once you have identified one or more potential topics for your inquiry, consider these questions:

- What strikes you as interesting about this topic?
- What about the topic seems like it might be engaging for your students?
- What prior knowledge and experience might your students have with the topic?

If you find overlap between your interest and your students', that's a good discovery and should help you develop a *compelling* compelling question.

Once you have decided on a topic for your inquiry, go ahead and insert it into the blueprint box that says "standards and practices." If your topic reflects a particular state or local standard, you can copy and paste that language into the box as well.

One other note: If your choice of topic inspires you to have some ideas about other elements of the blueprint, make a note about them as well. Inspiration can be unpredictable, so best to capture it when it hits!

IN YOUR CLASSROOM

COLLABORATION

Despite being surrounded by people, teaching can be a lonely profession. It need not be that way. Teachers can have productive relationships with their administrators, mentors, and colleagues.

Any of these people could offer assistance on your teaching practice. But you may find it useful to cultivate a relationship with one or more colleagues when working on an inquiry. If you are like most people, it may be hard to share your emerging ideas for fear of criticism and embarrassment; it's a natural reaction. But it's also one that we all need to overcome if we are to become better teachers and curriculum inquiry writers.

So, think about who you might want to be your inquiry "buddy" and begin building that relationship. (Hint: A good cup of coffee helps!)

Step 2: Developing a Compelling Question

Questions drive inquiry. Tasks and sources are important, of course. But without a question that propels those tasks and sources, there is no inquiry.

Not all questions are equally useful, however, in framing an inquiry. The value of a *compelling question* is that provides direction and a way to check the other pieces of the inquiry to see if they make sense. Recall how the tasks and sources in the Needs and Wants inquiry profiled in Chapter 10 worked together to enable students to answer the compelling question.

But for a compelling question to do its full job, it needs to hit two marks. One of those marks is on the academic side: A compelling question has to reflect a substantive topic, idea, or issue. That's why Step 1 speaks to the need to find a content angle.

A content angle is only one of the marks of a compelling question, however. The other is signaling the relevance of the inquiry to your students. Students care about a lot of things—fairness, conflict, friendships, rules. Developing a compelling question that gets under students' skin is no easy task. But it can make all the difference in whether an inquiry sings or flops.

▶️◀️ REFLECTION: WHAT DO STUDENTS CARE ABOUT?

> Deciding on a content angle can be challenging: There are so many options to choose from! Identifying the student relevance angle presents its own challenge: A teacher must know her students and what they care about. We offer a few suggestions above, but ask that you think about how to expand that list.
> ▶️◀️

Creating a compelling question that hits both of those marks is no easy task. You may be one of the lucky few for whom a rigorous and relevant question just pops. If that happens, great! Write it down fast and move on to the next section. If it doesn't, don't despair. We have worked with teachers who didn't settle on the final version of their compelling questions until their blueprints were nearly complete. At this stage, then, focus on developing a workable question, one that allows you to continue developing your inquiry and can be revised later on.

If you are ready, go ahead and insert your compelling question in the allotted space in the blueprint.

Step 3: Drafting Argument Stems

"Argument" is a tricky word. To many people, it means "an angry quarrel or disagreement" (Argument, n.d.) and so is something to be avoided. But argument has another definition: "A coherent series of reasons, statements, or facts intended to support or establish a point of view" (Argument, n.d.). It is this latter notion of argument that proves useful in social studies.

Democracy isn't easy, but it works best when people make their ideas clear and when they support those ideas with evidence. That combination—saying what you think and why you think it—is what making an argument is all about. Of course, passions can influence how loud an argument might be stated (or the evidence to support it). But as long as people are talking, progress is possible.

In IDM, a compelling question frames an inquiry; a summative argument closes it (unless a teacher decides to continue with an extension and/or a taking informed action sequence). In short, students answer a compelling question with their evidence-based arguments. It is helpful, however, for teachers to anticipate the kinds of arguments their students might make. One reason is to check the usefulness of the compelling question: If there is only one viable argument to be made, then the question really isn't *compelling*. Another reason that predicting students' arguments is useful is because it helps define the sources students will need. In other words, it is unlikely that students will be able to construct good arguments without relevant sources on which to draw.

For the Needs and Wants inquiry, recall that the teacher-authors wrote the following arguments based on what they know about kindergartners:

- We can get everything we need and want because my mom and dad will get it for me.

- We cannot get everything we want and need because stores can run out of stuff.

- We can get what we need, but not everything we want because there is not always enough money for what I want.

We call these statements *argument stems*. An **argument stem** has two parts—a stance and at least one claim. The **stance** is the "answer" to the compelling question; the **claim** is the reasoning behind that stance:

- We can get everything we need and want [Stance] because my mom and dad will get it for me [Claim].

- We cannot get everything we want and need [Stance] because stores can run out of stuff [Claim].

- We can get what we need, but not everything we want [Stance] because there is not always enough money for what I want [Claim].

Notice the word *because*: It is positioned as the first word after the stance in order to serve the role of providing a transition to the claim. An argument stem doesn't have to have a "because," but you may find it useful to use as you construct your first inquiries and as you teach students how to express their arguments.

RESOURCES: ARGUMENT STEMS

Writing argument stems demands that teachers know their students—how they think and reason, what their knowledge and experiential backgrounds are, how they make sense of the world. But even knowing your students well is no guarantee that you will have an easy time writing argument stems. So, check out the stems on a few of the inquiries on C3Teachers (www.c3teachers.org/inquiries). Seeing how other teacher-authors manage this task should prove helpful.

A word about "evidence." A claim supplies the reasoning behind an argument stance, but it is not the **evidence** for that stance. Instead, evidence is what one shows in order to support an argument in general or a claim in particular. For example, to support the second argument stem above, students might show a picture of empty supermarket shelves.

Making and supporting arguments may seem beyond the capacity of your youngest students. Yet, think about the children with whom you work: If they can say *what* they think about a topic (stance) and *why* they think that (claim), then they have the basics of argumentation. They may not be able to write a five-paragraph essay expressing their arguments yet, but that will come as they learn how to clearly express their argument stems.

Ready to take on the challenge of writing argument stems? There isn't a designated space on the blueprint for them (there's only so much one can put on one page!), so either enter them at the end of the blueprint if you are working online or on the back of your hardcopy version.

Step 4: Crafting Supporting Questions

If you are satisfied with the content angle, compelling question, and the argument stems you have drafted, then you are now ready to move to the middle portion of the IDM blueprint. The supporting questions, featured sources, and formative performance tasks provide your inquiry with the structure it will need to work well with your students.

Supporting questions function as the label implies: as a series of questions that provide scaffolding for the compelling question and the rest of the inquiry. They focus on definitions and explanations and offer students the opportunity to build the content knowledge they need to make their arguments.

The key thing to understand about supporting questions is that they need to follow logically, one after the other.[3] The supporting questions for some inquiries follow a chronological order. That is, the questions move from one event to the next over a period of time. The Call for Change inquiry features supporting questions that follow a chronological sequence directed toward the compelling question "What did it take for women to be considered 'equal' to men in New York?" (www.c3teachers.org/inquiries/call-for-change/). Another order to supporting questions is contrasting perspectives. Here, the idea is to have students view a range of viewpoints on a topic before deciding what they think. The Globalization inquiry, with the compelling question "Is sharing and trading across cultures always a good thing?" is an example of a contrasting perspectives sequence (www.c3teachers.org/inquiries/globalization/).

One other supporting question logic is called concept to analysis and it is this ordering that characterizes the Needs and Wants inquiry. The first supporting question asks about the key economic concepts of needs and wants; the second expands to another set of useful concepts—goods and services. Having explored these four concepts, students are now positioned to do some analysis by answering the supporting question, "What happens when there isn't enough for everyone?"

Students might have had some guesses about the answers to this question before they learned the concepts of needs and wants and goods and services. But with those ideas firmly in mind, they can now make arguments that are likely to be more sensible, more nuanced, and more complete.

▶|◀ REFLECTION: SUPPORTING QUESTIONS

To prod your thinking about supporting questions, pull up a couple different inquiries for your grade level and survey the supporting questions. As you do so, however, look at those questions from two directions—horizontally and vertically.

As you look horizontally—that is, from the first supporting question to the third or fourth—you should be able to detect an order or logic to the sequence.

If your horizontal scan looks okay, then look vertically—from the supporting questions to the compelling question. There, you should be able to see how each of the supporting questions *supports* the compelling question.
▶|◀

The teachers we work with say that crafting supporting questions can be harder than it looks. One problem is getting the list of questions in the right order, so that students can build their content knowledge sequentially. The second problem is that the questions need to support the compelling question, but not go beyond it. You can generate a lot of questions and even arrange them in a logical sequence, only to discover that they no longer speak to your compelling question!

If that is the case, don't panic. There are two possible fixes. One approach is to revise either the individual supporting questions or the order in which you have placed them. In fact, we have seen teachers solve their supporting question problem simply by moving what was the last question to the first position. The other fix has to do with the compelling question. If your list of supporting questions makes sense and it puts students in the right place content-wise, then consider tweaking your compelling question. Remember, it was just your best guess about a compelling question when you began constructing your inquiry. If you need to revise it now to make the relationship between your two sets of questions more coherent, then have at it!

Take a deep breath and start sketching out supporting questions, both individually and as a sequence, and don't hesitate to call on your inquiry buddy to check your work.

Step 5: Selecting Featured Sources

The next row of boxes on the blueprint is for the formative performance tasks. Working with teacher-authors, however, we have learned that when designing an inquiry it makes sense to go next to the featured sources boxes.[4]

Along with questions and tasks, sources are one of the three principal components of inquiry. Students' knowledge and experience are useful as they complete formative and summative tasks. But to fully answer compelling and supporting questions, they need to draw on sources outside of their own lives.

As we noted in Chapter 10, sources have three functions: to spark students' curiosity, to help them build their content knowledge, and to provide them with evidence to support their arguments. We also described how teachers can adapt sources for classroom use through excerpting, modifying, and annotating. The sources you select for your inquiry should address all three functions and you will likely need to consider, if not employ, all three kinds of adaptations.

But first you need to find some sources. Rather than searching the internet randomly, consider two questions:

- What information do I need to put in front of my students for them to answer the supporting questions?
- What type of source is likely to provide that kind of information?

Think back to the Needs and Wants inquiry. The teacher-authors wanted their students ultimately to understand the notion of scarcity. Rather than search aimlessly, they began looking for sources related to the preliminary concepts of needs and wants and goods and services. But not all sources. Knowing their kindergarten students have limited reading skills, the teacher-authors decided to focus on non-text sources. The internet is a wonderful resource. But you can drown in the number of hits it can generate. By asking themselves what information they wanted *and* what type of source they were looking for, they were able to narrow in on images of needs and wants and goods and services. They then followed a similar procedure to find sources related to scarcity.

▶️|◀️ REFLECTION: SOURCES

Having looked at a number of inquiries, you have seen all kinds of sources—visual, graphic, digital, and, of course, textual. Before you start the search for sources for your inquiry, take a few minutes to make some notes. What do your students need to know in order to answer each supporting question and what kinds of sources do you think might be most useful?

▶️|◀️

The sources you pull into your inquiry may work as is. More likely, however, you will have to take some adaptive actions to make them ready for your students. Textual sources may need the most work, especially for young learners. Providing an annotation or modifying some of the language may help. More likely, however, the length of a text may prove most challenging. Yes, we want students to be able to read and understand full-length sources. But until they build sufficient knowledge and confidence, they may give up on long pieces of text. Excerpting is recommended in that case. You may pull a paragraph or two from a document several pages long; you might even select only a single sentence! The idea is to put sources in front of your students that are both content-rich *and* accessible.

One more note about sources: Before you begin your search, understand that you will want to create a mix of sources that vary by perspective and complexity.

Because a compelling question can be answered with a variety of arguments, it is important to make sure that the sources you set in front of students reflect a range of perspectives on the topic. Think about it: If you choose sources that reflect only a single point of view, then you are limiting your students' abilities to think for themselves and to construct their own arguments. If you want students to all think in one particular way, then don't do an inquiry on that topic.

In addition to providing sources with different perspectives, think about choosing sources that vary in terms of complexity. The most obvious kind of source complexity is around text. **Lexile scores** offer a useful gauge of the text-based sources you are considering. In few third-grade classrooms, for example, do all the students read at a third-grade level. So, select sources that are accessible to students both above and below that level. If you want all students to engage with a challenging text, then consider organizing them into heterogeneous groups so that stronger readers can help their less able peers.

Although text-based sources can be the most challenging to young learners, other kinds of sources can present their own difficulties. Visual, graphic, and digital sources *seem* like they should be more accessible than texts. Not always. There may not be any words to decipher, but images can be just as complex to understand and students can be drawn to parts of a source that are irrelevant to the inquiry at hand. So, as you put together the sources related to each supporting question, consider varying the type of source so that students have a better chance to build the content knowledge they will need to address the compelling question.

Okay, enough thinking about sources, it's time to start selecting them! Be forewarned: This step can take a while. Finding sources that hit the content mark is one thing; making sure that they also vary by perspective and type may take some time. If you are struggling, don't forget to consult your inquiry buddy. But also remember that your school or district media person may be able to help as well.

Step 6: Constructing Formative Performance Tasks

The formative performance tasks complete the middle section of the blueprint. Working together with the supporting questions and featured sources, the formative tasks help teachers know if their students are building the requisite knowledge and skills to complete the inquiry.

Note the word *performance* in the phrase formative performance tasks. We use that word deliberately to indicate that we want students to demonstrate the knowledge and skills they are developing. To that end, the verbs one uses to write a formative performance task matter.

A lot of verbs curriculum writers use describe how students are thinking—evaluate, compare, analyze. These are important cognitive abilities. But what do they look like? How do you *know* if your students are analyzing? Because we cannot see directly into students' brains, we have to rely on approximations of their thinking. That's what a performance task (whether formative or summative) gives us—a direct insight into the knowledge and skills students are developing.

A formative performance task, then, has two parts: a verb and a product. The third formative performance task in the Needs and Wants inquiry, for example, asks students to "participate in a discussion of the options people have when faced with scarcity." The verb—participate—tells us what the teacher-authors wanted students to do; the product—a discussion—tells us in what form the task will be accomplished.

▶|◀ REFLECTION: FORMATIVE PERFORMANCE TASKS

There are lots of verbs to choose from in constructing formative performance tasks—sort, identify, define, make—and lots of products as well—charts, paragraphs, collages, claims. Go back to some of the inquiries you have looked at before and focus on the verbs and products identified in the formative performance tasks. You may find it helpful to make a list of each for later reference.

▶|◀

As you look at some of the inquiries on C3Teachers, you may notice something else about formative performance tasks—they get progressively more sophisticated from the first to the last. To that point, you won't see listing or defining as a last formative task and you won't see making a claim with evidence as a first task. Listing and defining are pretty low-level activities and so are suitable for addressing a first supporting question. Making a claim with evidence can only be accomplished once students have built up their content knowledge and skills, which typically occurs near the end of an inquiry.

Ready to write some tasks? Remember, each task is paired with a supporting question and a set of sources, so make sure that the tasks you construct enable students to answer the associated question while using the sources that you have selected.

Step 7: Staging the Compelling Question

With a set of formative performance tasks, the main body of your blueprint is now complete. You may still need to make some adjustments as you finish off your inquiry, but the heavy lifting is over. The next components of staging the compelling question, summative extensions, and taking informed action are important and useful to an inquiry. But they cannot substitute for a robust content angle, compelling question, and summative performance task and for logical sequences of supporting questions, featured sources, and formative performance tasks.

As we noted in Chapter 10, the staging activity is intended to jumpstart students' thinking about one or more of the core ideas behind an inquiry. A brief exercise—typically 15–20 minutes—it gives students a chance to engage their curiosity about the topic. It also provides teachers with an initial sense of what their students already know. In that way, then, the staging activity acts as a kind of formative task.

The brainstorming activity described in the Needs and Wants inquiry is an example of both of these intentions. First, it is likely to inspire considerable interest and excitement, as who doesn't like to talk about what they *need*! And second, as this initial exercise proceeds, teachers are likely to learn much about their students' conceptions of these important concepts.

RESOURCES: STAGING THE COMPELLING QUESTION

The staging activity is a chance to let your teacher's imagination run a little wild. As long as students are thinking about a key idea or two, the staging task can be as creative as you want. To get some more ideas about potential staging exercises, go to the C3Teachers website (www.c3teachers.org/inquiries) and check that component of the blueprint in a couple of inquiries above and below the grade you teach. Staging activities are rarely grade-specific, so give yourself a chance to explore.

A thought: If you have a challenging source that you want to use later in the inquiry, consider using it as part of the staging the compelling question activity. Doing so offers two advantages. The first is that it allows the students to encounter the source in a more relaxed atmosphere; the second is that students may find it less challenging when they work with it in response to a supporting question.

Okay—time to rev up those creative juices! Of course, the whole act of building an inquiry is a creative exercise. But the staging activity is a place to be a little more playful as you start your students on the path to inquiry.

Step 8: Establishing an Extension Task

As we have noted a couple of times now, an inquiry can end once students make their evidence-based arguments in response to the compelling question. But flexibility is built into the IDM approach. Summative extensions are one way in which teachers and their students can extend an inquiry.

The key word here is *extend*. An extension activity is not intended as a new teaching and learning situation. Instead, an extension offers students an opportunity to repackage their arguments for different audiences or to communicate those arguments using a different modality or technology. In other words, students are *extending* their original arguments rather than creating new ones.

Extensions are not simply busywork, however. Researchers (Nuthall & Alton-Lee, 1995) have long known that what students know can appear to change when given a different task. So having students rework their arguments in response to a new situation gives their teachers another opportunity to see what they know and can do.

Recall that, in the Needs and Wants inquiry, students created their original arguments in small groups; the extension called for them to create individual two-sided collages. Alert readers might wonder if it is okay to reverse the two tasks—i.e., have students do the collages as a way to answer the compelling question and then engage in a small group exercise as the extension. The answer—of course! A blueprint, like any curriculum plan, is always susceptible to change.

▶|◀ REFLECTION: EXTENSION TASKS

> Teachers have a general tendency to want to pack in a little more learning, so many inquiry writers will use the extension component as an opportunity to introduce more content. We understand that tendency, we really do. But there is value in having students linger with a set of ideas, letting them mature and grow stronger. So, consider using the extension task for its intended purpose—to give students a chance to try out their initial arguments in a new context.
>
>

We think extension activities have considerable value; they offer students additional experience of making and supporting arguments and they offer teachers additional occasions to understand their students' strengths and challenges. But time is never a teacher's friend. So, we acknowledge that the press of the classroom clock may mean that teachers have to cut them. Understand, however, that an extension task need not take a lot of classroom time. For example, if you had students write out their arguments, then consider a brief oral extension—that is, ask them turn to partners and explain their arguments in three minutes, call time, and then have the partners reciprocate. Six minutes and you have given all your students a second experience in making and supporting their arguments. Time will never be your friend, but you *can* cheat the clock!

Have you got an idea for a summative extension? If so, go ahead and log it in the appropriate box on your blueprint. If not, give your inquiry buddy a call and talk through the possibilities.

Step 9: Shaping a Taking Informed Action Sequence

Congratulations—you've almost completed your first blueprint! And now you get to develop what many students think is the coolest part of doing inquiry—taking informed action.

Typically, students' first complaint about social studies is that it's boring—all those meaningless names, dates, and places. Their second complaint is what to do with those names, dates, and places. The IDM addresses those grumbles in two different ways. One way is through the compelling question. A compelling question must have some academic meat, but it also must speak to the things students care about. So, if your compelling question is truly compelling, then students should be engaged throughout the inquiry. That leaves the question of what students can do with the knowledge and skills they build through an inquiry. And that is where the taking informed action component comes in.

Taking informed action gives students an opportunity to do something real, something that matters, with what they have learned. The Needs and Wants inquiry, for example, offers students a chance to determine something they need or want for their classroom, figure out ways to get that need or want, and choose a means of achieving that goal. Teachers could do this series of activities independent of the inquiry. But then it would not be *informed*! Think about how much richer the discussion will be at each stage of the sequence and how much more thoughtful the final decision will be if the students have a rich understanding of the concepts that surface in the inquiry. Students can get excited about taking any kind of action (especially if it means a break from doing a math worksheet!). But random and ill-informed action is often meaningless. Taking *informed* action demonstrates to students how important it is to act from a solid knowledge base.[5]

RESOURCES: TAKING INFORMED ACTION

Some teachers worry that doing action projects with their students will land them in trouble. Make no mistake—some will! But only if they are poorly designed, put students in difficult situations, or are illegal. That said, there are lots of things students can do to take action at the end of an inquiry that will enrich their lives and will not get you fired.

One suggestion is to back to the inquiries on C3Teachers (www.c3teachers.org/inquiries) and wander through them looking at the range of taking informed action sequences that experienced teacher-authors have created. You may not feel comfortable doing all of them—and that's okay. But you should see numerous examples of action activities that you could do with your students.

A second suggestion is to check out the teacher blogs on C3Teachers. Click on the "blogs" button in the top navigation line at www.c3teachers.org. Then click on the second filter ("all categories" is the default) and scroll down to "taking informed action." There you will see a dozen or so postings by teachers reflecting on their informed action efforts.

Returning to the problem of time, some teachers tell us that they would love to do informed action with their students, but they worry about the time it will take. We appreciate and understand that concern. Here are two ways to think about managing that dilemma:

- Rather than try to do a taking informed action sequence with every inquiry—and then feeling frustrated when you can't—consider planning for a limited number of action experiences throughout the school year. For example, you might have time for informed action opportunities four times a year—that is, once each marking period. But even if you are only able to schedule two experiences each year, you will have given your students an invaluable chance to make social studies real.

- A different way to manage the time crunch is to consider developing an **embedded action** inquiry. (See the blueprint template for an embedded action inquiry at www.c3teachers.org/inquiry-design-model.) The idea here is to double up the informed action steps by incorporating or embedding them in the supporting question sequence. This way students are building their capacity to take informed action at the same time they are building their knowledge and skills.

We have noted a couple of times now that an inquiry "officially" begins with a compelling question and ends with students making their evidence-based arguments. Summative extensions and taking informed action exercises are ways to enhance students' experiences, but they are no substitute for the powerful learning potential of a well-designed and well-taught inquiry. That said, engaging students in a set of taking informed action activities—even if only a couple times a year—adds a dimension to their social studies lives that has no peer.

So, get to it! Think about how to shape a set of taking informed action activities that enable your students to see the results of their learning in addressing a real-world issue. And, if you think you are getting too far out there, don't hesitate to bring in a consult with your inquiry buddy.

Step 10: Checking Your Inquiry

If all has gone swimmingly up to this point, maybe you're ready to teach your inquiry. But even if it has, it might be useful to take this last step in the IDM process and think through your inquiry one more time by looking at it vertically.

To this point, a good portion of your work has been horizontal. You have built a horizontal sequence of supporting questions, horizontal lists of featured sources, and a horizontal series of formative performance tasks. But a solid inquiry also has to be coherent vertically, that is, up and down the blueprint. To that end, we suggest two vertical alignment checks.

One of those checks involves the compelling question, summative argument, and argument stems; the second looks at the relationships between each of your supporting questions, formative performance tasks, and featured source sequences.

Once again, an inquiry is primarily defined by the compelling question and summative argument. The pieces in between—supporting questions, featured sources, and formative performance tasks—are important, but if the primary relationship between compelling question and argument isn't working, then it really does not matter if those other components do.

Argument stems are the key to assessing the vertical alignment between the compelling question and summative argument. Those stems (a stance and at least one claim) should demonstrate that your students can answer the compelling question in at least two or three valid ways. From the vantage point of having completed a first full draft of a blueprint, you should now be able to go back and assess how well your compelling question, summative argument, and argument stems work together.

The second kind of alignment that we think is worth checking is in the middle of your blueprint. Yes, supporting questions, featured sources, and formative tasks need to be well sequenced across the page. But they also need to work with one another. That is, look vertically at your first supporting question, set of sources, and formative task. If your students use the sources to complete the task, will doing so answer the supporting question? If your answer is yes, then move to the next question/source/task relationships and determine if they, too, make sense. If they don't—time to revise.

Of course, having a beautifully coherent blueprint is no guarantee of class-room success: Teaching and learning are simply too complex for anything to be a sure thing. But good planning generally leads to good instructional outcomes.

▶️◀ REFLECTION: CHECKING YOUR INQUIRY

If it is still not clear what we mean when we talk about the vertical alignment of your inquiry, go back to the Needs and Wants blueprint (or any of the others at the C3Teachers' site) and check out the two kinds of alignment we describe above.

This would also be a good time to bring in your inquiry buddy to assess the overall flow of your blueprint. The more eyes you have on your plan, the better.
▶️◀

If you are now satisfied with the inquiry represented in your blueprint, give yourself a pat on the back! Inquiry writing is no easy task, so to complete one that makes sense is no small achievement. If you continue to design your own inquiries, terrific! But if you decide to use and modify already published inquiries, we know that you will do so standing on much firmer instructional ground.

▶|◀ REFLECTION: BLOGGING ABOUT INQUIRY

Now that you have completed an inquiry, we hope that you will consider adding your voice to those who have been blogging about their own experiences in creating and teaching inquiries. Check out the blog site at www.c3teachers.org/blog. If you are interested in contributing your own story, then hit the "join" button at the top of the page, sign up to be a C3Teacher (it's free), and join the conversation.
▶|◀

So that's it. We have taken you through the ten steps to building a fully complete blueprint and a great inquiry. Of course, there is one more step—that's teaching your inquiry and seeing your students' faces light up. Good luck!

Chapter Summary

1 **What are the design steps of the Inquiry Design Model?** The ten design steps are: 1) deciding on a content angle, 2) developing a compelling question, 3) drafting argument stems, 4) crafting supporting questions, 5) selecting featured sources, 6) constructing formative performance tasks, 7) staging the compelling question, 8) establishing extension tasks, 9) shaping a taking informed action sequence, and 10) checking your inquiry.

2 **How can you check the alignment of your blueprint?** One way to check a blueprint is horizontally. The idea here is to look at each sequence of supporting questions, formative performance tasks, and featured sources to ensure that they proceed logically, making sense individually and as a group. The other way to check a blueprint is vertically. There, the idea is to look at clusters of components, most notably the relationship a) between the compelling question and argument stems, and b) from each supporting question to the associated featured sources and formative performance tasks.

3 **Where can I go for resources related to constructing inquiries for my classroom?** The C3Teachers site offers a range of resources including hundreds of downloadable inquiries, publications, and blogs.

4 **How can I join the conversation around inquiry-based teaching and learning?** The easiest way is to join C3Teachers and become a blogger.

Notes

1   This chapter draws heavily on the books by S.G. and his colleagues on the design process of IDM entitled *Inquiry Design Model: Building Inquiries in Social Studies* (Swan, Lee, & Grant, 2018) and the *Inquiry Design Model: The Workbook* (Grant, Swan, & Lee, 2018).

2   Note that the ten steps to designing an inquiry include all the blueprint elements, but do not necessarily present them in the same order as the blueprint shows.

3   Readers will notice that the blueprint on p. 267 features three supporting questions. There is also a four-question version of the blueprint on the C3Teachers website (www.c3teachers.org/inquiry-design-model).

4   As noted in Chapter 10, the term "featured" indicates that these are only some of the possible sources a teacher might use in developing an inquiry. Recall that in Chapter 8, we suggested that trade book literature is a terrific place to look for relevant sources.

5   Alert readers will recall that we made mention of examples of taking informed action in earlier chapters. See, for example, the actions students might take in response to the idea of creating a new town park in Chapter 8.

Teaching Resources

Print Resources

Grant, S.G., Swan, K., & Lee, J. (2018). *Inquiry Design Model: The workbook*. Raleigh, NC: C3Teachers. A companion to the title below, the *workbook* offers a series of practical exercises that teacher-writers can do to help them construct their own inquiries.

Swan, K., Lee, J., & Grant, S.G. (2018). *Inquiry Design Model: Building inquiries in social studies*. Silver Spring, MD: National Council for the Social Studies. This book provides an in-depth presentation regarding the ten-step process of building inquiries.

As mentioned at the end of Chapter 10, two additional print resources for inquiries are *Social Studies and the Young Learner* and *Social Education*, both publications of the National Council for the Social Studies.

Technology Resources

The most comprehensive resource for all-things-inquiry is the C3Teachers website:

■   www.c3teachers.org

There, readers will see some 300 fully-developed and vetted inquiries (under the "Inquiries" tab), additional inquiries (under the "Hubs" tab), a series of publications exploring a range of topics around inquiry-based teaching and learning (under the "Publications" tab), and a place to read the blogs of teachers and other educators who are working with inquiry (under the "Blogs" tab).

Becoming a Reflective Social Studies Teacher

In the preceding chapters, we have seen how powerful and ambitious social studies teaching in elementary school requires careful attention to the four commonplaces. Such teaching also requires **reflective practice**: regular examinations of and introspection into what, who, and how you're teaching, and why you choose to do what you do. The decisions you make should be based on careful attention to your classroom practices and environment, student learning goals and the evidence of that obtained from your assessment efforts, and a solid goal framework.

Being reflective and thoughtful about your teaching practice is essential to becoming an effective elementary social studies teacher; in fact, some argue that it is the key to becoming a great teacher in any subject matter. Reflective teachers think hard about their teaching practices, the learners in front of them, the social studies subject matter they teach, and the learning community they build in their classrooms. They also consider the larger school community context within which their reflective practice occurs and is shaped. Given its centrality to all that is good teaching, we close this book with a discussion of teacher reflection.

When you have completed this chapter, you should be able to answer these questions:

1   What does it mean to be reflective?
2   What does reflection entail?
3   What are the different types of reflection?

Defining Reflective Practice

When we talk about reflection, we mean—to paraphrase John Dewey (1933)—conscious, repeated, and careful thought about your beliefs and teaching practices (and all the other commonplaces that revolve around them), including why you follow them and how they influence what you might believe and do in the future. In part, this definition is particularly personal. It points inward toward an analysis of what you believe and do and the reasons you hold for thinking and acting in these ways. It also points outward toward a consideration of how your beliefs and actions will influence your students, the subject matter you teach, and the classroom learning opportunities and structures you create, including assessments. Let's consider first the inward view and look at it in relationship to how, as Dewey indicates, it inevitably points outward.

Personal Growth

Continual inward self-assessment is essential to growth as a teacher; without it, you atrophy. You simply lose your interest in teaching, and then you will badly serve your students. Learning to teach is something we never quite master; it's an ongoing, lifelong pursuit. The best social studies teachers we know are those who are quickest to say that they have much to learn, even though they may have been teaching for 20 years or more.

The key for these teachers, if you ask them, is their ability to constantly challenge themselves through the reflective self-assessment process. They know they have chosen no easy path, but they live for the journey and they love the opportunity for continued development as teachers and human beings. Sometimes it's difficult and downright intimidating to question and assess what you do and believe. Even so, we can't stress enough the important connection between looking inward at your beliefs and actions and your success as an ambitious social studies teacher.

It is essential to keep asking, for example, whether or not you know enough about the social studies subject matter you are teaching. If you think not, you embark on a journey to learn more by reading and taking classes and by borrowing thoughts and ideas from your colleagues. These actions are examples of what we mean by personal growth: using the self-reflection, question-asking process to change and grow as a social studies teacher. The teachers who regularly engage in this process continue to love teaching. Through the growth process of self-reflection, they continually remake themselves as thoughtful and caring teachers.

Professional Responsibility

As Dewey intimates, however, there is more to being reflective than your personal growth. Reflective practice has an outward, public dimension as well. In the end, teaching is essentially a moral endeavor, for the many teaching decisions you make affect the lives of children, often in quite profound ways. You have a moral obligation and professional responsibility to do the best you can by them, *to make the best choices on their behalf*. Although making choices may often feel like a solitary effort, teachers perform on the drive to school in the morning or during a planning period, decision-making does happen within a broader context. Here's how.

FIGURE 12.1 Personal growth can take many forms—quiet reflection, journal writing, reading, and the like. But there is much to be said for reflection growing out of interactions with other adults, in which we try out our ideas on others, listen to their responses, reform our ideas, and then try them out again.

As a teacher, you are a professional educator, part of the larger teaching profession comprising many who, like you, pride themselves on being up to date about what they know and do. Therefore, you have to pay attention to teachers' **craft knowledge**, those practices teachers regularly use in the classroom. As our profession's understanding of that craft develops, you must stay abreast of it by continually reading, conversing with colleagues, taking college course work, and engaging in other professional development activities.

The commonplaces are a useful way to check your understandings. You need to stay in close touch with your students, learning about them individually and as an age-related group. The first you accomplish through regular attention to the many ways your individual students think about and express their ideas, hopes, and ambitions. The latter you develop by interacting with your colleagues and through reading and studying research on how children learn and grow. You must attend to the social studies subject matter through what you know and continue to learn, and by understanding the curricular demands within your school district and state. And finally, you should monitor your classroom community and attempt to keep your goals and aims there aligned with your practices. As a teacher, you will find that 80 percent of your attention will be outward-focused and 20 percent inward. See Figure 12.3.

Having as much knowledge as possible about the commonplaces, and continuing to seek more, can enhance the quality of your teaching choices. Reflection

FIGURE 12.2 Just as we want students to become lifelong learners, important too is the notion that teachers see themselves as learners. To that end, continuing professional development is an increasingly vital part of teachers' lives.

FIGURE 12.3 Teachers' inward and outward focus.

is the vehicle by which enhancing this knowledge and understanding can take place, for it helps frame good questions that can enable you to maximize your personal and professional growth.

RESOURCES: PROFESSIONAL GROWTH

The following site provides a wide range of materials on which teachers can draw for professional growth, reflection, and development:

- www2.ed.gov/teachers/dev/contedu/edpicks.jhtml

▶️◀ REFLECTION: WHAT IS REFLECTIVE PRACTICE?

What do you think of when you hear someone talk about reflective teaching practice? How does this compare or contrast with our discussion of reflection as defined by John Dewey? Do you agree or disagree with Dewey?

■ SECTION SUMMARY: DEFINING REFLECTIVE PRACTICE

- Reflection involves conscious, repeated, and careful thought about your beliefs and teaching practices, including why you follow them and how they influence what you might believe and do in the future.

- Reflection moves in two directions at the same time. Looking inward, teachers' reflections contribute to their personal growth. Looking outward, teachers' reflections contribute to their growth as professionals with responsibilities to others.

Reflectiveness in Teaching: An Illustration

We realize that what we describe above is a tall order. This view of reflection, although complete with wonderful personal opportunities, also means powerful obligations and responsibilities, especially to the children who are your students. To put some substance around these ideas and to further depict various aspects of reflection, let's consider how we, Bruce and S.G., discussed one aspect of how Bruce taught a piece of his elementary-school social studies course. This illustration of reflective practice, although not comprehensive, allows us to show you how it works, how it can be a natural, regular outgrowth of the interactions you have with your students and other professionals.

The Context

Bruce teaches a course to prospective teachers on learning to become an elementary-school social studies teacher. Each time he teaches this course he modifies the syllabus as a result of what he's done in the past, how well he thinks the course succeeded in fostering learning among his students, and questions he has about how to enhance the experience for the prospective teachers. The path down this road has been bumpy and criss-crossed. No big surprise there: Teaching is a never-ending quest to reflect and improve on practice, regardless of the level.

In the course, Bruce uses a book titled *Teaching and learning history in elementary schools* (Brophy & VanSledright, 1997), which includes detailed case studies of three fifth-grade teachers teaching American history: Mary Lake, Ramona Palmer, and Sara Atkinson (we have discussed two of these teachers in earlier chapters). After assigning readings related to these teachers, Bruce encourages his students to focus on trying to understand the teachers and make sense of their social studies teaching practices and decision-making.

The three teachers present significantly different cases, from which Bruce hopes his students will learn much about teaching social studies. Mary Lake's version of teaching history hinges on her storytelling approach. She conveys the American past by engaging her students in detailed, sometimes mesmerizing accounts of the historical actors' activities. Lake searches out dramatic and human-interest elements of the historical record that she can narrate to her students to provoke their curiosity and encourage their understanding. She typically follows the scripts provided by her textbook—the common celebrations of American nation building and achievement told through the perspectives of European Americans—and reconstructs them using her own dramatic flourishes.

Ramona Palmer, whom you met earlier, sees American history as a series of cause-and-effect relationships that plays out over and over again. In her view, for example, the American Revolution is the *effect* caused by economic and political differences between the colonists and England. Some of these differences were caused by the French and Indian War, which was settled only a few years before the Revolution. The *effect* of the war was to leave the English saddled with significant debt, which they tried to collect in part from the colonists. Unlike Lake, Palmer is not interested in telling dramatic stories per se. She wants to help her students understand historical cause-and-effect relationships.

Sara Atkinson, another teacher you've already met, views American history as a story about choices in which Americans made mistakes, acknowledged them, and made other choices to correct those mistakes. For example, she sees the amendments to the Constitution as clear illustrations of this effort to use history to learn from errors in judgment. She teaches the chronology of American history to help her students understand the importance of decision-making reform, how it plays out over time, and how they can play a role in changing society.

Each teacher approaches teaching American history differently and therefore displays goals that vary from the others (see Chapter 9). Likewise, each teacher's teaching practices vary, as do the learning communities each strives to create. No teacher can do it all. Therefore, choosing an approach to teaching history influences student learning in particular ways and produces trade-offs in the classroom. For example, Atkinson is critical of choices that American leaders have made (for example, she noted the weaknesses of the Articles of Confederation, the fact that women and Blacks were barred from voting, and the like), and she shows her students how remedies for these choices were conceived. Unlike Lake, she engages in no storytelling practices. On the other hand, Lake motivates and engages her students in a subject that many find lifeless. However, she seldom if ever asks her students to develop a critical, questioning attitude or approach to the study of history.

Bruce wants his prospective teachers to understand the differences among the three teachers and the trade-offs embedded in their practices. He expects his students to use the cases to analyze and reflect on their own thinking about teaching, learning, subject matter, and classroom environment. After three weeks of studying each case, Bruce asks his students a seemingly simple question: Of the three teachers, who do you like best and why?

This question provokes a flurry of in-class commentary. Some students choose Lake, others choose Palmer, and still others choose Atkinson. Vigorous defenses support each choice. The prospective teachers often put themselves in the places of their favorite teachers as they argue on their behalf and supply reasons for the trade-offs made by their choice teacher. Things build up to fever pitch until the third class ends.

After the first time this discussion took place, Bruce immediately emailed S.G., who teaches a similar class at his institution. Bruce explained what had happened, much as it is conveyed here. S.G. responded within a few hours, and the ensuing exchange lasted about a week. In effect, Bruce asked S.G. to help him reflect on what occurred, to assist him in sorting out the many details, and to help him find ways to enhance this learning experience for students the next time around.

The Conversation

After giving S.G. the details of the experience from his perspective, Bruce raved about how intense the in-class discussion had become, to the point where the class took over the direction of the conversation and he became a relatively passive participant. Bruce rejoiced in the idea that students could become this animated and personally involved, but, like many teachers, he worried about what understandings they were developing. Are these three teachers truly such model teachers that any one of them is fine to emulate? None of his students suggested that they wouldn't endorse any of the three because they had a different, more exemplary teacher in mind. Was this a problem? How could he encourage his students to become even more critically thoughtful about these teachers and therefore about the teachers they would become?

Based on these questions, S.G. and Bruce had the following exchange:

SG: The notion of a "teaching model" seems both helpful and problematic. Did both ideas surface in the class discussion? What sense, if any, did your students make of this?

BV: Actually, *model* is my word. None of the students used that term. I think the term cases is probably a better way to think about this. But I did use the word *model*, didn't I? I think I was getting at this idea of helping them build a mental structure around particular ways of teaching history at fifth grade—different ways of thinking about history subject matter, kids, and learning communities. My students often tell me that they never see social studies taught. With these three cases, I was hoping to give them examples, ones that they don't see in the field. I think I need to go back and point out how the term *model* is both useful and problematic. How do *you* think it's both?

SG: Your note makes me think of two things. One is this conundrum of social studies being left out of the elementary-school day. I just don't get it. Given that social studies is about how and why people do the things they do *and* that we all seem to be innately interested in this stuff, how can teachers just leave it out? My guess is that what teachers see in their textbooks looks only remotely interesting and so, when pressed for time, it becomes easier to put social studies off. It doesn't have to be that way, and that's why I like the idea of using cases of teachers like the ones you describe (I like *cases* better than *models*, but more on that in a minute). The Palmer and Atkinson cases show me that elementary teachers and kids can engage in real and thoughtful discussions. The Lake case shows me that one way to make more time for social studies stuff is by forging a strong connection to one's literacy instruction—historical fiction is a way to teach *both* history and reading. In these ways, the cases of these teachers serve as models, that is, instances of wise practice that are worth emulating. What seems especially important about these teachers is that none does her work flawlessly. Looking at the successes these teachers have made is even more instructive and important when we consider the challenges they face. None of us (least of all you and me!) do things perfectly, and so presenting the full scope of these teachers' efforts seems critical. Now, maybe I'm just being too particular, but *model* implies a focus on only the good stuff, a "here's what I did and you should do the same" kind of thing. A case, on the other hand, implies a fuller consideration of a teacher's actions, the good parts as well as the problems. Moreover, a case usually suggests the importance of the context in which the teacher works. Models are supposed to work regardless of the context. Cases are context-specific; the implication is that another teacher in another context can expect differences to surface. And that seems like an important thing to remember. I'm probably rambling, but the point I want to make is that if your students see these three teachers as one-dimensional success stories or models, rather than as full, rich, complex cases, I think they're only getting half the value of them. But all this makes me think about another question: How do you know what sense your students are making of all this? I really struggle with this question in my own classes.

BV: I, too, am troubled by how little social studies appears in the elementary-school curriculum. Science suffers the same fate. I wonder if it has something to do with the heavy subject matter demands these topics make on teachers. When I see reading and math taught, it's largely skills-based. On the surface, I think teachers might think math and reading are easier because you can teach these distinct skills in a particular order. Progress seems equally easy to measure. Social studies, on the other hand, requires a large pool of conceptual understandings to teach it well. That may scare teachers away. These three cases, I think, are encouraging because they show teachers diving into the history subject matter and bringing their kids along. Some students liked Lake because they could see how she integrated reading and history, but they weren't especially quick to notice (judging by classroom comments) that her approach was rather narrow and didn't allow her students to see history from perspectives other than the celebration stories she told and had them read. Your thoughts about cases are almost exactly what I thought about the three teachers. They're hardly perfect. In fact, after the discussion I worried a great deal about my students picking one of them as their model social studies teacher. So perhaps asking them to pick a teacher they liked best was not such a good idea, despite all the great discussion that followed. That "model" idea is so tempting for me, though, and I suspect for my students. Teachers want magic bullets, the way that will work, regardless of context and setting. I need to do a better job of helping them to see how learning varies by class and students, how the learning community must shift accordingly, and how subject-matter representations and content need adjusting also. I must stress the moral dimension of teaching, how teachers constantly choose different courses of action based on their assumptions and understandings of the context. Using these three teachers as different cases of decision-making is probably a better approach. As to the question you asked at the end, I, too, wonder how to get a grip on what my students understand from these cases. I listen to them very carefully in class. I puzzle aloud with them. I ask them more questions and listen again carefully, but how can I know what sense they make? How long do their understandings last before they are changed, say, by a school practicum setting where they see a teacher teach social studies in yet another way? I think this discussion is helping me see that I need to develop some form of assessment (an essay they write analyzing the cases?) that can help me get a better idea about their thinking. Any thoughts on this?

At this point, the conversation begins to broaden out into the larger terrain of teaching. As reflective talk goes, this is pretty common. One set of ideas can lead to a wide scope of practice-related concerns. Because teaching results often are uncertain, you shouldn't be surprised that S.G. and Bruce end up reflecting considerably on their anxieties concerning this uncertainty.

SG: As usual, you make some nice points that help me think harder about what I do and why. But those points also raise more anxieties about whether or not I'm being as helpful as I can be. I suppose you can't have one without the other, so let me try out a little more of my thinking on you. First, I suspect you're right about the discomfort elementary-school teachers seem to feel about teaching social studies. I wonder how much teachers' knowledge of social studies plays into their reluctance. I survey my class as to their undergraduate majors (remember that our teacher preparation program is largely at the post-BA level) on the first night of class. Few come with anything like a social studies major (for example, in history, political science, or sociology). Not only that, but most come with a pervading sense that social studies, and history in particular, is just one long and dull list of people, places, and dates. There's a double whammy: Not only do my students come with little content knowledge, they also come with few positive experiences as social studies learners. If that generalization holds for the wider population, no wonder many practicing elementary-school teachers avoid social studies instruction if they can. Second, on your point about your students wanting magic bullets, who doesn't? Even though we say several times in our book that there is no such thing, that doesn't stop me from wanting a plain and simple answer to the complicated messiness of teaching and learning. That messiness is truly why I love this field, but sometimes it's a big pain in the butt! And that brings me to your last point about how to know what our students know. Sometimes, I think this is the most difficult job teachers face. Planning lessons and units is hard, but truly understanding what sense one's students make of those activities is a daunting task. And what makes it especially problematic is that, as you point out, teaching social studies offers no simple progression of ideas and skills. For example, I teach my students the commonplaces on the first night of class. At that point, I'm fairly confident that if I gave them a multiple-choice test (for example, using an item that stated, "The ___ commonplace that deals primarily with students: a) learners and learning; b) teachers and teaching; c) subject matter; or, d) classroom environment"), most would do pretty well. It's hardly enough, however, to be able to identify differences between subject matter and classroom environment. So, we keep coming back to these constructs in different contexts throughout the semester, each time (hopefully) stretching and deepening our understanding of them. That recursiveness—the idea of continually coming back to an idea—makes a lot of sense to me, but it also means that what my students know at any one time is likely to be different from what they know at another time. Determining if and when they finally get it is terribly difficult. Like you, I raise a lot of questions in class and listen as hard as I can. I'd be interested in your thoughts about a couple other things that I also do. One is that I put my students in a lot of different situations, hoping that the more they talk about ideas, the more sense those ideas will make. For example, I like to use flexible grouping—partners and small groups—as well as whole-class settings to talk about ideas. My thought here is that those students who are reluctant to try out their thinking in the large group may be more likely to do so in more intimate settings. I also have students write about their ideas. Sometimes that takes the form of in-class fastwrites, but I also require that students keep a class journal. I like this because it's a good place for students to write about the readings and class discussions. I especially like it because students (and I) can look back and see how their ideas mature as the semester unfolds. Journals are a great source of insight into students' thinking, especially those students who may not say a lot in class. In addition, I require a reflective narrative as part of the course unit plan assignment. I like this because it provides a place for students to think back on what they've learned and to pull together some of the themes that stand out. I like all these efforts, but to tell the truth, I still can't shake the feeling that I really don't understand what my students know, and maybe more importantly, what they will do with all this stuff once they begin teaching. What do you think?

Let's stop here and take a closer look at several features of reflection in general and this reflective conversation specifically. But first, take a moment to reflect on this email conversation yourself.

▶I◀ REFLECTION: OF WHAT SHOULD REFLECTION CONSIST?

What do you think of the exchange between Bruce and S.G.? Does it meet your expectations for productive reflection? How does it stack up against Dewey's ideas about reflection? Does it contain both the inward-looking and outward-looking elements?

Analyzing the Conversation: Five Types of Reflection

In the section that follows, we reconsider our exchange above in light of Linda Valli's (1997) framework for understanding teacher reflection. Valli identifies five types of reflection: **technical reflection, reflection-in-action, deliberative reflection, personalistic reflection,** and **critical reflection** (see Figure 12.4 for summary definitions).

Technical Reflection

One common type of reflection, perhaps the most frequent in teacher talk about their practice, involves what Valli calls technical reflection. In this form, teachers try to answer the question "Did I use the right teaching method?" Bruce's concern over how he used the cases of the three teachers to spur discussion is, in some ways, an example of technical reflection. Bruce wonders whether his method or technique—asking his students to grapple with issues related to which teacher's style they prefer and why—is the most effective in helping them think about the teachers they are and wish to become. S.G. subsequently presses Bruce to think more deeply about his practice.

Type of reflection	Description
Technical reflection	Trying to answer the question "Did I use the right teaching technique?"
Reflection-in-action	Thinking about, assessing, and adjusting your practice as you teach
Deliberative reflection	Concerning yourself with a variety of issues involved in teaching, from subject matter and learners' understanding of it, to teaching method and its relationship to classroom milieu
Personalistic reflection	Using and expanding your personal knowledge and that of others to enhance growth as a teaching professional
Critical reflection	Focusing on the social, moral, and political dimensions of teaching and schooling

FIGURE 12.4 Types of reflection in teaching (adapted from Valli, 1997).

Reflection-in-Action

Technical reflection is important, but it can be rather narrowly conceived. As we have noted throughout this book, and as our reflective conversation suggests, no method or technique really achieves magic-bullet status. Methods are context specific: You have to know your students. You have to adjust your methods as you go, sometimes in the thick of the action of actual teaching, or on the fly, and almost certainly after you have assessed your students (see Chapter 6).

Valli describes this process as reflection-in-action. Teachers do this all the time, often without being entirely aware of it. Good teachers, we think, consciously and deliberately adjust their teaching methods, or pedagogy, as class circumstances, assessment evidence and learners' reactions dictate. Our reflective conversation above cannot provide examples of this because the discussion occurred in the week after the teaching episode. But good cases that describe in detail teaching as it proceeds (such as those of Lake, Palmer, and Atkinson) illustrate how this reflection-in-action occurs.

Deliberative Reflection

The conversation about Bruce's teaching episode contains considerable talk about what Valli refers to as deliberative reflection. This type of reflection covers a variety of issues involved in teaching, from concerns over subject matter and learners' understanding of it, to teaching method and its relationship to classroom environment. S.G. and Bruce reflect on the limited role social studies appears to play in the elementary-school curriculum, on teachers' knowledge of social studies, and on their experiences of learning social studies. They also discuss various strategies for helping students to connect their prior knowledge to what goes on in class (for example, S.G.'s fastwrites, journals, and group work).

Finally, they talk of assessing student knowledge and how difficult it is to construct good assessment tools to help teachers understand what sense students make of things. Each of these types of talk suggests a deliberative form of reflection. Deliberative reflection often arises from technical reflection if both are done intentionally. Technical reflection, as we noted, can be limited. Deliberative reflection opens up the terrain and serves to enhance what we learn from being reflective by encouraging talk about alternative teaching approaches and competing viewpoints. As a result, it can't help but improve practice.

Personalistic Reflection

A fourth type of reflective talk is what Valli calls **personalistic reflection**. Much of Bruce and S.G.'s conversation brings their own understandings into play. We referred to this earlier as looking inward. Both want to improve what they do. They talk about their personal understandings of what happens in their classrooms with their students in an effort to sort out the complexities of teaching. Each tries to use his own knowledge and that of the other to enhance his personal growth as professionals. Doing so is a fundamental aspect of teaching. The practice of teaching is something we never quite master. We are always learners, seeking to become more capable educators. Personalistic reflection is crucial to this process.

Critical Reflection

Finally, S.G. and Bruce reflect on several dimensions of their teaching experience that have ethical repercussions. They both worry about the reduced role of social studies in elementary school and the possible impact that role may have on the intellectual and personal growth of youngsters. They express concern that the emphasis on other subjects such as reading and mathematics and the choices school districts make to put more resources into those subjects could effectively eliminate key social studies learning opportunities for students. They worry about how teachers may contribute to those losses if they value social studies less than other subjects because of their poor experiences with social studies. Valli calls this type of exchange critical reflection because it focuses on the social, moral, and political dimensions of teaching and schooling. It centers on the goals and purposes of what teachers and schools do (or fail to do) that contribute to providing students with equal (or unequal) opportunities to learn.

These five different types of reflection—technical, in-action, deliberative, personalistic, and critical—are important to the growth of professional teachers. None is really more important than the others. One focuses on looking inward (personalistic); the other four focus on looking outward. That seems like the right balance to us; teaching should be more about serving others—students, students' parents, communities, culture—than serving one's self. Nevertheless, all five are fundamental. They simply serve different purposes and focus reflection on different aspects of teaching. We only tease them apart here to call your attention to their different features and goals and to persuade you to engage all of them frequently and deliberatively.

▶❙◀ REFLECTION: EVOLUTION OF REFLECTION

Here again, take a moment to stop and think: What do you think about the ratio of reflectivity being one part inward looking to four parts outward looking? Do you agree with our claim here? Why or why not?

Consider this situation as well: Some studies on how teachers learn to teach across their careers indicate that, for the first two to three years, new teachers focus almost exclusively on forms of personalistic reflection and only later aim their reflections on the other four types. What do you think of this observation? Granting the research point for a moment, why do you think reflection in learning to teach evolves this way, from inward-looking, personal forms to outward-looking ones? What might this mean for you as a new teacher?

▶❙◀

■ SECTION SUMMARY: TYPES OF REFLECTION

- Reflection, both self-reflection and reflection with others, is a powerful means of improving one's teaching practice.

- Reflection takes many forms. *Technical reflection* focuses on whether or not the right teaching strategies were used; *reflection-in-action* emphasizes thinking about, assessing, and adjusting one's practice during the teaching act; *deliberative reflection* is concerned with issues such as teaching, subject matter, learners, and environment; *personalistic reflection* emphasizes the growth of personal knowledge; and *critical reflection* focuses on the social, moral, and political dimensions of teaching and schooling.

Reflection and the Social Context of Teaching

The most common approach in our culture to organizing schools is to build large buildings and to divide them up into smaller egg-crate-like units. We typically see lone teachers in classrooms with 20 to 30 students. This situation makes teaching a mighty solitary affair. On the one hand, many teachers enjoy the feel of greater personal autonomy over their practice. They can teach about the geography of the Great Plains, or the causes of the American Revolution, or the unique roles of people in our local communities in whichever way they choose. On the other hand, some teachers feel quite isolated from their professional colleagues and collective knowledge sharing, and thus remain fairly silent about what they do. We believe that few teachers want to be silent about their practices; we think those silences spring from how schools are organized and the teacher isolation that often results.

Breaking the Silences around Teaching Practice

Our exchange regarding Bruce's teaching demonstrates the potential benefits of breaking through professional silence. Teachers are social creatures, and their professional growth and understanding are enhanced considerably when they talk with others who share in their commitments. In fact, some research suggests that the most powerful learning occurs in social contexts such as group discussions, small and large, and in one-on-one reflection exercises where the participants are knowledgeable and the focus of the talk is considered mutually shared and important by the discussants (Eraut, 2004; Johnson, Johnson, & Holubec, 2009).

We encourage you to avoid the tendency toward professional isolation and the resulting silence about teaching practice. Engage in these various forms

FIGURE 12.5 Self-assessment and lifelong learning are key to one's growth as a teacher.

of reflection not only in your own thoughts, but also *with* others—teachers, administrators, parents, and university professors—in professional communities that strive to assist participants in enhancing their professional growth. We hope that you can locate such a reflective, conversational community.[1] If you find none readily available, create one with those who share your passions about teaching and learning.

RESOURCES: USING ONLINE DISCUSSION CENTERS, FORUMS, AND BLOGS

To help break some of the silences around teaching, several educational organizations have created online discussion centers, forums, and blogs where teachers can raise and conduct ongoing discussions of an unlimited range of issues, including recently some discussion about how to handle the growing pressure of high-stakes assessments and what this might mean for teaching social studies in elementary schools. You can find links to different types of forums and blogs at the following website:

http://forums.atozteacherstuff.com

▶❙◀ REFLECTION: ISOLATION VERSUS COLLABORATION

In your experiences observing teachers in school, do you see the isolation we discussed? Or do you see more collaboration between and among teachers, more sharing of ideas about teaching practice? If you have seen much more of the latter, what do you think accounts for the more collaborative processes you have witnessed? Do these more collaborative environments among teachers attract you, or are they intimidating?
▶❙◀

Five Examples of Activities that Promote Reflective Practice

Now that we have laid out what we believe constitutes reflectiveness in teaching, we want to suggest some examples of activities that promote the sorts of reflections we have been describing. For our purposes here, we assume that you are a prospective teacher who, in addition to taking a social studies teaching methods course, has a practicum placement in a school where you have opportunities to watch your mentor teacher teach, to work with students, and perhaps to engage in some teaching yourself.

- Video-record a lesson that you teach, study it afterwards, and write up an analysis in which you focus on several different aspects of your practice (e.g., how you engaged students in the social studies compelling question, how you stimulated discussion, what you were thinking about at various points in the lesson). Share your analysis with your mentor teacher, and schedule a discussion with him or her after school one day. This is a reflective practice that a number of teachers have used to great effect. Yes, it can be intimidating to have the video-recorder running in the back of the room and later see yourself in action. However, this practice helps you "see yourself" as a teacher, and it promotes an array of analytic reflections about what you do, how you do it, and what you think about as you teach.

■ Organize some of your fellow prospective teachers into a small discussion group in which you talk about key issues facing you in the classroom. We would suggest that you discuss how you are thinking about representing the big ideas and compelling questions you choose to work with, how you anticipate students' responses to your efforts—and then reflect on how they responded, what you might choose to do or think about differently if you were to teach a certain topic again, and so on. These discussion groups, if used for more than "complaint sessions," can promote deep reflection about your teaching practice in all five areas we have described.

■ Have your mentor teacher or a prospective-teacher colleague observe your teaching. You might wish to design a short list of focus questions that can guide her toward the issues you may want to think about later. Ask her to write out an analysis of what she has seen, much as we described under the preceding suggestion for a video-recorded lesson. Schedule a time to discuss this analysis with your mentor teacher or colleague.

■ Negotiate an experience in which you can work with a small group of students in a quiet room away from the rest of the class. Plan to audio-record the session. If you plan this experience shortly before you teach a certain topic, you could interview the students about their prior knowledge of that topic. Listen to or transcribe the audio-recording. Use what you learn to reflect on how you might construct your lesson. This approach can promote deep deliberative reflection.

■ Choose a student who is ethnically or racially different than you are. Arrange to shadow this student as much as is practically possible for a week. If possible, perhaps you can even visit the student's home. The idea is to construct a descriptive case study of who this student is as a means of becoming more deliberatively, personally, and critically reflective about how to teach students who are different from you. This exercise can be important because classroom populations across the country are becoming increasingly diverse while the teaching profession continues to be dominated by European-American teachers. Part of your reflective task will be to avoid overlaying your observations with stereotypes and unwarranted assumptions about who this child is. You will need to concentrate to spot the assumptions you make about those who are not like you. This exercise, if done carefully and thoughtfully, can teach you much about both yourself and the child. And that's precisely the type of thing that reflection about teaching best serves. It can help make you a more sensitive and effective teacher, especially when many of your charges come from backgrounds that are outside your own experience.

Be sure not to overlook the many opportunities to reflect and collaborate with other teachers. As Figure 12.6 shows, this important activity can take place in a number of different settings. You can participate within your own school in discussions about teaching and curricular issues. You can get to know other teachers in your school system by volunteering for curriculum advisory or curriculum revision committees. Many states have social studies organizations that convene once a year; share email addresses with those you meet at these events and build relationships electronically.

Also consider getting involved in the national scene by attending the annual meeting of the National Council for the Social Studies. In general, activities closer to home may allow you to participate more often, but will not introduce you to as many other new and experienced teachers as you will meet if you travel outside your area or participate in electronic forums and bulletin boards. You may be surprised to find how similar the challenges are among teachers from vastly different regions, or how the perspective of someone well outside your situation can give you a fresh outlook on a problem back home.

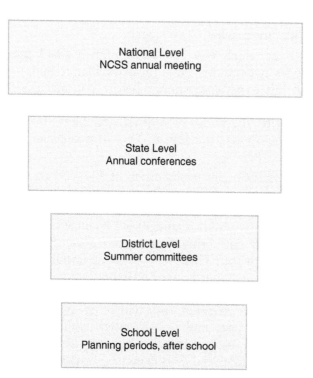

National Level
NCSS annual meeting

State Level
Annual conferences

District Level
Summer committees

School Level
Planning periods, after school

FIGURE 12.6 Opportunities for collaborating with other teachers.

Review of Key Themes: Some Parting Thoughts

With all this talk of reflection, this is a good place to review some of the themes percolating throughout the preceding chapters.

The Commonplaces of Education

The first theme is the power of the *commonplaces of education*—learners and learning, subject matter, teachers and teaching, and classroom environment. Taken individually, each of the commonplaces provides a useful lens focused on a central dimension of your teaching practice. Taken together, however, they are even more powerful, for they provide a wide-angle lens that is especially useful when tackling classroom problems, constructing teaching unit plans, assessing, and, as we have seen, reflecting on what one knows.

Constructivist Learning Theory

We introduced and explained a *constructivist theory of learning* social studies subject matter. We think this theory best explains how your students learn. Children are active, meaning-making human beings who are eager to make sense of the interesting ideas and topics you teach them. They come to you with already developing ideas about these topics based on their out-of-school life experiences. In the classroom, you will interact with the understandings they already possess as you help them construct and shape new ideas. Paying attention to children's prior knowledge by asking questions and listening carefully is crucial to knowledge construction and to your students' success as they make new meaning from the learning opportunities they encounter.

Inquiry and the Subject Matter Threads

Third, we believe that working with compelling questions in social studies is pivotal to powerful teaching. Social studies is a broad area filled with myriad facts and concepts and people and events. It's easy to get lost in an effort to feed these to students as though all of them were equally important. The rub is that, even if they were indeed equally important (needless to say, we don't think they are), you would never find the time to teach all of them well. Instead, you must pick and choose. We encourage you to use the Inquiry Design Model to focus on the big, rich social studies ideas that can lead to the most powerful learning experiences for your children.

This recommendation raises the question about where to find the kinds of ideas and questions that can rouse your students' social studies selves. You can find the beginnings of many such ideas among the *threads* of social studies, which draw on the disciplines of history and the social sciences. Not only do the threads offer potential ideas and questions, but the greater the number of thread linkages you make, the more powerful your social studies instruction will be.

Another good source is a book S.G. and a colleague edited (Grant & Gradwell, 2010) entitled *Teaching History with Big Ideas*.

Ambitious Teaching

A focus on *ambitious teaching* also plays a central role in what we have been advocating. As we have noted many times, much of what passes for social studies teaching and learning in public schools is vapid and lifeless. You can change that. We encourage you to pull out the stops, grab on to big, powerful social studies ideas, and invite and challenge your students to make sense of them through an inquiry-based practice. Social studies is a rich, fascinating, and mind-expanding subject matter, one that when taught well is deeply stimulating and wholly engaging to elementary-school children.

Powerful Assessments

We have argued that designing and using strong, powerful assessment strategies can be an integral key to good practice. It helps you better diagnose the ways in which your students learn. This approach, in turn, allows you to adjust your teaching practices to enhance that learning of the social studies subject matter you teach them. In many respects, this is the core of what you are doing—attempting to improve your students' thinking and thus their understanding of the socio-cultural world they live in. Being equipped with those deeper understandings enables learners to better navigate that world.

Genuine Classroom Communities

We have suggested the importance of building a genuine classroom community with your students. Such a community is marked by the presence of big ideas and questions and the discourse, classroom organization, and dispositions to pursue knowledge construction via individual and collective meaning-making. We mean a community characterized by powerful learning opportunities, wherein children wrestle with ideas, ask many questions and inquire into the subject matter, talk a lot to you and to each other about their emerging understandings, listen respectfully to new approaches and thoughts, and demonstrate deep interest and engagement in what you ask of them and what they in turn ask of each other.

Goal-Mindedness and Reflection

Finally, we believe that thoughtful teachers display two additional characteristics. One is that they are *goal-minded*. By this, we mean teachers who, despite competing views of what constitutes good citizenship and what it means to teach children about it, push themselves to construct a coherent and workable perspective that frames their social studies practice. We recognize that this is no easy task and that teachers' perspectives on such goal-oriented matters may well change over time and with experience. With that assumption in mind, we offer the second characteristic of good teaching, namely, *reflection*. Reflective teachers do not know everything about teaching, learning, subject matter, and classroom environment. Who could? They do, however, know that their effectiveness as a teacher is rooted in their willingness to think hard, listen hard, and try hard to be the best teacher they can be. These are the teachers who most often receive the greatest compliment, the student who says, "Thanks. You really helped me learn." We hope you will strive to be just that kind of teacher.

Chapter Summary

1   **What does it mean to be reflective?**
    To paraphrase John Dewey, reflection means conscious, careful, and repeated thought about your beliefs and teaching practices, including your reasons for them and how they influence what you might believe and do in the future.

2   **What does reflection entail?**
    Reflection generally points in two directions. Personal growth generally develops as teachers look inward. Professional growth develops as teachers cast their gaze outward toward the people with whom they work and the contexts in which they work. Reflection can take many forms. It can be in a subvocal conversation you have with yourself in the mirror before school in the morning, or it can be in a conversation with another teacher who values open reflection on teaching practice.

3   **What are the different types of reflection?**
    Linda Valli (1997) outlines five types of reflection: technical reflection, reflection-in-action, deliberative reflection, personalistic reflection, and critical reflection.

Note

1   To read more on the power of conversational community, see Grant and VanSledright (1992).

Teaching Resources

Print Resources

Fraenkel, J. (1973). *Helping students think and value: Strategies for teaching the social studies*. Englewood Cliffs, NJ: Prentice-Hall.
An older but still valuable discussion of approaches to teaching social studies.

Jackson, P., Boostrom, R., & Hansen, D. (1993). *The moral life of schools*. San Francisco: Jossey-Bass.

Tom, A. (1984). *Teaching as a moral craft*. New York: Longman.

These latter two books, both classics, explore the notion of teaching and schooling as moral endeavors.

Technology Resources

■   https://creativeeducator.tech4learning.com/21st-century-classrooms

This site features a wide range of topics, lessons, and advice for twenty-first-century teachers interested in being reflective about advancing their professional growth.

Content Resources from Children's Literature

In Chapters 5 and 8, we discussed the use of literature in the context of social studies units to help children develop a richer understanding of ideas than can be found routinely in textbooks. What follows is a listing of recent children's book titles, both fiction and nonfiction. We organized these books to correspond with the unit ideas we have described throughout the book.

The list that follows comes with two caveats. First, with so many children's titles available, this list is meant to be illustrative rather than exhaustive. And second, a list like this one soon becomes outdated as new titles are added each year. One good source of new books is *Social Education*, which publishes an annual review of children's titles.

American Revolution

Bober, N. (1998). *Abigail Adams: Witness to a revolution.* New York: Aladdin.

Cox, C. (1998). *Come all you brave soldiers: Blacks in the Revolutionary War.* New York: Scholastic.

Davis, B. (1992). *Black heroes of the American Revolution.* San Diego, CA: Harcourt Brace.

Forbes, E. (2011). *Johnny Tremain.* New York: Houghton Mifflin Harcourt.

Fritz, J. (1997). *Will you sign here, John Hancock?* New York: Putnam Juvenile.

McGovern, A. (1990). *Secret soldier: The story of Deborah Sampson.* New York: Scholastic.

Moore, K., & O'Leary, D. (1997). *If you lived at the time of the American Revolution.* New York: Scholastic.

Osborne, M., & Osborne, N. (2004). *Magic tree house research guide: American Revolution.* New York: Random House.

Stevenson, A., & Garriott, G. (1986). *Molly Pitcher, young patriot.* New York: Aladdin.

Bill of Rights/Citizenship

Beier, A. (2004). *The importance of being an active citizen.* New York: Rosen.

Fritz, J. (1997). *Shh! We're writing the Constitution.* New York: Puffin. (Original work published 1987).

Levy, E. (1987). *If you were there when they signed the Constitution.* New York: Scholastic.

Loewen, N., & Wesley, O. (2003). *We live here too! Kids talk about good citizenship.* Minneapolis, MN: Picture Window.

Swanson, J. (2007). *I pledge allegiance (Revised Edition).* Minneapolis, MN: Millbrook Press.

Canada

Greenwood, B. (2007). *The kids book of Canada (Revised Edition).* Toronto, ON: Kids Can Press.

Civil War

Beatty, P. (1989). *Charley Skedaddle.* New York: Troll.

Elliott, L. (2004). *Annie, between the states.* New York: HarperCollins.

Ford, C. (2013). *The Emancipation Proclamation, Lincoln, and slavery through primary sources.* Berkeley Heights, NJ: Enslow.

Hansen, J. (1986). *Which way freedom?* New York: Walker.

Murphy, J. (1990). *The boys' war: Confederate and Union soldiers talk about the Civil War.* New York: Clarion.

Reeder, C. (1998). *Across the lines.* New York: Avon.

Reit, S. (1991). *Behind rebel lines: The incredible story of Emma Edmonds, Civil War spy.* San Diego, CA: Harcourt Brace.

Colonization/Colonial America

Fritz, J. (1997). *Where do you think you're going, Christopher Columbus?* New York: Putnam Juvenile.

Grace, C., & Bruchac, M. (2001). *1621: A new look at Thanksgiving.* Washington, DC: National Geographic Society.

Hall, D. (1983). *Ox-cart man.* New York: Viking.

Keehn, S. (1991). *I am Regina.* New York: Philomel.

Parker, L. (2003). *English colonies in the Americas.* New York: Rosen.

Penner, L. (1991). *Eating the plates: A Pilgrim book of food and manners.* New York: Simon & Schuster.

Roop, C., & Roop, P. (Eds.). (1995). *Pilgrim voices: Our first year in the new world.* New York: Walker.

Samford, P., & Ribblett, D. (1995). *Archaeology for young explorers: Uncovering history at colonial Williamsburg.* Williamsburg, VA: Colonial Williamsburg Foundation.

Smith, R. (2005). *Spotlight on America: Colonial America.* Westminster, CA: Teacher Created Resources.

Speare, E. (2011). *Sign of the beaver*. New York: Houghton Mifflin Harcourt.
Stanley, D. (2004). *Thanksgiving on Plymouth Plantation*. New York: HarperCollins.

Family History

Adoff, A. (1973). *Black is brown is tan*. New York: Harper & Row.
Flournoy, V. (1985). *Patchwork quilt*. New York: Dial.
Garland, S. (1997). *The lotus seed*. New York: Harcourt Brace.

Immigration

Knight, M. (1993). *Who belongs here? An American story*. Gardiner, ME: Tilbury House.
Kuklin, S. (1992). *How my family lives in America*. New York: Simon & Schuster.
Lawlor, V. (Ed.). (1995). *I was dreaming to come to America: Memories of the Ellis Island oral history project*. New York: Viking.
Levine, E. (1994). *If your name was changed at Ellis Island*. New York: Scholastic.
Mohr, N. (1999). *Felita*. New York: Puffin.
Sandler, M. (1995). *Immigrants*. New York: HarperCollins.
Sandler, M. (2003). *Island of hope: The story of Ellis Island and the journey to America*. New York: Scholastic.
Surat, M. (1983). *Angel child, dragon child*. New York: Scholastic.

Maps and Mapmaking

Gackenbach, D. (1989). *With love from Gran*. New York: Clarion.
Gershator, D., & Gershator, P. (1995). *Bread is for eating*. New York: Holt.
Hartman, G. (1993). *As the crow flies: A first book of maps*. New York: Aladdin.
Holling, H. (1984). *Paddle-to-the-sea*. Boston: Houghton Mifflin.
Leedy, L. (2003). *Mapping Penny's world*. New York: Holt.
Rabe, T. (2002). *There's a map in my lap*. New York: Random House.
Ritchie, S. (2009). *Follow that map! A first book of mapping skills*. Toronto, ON: Kids Can.

Native Americans

Bruhac, J. (1993). *First strawberries*. New York: Dial.
Bruhac, J. (1999). *Eagle song*. New York: Dial.
DePaola, T. (1986). *The legend of the bluebonnet*. New York: Putnam.
Goble, P. (1991). *Star boy*. New York: Aladdin.
Harjo, J. (1996). *The woman who fell from the sky: Poems*. New York: Norton.
Jeffers, S. (1991). *Brother eagle, sister sky*. New York: Dial.
McDermott, G. (1999). *Coyote: A trickster tale from the American southwest*. New York: Harcourt Brace.
Neihardt, J. (2014). *Black Elk speaks*. Lincoln, NE: University of Nebraska Press.

O'Dell, S. (2010). *Thunder rolling in the mountains*. San Anselmo, CA: Sandpiper.

Ortiz, S. (1988). *The people shall continue*. San Francisco: Children's Book Press.

Rain Forest

Amstutz, L. (2012). *Rain forest animal adaptations*. Mankato, MN: Capstone.

Baker, L. (1993). *Life in the rain forest*. New York: Scholastic.

Cherry, L. (2000). *The great kapok tree*. New York: Houghton Mifflin Harcourt.

Cherry, L., & Plotkin, M. (1998). *The shaman's apprentice: A tale of the Amazon rain forest*. San Diego, CA: Harcourt Brace.

Osborne, W. (2001). *Rain forests: A nonfiction companion to Afternoon on the Amazon*. New York: Random House.

Slavery/Underground Railroad

Anderson, L. (2008). *Chains: Seeds of America*. New York: Simon & Schuster for Young Readers.

Bial, R. (1995). *The underground railroad*. Boston: Houghton Mifflin.

Fox, P. (1973). *Slave dancer*. New York: Yearling.

Johnson, D. (1997). *Now let me fly: The story of a slave family*. New York: Aladdin.

Johnson, P., & Kamma, A. (2004). *If you lived when there was slavery in America*. New York: Scholastic.

Lester, J. (1998). *From slave ship to freedom road*. New York: Dial.

Winter, J. (1988). *Follow the drinking gourd*. New York: Knopf.

Yates, E. (1989). *Amos Fortune, free man*. New York: Puffin.

Glossary

adaptation working with sources in order to meet students' differing academic needs. Three types of adaptions are excerpting, modifying, and annotating.

affective outcome a desired goal that emphasizes students' personal development.

argument one or more evidence-based claims that build to a reasonable conclusion.

argument stem a possible student's "answer" to a compelling question. Argument stems have two parts—a stance and one or more claims.

assessment a general term used to describe approaches to understanding what students know and can do.

assessment pillars refers to three key columns that form the basis on which to design powerful assessment tools and tasks. They include cognition (what thinking about and understanding ideas looks like), observation (tasks that allow teachers to "see" evidence of students thinking and understanding), and interpretation (relying on uniform means to make sense of what observations are saying about thinking and understanding).

authentic assessment activities designed to allow students to demonstrate their understanding in real and genuine ways.

autonomy the relative freedom of teachers to make content, instructional, and assessment decisions in their classrooms.

behaviorism a psychological theory that explains behavior in terms of stimulus–response interactions.

big book an oversized text, usually written by and for young students.

big idea a question or generalization that helps a teacher decide what to teach and how to teach it.

blank slate the idea that children's minds are empty until someone inscribes something on them.

blueprint a one-page representation of the common elements of inquiry-based practice—questions, tasks, and sources.

book talk a brief presentation in which a student provides a synopsis of a whole book or a key element or concept.

brainstorming a teaching strategy designed to elicit the widest array of ideas students can generate around a topic, question, or issue.

claim an evidence-based assertion made to support an overall argument.

C3 Framework a document created by the National Council for the Social Studies to help states and school districts to craft their own curriculum standards.

classroom management the range of approaches teachers take to monitor and control children's classroom behavior.

classroom organization the ways in which learning activities are structured.

cognitive outcome a desired goal that emphasizes students' academic or knowledge growth.

commonplaces of education a conceptual framework consisting of *learners and learning, teachers and teaching, subject matter*, and *classroom environment* designed to help educators analyze classroom situations and understand classroom problems.

compelling question a question that is both academically rigorous *and* attends to the things that learners care about.

concept a way of expressing a complex set of ideas, such as "change" or "justice."

conflation the idea that children will mix historical details from one event with another.

constructivism a psychological theory that asserts that people actively construct their understandings based on a wide range of internal and external influences.

content angle the topic of an inquiry.

contextualization the idea that readers need to understand where and when a text was created.

cooperative learning an approach to group learning that emphasizes specific roles and responsibilities for group members.

corroboration represents the idea that readers need to consider any text in relation to others on the same topic.

counter-claim an assertion that presents a different perspective than one stated earlier in a piece of writing.

craft knowledge those practices in which teachers regularly engage in the classroom.

critical reflection a form of reflection that focuses on the social, moral, and political dimensions of teaching and schooling.

cultural toolkit the knowledge that individuals and societies hold that enables them to function.

curriculum framework see "curriculum guide."

curriculum guide a generic term for a document that expresses a set of subject-matter goals and objectives.

curriculum materials a general term for a range of instructional resources, such as textbooks, trade books, maps, globes, and computer programs.

curriculum standards documents produced by state and national entities that specify a course of study.

deliberative reflection a form of reflection where one examines a variety of issues involved in teaching, from subject matter and learners' understanding of it, to teaching method and its relationship to classroom environment.

developmental stages the idea that children progress through a series of clearly identifiable and mutually exclusive levels of intellectual growth.

Dewey, John a philosopher who promoted, among other things, ideas about the linkages between learning and culture and between children and subject matter.

diagnostic assessment any assessment tasks or processes that allow teachers to gauge where students might be along a learning trajectory from knowing and being able to perform very little to knowing and performing competently.

digital citizenship refers to the practice of appropriate and responsible use of technology.

dilemma a classroom situation for which there is no one right or best solution.

discourse the nature of the talk that occurs in a classroom.

Disney effect the idea that children may take what they see in various media presentations as authoritative.

dispositions the values and attitudes teachers and their learners create and practice during classroom activity.

embedded action inquiry an IDM blueprint that makes the taking informed action activities part of the supporting question sequence.

empathy the attempt to perceive a situation through the perspective of another.

evaluation a particular form of assessment that emphasizes the judgment of students' efforts.

evidence the support one marshals in defense of an argument.

expanding communities a curriculum scope and sequence developed by Paul Hanna that grows outward from the student to the world.

explanation a straightforward account or description of an individual, action, or event.

extension an exercise that offers students an opportunity to present their arguments in a new format.

fact a means of expressing ideas that are provable and accepted by most people, such as "George Washington was the first president of the United States."

factory model of schooling a conception of schooling in which teachers push students to accumulate as much knowledge as possible and then test them to see whether they have succeeded.

formative assessment a form of assessment used by teachers in an ongoing, frequent way to make sure learning growth is occurring.

formative performance tasks exercises through which students build their content knowledge and skills in answer to supporting questions.

Freud, Sigmund a psychologist who specialized in trying to understand the inner forces that shape people's behavior and developed the theory of the unconscious.

genuine classroom community a classroom environment where ambitious teaching is sensitive to the needs of learners and the subject matter and where discourse, classroom organization, and dispositions encourage the development of thoughtful, caring, active human beings.

generalization a broad statement that effectively summarizes a set of conditions.

goal a specific aim that teachers hold.

goal framework a cluster of aims that help teachers decide how to design learning opportunities, what the opportunities should consist of, when to put them in place and in what order, and how to explain why engaging these opportunities is important. In social studies, goal frameworks typically express a view of good citizenship.

good citizenship although subject to many different definitions, this aim is a fundamental part of social studies education.

grading the assignment of a number or letter evaluation to a piece of student work or a performance.

historical fiction a form of narrative that employs fictional and real characters to dramatize a historical event.

IRE a form of classroom recitation that represents teacher Initiation–student Response–teacher Evaluation.

individual assignment an instructional activity designed to be done by each student independently.

informal assessment the information collected in order to understand what sense learners are making of the material so that one can make instructional adjustments if necessary.

informational text books and other documents that present fact- and evidence-based accounts.

inquiry an approach to teaching and learning that emphasizes questions, tasks, and sources.

Inquiry Arc a description of the four dimensions of inquiry-based teaching and learning. Those dimensions are 1) Developing questions and planning inquiries, 2) Applying disciplinary concepts and tools, 3) Evaluating sources and using evidence, and 4) Communicating conclusions and taking informed action.

Inquiry Design Model (IDM) an approach to constructing an inquiry-based curriculum featuring questions, tasks, and sources.

instructional strategies the range of approaches teachers consider and use in planning and enacting their lesson and unit plans.

interdisciplinary refers to the practice of linking ideas across subject matter and/or disciplinary boundaries.

issues-centered social studies an approach to defining good citizenship that focuses on the need to address public issues.

jigsaw activity an instructional activity in which each member of a small group becomes an "expert" on one idea, which she or he shares with other group members.

journal a notebook in which students make regular entries based on a prompt offered by a teacher or on a personal reflection.

K-W-L a teaching strategy that highlights what students Know, what they Want to know, and what they have Learned.

learning center an area designated within a classroom where teachers place a range of instructional materials and activities.

learning log a folder where students can record their thoughts and ideas.

Lexile score a measure of a text's complexity.

media literacy the practices that enable people to access, evaluate, and create media.

multicultural education an approach to defining good citizenship that focuses on creating a greater awareness of the ethnic and racial diversity of our culture.

narrative a form of story that usually features a chronological and causal retelling of an event.

narrative text a subset of literary text that highlights the telling of a story. An example is historical fiction.

objective-type test an assessment that emphasizes factual recall, such as multiple-choice, fill in-the-blank, and matching questions.

open-ended task an assessment that asks students to consider broader questions and to respond in more complete expressions, such as essays and journal entries.

organizational influences factors such as roles and responsibilities, norms and expectations, and resources that can shape teachers' pedagogical thinking and actions.

pedagogical plan a teaching plan that gives attention to instructional strategies, curriculum materials, and assessment.

pedagogical reasoning the approach teachers take in transforming the curriculum into instructional representations that reflect attention to both the subject matter and the learners at hand.

performance-based assessment activities designed to allow students the opportunities to demonstrate what they know and can do.

personal influences factors such as teachers' knowledge, beliefs, and experiences that represent their lived experience.

personal outcome the types of interests learners demonstrate in the ideas they are working with.

personalistic reflection a form of reflection that emphasizes using and expanding one's personal knowledge and that of others to enhance one's growth as a teaching professional.

Piagetian theory the work of Swiss psychologist Jean Piaget, who argued that children pass through identifiable and age-dependent stages of intellectual development.

policy documents such as curriculum frameworks, tests, and policy statements that can shape teachers' thinking and actions.

portfolio a collection of student work used to demonstrate learning over time.

positive reinforcement a reward for expected behavior.

post-test an examination given at the end of an instructional unit to assess students' learning.

pre-test an examination given before any instruction to assess students' prior knowledge.

prior knowledge the ideas, beliefs, and experiences that one brings to a new learning situation.

procedural knowledge see "syntactic knowledge."

propositional knowledge the accumulative ideas, concepts, and theories in an academic discipline.

psychic reward the gratification teachers experience when they believe they have positively influenced learners.

recitation a form of classroom discourse that emphasizes fact-based questions and answers.

reflection-in-action a form of reflection that emphasizes thinking about, assessing, and adjusting your practice as you teach.

reflective practice making decisions about the who, what, how, and why of teaching based on purposeful, ongoing introspection into the alternative beliefs and choices available and with reference to future possibilities.

repair strategies approaches researchers take to make a text more comprehensible to students.

response a reaction to a stimulus.

role-playing a teacher-created situation in which students assume roles different from those they normally play.

rubric a scoring guide that allows teachers to examine and evaluate students' work across a range of criteria.

scaffold a conceptual framework for understanding an idea, issue, or topic.

scope and sequence see "curriculum guide."

simulation a teacher-created situation in which students are confronted with a series of problems and decisions.

Skinner, B.F. a psychologist who developed a range of theories in support of a behavioral view of psychology.

small-group activity an instructional activity in which children work together, usually in groups of two to five students.

social outcome a desired goal that focuses on how students work, especially how they interact with one another.

social science disciplines the formal study of subjects such as anthropology, geography, economics, political science, psychology, sociology, and international relations.

sources human creations that can be used to build inquiries.

sourcing the idea that readers need to know and consider a document's source and purpose.

staging the compelling question a type of formative task that is intended to surface students' initial ideas about the topic of an inquiry.

stance the first part of a student's argument.

standardized test an assessment of student learning developed by either state departments of education or commercial test-publishing companies that is given to large numbers of students.

stimulus any catalyst for behavior.

story grammar the elements of a narrative account.

structural factor see "organizational influences."

substantive knowledge see "propositional knowledge."

summative assessment a form of classroom-based assessment that attempts to measure learning growth at the end of a long teaching cycle such as a unit, a marking period, or a semester.

summative performance tasks exercises that enable teachers to see how their students have made sense of the inquiry taught.

supporting questions questions that highlight the content students need to learn in an inquiry. Supporting questions typically focus on definitions and examples.

survey an assessment of what a group of people think about a topic at a particular point in time.

syntactic knowledge the ideas people within academic disciplines hold about developing new understandings.

taking informed action an exercise that enables students to apply the content they learn through an inquiry in a civic form either inside or outside of the classroom. The three phases of a taking informed action sequence are: understand, assess, and act.

T-chart activity an instructional activity in which students record their ideas, usually in a comparative sense, on a divided chart.

teaching strategy see "instructional strategies."

technical reflection a form of reflection that tries to answer the question "Did I use the right teaching technique?"

test-based assessment see "evaluation."

text complexity a term that refers to the qualitative, quantitative, and reader/text/task elements of a text.

text comprehension a term that refers to the ability of students to understand what they read.

think-aloud protocol an approach to research where students are asked to talk about the sense they are making as they read a piece of text.

threads of social studies a conceptual framework consisting of *geographic, political, economic, sociocultural,* and *global* concepts designed to help teachers think about and organize the content they teach.

topic a means of labeling a large amount of information, such as "American Revolution."

trade books a generic term for commercially published books, fiction or non-fiction, that are geared toward children.

traditional assessment see "evaluation."

traditional classroom setting a classroom environment where teacher-centered instruction focuses on the quiet, orderly, and individual acquisition of knowledge.

Vygotsky, Lev a psychologist focused on the construction of meaning who created the concept of the "zone of proximal development."

WebQuest an inquiry-based research project designed to draw upon Internet resources.

whole-group activity an instructional activity in which the entire class participates.

zone of proximal development the cognitive area between a child's prior knowledge and the ideas and expertise the child can attain with the help of knowledgeable teachers.

References

Adelson, J., & O'Neil, R. (1966). Growth of political ideas in adolescence: The sense of community. *Journal of Personality and Social Psychology, 4,* 295–306.

Adler, D. (1991). *A picture book of Christopher Columbus.* New York: Scholastic.

Afflerbach, P., & VanSledright, B.A. (1998, December). *The challenge of understanding the past: How do fifth-grade readers construct meaning from diverse history texts?* Paper presented at the annual meeting of the National Reading Conference, Austin, TX.

Akinbode, A. (2013). Teaching as lived experience: The value of exploring the hidden and emotional side of teaching through reflective narratives. *Studying Teacher Education, 9*(1), 62–73.

Angell, A. (1991). Democratic climates in elementary classrooms: A review of theory and research. *Theory and Research in Social Education, 19*(3), 241–266.

Ankeney, K., Del Rio, R., Nash, G., & Vigilante, D. (1996). *Bring history alive! A sourcebook for teaching United States history.* Los Angeles: UCLA.

Anyon, J. (1981). Social class and school knowledge. *Curriculum Inquiry, 11*(1), 3–42.

Apple, M. (1993). The politics of official knowledge: Does a national curriculum make sense? *Teachers College Record, 95,* 222–241.

Argument (n.d.). In *Merriam-Webster collegiate dictionary.* Retrieved from www.merriam-webster.com/dictionary/argument.

Baker, J. (1999). Teacher–student interaction in urban at-risk classrooms: Differential behavior, relationship quality, and student satisfaction with school. *Elementary School Journal, 100*(1), 57–70.

Banks, J. (1994). *An introduction to multicultural education.* Boston: Allyn & Bacon.

Banks, J. (2001). *Cultural diversity and education: Foundations, curriculum, and teaching.* Boston: Allyn & Bacon.

Banks, J., & Nguyen, D. (2008). Diversity and citizenship education: Historical, theoretical, and philosophical issues. In L.S. Levstik & C. Tyson (Eds.). *Handbook of research in social studies education* (pp. 137–153). New York: Routledge.

Barton, K.C. (2008). Research on students' ideas about history. In L.S. Levstik & C. Tyson (Eds.). *Handbook of research in social studies education* (pp. 239–258). New York: Routledge.

Barton, K., & Levstik, L.S. (1996). "Back when God was around and everything": Elementary students' understanding of historical time. *American Educational Research Journal, 33,* 419–454.

Beck, I., McKeown, M., & Gromoll, E. (1989). Learning from social studies texts. *Cognition and Instruction, 6,* 99–158.

Berti, A., & Bombi, A. (1988). *The child's construction of economics.* Cambridge: Cambridge University Press.

Bickmore, K. (2008). Social justice and the social studies. In L.S. Levstik & C. Tyson (Eds.). *Handbook of research in social studies education* (pp. 155–171). New York: Routledge.

Bloom, B. (Ed.). (1956). Taxonomy of educational objectives: Book 1/Cognitive domain, 2nd ed. New York: Addison-Wesley-Longman.

Bluestein, N., & Acredolo, L. (1979). Developmental changes in map-reading skills. *Child Development, 50,* 691–697.

Brophy, J. (1990). Teaching social studies for understanding and higher order applications. *Elementary School Journal, 90,* 351–418.

Brophy, J., & Alleman, J. (1997). Second graders' knowledge and thinking about shelter as a cultural universal. *Journal of Social Studies Research, 21,* 3–15.

Brophy, J., & Alleman, J. (2008). Early elementary social studies. In L.S. Levstik & C. Tyson (Eds.). *Handbook of research in social studies education* (pp. 33–49). New York: Routledge.

Brophy, J., Alleman, J., & O'Mahoney, C. (2003). Primary-grade students' knowledge and thinking about food production and the origins of common foods. *Theory and Research in Social Education, 31,* 10–50.

Brophy, J., & VanSledright, B.A. (1997). *Teaching and learning history in elementary schools.* New York: Teachers College Press.

Brophy, J., VanSledright, B.A., & Bredin, N. (1993). What do entering fifth graders know about American history? *Journal of Social Studies Research, 16/17,* 2–22.

Brown, A., & Campione, J. (2002). Communities of learning and thinking, or context by any other name. In P. Woods (Ed.), *Contemporary issues in teaching and learning* (pp. 120–126). New York: Routledge.

Bruner, J. (1996). *The culture of education.* Cambridge, MA: Harvard University Press.

Buckles, S., Schug, M., & Watts, M. (2001). A national survey of state assessment practices in the social studies. *The Social Studies, 90*(4), 141–146.

Bullough, Jr., R.V. (2008). *Counternarratives: Studies of teacher education and becoming and being a teacher.* Albany, NY: SUNY Press.

Butts, R.F. (1980). *The revival of civic learning.* Washington, DC: Phi Delta Kappa Educational Foundation.

California Board of Education. (1988). *History–social science framework for the California public schools.* Sacramento, CA: California Department of Education.

Center for Civic Education. (1994). *National standards for civics and government.* Calabasas, CA: Author.

Cherry, L. (1990). *The great kapok tree.* New York: Gloucester Press.

Cimbricz, S. (2002). State testing and teachers' thinking and practice: A synthesis of research. *Educational Policy Analysis Archives, 10*(2). Available online at: https://epaa.asu.edu/ojs/article/view/281/407.

Clark, C., & Peterson, P. (1986). Teachers' thought processes. In M. C. Whitrock (Ed.), *Handbook of research on teaching* (3rd ed., pp. 255–296). New York: Macmillan.

Cohen, D. (1989a). Practice and policy: Notes on the history of instruction. In D. Warren (Ed.), *American teachers* (pp. 393–407). New York: Macmillan.

Cohen, D. (1989b). Teaching practice: Plus ça change ... In P. Jackson (Ed.), *Contributing to educational change: Perspectives on research and practice* (pp. 27–84). Berkeley, CA: McCutchan.

Cohen, D. (2011). *Teaching and its predicaments.* Boston: Harvard University Press.

Cohen, D., & Barnes, C. (1993). Pedagogy and policy. In D. Cohen, M. McLaughlin, & J. Talbert (Eds.), *Teaching for understanding: Challenges for policy and practice* (pp. 207–239). San Francisco: Jossey-Bass.

Coles, R. (1986). *The political lives of children.* Boston: Houghton Mifflin.

Coles, R. (2010). *The story of Ruby Bridges.* New York: Scholastic.

Connell, R. (1971). *The child's construction of politics.* Carlton, Australia: Melbourne University Press.

Cuban, L. (1984). *How teachers taught: Constancy and change in American classrooms, 1890–1980.* New York: Longman.

Cuban, L. (1991). History of teaching in social studies. In J. Shaver (Ed.), *Handbook of research on social studies teaching and learning* (pp. 197–209). New York: Macmillan.

Delpit, L. (1988). The silenced dialogue: Power and pedagogy in educating other people's children. *Harvard Educational Review, 58*(3), 280–298.

Dewey, J. (1902/1969). *The child and the curriculum.* Chicago: University of Chicago Press.

Dewey, J. (1933). *How we think.* Chicago: Henry Regnery.

Dewey, J. (1938). *Experience and education.* New York: Collier.

Donovan, S., & Bransford, J. (2005). *How students learn: History in the classroom.* Washington, DC: National Academies Press.

Dorros, A. (1990). *Rain forest secrets.* New York: Scholastic.

Duffin, L., French, B., & Patrick, H. (2012). The teachers' sense of efficacy scale: Confirming the factor structure with beginning preservice teachers. *Teaching and Teacher Education, 28*(6), 827–834.

Edwards, A., & Westgage, D. (1987). *Investigating classroom talk.* Philadelphia: Falmer.

Engle, S., & Ochoa, A. (1988). *Education for democratic citizenship: Decision making in the social studies.* New York: Teachers College Press.

Epstein, T. (2009). *Interpreting national history: Race, identity, and pedagogy in classrooms and communities.* New York: Routledge.

Eraut, M. (2004). Informal learning in the workplace. *Studies in Continuing Education, 26*(2), 247–273.

Evans, R., & Saxe, D.W. (1996). *Handbook on teaching social issues.* Washington, DC: National Council for the Social Studies.

Farquhar, M. (1962). *Colonial life in America.* New York: Holt.

Fell, B. (1976). *America B.C.: Ancient settlers in the new world.* New York: Quadrangle/New York Times Book.

Fillpot, E. (2012). Historical thinking in third grade. *Social Studies, 103*(5), 206–217.

Finch, F. (1991). The blue and the gray. In D. Ravitch (Ed.), *The American reader: Words that moved a nation* (p. 159). New York: Harper Perennial.

Fitzgerald, F. (1980). *America revised.* New York: Vintage.

Freire, P. (1998). *Pedagogy of freedom: Ethics, democracy and civic courage.* Lanham, MD: Rowman & Littlefield.

Furth, H. (1980). *The world of grown-ups.* New York: Elsevier.

Gay, G. (2000). *Culturally responsive teaching.* New York: Teachers College Press.

Goodlad, J. (1984). *A place called school.* New York: McGraw-Hill.

Goodman, J. (1992). *Elementary schooling for critical democracy.* Albany, NY: SUNY Press.

Grant, S.G. (1996). Locating authority over content and pedagogy: Cross-current influences on teachers' thinking and practice. *Theory and Research in Social Education*, 24(3), 237–272.

Grant, S.G. (1998). *Reforming reading, writing, and mathematics: Teachers' responses and the prospects for systemic reform*. Mahwah, NJ: Lawrence Erlbaum Associates.

Grant, S.G. (2000). Teachers and tests: Exploring teachers' perceptions of changes in the New York state testing program. *Educational Policy Analysis Archives*, 8(14). Available online at: https://epaa.asu.edu/ojs/article/view/405/528.

Grant, S.G. (2001). An uncertain lever: The influence of state-level testing in New York State on teaching social studies. *Teachers College Record*, 103(3), 398–426.

Grant, S.G. (2007). Understanding what children know about history: Exploring the representation and testing dilemmas. *Social Studies Research and Practice*, 2(2), 196–208. Available online at: www.socstrp.org.

Grant, S.G. (2018). Teaching practices in history education. In S. Metzger & L. Harris, (Eds.), *Handbook of history teaching and learning*, (pp. 419–448). New York: John Wiley and sons.

Grant, S.G., & Gradwell, J. (2010). *Teaching history with big ideas: Cases of ambitious teachers*. Lanham, MD: Rowman & Littlefield.

Grant, S.G., Swan, K., & Lee, J. (2017). Questions that compel and support. *Social Education*, 81(4), 200–203.

Grant, S.G., Swan, K., & Lee, J. (2018). *Inquiry-based practice in social studies education*. New York: Routledge and C3Teachers.

Grant, S.G., Swan, K., & Lee, J. (2018). *Inquiry Design Model: The workbook*. Raleigh, NC: C3Teachers.

Grant, S.G., Swan, K., & Lee, J. (in press). The Civil War and the Inquiry Design Model. In M. Karpyn, (Ed.), *Teaching the causes of the Civil War*. New York: Peter Lang.

Grant, S.G., & Tzetzo, K. (1997). Mixed messages and unanswered questions. *Theory and Research in Social Education*, 25(4), 521–531.

Grant, S.G., & VanSledright, B.A. (1992). The first questions of social studies: Initiating a conversation. *Social Education*, 56, 141–143.

Greene, B. (1995). *From forge to fast food: A history of child labor in New York State*. Troy, NY: Council for Citizenship Education.

Gregg, M., & Leinhardt, G. (1994). Mapping out geography: An example of epistemology and education. *Review of Educational Research*, 64, 311–361.

Hahn, C., & Alviar-Martin, T. (2008). International political socialization research. In L.S. Levstik & C. Tyson (Eds.), *Handbook of research in social studies education* (pp. 81–108). New York: Routledge.

Hakim, J. (2007). *A history of US*. New York: Oxford University Press.

Haladyna, T., & Shaughnessy, J. (1985). Research on student attitudes toward social studies. *Social Education*, 49(8), 692–695.

Hanna, P. (1963). Revising the social studies: What is needed. *Social Education*, 27(4), 190–196.

Hansen, J. (1994). *The captive*. New York: Scholastic.

Hauver, J. (2019). *Young children's civic mindedness: Democratic living and learning in an unequal world*. New York: Routledge.

Hawkins, D. (1974). I, thou, and it. In D. Hawkins (Ed.), *The informed vision: Essays on learning and human nature* (pp. 48–62). New York: Agathon Press.

Heffron, S., & Downs, R. (Eds.). (2012). *Geography for life: National geography standards* (2nd ed.). Washington, DC: National Geographic Society.

Hirsch, E.D. (1987). *Cultural literacy: What every American needs to know*. Boston: Houghton Mifflin.

Hirsch, E.D. (1999). *The schools we need and why we don't have them*. Lake Forest, CA: Anchor Books.

Hoban, T. (1987). *I read signs*. New York: Greenwillow Books.

Holt, T. (1990). *Thinking historically: Narrative, imagination, and understanding*. New York: College Entrance Examination Board.

Howard, T. (2003). Culturally relevant pedagogy: Ingredients for critical teacher reflection. *Theory into Practice, 42*, 195–202.

Jahoda, G. (1984). The development of thinking about socioeconomic systems. In H. Tajfal (Ed.), *The social dimension* (Vol. 1, pp. 69–88). Cambridge: Cambridge University Press.

Johnson, D., Johnson, R., & Holubec, E. (2009). *Circles of learning: Cooperation in the classroom* (6th ed.). Edina, MN: Interaction Books.

Kahne, J., & Sporte, S. (2008). Developing citizens: The impact of civic learning opportunities on students' commitment to civic participation. *American Educational Research Journal, 45*, 738–766.

Kalman, B. (1992). *A colonial town, Williamsburg*. New York: Crabtree.

Koeppen, K.E. (2010). Issue-centered social studies unit sampler. In E. Heilman (Ed.), *Social studies and diversity education: What we do and why we do it* (pp. 246–248). New York: Routledge.

Kozol, J. (1991). *Savage inequalities: Children in America's schools*. New York: Crown.

Krensky, S. (1991). *Christopher Columbus*. New York: Random House.

Kubelick, C. (1982). Building a just community in the elementary school. In L.W. Rosenzweig (Ed.), *Developmental perspectives on the social studies* (pp. 15–29). Washington, DC: National Council for the Social Studies.

Ladson-Billings, G. (1994). *The dreamkeepers: Successful teachers of African American children*. San Francisco: Jossey-Bass.

Lapp, M., Grigg, W., & Tay-Lim, B. (2002). *The nation's report card: US History 2001*. Washington, DC: US Department of Education, National Center for Educational Statistics.

Larkins, A., Hawkins, M., & Gilmore, A. (1987). Trivial and noninformative content of elementary social studies: A review of primary texts in four series. *Theory and Research in Social Education, 15*, 299–311.

Lee, P., & Ashby, R. (2000). Progression in historical understanding among students ages 7–14. In P. Stearns, P. Seixas, & S. Wineburg (Eds.), *Knowing, teaching and learning history: National and international perspectives* (pp. 199–222). New York: New York University Press.

Levine, E., & Johnson, L. (1993). *If you traveled on the underground railroad*. Washington, DC: Scholastic.

Levstik, L.S. (1989). Historical narrative and the young reader. *Theory into Practice, 28*, 114–119.

Levstik, L.S. (1993). Building a sense of history in a first-grade classroom. In J. Brophy (Ed.), *Advances in research on teaching* (Vol. 4, pp. 1–31). Greenwich, CT: JAI.

Levstik, L.S. (2008). What happens in social studies classrooms? Research on K–12 social studies practice. In L.S. Levstik & C. Tyson (Eds.). *Handbook of research in social studies education* (pp. 50–64). New York: Routledge.

Levstik, L.S., & Barton, K. (2011). *Doing history: Investigating with children in elementary and middle schools* (4th ed.). New York: Routledge.

Levstik, L.S., & Pappas, C.C. (1987). Exploring the development of historical understanding. *Journal of Research and Development in Education, 21*, 1–15.

Levstik, L.S., & Tyson, C. (Eds.) (2008). *Handbook of research in social studies education.* New York: Routledge.

Liben, L., & Downs, R. (1989). Understanding maps as symbols: The development of map concepts in children. In H. Reese (Ed.), *Advances in child development* (pp. 145–201). New York: Academic.

Loewen, J. (2010). *Teaching what really happened: How to avoid the tyranny of textbooks and get students excited about doing history.* New York: Teachers College Press.

Lortie, D. (1975). *Schoolteacher.* Chicago: University of Chicago Press.

McCabe, P. (1993). Considerateness of fifth-grade social studies texts. *Theory and Research in Social Education, 21*, 128–142.

McDonough, G. (2005). Moral maturity and autonomy: Appreciating the significance of Lawrence Kohlberg's Just Community. *Journal of Moral Education, 34*(2), 199–213.

McGowan, T., Sutton, A., & Smith, P. (1990). Instructional elements influencing student attitudes toward social studies. *Theory and Research in Social Education, 18*, 37–52.

McKeown, M.G., & Beck, I.L. (1990). The assessment and characterization of young learners' knowledge of a topic in history. *American Educational Research Journal, 27*, 688–726.

McKeown, M.G., & Beck, I. (1994). Making sense of accounts of history: Why young students don't and how they might. In G. Leinhardt, I. Beck, & C. Stainton (Eds.), *Teaching and learning in history* (pp. 1–26). Hillsdale, NJ: Erlbaum.

Marshall, H. (1990). Beyond the workplace metaphor: The classroom in a learning setting. *Theory into Practice, 29*, 94–107.

Martin, A. (1990). Social studies in kindergarten: A case study. *Elementary School Journal, 90*(5), 305–317.

Menzies, G. (2003). *1421: The year China discovered America.* New York: HarperCollins.

Miller, S., & VanFossen, P. (2008). Recent research on the teaching and learning of pre-collegiate economics. In L.S. Levstik & C. Tyson (Eds.), *Handbook of research in social studies education* (pp. 284–304). New York: Routledge.

Monte-Sano, C., & Reisman, A. (2016). Studying historical understanding. In L. Corno & E.M. Anderman (Eds.), *Handbook of educational psychology* (3rd ed.) (pp. 281–294). New York: Routledge.

Moore, S., Lare, L., & Wagner, K. (1985). *The child's political world: A longitudinal perspective.* New York: Praeger.

Morgan, T. (1993). *Wilderness at dawn.* New York: Simon & Schuster.

Mueller, R. (2017). Calibrating your "compelling compass": Teacher-constructed prompts to assist question development. *Social Education, 81*(6), 343–345.

National Board for Professional Teaching Standards. (1994). *Social studies–history: Draft standards for National Board certification.* Detroit, MI: Author.

National Center for History in the Schools. (1996). *National standards for history, basic edition.* Los Angeles: Author.

National Council for the Social Studies. (1993). Definition of the social studies. *The Social Studies Professional, 114*, 7.

National Council for the Social Studies. (1994). *Curriculum standards for social studies: Expectations of excellence.* Washington, DC: Author.

National Council for the Social Studies (2010). *National curriculum standards for social studies: A framework for teaching, learning, and assessment.* Silver Spring, MD: Author.

National Council for the Social Studies. (2013). *The college, career, and civic life (C3) framework for Social Studies state standards.* Silver Spring, MD: Author.

National Council on Economic Education. (1997). *Voluntary national content standards in economics*. New York: Author.

National Governors Association Center for Best Practices and Council of Chief State School Officers. (2010). *Common core state standards for English language arts and literacy in history, social studies, science, and technical subjects*. Washington, DC: Author.

National Geographic Society. (1994). *Geography for life: National geography standards*. Washington, DC: Author.

Naylor, D., & Diem, R. (1987). *Elementary and middle school social studies*. New York: Random House.

Neihardt, J. (1988). *Black Elk speaks*. Lincoln: University of Nebraska Press.

New York State Education Department. (1998). *Social studies resource guide*. Albany, NY: Author.

Nickell, P. (1992). "Doing the stuff of social studies": A conversation with Grant Wiggins. *Social Education, 56*(2), 91–94.

Ningsih, S., & Budi Eko, S. (2017). Improving the students' activity and learning outcomes on social sciences subject using round table and rally coach of cooperative learning model. *Journal of Education, 8*(11), 30–37.

Nuthall, G., & Alton-Lee, A. (1995). Assessing classroom learning: How students use their knowledge and experience to answer classroom achievement test questions in science and social studies. *American Educational Research Journal, 32*(1), 185–223.

Ogle, D. (1986). K-W-L: A teaching model that develops active reading of expository text. *Reading Teacher, 39*, 564–570.

Ortiz, S. (1988). *The people shall continue*. New York: Children's Book Press.

Parker, W.C. (2008). Knowing and doing in democratic citizenship education. In L.S. Levstik & C. Tyson (Eds.), *Handbook of research in social studies education* (pp. 65–80). New York: Routledge.

Pellegrino, J., Chudowsky, N., & Glaser, R. (2001). *Knowing what students know: The science and design of educational assessment*. Washington, DC: National Academies Press.

Priestley, M., Edwards, R., Priestley, A., & Miller, K. (2012). Teacher agency in curriculum making: Agents of change and spaces for manoeuvre. *Curriculum Inquiry, 42*, 191–214.

Ravitch, D., & Finn, C., Jr. (1987). *What do our 17-year-olds know? A report on the first National Assessment of History and Literature*. New York: Harper & Row.

Reisman, A. (2012). The "Document-Based Lesson": Bringing disciplinary inquiry into high school history classrooms with adolescent struggling readers, *44*(2). Available online at: www.tandfonline.com/doi/full/10.1080/00220272.2011.591436.

Rock, T.C., Heafner, T., O'Connor, K., Passe, J., Oldendorf, S., Good, A., & Byrd, S. (2006). One state closer to a national crisis: A report on elementary social studies education in North Carolina schools. *Theory and Research in Social Education, 34*(4), 455–483.

Rothstein, R. (2004). We are not ready to assess history performance. *Journal of American History, 4*, 1381–1391.

Rubin, B. (2011). *Making citizens: Transforming civic learning for diverse social studies classrooms*. New York: Routledge.

Schwab, J. (1978). The practical: Translation into curriculum. In I. Westbury & N. Wilkop (Eds.), *Science, curriculum, and liberal education: Selected essays* (pp. 365–383). Chicago: University of Chicago Press.

Segall, A., & Helfenbein, R. (2008). Research on K–12 geography education. In L.S. Levstik & C. Tyson (Eds.), *Handbook of research in social studies education* (pp. 259–283). New York: Routledge.

Shaver, J., Davis, O.L., & Helburn, S.W. (1980). An interpretive report on the status of precollege social studies education based on three NSF-funded studies. In National Science Foundation (Ed.), *What are the needs in precollege science, mathematics, and social science education? Views from the field* (pp. 3–18). Washington, DC: Author.

Shulman, L. (1987). Knowledge and teaching: Foundations of the new reform. *Harvard Educational Review, 57(1)*, 1–22.

Sleeter, C., & Grant, C. (1994). *Making choices for multicultural education: Five approaches to race, class, and gender* (2nd ed.). New York: Macmillan.

Smith, J., & Niemi, R. (2001). Learning history in school: The impact of coursework and instructional practices on achievement. *Theory and Research in Social Education, 29(1)*, 18–42.

Speare, E. (1983). *Sign of the beaver*. Boston: Houghton Mifflin.

Swan, K., Lee, J., & Grant, S.G. (2018). *Inquiry Design Model: Building inquiries in social studies*. Silver Spring, MD: National Council for the Social Studies and C3Teachers.

Taylor, M. (1976). *Roll of thunder, hear my cry*. New York: Penguin.

Terry, A., & Panter, T. (2010). Students make sure that the Cherokees are not removed… again: A study of service-learning and artful learning in teaching history. *Journal for the Education of the Gifted, 34(1)*, 156–176.

Thornton, S.J. (2004). *Teaching social studies that matters: Curriculum for active learning*. New York: Teachers College Press.

Turiel, E. (1983). *The development of social knowledge*. Cambridge: Cambridge University Press.

Valli, L. (1997). Listening to other voices: A description of teacher reflection in the United States. *Peabody Journal of Education, 72*, 67–88.

Van Sertima, I. (1976). *They came before Columbus: The African presence in ancient America*. New York: Random House.

VanSledright, B.A. (1995). "I don't remember—the ideas are all jumbled in my head": Eighth-graders' reconstructions of colonial American history. *Journal of Curriculum & Supervision, 10*, 317–345.

VanSledright, B.A. (1997). And Santayana lives on: Students' views on the purposes for studying American history. *Journal of Curriculum Studies, 29*, 529–557.

VanSledright, B.A. (2002). *In search of America's past*. New York: Teachers College Press.

VanSledright, B.A. (2014). *Assessing historical thinking and understanding: Innovative designs for new standards*. New York: Routledge.

VanSledright, B.A. (2015). Individual differences in reading history. In P. Afflerbach (Ed.), *Handbook of individual differences in reading* (pp. 245–258). New York: Guilford.

VanSledright, B.A., & Afflerbach, P. (2005). Assessing the status of historical sources: An exploratory study of eight elementary students reading documents. In P. Lee (Ed.), *Children and teachers' ideas about history: International research in history education* (Vol. 4, pp. 1–20). London: RoutledgeFalmer.

VanSledright, B.A., & Brophy, J. (1992). Storytelling, imagination, and fanciful elaboration in children's reconstructions of history. *American Educational Research Journal, 29*, 837–859.

VanSledright, B.A., & Grant, S.G. (1994). Citizenship education and the persistence of classroom dilemmas. *Theory and Research in Social Education, 22(3)*, 305–339.

VanSledright, B.A., & Kelly, C. (1998). Reading American history: The influence of using multiple sources on six fifth graders. *Elementary School Journal, 98*, 239–265.

VanSledright, B.A., & Limon, M. (2006). Learning and teaching in social studies: Cognitive research on history and geography. In P. Alexander & P. Winne (Eds.), *The handbook* of educational psychology (2nd ed.) (pp. 545–570). Mahwah, NJ: Lawrence Erlbaum Associates.

Von Zastrow, C., & Janc, H. (2004). *Academic atrophy: The condition of the liberal arts in America's public schools.* Washington, DC: Council for Basic Education.

Wahlgren, E. (1986). *The Vikings and America.* New York: Thames & Hudson.

Wiggins, G. (1989). The futility of trying to teach everything of importance. *Educational Leadership, 47,* 44–59.

Wiggins, G. (1993). *Assessing student performance: Exploring the purpose and limits of testing.* San Francisco: Jossey-Bass.

Wilen, W., & White, J. (1991). Interaction and discourse in social studies classrooms. In J. Shaver (Ed.), *Handbook of research on social studies teaching and learning* (pp. 483–495). New York: Macmillan.

Wilson, S.M. (1990). *Mastodons, maps, and Michigan: Exploring uncharted territory while teaching elementary school social studies.* (Elementary Subjects Center Paper No. 24). East Lansing: Michigan State University, Institute for Research on Teaching, Center for the Learning and Teaching of Elementary Subjects.

Wineburg, S.S. (1991). On the reading of historical texts: Notes on the breach between school and academy. *American Educational Research Journal, 28*(3), 495–519.

Wineburg, S.S. (1996). The psychology of teaching and learning history. In R. Calfee & D. Berliner (Eds.), *Handbook of educational psychology* (pp. 423–437). New York: Macmillan.

Wood, G. (1990). Teaching for democracy. *Educational Leadership, 48*(3), 32–37.

Index

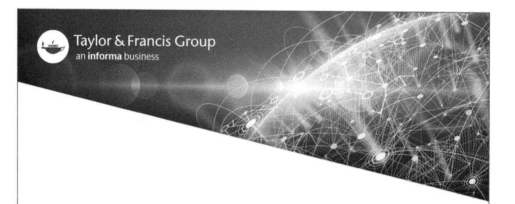

Lightning Source UK Ltd.
Milton Keynes UK
UKHW030837190722
406049UK00013B/176